P9-CLU-382

WHY DO SOME SHOES SQUEAK?

AND
568 OTHER
POPULAR QUESTIONS
ANSWERED

BY GEORGE W. STIMPSON

BELL PUBLISHING COMPANY
NEW YORK

Dedicated

To

FELIX T. COTTEN

Copyright © 1984 by Crown Publishers, Inc., All rights reserved.

This 1984 edition is published by Bell Publishing Company,
distributed by Crown Publishers, Inc.
225 Park Avenue South, New York, New York 10003.

Manufactured in the United States of America

Library of Congress Cataloging in Publication Data
Stimpson, George W., 1896–
Why do some shoes squeak and 568 other popular
questions answered.
Includes index.
1. Questions and answers. I. Title.
AG195.S74 1984   031'.02   84-18563
ISBN: 0-517-455749

o   n   m   l   k

FOREWORD

"Ignorance never settles a question."

—BENJAMIN DISRAELI

When you stop to think a moment, you realize that there are many unanswered questions that stand as small mysteries in our daily lives. Do rainbows ever appear as complete circles? Why does salt melt snow? What is the gold standard? Why are maps made with north at the top? How did the term "throwing the hat in the ring" originate? Why is time indicated on shipboard by bells? How did "Mind your P's and Q's" originate? Why is thirteen called a baker's dozen?

Though we live with these concepts as an integral part of our customs and culture, most of us would be hard pressed to answer any of the preceding questions. *Why Do Some Shoes Squeak? and 568 Other Popular Questions Answered* is a truly invaluable book because it gives solid and complete answers to these everyday mysteries. The book solves the dilemma of where to look for an explanation to something that is commonplace, yet, at the same time, obscure. Why *do* some shoes squeak? The answer to this question, as well as to hundreds of others, is fully and intelligently discussed in this handy volume.

PREFACE

Perhaps the basic characteristic of this work is in the nature of the questions, the fact that they are such as continually occur to all sorts and conditions of people. Nevertheless, the author has tried to impart to it another in the reliability of the answers. He has spared no effort to obtain the facts, though the search often led him through many labyrinths in the stores of knowledge.

The questions have been selected with regard to variety, quality, and popular interest; and it is hoped that they will appeal not only to the general reader but also to teachers, students, editors, writers and others to whom a book of this kind should be a practical manual. The prevalent interest in science and natural history is reflected in the large number of questions on these subjects, while superstition, legend, tradition, and popular misconception and belief come in for liberal treatment.

In this work, a volume based on the rich materials at the author's disposal, the subject matter has not been classified. The arrangement adopted, it is believed, presents the information in the simplest and most interesting manner.

Not all of the questions dealt with admit of definite answers. The fact that a definite answer is not obtainable, however, has not been deemed sufficient reason for excluding the question. Frequently, it is of value, and aids in dispelling misconceptions, to know just what authentic information is available on a particular subject. The author's policy has been to take the questions as they have been repeatedly presented to him, and in each case to endeavor to give, in the clearest language at his command, the best information obtainable by painstaking research.

Lack of space makes it impossible to cite all the authorities and sources consulted. When an authority is occasionally cited it should not be understood that the author has relied entirely on that source. He has sought to confirm such statements by comparing them with

v

collateral evidence.

The reference value of the work has been greatly enhanced by a thorough index. An index, to paraphrase Pope, holds the eel of knowledge by the tail, and there would be little excuse for publishing a book of this kind without such a key to its contents. Not infrequently several related and equally important questions are answered in the discussion under a leading question, and the index has been compiled with a view of making all this information readily accessible.

The author regrets that space does not permit a special acknowledgment to all those who have assisted him in the preparation of this work. He does, however, wish to express grateful appreciation for the helpful criticism and counsel of Mr. Edward Cullom and Mr. Maurice Splain, and wishes to thank Mr. J. D. Hufham and Mr. Charles Bullen for their aid in the laborious task of correcting the proof.

GEORGE W. STIMPSON

WHY DO SOME SHOES SQUEAK?
AND
568 OTHER POPULAR
QUESTIONS ANSWERED

Have human beings ever been crossed with animals?

There is no authentic record of a cross between the human race and lower animals of any species whatever. According to the Smithsonian Institution, numerous reports of crosses between human beings on the one hand and apes, bears, dogs and other animals on the other have invariably proved groundless when investigated by competent scientists.

What is the oldest city in the world?

It is generally supposed that Damascus, the chief city of Syria, is the oldest city in the world. Although positive evidence is wanting, there is some reason for believing that its site has been continuously occupied by a city longer than any other spot on the earth. The Jewish historian Josephus, who probably based his assertion on Hebrew tradition, attributed the foundation of Damascus to Uz, the son of Aram and the great-grandson of Noah. In *Genesis 14* it is related that Abraham pursued the routed kings to Hobah, "which is on the left hand of Damascus." While this statement is not conclusive, the evidence indicates that Damascus was a place of importance already in the time of Abraham, who, it is supposed, lived 2,000 years or more before Christ.

Why do a cat's eyes shine in the dark?

The luminous appearance of a cat's eyes in the dark is due to the reflection of light by the tapetum lucidum, which is part of the membranous layer between the retina and the outer covering of the pupils of the eyes. This remarkable layer is distinctly differentiated from the choroid layer only in certain animals. It is the tapetum lucidum that enables members of the feline family and other nocturnal animals to see even when there is very little light. Some authorities believe this layer reflects the light rays through the retina a second time. In the domestic cat the tapetum lucidum is brilliant green or blue in color and has a metallic luster. The well known glare is especially noticeable when artificial light is thrown on a cat in a dark corner, or when a cat in a dark place is observed through an opening, light entering the darkness through the opening being reflected from the cat's eyes as from a mirror.

When does a new administration begin?

Technically a new Presidential administration starts at the beginning of March 4, that is, immediately after midnight March 3, and the President is paid his salary on that basis. The same is true of a new Congress. But since the beginning of the Federal Government it has been assumed for convenience that the Presidential and Congressional terms do not expire until noon March 4. Accordingly it is customary for the outgoing President to perform the functions of the office until his successor takes the oath at the formal inauguration on March 4, or March 5 when March 4 falls on Sunday. If Congress does not complete its work by noon March 4, the clock is set back. This is merely a legal fiction dating back to the early days of the Government. Bills signed by the outgoing President on March 4 are dated March 3, and he receives no salary for his services after midnight March 3.

Did Sir Walter Raleigh ever visit America?

Sir Walter Raleigh never set foot on the mainland of North America. Queen Elizabeth's infatuation for her favorite prevented his going to Virginia with his first expedition for colonization. It is said that she promised to pay all the expenses of the expedition if Raleigh would not go in person. In 1595, having heard the stories of El Dorado, Raleigh made a voyage to South America with the object of finding a gold mine, and on his return he published an account of the voyage under the title *The Discoverie of Guiana,* which is a brilliant mixture of fact and romance. In 1617 he again sailed with an expedition to find a gold mine on the northern coast of South America, but he himself remained in Trinidad while he sent several vessels up the Orinoco River. On his way back to Europe he stopped a short time on the island of Newfoundland. That was the nearest he ever got to the North American mainland.

Where in the New World does the sun rise in the Pacific?

To observers on parts of the Isthmus of Panama the sun rises in the Pacific and sets in the Atlantic. The Isthmus turns and twists in such a manner that the end of the Panama Canal farthest east touches the Pacific and the end farthest west touches the Atlantic. This is contrary to what one unfamiliar with the Isthmus would suppose, because the majority of people imagine that the Canal runs east and west when as a matter of fact it runs in a northwesterly-southeasterly direction. Balboa, at the Pacific entrance, is farther east than Cristobal, at the Atlantic entrance.

Who served in Congress the longest?

Joseph Gurney Cannon of Illinois, familiarly known as "Uncle Joe," served in the House of Representatives longer than any other person who has served in either or both branches of Congress. During the fifty years from March 4, 1873, to March 3, 1923, when he voluntarily retired, he served forty-six years in the House of Representatives. He was defeated for the terms beginning March 4, 1891, and March 4, 1913, respectively. Justin Smith Morrill of Vermont served *continuously* in Congress for a longer period than any other member. He became a member of the House March 4, 1855, and served in that body until March 3, 1867, when he became a member of the Senate, in which he remained until his death December 28, 1898. His continuous service in the House and Senate combined covered a period of forty-three years nine months and twenty-four days. William Boyd Allison of Iowa served *continuously* in the Senate for a longer period than any other member of that body. He served from March 4, 1873, until his death August 4, 1908—a period of thirty-five years and five months. However, the total service of Francis Emory Warren of Wyoming in the Senate was longer than that of any other Senator—more than thirty-six years. He served in the Senate first from November 18, 1890, until March 4, 1893, and then continuously from March 4, 1895, until his death November 24, 1929, his continuous service being a little less than thirty-four years and nine months. Henry Harrison Bingham of Pennsylvania served *continuously* in the House of Representatives longer than any other man who has served in that body. He served from March 4, 1879, until his death March 22, 1912—thirty-three years and nineteen days.

Is the backbone of a camel curved upward in the middle?

The backbone of the single-humped camel is not curved upward in the middle, as many people suppose. It is as straight as the backbone of a horse or an elephant. Humps on camels are composed chiefly of fat, and they vary in size according to the physical condition of the animals. When camels are worked hard and poorly fed their humps shrivel up and become flaccid. Much of their ability to travel long distances over the desert without food and water is due to the reabsorption of the extra fat carried in the humps. Thus the hump serves as a sort of commissary department from which the camel receives sustenance in time of famine. Similarly, in certain breeds of sheep extra fat is stored in the tail.

Does any species of fish give birth to living young?

Many fishes give birth to living young. There are three general types of reproduction among fishes—oviparous, viviparous and ovoviviparous. Each of these types has many minor characteristics in the fertilization, deposition and development of the eggs. The great majority of fishes are oviparous and lay their eggs in the water, where they are fertilized externally by the males. But some species, in fact entire families, are viviparous and produce living young from within the body. However, most so-called viviparous fishes are really ovoviviparous, that is, living young are produced from eggs fertilized by copulation and retained within the body during their development, but they do not form an attachment to the oviduct or derive nourishment from the mother. In this class are most of the rays, as well as numerous members of several other families. The true viviparous fishes, such as the moonfishes, Mexican swordtails, surf fishes, guppies and the common top minnows, not only give birth to living young hatched from eggs fertilized by copulation, but the young arc nourished in the body through placental connection with the mother. Female swordtails have been known to produce as many as one hundred young at a birth. The young are capable of taking care of themselves immediately and in most cases they are compelled to seek shelter from their cannibalistic mothers who try to devour them.

Can a Supreme Court judge be removed for incompetency?

There is no Constitutional method by which justices of the Supreme Court of the United States can be removed for mere incompetency. These officials can be removed only for improper conduct in office, such as treason, bribery and other high crimes and misdemeanors. Impeachment by the House of Representatives and trial by the Senate is the only method of removal prescribed by the Constitution. Even an insane judge would have a legal right to remain on the bench, unless it became necessary to incarcerate him. In fact there has been one case of this kind. Associate Justice Henry Baldwin of Pennsylvania, who was a member of the Supreme Court from 1830 to 1844, often exhibited an alienation of mind, according to notes left by John Quincy Adams and Daniel Webster. Notwithstanding his impaired mental faculties Justice Baldwin was permitted to remain on the bench and regularly to take part in the decisions until his death. The danger to the course of justice was not great, because the deranged member of the court had only one vote and his colleagues could easily prevent any undesirable effect his opinion might have on the decisions.

Did Hoover call prohibition *a noble experiment?*

Herbert Hoover never referred to prohibition as *a noble experiment* in those exact words. The common belief that he did arose from a letter which he wrote to Senator William E. Borah of Idaho on February 23, 1928. Borah had sent a questionnaire on the subject of prohibition to several of the leading men then seeking the Presidency. "Our country," replied Hoover in part, "has deliberately undertaken a great social and economic *experiment, noble in motive* and far-reaching in purpose." This statement was the original source of the popular expression frequently attributed to Hoover. Later Hoover quoted part of his letter to Borah in his address of acceptance at Stanford University, California.

How often does one born February 29 have a birthday?

A person born on February 29 in leap year has a birthday only once every four years so far as the calendar is concerned. It is, however, purely a calendar problem. In reality there is no problem at all, because none of us observe our birthdays on exactly the proper twenty-four hours, owing to imperfections in the calendar. Every four years the calendar is about twenty-four hours behind the astronomical or true solar year. This difference is made up by adding an extra day to February every four years, making leap year. According to our present calendar, every year represented by a number divisible by four is a leap year, except those represented by numbers divisible by 100 but not by 400. This arises from the fact that the addition of a whole day every fourth year is a few minutes too much to make the calendar come out even. A person born on February 29 in leap year would be one year old exactly a year later, and his true birthday would begin then and would last for twenty-four hours, regardless of the calendar. The same holds true of a person born on any other date. But it is customary to adopt as one's birthday the entire calendar day nearest the astronomical date. Those born on February 29 have a choice of observing their birthdays on February 28 or March 1, except in leap years.

What States comprise the Middle West?

This term is indefinite and opinion differs as to just what States constitute the region popularly referred to as the Middle West. It depends a great deal on the viewpoint of the individual using the term. The United States was settled from the Atlantic seaboard and the terms *East, Middle West, West* and *Far West* were applied to different sections as the frontier was pushed toward the Pacific. This accounts for the present lack of uniformity in usage. In the broadest sense, the Middle West consists of that part of the United States lying between the Appalachian and Rocky mountains on one hand and the Mason and Dixon line

and the Canadian border on the other. This section comprises
Ohio, Michigan, Indiana, Wisconsin, Illinois, Minnesota, Iowa,
Nebraska, Kansas, North Dakota, and South Dakota. Frequently
the term also embraces Kentucky and Missouri. Many people,
however, restrict the term to Ohio, Michigan, Indiana, Illinois
and Wisconsin, and class all the States west of the Mississippi
river as *West* or *Far West*. In 1929 the Chicago *Tribune* announced
that henceforth it would use *Central States* in place of *Middle
West* on its editorial pages. The term *Middle West,* said that paper,
has lost is original geographical meaning and "it connotes colonial-
ism and inferiority."

Do tornadoes actually drive straws into boards?

The velocity of the wind in the whirl of a tornado is terrific.
It probably sometimes attains a speed of more than three hundred
miles an hour. That such wind frequently drives quills, straws
and splinters into solid boards and tree trunks is well established.
"Straws," wrote the director of the U. S. Weather Bureau to
the author in 1925, "have been driven by tornadoes short distances into the bark of trees and in some cases into the surface
of wooden boards or the wooded parts of trees. Many witnesses
have testified to these facts, and photographs of the phenomena
are rather common. There is some uncertainty as to the depth of
penetration in most cases, also as to the real hardness of the small
surface of materials thus penetrated, but there is no question
that wind does sometimes drive straws into wood." According
to the National Geographic Society, tornadoes have been known to
drive planks all the way through the trunks of trees. A tornado-like
waterspout at Calcutta, India, once drove a bamboo cane completely through a six-foot wall faced on both sides with brick.
These phenomena are no mystery to physical science. The velocity
of a straw, splinter or other small object may be so great that it
will penetrate a harder body before it is crushed itself. It is the
energy with which a body strikes another that determines its
piercing effect. A small fast-moving object may possess far greater
kinetic energy than a large slow-moving body. The straw hurled
through space at a tremendous speed expends its kinetic energy
in penetrating the harder object, and this happens so quickly that

the inertia of the straw prevents it from crumpling until it has penetrated some distance. Because of the same principle wax candles can be shot with a rifle through solid boards. An Army officer reported that he fired six-inch wax candles through four pine boards placed a foot apart. Each board was cleanly perforated at a range of twenty-five yards.

What two Old Testament characters never died?

The prophet Elijah and Enoch, the father of Methuselah, never saw death, according to the Bible. *II Kings 2: 11* says: "And it came to pass, as they [Elijah and Elisha] still went on and talked, that, behold, there appeared a chariot of fire, and horses of fire, which parted them both asunder; and Elijah went up by a whirlwind into heaven." This, it is presumed, is merely a figurative way of saying that the prophet passed from earth by miraculous translation instead of through the gates of death. Likewise Enoch never saw death, according to *Hebrews 11: 5.* "By faith," that passage says, "Enoch was translated that he should not see death; and he was not found, because God translated him: for before his translation he had this testimony, that he pleased God." This is the basis for the popular but misleading statement that Methuselah, the oldest man mentioned in the Bible, died before his father did. As a matter of fact, according to the Biblical account, Methuselah's father never died at all. *Genesis 5: 25* says simply: "And Enoch walked with God: and he was not; for God took him."

Why is winter colder than summer?

It is a common fallacy to suppose that it is colder in winter because the sun is then farther from the earth. As a matter of fact the sun is farthest from the earth in summer and closest in winter. In astronomy the point of nearest approach of a body to the sun is called perihelion, and the earth is at perihelion about January 3. Likewise the earth is farthest from the sun early in July. The seasons, spring, summer, fall and winter, occur because of the inclination of the earth's axis while the earth moves around the sun; that is, the seasons are produced mainly by the relative positions of the earth's axis in respect to the sun. The principal reason for the difference in temperature between summer and winter is the angle at which the rays of the sun strike the earth, coupled with the longer duration of daylight in summer. The imaginary line from pole to pole which is known as the axis and around which the earth rotates is slightly tilted. As the earth moves in its annual orbit the Northern Hemisphere is tilted toward the sun half the year and away from it the other half. It is summer in the Northern Hemisphere when that portion of the earth is tilted toward the sun. The sun, while actually farther away then, is more directly overhead. It is winter in the Northern Hemisphere when that part of the earth is tilted away from the sun. Then the sun, while actually closer to the earth, is lower in the sky and its rays strike the earth at a much greater slant than they do in summer. This means that the rays of the sun must pass through a greater distance of atmosphere in the winter. In the Southern Hemisphere the seasons are reversed. It is winter there while it is summer in the Northern Hemisphere, because the Southern Hemisphere is inclined away from the sun while the Northern Hemisphere is inclined toward it. There would be no seasons if the earth's axis were perpendicular to the plane of its orbit. Perpetual summer would exist on a belt near the Equator, while perpetual winter would exist on the parts nearer the poles.

Where is the American flag flown continuously?

According to recognized flag etiquette, the American flag should generally be displayed only from sunrise to sunset, indicating the beginning and the cessation of "the activities of the day." This rule governs the flags flown at Army posts and Navy stations and on ships of war at anchor, as well as nearly all the flags flown over Federal buildings. The authorities, however, sometimes specify different hours. The National Capitol at Washington is the only building in the United States over which the American flag is officially flown continuously, both day and night, throughout the year. Several years ago it was officially decided that there should be one place in the nation where the National emblem is always displayed. Accordingly the two flags over the east and west fronts of the central part of the Capitol are never taken down except to replace them with new ones. The flags over the wings of the same building are governed by the sittings of Congress. Flags are flown over the Senate Chamber and the Hall of the House of Representatives when these branches are sitting, either actually or technically, and they are not lowered at night except in case of adjournment at that time. When Congress recesses these flags are kept up, even during the night, until the recess ends. The flags over the Senate Office Building and the House Office Building are supposed to be displayed only from sunrise to sunset. At the Library of Congress the "activities of the day" do not cease at sunset and accordingly the flag is kept up over that building until 10 : 00 P. M. A flag is flown over the White House every day from sunrise to sunset when the President is in Washington. It is not flown when the President is absent from the Capital.

Does the sap of a tree rise in the spring?

That the sap of a tree rises in the spring and goes down in the fall is a common but erroneous notion. In the spring there is an increased circulation of liquids through the tissues of the tree and the food materials stored in the trunk and branches are dissolved and carried to the buds and root tips where first growth begins. It is this increased activity preceding the bursting of the buds and the development of visible growing parts which is so often taken for the rise of sap. In sugar maple trees the circulation of liquid through the stem in the spring is attended by considerable pressure. If one of these trees is wounded in the spring it bleeds more freely than if it is wounded at any other season and this is taken by many as positive proof that there is more moisture in the tree in the spring than at any other time. It is also accepted as evidence that the sap goes up in the spring and down in the fall. As stated above, such is not the case. The sap does not go down at any time. At any given point above the ground the moisture content between the inner and outer zones of living wood may vary from month to month and from season to season. A British investigator found that in the fall the center of a tree is very wet, and the outer regions are comparatively dry, while in the spring this condition is reversed. He concluded that if we desire to make our language conform with the fact we should not say that the sap is up in the spring and down in the fall, but that it is out (near the bark) in the spring and in (toward the center) in the fall.

Analysis shows that pieces of wood cut from trees in the winter sometimes have a moisture content just as high or even higher than pieces cut in the spring or early summer.

Who was the first woman nominated for President?

It is often said that Belva Lockwood, who headed the ticket of the Equal Rights Party in 1884 and again in 1888, was the first woman nominated for the Presidency of the United States. Such is not the fact. That honor belongs to Mrs. Victoria Claflin Woodhull (later Martin), who in 1872 was nominated for the Presidency at Vineland, New Jersey, by a convention styling itself the Equal Rights Party. Frederick Douglass, the Negro reformer, was the candidate for Vice President. The head of the ticket, however, spent election day that year in Ludlow Street Jail in New York City, where she had been confined after being charged with circulating obscene literature. Mrs. Woodhull, like Mrs. Lockwood, received no electoral votes and only a few scattered popular votes. Her supporters adopted the following campaign song, sung to the tune of *Comin' Thro' the Rye:*

> Yes! Victoria we've selected
> For our chosen head:
> With Fred Douglass on the ticket
> We will raise the dead.
>
> Then around them let us rally
> Without fear or dread,
> And next March, we'll put the Grundys
> In their little bed.

Why are three golden balls the pawnbroker's sign?

Three golden balls as the sign of the pawnbroker are supposed to be derived from the device of the famous Medici family of Florence. A pawnbroker lends money on personal pledges left in his possession as security. This trade first flourished in Italy, and during the Middle Ages pawnshops were operated almost exclusively by the Jews and the Lombards. The first money-lenders of London were Lombards from Florence who established themselves on Lombard Street, which became proverbial as the "money market." Among the principal Lombard bankers and pawnbrokers were the members of the Medici family. Formerly, as their name indicates, the Medicis were engaged in the medical profession. Averardo de Medici was an officer under Charlemagne, and, according to a legend, he slew a giant named Mugello, on whose mace were three gilded balls. Averardo, to perpetuate his exploit, adopted the three golden balls as the device of his family. The family was so prominent that the device became the symbol of the whole profession of medicine, and a legend grew up that the three golden balls represented three gilded pills. Later, however, the Medicis became bankers and pawnbrokers and gradually the device was transferred from the medical profession to the pawnbroker's trade.

Is there a flying snake?

No known species of snake actually flies. However, *Chrysopelea ornata,* a species of arboreal constrictor found in India, southeastern Asia and the Malay archipelago, is known as the flying snake. Although this species cannot fly in the ordinary sense of the term, it can glide through the air for some distance from an elevation to a lower altitude. The so-called flying snake accomplishes this feat by flattening out its body to check its fall. It holds itself rigid and straight, with ribs pushed outward and belly drawn in to form a concave surface, which enables it to descend with safety from a considerable height. Major Stanley Flower of the London Zoological Society reported that he saw one of these snakes *fly* eight feet, and another parachuted or glided to the ground from a height of twenty feet. It is doubtful whether the snake ever resorts to this method of travel except in emergencies. *Chrysopelea* feeds chiefly on lizards and is reputed to be very fierce, resisting capture by striking and biting furiously. This species is variable in color. The body, says the curator of reptiles at the New York Zoological Park, may be black or green, ornamented with yellow, red or orange; the head is black with yellow markings.

What causes the holes in Swiss cheese?

The characteristic holes or *eyes* in Swiss cheese are produced by the liberation of gases generated by bacterial action during the process of fermentation. These eyes or gas-holes are sometimes more than half an inch in diameter, and when they have glassy interiors and are regularly formed they denote a cheese of good quality and flavor. This type of cheese originated in the mountains of Switzerland and it was formerly believed that the atmosphere and grass of that region were essential to the development of the eyes. The U. S. Department of Agriculture has shown that good Swiss cheese can be produced in other parts of the world by employing a bacteria starter. Although the organisms which cause the gas-holes are fairly well understood and may be introduced artificially, it is probable that the atmosphere and pasture of the particular region may have a general influence upon the formation of the eyes.

Why is it considered unlucky to light three cigarettes with the same match?

Two theories have been advanced to explain the origin of the superstition that it is unlucky to light three cigarettes with the same match. According to one, the superstition originated during the World War and arose from the real danger incident to keeping a match lighted in the trenches long enough to light three cigarettes. If a match were made to do triple duty it might not only attract the enemy's attention but give him time enough for his aim. But a match extinguished quickly after lighting one or two cigarettes would not give the enemy sufficient time to direct his fire. The continual caution on this point, it is said, gave rise to the odd superstition now so common. According to the other theory, the superstition originated in eastern Europe in connection with the funeral service in the Russian church in which three altar candles are lighted with one taper. The Russians, this story has it, regarded it as sacrilegious and impious to make any other lights in groups of three and hence the superstition that ill luck will befall anybody who lights three cigarettes with the same match, or anybody who even accepts such a light.

What is a moonless month?

Moonless month is the name popularly given to a month in which no full moon occurs. Under our present calendar February is the only month that is shorter than the lunar cycle and consequently it is the only month that can have fewer than four moon phases. The absent phase, however, need not necessarily be the full moon, but may be any one of the four. Likewise five phases of the moon occasionally fall in the other months. The average time from one full moon to another is 29½ days, and the time from one phase to the next varies from less than seven days to more than eight. About every six years February has only three phases; it is, of course, without a full moon much less frequently. In 1866 February had no full moon while the preceding January and the following March had two full moons each. This remarkable sequence, astronomers estimate, will not occur again for some 2,500,000 years. February was without a full moon in 1885 and 1915, and from approximate computations made by the U. S. Naval Observatory that month will be without a full moon in 1934 and 1961. Februaries without new moons or either of the other two phases occur at about the same intervals, but, of course, in different years.

How can insects fly about in a moving train?

Flies can fly about in a closed car while it is moving almost as readily as when it is stationary. This is because the air in which the insects are moving is traveling with the car. If an insect were to fly slowly above a fast-moving flat car it would soon be left behind with that portion of the atmosphere in which it was flying. Likewise, if a man in a moving Pullman jumps straight up he will alight in about the same spot from which he jumped. His motion through space is the same as that of the train. He moves with the car, and since the air in the closed car moves with it also, there is no friction to hold him back while he is in the air. If a man did the same thing on an open car he would be held back by the friction of the air and would alight slightly farther to the rear of the spot from which he jumped. The U. S. Bureau of Standards estimates that if a person jumps straight up three feet on an open car traveling seventy miles an hour when there is no natural wind he will alight about fifteen inches farther back. Many people have the erroneous notion that a bird or aviator flying high in the sky is left behind by the ground below as the earth rotates on its axis. Such, of course, is not the case. If it were, Charles A. Lindbergh could have gone north to the proper latitude, ascended to a considerable altitude and remained in the same vicinity until Paris passed beneath him! The atmosphere in which we move is just as much a part of the earth as the solid ground on which we walk. The entire earth, including the blanket of air around it, is rotating upon its axis and revolving around the sun. It is absurd to suppose that the earth moves through the atmosphere. If such were the case, a terrific gale would be created by the earth speeding through space and every un-attached object would be swept off. The atmosphere is held to the rest of the earth by gravity and goes with it because there is nothing in space to hold it back.

Do eagles ever carry off children?

Hardly a year passes that the newspapers do not publish re-ports of a child being carried away by an eagle in Switzerland or some other part of the world. Most of these reports are no doubt made up out of whole cloth and may be dismissed as pure fiction. The U. S. Biological Survey states that it has been unable to find a single authentic instance of this kind so far as North America is concerned. It is possible, however, that some of the larger eagles have, under unusual circumstances, seized and carried away small children. The golden eagle, it is estimated, can carry a weight of from twelve to fifteen pounds and it often preys upon lambs, fawns and kids. From time immemorial the Kirghiz Tartars have trained golden eagles to hunt antelopes, foxes, wolves and other game. Dr. W. Reid Blair says that the harpy eagle of Central and South America "attacks and kills animals of more than three times its own size and weight. Turkeys, fawns, foxes, sloths and monkeys alike fall victims to this powerful bird's claws." There is reason to suppose that such a bird, when hungry, might prey upon an un-protected baby.

What was the longest reign in history?

It is believed that the reign of Pepi II of the sixth Egyptian dynasty is the longest on record. According to James Henry Breasted, Pepi II ascended the throne of Egypt about 2566 B. C., when he was only six years of age, and reigned ninety-one years. Some of the ancient writers estimated the length of this reign as high as one hundred years. The reign of Louis XIV of France is the second longest on record. He ascended the throne in 1643 at the age of five and reigned until his death in 1715—a period of seventy-two years. Francis Joseph of Austria-Hungary reigned nearly sixty-eight years—1848 to 1916. The longest reign in the annals of English history was that of Victoria who ascended the throne in 1837 and reigned until her death in 1901—sixty-four years. Her nearest rival in this respect was George III, who reigned from 1760 to 1820—a period of sixty years. The reign of Pedro II of Brazil was also a long one. He was emperor for 58 years— from 1831 to 1889. Alphonso XIII of Spain was born in 1886. He was the posthumous son of Alphonso XII and was proclaimed king at birth. Accordingly he already has had one of the long reigns of history.

Why is China called the Flowery Kingdom?

Flowery Kingdom is a translation of the Chinese *Hua Kuo* and is the most ancient name of China. Whether it originally referred to flowers in the literal sense is not known for certain. It probably did not. *Hua* means flowery, elegant, glorious, distinguished. The ancient Chinese so designated their country, it is supposed, because they regarded their people as the most polished and civilized nation in the world. The term, however, may have been once employed in the sense of "country full of flowers." According to one theory, the Chinese originally lived in central Asia, which is a very barren region, and they called their new country *flowery* in contrast to their old home in the desert.

What is a human body worth?

If the chemical elements composing an average human body were isolated and sold at commercial prices they would be worth only about one dollar. The U. S. Bureau of Chemistry and Soils supplies the following careful estimate of the average percentage of the different elements in the human body: oxygen, 65; carbon, 18; hydrogen, 10; nitrogen, 3; calcium, 1.5; phosphorus, 1; potassium, 0.35; sulphur, 0.25; sodium, 0.15; chlorine, 0.15; magnesium, 0.05; iron, 0.004, and iodine, 0.00004. The body also contains minute quantities of fluorine and silicon, and perhaps manganese, zinc, copper and aluminum. Even arsenic has been discussed as being possibly an essential constituent of a normal human body. Those who have attempted to evaluate the elements composing an average human body have met with many difficulties and their figures are nothing more than rough estimates.

How can one tell by the tracks which way a rabbit has run?

The triangle formed by the tracks of a rabbit in the snow points in the direction opposite that in which the animal was running. When a rabbit runs it touches the ground with both small front feet close together and then strikes with the two large hind feet apart and ahead of the front feet, forming the base of the triangle with the hind feet and the apex with the front ones. In other words, the hind feet strike the ground last and leave it last with each leap, but they strike far ahead of the front feet, and consequently the two foremost and most widely separated tracks are made by the hind feet, not by the front ones as so often supposed. Unless one understands the relative position of the rabbit's feet while in motion it is sometimes hard to tell by its tracks which way it has run, because the feet are covered with hair to such an extent that the toes do not always show in the tracks.

Does Washington cover the entire District of Columbia?

Legally the City of Washington and the District of Columbia occupy the same area. The City is not independently incorporated and it has no boundaries which are not also the boundaries of the District. Such, however, was not always the case. Georgetown was incorporated in 1789 as a separate town with its own municipal government. In 1802 Washington was also incorporated as a town with a mayor, board of aldermen and a common council. Thus from that date until 1871 there were two incorporated towns in that part of the District of Columbia which was ceded to the Federal Government by the State of Maryland. The charters of both Washington and Georgetown were revoked in 1871 and the two towns were merged. Since then Washington and the District have been coextensive in area and have been governed by the same officials and by the same laws. Notwithstanding this fact, the City of Washington proper covers only part of the 69¼ square miles known as the District of Columbia. This situation exists because a certain tract was set aside for the site of the Federal city and the actual city has not yet occupied all of this tract. There are some differences in taxation in the rural and urban sections of the District.

What birds can fly immediately after being hatched?

The mound builders, a family of birds inhabiting Australia and certain South Sea Islands, are unique in that the young are hatched fully feathered and are able to fly and live an independent life from the moment they emerge from the shell. These birds are called megapodes because of their large feet. Most species lay their eggs in large mounds constructed of loose soil, leaves, grass, twigs, etc. Not infrequently the mounds are ten or twelve feet high and contain several wagon-loads of material. After the eggs are deposited they are left to hatch out by the heat of the decaying vegetable matter. The brush turkeys are the most common of the mound builders. One species of megapodes lays its eggs in the sand on the seashore and leaves them to be hatched by the heat of the sun.

Can snakes bite through leather shoes?

Such snakes as the bushmaster, rattlesnake and Gaboon viper have long, powerful fangs and are able, under favorable circumstances, to bite through soft leather and rubber of the thickness generally used in making shoes, boots and leggings. No species of snake, however, is able to bite through the hard, thick leather used in heavy boots, leggings and puttees, and ordinary boots and leggings are a great protection against most snakes. Any leather ceases to be an absolute protection against venomous snakes after it becomes thin and soft from repeated wear. Hunters in the Southern States, says the U. S. Biological Survey, find that leather leggings afford sufficient protection against the poisonous snakes in that region, and a specially constructed rubber boot, with a shank including several layers of canvas, widely used by quail hunters in Florida, is a perfect protection for the parts it covers. Raymond L. Ditmars, curator of reptiles at the New York

Zoological Park, says he would feel perfectly safe from snake bites if he were provided with very stiff canvas leggings. Rattlesnakes seldom strike a person above the knee.

Why are criminals executed on Friday?

In Europe the custom of executing criminals on Friday dates back at least to the Middle Ages. Because of this custom Friday used to be popularly known as *hangman's day*. Although the practice is not so prevalent as formerly, an examination of current newspaper files indicates that Friday is still the favorite day in the United States for the execution of persons condemned to capital punishment. No adequate explanation has ever been offered as to why the sixth day of the week should be preferred as the day for hanging or electrocuting criminals. Some authorities say the custom undoubtedly arose from the fact that Jesus was executed by crucifixion on Friday, the sixth day of the week according to the old Jewish calendar. Since then, they say, it has been the practice to set the date of an execution so it will fall on that day. This, of course, is mere speculation. It is generally assumed, with some reason, that the ill luck associated with Friday by superstitious people arose from the connection of that day with the crucifixion of Jesus. However, the superstition may have been suggested by the fact that Friday was hangman's day; or, on the other hand, criminals may have been put to death on that day because of the ill luck already associated with it. Curiously enough, the ancient Scandinavian peoples, as well as the Hindus, regarded Friday as the luckiest day of the week.

Does speed affect the mileage obtained from gasoline?

Other things being equal, more mileage is obtained from a gallon of gasoline when the automobile is driven at moderate speed than when it is driven at high speed. Accordingly the motorist who speeds up to reach a filling station before his gasoline supply is exhausted is generally fooling himself. The following careful statement concerning the relation between fuel economy and automobile speed was prepared for the author by the U. S. Bureau of Standards: "More force is required to propel a car at high speed than at low speed, chiefly because wind resistance increases approximately as the square of the speed. The mileage from a gallon of gasoline will be better at low speeds, therefore, if the fuel-air ratio furnished at both speeds is the same. If, as frequently happens, the mixture furnished by the carburetor is different for different speeds, the actual mileage obtained in service may increase or decrease with speed, depending upon the carburetor characteristics."

What Indian is pictured on the buffalo nickel?

No particular Indian, according to the Treasury Department, posed for the design on the United States five-cent piece. The head is the composite of several models and is the sculptor's ideal of an American aborigine. James Earle Fraser, an American sculptor, designed the nickel, which was first issued in 1913. "The head," says Fraser himself, "is an idealized portrait and represents no particular Indian." Several Indians have obtained considerable publicity by being introduced in different parts of the country as "the chief whose likeness appears on the buffalo nickel."

What English queen had seventeen children?

Queen Anne, who reigned over England from 1702 to 1714, gave birth to seventeen children, not one of whom survived her. Several of them were still born. The queen's life has been described as a mournful series of childbirths, miscarriages and infant funerals. She, her husband and the seventeen children are buried in a single tomb in Westminster Abbey. Anne was the second daughter of James II and Anne Hyde. In 1683 she was married to Prince George of Denmark. Only one of the seventeen children born of this union survived infancy. This was William, the Duke of Gloucester, who died in 1700 at the age of eleven.

Do bears hug their enemies to death?

The proverbial hugging propensity of bears is probably a myth, notwithstanding a vast amount of alleged testimony to the contrary. Literature, reference works, and books on natural history contain numerous references to the "crushing embrace" or "deadly hug" of bears. Pope says: " 'Tis a bear's talent not to kick, but hug." Nearly all careful observers are agreed that this notion is erroneous. It no doubt arose from faulty observation. In his book entitled *In the Zoo,* Dr. W. Reid Blair, director of the New York Zoological Park, says on this subject: "In regard to the proverbial *hug,* the story is apparently devoid of foundation. A bear, on account of its anatomical structure, strikes round with its paws as if grasping, and the blow of its powerful arm drives its claws into the body of its victim, which action apparently gave rise to its *hugging* reputation."

Do Japanese flowering cherries bear fruit?

Japanese flowering cherries differ widely in fruiting habits, depending on the variety of the tree and on the climate. So far as known, the double-flowered varieties never produce fruit, and only occasionally is fruit borne by the semi-double forms. The single-flowered varieties, which grow wild in Japan, do bear fruit, but very sparingly except in certain restricted regions. For centuries the Japanese have looked upon these ornamental cherries with an admiration bordering on reverence, and their horticulturists have devoted much time to the development of new varieties. Although such trees were brought to the United States as early as 1863, and there are now many collections in this country, the best known and most popular collection is in Potomac Park, Washington, D. C. The first Japanese flowering cherry trees planted on public ground in Washington were purchased in 1909 by Mrs. William Howard Taft. In 1910, upon the suggestion of the Japanese consul general at New York, the City of Washington received two thousand trees as a gift from the City of Tokyo. This entire consignment, however, was ordered burned by the Federal Government because the trees were infested with insect pests and plant diseases. Tokyo then sent another consignment of more than three thousand trees, most of which were planted in Potomac Park. Of these trees the U. S. Bureau of Plant Industry says: "The earliest flowering variety of this collection, the Yoshino, which encircles the Tidal Basin with its nearly one thousand trees, bursts into bloom usually late in March or early in April. The other eleven varieties growing along the East and West Drives open their flowers in rapid succession about the time the Yoshino has ceased blooming, making a continuous display for over a month." The different varieties were carefully selected for successive blooming so that blossoms might be seen continuously for a period of a month or six weeks. Of course the actual date when the first blossoms appear in the spring depends on the advancement of the season. None of the flowering cherries in Washington bear fruit, except in rare instances, but the single-flowered trees in the Government garden at Chico, California, bear a crop of fruit nearly every year, and the same is true of these varieties growing in the Arnold Arboretum, Jamaica Plain, Massachusetts.

What flag has endured longest without change?

The Danish flag, consisting of a large white cross on a red field, is the oldest unchanged national flag in existence. About 1218 King Valdemar II of Denmark led a crusade against the pagans who were continually attacking his colonies on the Baltic. The Danes were surprised in their camp near what is now Reval in Estonia and only the personal exertions of the king himself saved them from disaster. According to a legend, a red banner bearing a white cross appeared in the sky at the most critical moment of the battle. This was taken by Valdemar as an answer to his prayers and a promise of aid from heaven. After routing the enemy the king adopted the banner as the standard of the Danes and called it *Dannebrog,* literally meaning Danes' Cloth. Apart from this legend, however, there is unquestioned proof that this flag has been in continual existence as the national emblem of Denmark since the thirteenth century.

Do tall buildings sway with the wind?

Tall buildings such as modern skyscrapers are moved back and forth by the force of the wind, but the movement is very slight and is probably never perceptible to the senses. This movement is due to vibration set up by wind and is not correctly described as a sway. The common impression that tall structures, like the Woolworth Building, for instance, weave back and forth several inches when a strong wind blows is erroneous. All building material has a certain amount of resilience. Engineers take this into consideration and make provisions for wind-bracing. A tall building, tower, monument or chimney, from the standpoint of the physicist, is really an elastic cantilever held by the earth at one end and left free to vibrate at the other. Heavy gusts of wind striking the structure will sometimes cause it to vibrate back and forth, much as the tines of a tuning fork can be made to vibrate by striking them. But in the case of a high office building this motion back and forth usually cannot be measured in inches or even in the larger fractions of an inch. Many engineers and architects doubt whether the motion is ever sufficient to be perceptible to the senses of the occupants of the building, although they may feel a slight jar due to the vibration. Cass Gilbert, architect of the Woolworth Building, made tests and took measurements and concluded that there is no appreciable so-called sway in that structure at any time, notwithstanding numerous reports to the contrary. Readings taken with delicate instruments over a long period show that during the heaviest winds the vibration in the tallest office buildings does not produce a movement of more than an inch, which is only half an inch off the vertical each way. Pranks played by rocking chairs, hanging fixtures, pendulum clocks and water in bathtubs can usually be explained by the fact that a comparatively mild vibration in the building itself often sets up a violent vibration in loose objects in it. A building that vibrates off the vertical a quarter of an inch may cause a fixture to sway six or eight inches or even more. Many people confuse the movement due to vibration with what is known as bending or leaning in buildings, which is caused chiefly by changes in temperature. Such changes cause all tall structures to lean out of the vertical slightly. When the sun shines on one side of a building and the other side is cool the warm side will naturally expand and cause the top to lean away from the sun. A warm wind may have the same effect. The Washington Monument in Washington, D. C., sometimes leans as much as an inch off the vertical as the result of changes in temperature.

Why is artificial silk called rayon?

In 1923 the National Retail Dry Goods Association of the United States invited a number of associations to form a committee for the purpose of selecting a substitute for the name *artificial silk,* which was deemed inadequate and misleading. After considering many suggestions submitted by the public, *glos* was adopted by the committee on January 25, 1924. This term, however, failed to meet with general approval, and, therefore, another committee was appointed to select a more euphonious word. This second committee consisted of twenty men, who represented the leading manufacturers and consumers of artificial silk. The chairman of this committee was Mr. S. A. Salvage, president of the Viscose Company, pioneer rayon manufacturers in the United States. In a statement dated September 4, 1928, and addressed to the author, Mr. Salvage explained how *rayon* was coined:

We started with no ideas, but we felt that a two-syllable word would be preferable, and a member of the committee suggested that as the product had a brilliant luster, one syllable should denote brilliancy, and also suggested that that syllable be *ray,* and we finally concluded to tack *on* to it, and thus the word *rayon* was born. There was no connection with the French word *rayon,* and we felt at the time there would not be much confusion over the two words on account of the different pronunciation, but we now know that there would already have been a world-wide adoption of the term *rayon* had it not conflicted with the French word.

The National Retail Dry Goods Association officially adopted the new word on May 23, 1924, and other interested organizations soon followed suit. It was later adopted by the Federal Trade Commission, the Department of Commerce, and the Department of Agriculture, as well as by other Federal agencies.

What is meant by the keys of the city?

Frequently we read that a noted visitor has been presented with the keys of a certain city. This is merely a figurative way of saying that he has been given an official welcome or has been honored with the freedom of the city. The expression and the ceremony are survivals of the time when every important town in Europe was fortified with walls and people could enter or leave the inclosure of the city only through gates which were generally closed and locked at sundown. The keys to the gates were kept by the mayor or military commander and when the city surrendered the keys were formally turned over to the victors. This ceremony suggested the common practice of presenting distinguished visitors with the keys of the city as a token of honor and esteem, just as a private person might give a friend the key to his house to express complete confidence in him. Figuratively speaking, the city is surrendered to the eminent person who honors it by his visit. Occasionally a modern city presents an actual key or set of keys to symbolize the ancient ceremony of presenting the keys of the city.

Who invented the gasoline automobile?

The gasoline automobile is not the product of a single inventor and it would be impossible to assign a definite date to its invention. Several inventors working in different parts of the world arrived at similar results at about the same time. After it was found that steam-driven carriages were impractical on ordinary roads various oils began to be considered as possible sources of motive power for self-propelling vehicles. It is stated, without conclusive proof, that in 1875 an Austrian named Siegfried Narkus built and operated a four-wheeled carriage driven by a crude internal combustion engine. Be that as it may, it is certain that in 1885 Dr. Karl Benz of Munich constructed a tricycle driven by such a motor. In 1891 Benz built what is believed to have been the first gasoline-driven automobile made in Germany. Gottlieb Daimler, also a German, installed a gasoline engine in a bicycle in 1885, and two years later he patented a high-speed internal combustion engine. A Frenchman named Levassor, seeing the possibilities of this engine, bought the French rights from the inventor and a few years later began to manufacture automobiles. The gasoline automobile as a practical machine may be said to date from 1894. In that year a man named Krebs in France designed a Panhard motor car which contained most of the essential features of the modern automobile. It had a chassis similar to those now used and was driven by a vertical engine under a hood at the front. In the same year Elwood Haynes obtained patents on a gasoline-driven car perfected in the Apperson wagon works at Kokomo, Indiana. This machine was given its initial trial July 4, 1894, when it traveled at a speed of six or seven miles an hour. The original model, as altered during the next two years, is now in the National Museum in Washington. It is difficult to determine who actually constructed the first gasoline automobile in America. The evidence is conflicting and new claims for the honor are being advanced continually. Several impractical buggy-like vehicles equipped with crude gasoline motors were built in different parts of the country during the five years preceding 1894. The most successful of these was the motor car tested sometime before July 8, 1892, by Charles E. Duryea at Springfield, Massachusetts.

Where is the Mason and Dixon line?

The Mason and Dixon line is the boundary between Pennsylvania on the one hand and Maryland and part of West Virginia on the other and is perhaps the most famous boundary line in America. It received its name from the fact that the greater portion of it was originally surveyed between 1763 and 1767 by two English mathematicians, Jeremiah Mason and Charles Dixon, who ran the line to a point about 244 miles west of the Delaware River and about thirty miles beyond the extreme northwest corner of Maryland. A dispute of long standing between the proprietors of Pennsylvania and Maryland was finally settled by this survey. In 1779 commissioners from Virginia and Pennsylvania agreed that "the line commonly called Mason's and Dixon's line be extended due west" to complete the southern boundary of Pennsylvania. Thus the Mason and Dixon line proper is merely the southern boundary of Pennsylvania, exclusive of the arc-boundary between that State and Delaware which was originally surveyed in 1701 and merely verified by Mason and Dixon. All but the extreme western part of the line surveyed by Mason and Dixon was marked by milestones, every fifth one of which bore the arms of William Penn on one side and the arms of Lord Baltimore on the other. The line was locally known as Mason's and Dixon's line before the Revolution, but it did not become nationally so known until after all the States north of it had abolished slavery and none of those to the south had taken such action. During the debates on slavery and the Missouri Compromise in 1819 and 1820 John Randolph of Roanoke and other public men frequently referred to the Mason and Dixon line as the dividing line between free and slave territory. Gradually people began to regard the Mason and Dixon line as the line of separation between the North and the South, and even today there are many who have a hazy notion that this famous line extends from the Atlantic to the Pacific, dividing the States that were free immediately before the Civil War from those that had slavery.

Can the President veto a declaration of war?

Under the Constitution the President has the power to veto an act declaring war and Congress has the power to pass it over his veto. No part of the Constitution is more generally misunderstood than the clause providing that, "Congress shall have power . . . to declare war." A great number of people erroneously believe the founders of our government intended to emphasize the fact that formal declarations of war should be initiated exclusively by the legislative branch of the government so that no one man could plunge the country into war as the absolute monarchs of that time were in the habit of doing. The framers of the Constitution were forming a federal republic out of a group of more or less independent States and they intended merely to make clear that the power to declare war is vested in the Federal Government rather than the States. When they stated that "Congress shall have power to declare war" they meant exactly what they would have meant if they had said that "The Federal Government, not the separate States, shall have power to declare war." At the same time it was provided that, "No State shall, without the consent of Congress, . . . engage in war, unless actually invaded, or in such imminent danger as will not admit of delay." There was obviously no intention to make the power of Congress to declare war more exclusive than its other legislative powers. This power is included in a long list of powers vested solely in the Federal Government, such as the power to coin money and to establish post offices. A bill or joint resolution declaring war does not differ from any other ordinary bill or joint resolution and cannot become effective until it has been presented to the President and approved by him or repassed over his veto by two thirds of the Senate and House of Representatives. No President has ever vetoed an act declaring war and evidently it would be bad policy for Congress to pass such an act without the approval of the official who, by virtue of his office, is commander-in-chief of the Army and Navy and who would be charged with the prosecution of the war. As a matter of fact, it is customary for Congress to pass an act declaring war only after the President has recommended such a step. The President cannot formally declare war, but when he finds an actual state of war in existence he may take the necessary military steps in the absence of Congressional action, and he is the sole judge whether such a condition exists.

Who was the first President to wear long trousers?

James Madison was the first President of the United States who habitually dressed in long trousers while he was Chief Executive. Washington, the elder Adams and Jefferson wore knee breeches during their administrations. Trousers or long pants were adopted in France in 1789 by the supporters of the revolution. For that reason the revolutionists were known as *sans-culottes,* which literally means *without breeches,* that is, without the knee breeches worn by the royalists. Many Americans adopted long pants in token of their sympathy with the French revolution. Between 1790 and 1800 trousers gradually came into vogue among the common people in America, but it was not until ten or twelve years later that they were substituted for breeches on dress occasions. Although the Duke of Wellington is said to have worn trousers in England after the Peninsular campaign, Beau Brummell is usually credited with having popularized trousers in that country.

Why do the eyes of some portraits follow the observer?

If an artist represents the eyes of a portrait as gazing directly forward they will appear to look directly at an observer standing at any point in front of the picture where a view is possible. The same effect is obtained in photography when the subject looks straight into the camera. On the other hand, if the eyes of a picture are not painted or photographed to look directly at the observer they will not do so even if he stands at the point toward which the eyes seem to be directed. This is because the picture is on a flat surface and has only two dimensions. Suppose, by way of illustration, a portrait represents a person with his face turned somewhat to the observer's right and his eyes fixed directly at the observer. If the observer moves to the left he does not get a different view of the picture; that is, he does not obtain a profile view as he would in real life. He merely sees the same picture narrowed somewhat in perspective. The picture of the face, though elongated in proportion to the angle at which it is viewed, possesses all the same lines that it did when seen in front, and the eyes still look directly forward and consequently at the observer. In other words, if the eyes of a portrait on a flat surface are represented as looking directly forward they will appear to follow the observer no matter what the angle may be at which the picture is viewed; and if the eyes are represented as looking in some other direction the observer cannot place himself in a position so they will appear to look at him. The same thing occurs in two-dimension motion pictures. An observer at the extreme left side of a theater sees the same scenes, though slightly distorted, that are seen by a person on the extreme right side.

What is the function of a cat's whiskers?

There is an old belief that a cat uses its whiskers to determine whether it can squeeze through a small hole or opening. According to this notion, the whiskers are exactly the same width as the animal's body and if they touch the sides of the hole the cat will not attempt to enter. Although not strictly true, there is a grain of truth in the belief. The large facial hairs, known scientifically as *vibrissæ*, serve as feelers or organs of touch and they contribute materially to the cat's ability to move about in the dark. These hairs themselves, of course, are not sensitive, but the roots are provided with sensitive nerve-endings. John Fiske, in *Through Nature to God,* writes as follows of these remarkable tactile organs: "The most perfect organs of touch are the *vibrissæ* or whiskers of the cat, which act as long levers in communicating impulses to the nerve fibers that terminate in clusters about the dermal sacs in which they are inserted. These cat-whiskers are merely specialized forms of such hairs as those which cover the bodies of most mammals, and which remain upon the human skin imbedded in minute sacs." Facial hairs of this type are particularly well developed, both in number and size, in those predatory species which hunt chiefly in jungles and other thick undergrowth. In the vegetable-eating bears the whiskers are few in number, small in size and apparently without any functon. There may be a relationship between a cat's whiskers and its sense of sight. A naturalist found that cats with their whiskers cut short were unable to judge distances accurately. In experiments cats without whiskers would repeatedly miss their prey when springing for it. The investigator concluded that the facial hairs aid the animal to fix its eyes on its prey and that it is undoubtedly injurious to remove the whiskers from a cat which must hunt for a living.

Why can't the people of Washington vote?

The National Capital occupies a peculiar position in the American commonwealth. It is in the nature of a Federal reservation without the status of either a State or a Territory. The tract of land known as the District of Columbia, which is coextensive in area with the City of Washington, was acquired by the Federal Government in 1789 from Maryland in pursuance of Article I, Section 8, Clause 17 of the Constitution, which provides that Congress shall have power "to exercise exclusive legislation in all cases whatsoever" in a district which may become "the seat of the government of the United States." There were definite reasons for giving Congress absolute control over the District of Columbia. Such control was deemed necessary in order to safeguard the best interests of the National Government. On June 21, 1783, the Continental Congress, then sitting in Philadelphia, was surrounded by a band of unpaid Continental troops, who broke up the session by pointing their muskets through the windows, hooting at and otherwise threatening the members. The governor of Pennsylvania either could not or would not provide protection, and the result was that the seat of government was removed from Philadelphia, first to Princeton and then to Annapolis. The framers of the Constitution had this unpleasant incident in mind when they determined to build a Capital in a territory over which the Federal Government should have exclusive jurisdiction. Their ideal was a Federal Capital without local politics, where the local authorities could not bully the Federal authorities. Washington does not belong to its residents, but to all the people of the United States, who govern it through their representatives in Congress. Congress can and does delegate its powers over the District to some extent, but it cannot abandon these powers without a change in the Constitution. For instance, a Constitutional Amendment establishing the District of Columbia as a State would be necessary before it could be given representation in the electoral college and the citizens the privilege of voting for President and Vice President. The privilege of voting—even for President—is not conferred upon citizens of the United States by the Constitution, but by the States in which they live. But Congress could, if it desired, confer upon the citizens of the District of Columbia some measure of local self-government, just as it does in the case of Hawaii, Alaska, the Philippines and Porto Rico, all of which elect their own legislatures and send delegates or commissioners to Congress with the power to speak but not to vote on bills. No Territory or dependency, however, can participate in a Presidential election. At the outset Congress delegated the government of the District of Columbia to three commissioners. Georgetown was incorporated in 1789 as a separate town with its own municipal government. In 1802 Washington was also incorporated, with a mayor, board of aldermen and a common council. But in 1871 Congress revoked the charters of both Washington and Georgetown and established a territorial form of government over the entire District. The new government consisted of a governor, a council appointed by the President, a house of delegates, and a delegate in the Federal House of Representatives elected by the voters. Congress in 1874 abolished the territorial government and restored government by itself through commissioners appointed by the President and confirmed by the Senate. Four years later this form of government was made permanent. Under this system the citizens of the District of Columbia cannot vote in National elections, and there are no local elections. They not only have no voice whatever in the management of their public affairs, but they are taxed without representation. Of course many temporary residents of the District retain their legal residence elsewhere and either go home to vote or vote by mail in those States where that method is permitted. Nevertheless a citizen of the District is a citizen of the United States and is eligible to Federal offices. The original District of Columbia, which was ten miles square, included a tract south of the Potomac ceded by Virginia. No public buildings were erected on that tract and in 1846, upon petition of the inhabitants, it was receded by Congress to the parent State.

Does corn grow faster at night?

Other things being equal, corn probably grows most rapidly on warm nights. Many plants, including corn or maize, continue to grow after dark, notwithstanding the fact that photosynthesis takes place only while the plants are receiving sunlight. The rate of growth in plants, says the U. S. Bureau of Plant Industry, is influenced by many factors other than the formation of food materials through photosynthesis, and the photosynthetic products themselves may require further change before being utilized in growth. Thus it happens that some plants not only continue to grow after nightfall but actually grow more rapidly at night under ordinary conditions than they do during the day. Apparently, however, this is not true of all plants. There is no particular period in the course of the twenty-four hours of the day during which all plants grow most rapidly. Even among those that reach their maximum rate of growth in the night the period of most rapid growth in some species seems to begin in the early part of the night, while in other species it does not begin until after midnight. Certain plants will continue to elongate rapidly even in prolonged darkness, but in such cases the type of growth differs materially from that which takes place when the plants are exposed to sunlight.

What is the size of the smallest fish in the world?

According to the U. S. Bureau of Fisheries, the smallest fish in the world reaches an average length of $\frac{6}{16}$ of an inch and a maximum length of $\frac{7}{16}$ of an inch. It is about the size of an ant and is probably the tiniest back-boned creature which has ever been called to the attention of science. The species is found in certain creeks in the Philippines and is known scientifically as *Pandaka pygmea*. Specimens are not numerous. The bodies of these fish are slender and almost transparent, the comparatively large eyes being the only features clearly visible. The next fish in respect to size is *Mistichthys luzonensis* and is also found in the Philippines. Its average length is about $\frac{1}{12}$ of an inch greater than that of *Pandaka pygmea*. Fish of this species are so numerous in Lake Buhi, Luzon, that the natives catch them for food. *Sinarapan* is the local name for the species.

Do Southerners use *you-all* in the singular?

In the Southern part of the United States *you-all* with emphasis on *you* is used colloquially as a plural of *you*. Many people in the North have the erroneous impression that Southerners employ *you-all* in reference to one person. *You-all* is probably never used in the singular except when the speaker is attempting to be humorous, although it is said that it is so used occasionally by the most ignorant, which is very doubtful. This phrase is used in addressing two or more persons, or one person representing others either actually or by implication. Joel Chandler Harris, Thomas Nelson Page and many other Southern writers declared that they never once heard *you-all* used when the speaker did not have in mind more than one individual, although he may have been addressing only one. Harris wrote: *"You-all, we-all, you-uns* and *we-uns* invariably refer to more than one individual."* For instance, one Southerner might ask another: "Did you-all catch any fish?" But the speaker would have in mind not only the person spoken to, but also another person or other persons who had also gone fishing. A person not thoroughly acquainted with this usage might easily suppose that the speaker referred to only the person spoken to. This no doubt accounts for the fact that many uninitiated Northerners feel absolutely certain that they have heard Southerners use *you-all* as a singular. The use of *you-all* is merely an effort to differentiate *you* as a plural from *you* as a singular. It simply means *you jointly* as opposed to *you* in the singular sense of *thou*. It has been stated that *you-all* as used in the South was repeatedly employed by Shakespeare and other classical writers. But *you-all* as used by Southerners differs in meaning from *you all* in the ordinary sense of *all of you,* which was used frequently by Shakespeare. In the latter case *all* instead of *you* is emphasized. When Antony in *Julius Cæsar* says, "You all did see that on the Lupercal I thrice presented him a kingly crown," the speaker emphasizes the *all* and means that everybody present saw him offer Cæsar the crown.

Likewise St. Paul emphasizes the *all* when, according to *Romans 1: 8*, he says, "I thank my God through Jesus Christ for you all." The following sentence illustrates the difference in usage: "I told *you*-all to bring your rifles but I see that you *all* did not do so."

What is Yiddish?

Yiddish is a corruption of German *Jüdisch,* meaning Jewish. Yiddish is the native language of those Jews whose ancestors left the Rhineland section of Germany during the Middle Ages and settled in Poland, Russia and other Slavic countries. These emigrants from Germany retained their Low German language but wrote it in Hebrew characters. They were isolated so many centuries from those who spoke German that their language absorbed much from the local dialects and gradually became irregular in grammar, spelling and pronunciation, finally evolving into a distinct folk-tongue. It acquired many Hebrew, Polish and Russian words, as well as a sprinkling of words of Latin origin. Thus Yiddish is essentially a Low German dialect which has developed under Slavic influences and which has been carried to all parts of the world by Jews from eastern Europe. A student in one of Professor B. F. Williams's English classes at Valparaiso University accidentally stumbled upon an apt although facetious definition of Yiddish when he defined it as "crucified German." It is now so widely spoken by Jews that it serves as a sort of international language for them. The Hebrew characters employed in writing and printing give written Yiddish more the appearance of Hebrew than German. Roughly speaking, however, the vocabulary contains 70 per cent of German words, 20 of Hebrew, and 10 of Slavic. During the nineteenth century Yiddish grammar and spelling were made more uniform and there is now an extensive literature printed in the language.

How large was the largest nugget of gold ever found?

Nugget is the common name given to a large, rounded mass of gold found in the native or free state. The largest nugget of which there is authentic record was the Welcome Stranger, which was found February 5, 1869, in a shallow cart rut near Moligul, Victoria, Australia. Authorities differ as to its exact weight, but it undoubtedly weighed between 2,250 and 2,500 troy ounces. Of course larger masses of gold in a more or less pure state have been taken from mines, but they are not correctly described as nuggets. What is popularly known as the Welcome nugget (often confused with the Welcome Stranger), weighed 2,195 ounces and was found 180 feet below the surface of Bakery Hill, Ballarat, also in Victoria, June 11, 1858. It was about 99 per cent pure gold. Perhaps the largest mass of gold ever found was the so-called Holterman nugget which was extracted in 1872 from Holterman's claims northwest of Bathurst, New South Wales. It contained about 3,000 ounces of gold and today would be worth $60,000. In 1860 a mass of gold weighing 1,596 ounces was taken from the Monumental mine in Sierra County, California.

What Cabinet officer's son was hanged at sea?

Philip Spencer, a midshipman in the American Navy, was hanged at sea while his father, John C. Spencer of New York, was Secretary of War in the Cabinet of President Tyler. The young midshipman was convicted of attempting to organize a mutiny on the U. S. S. *Somers* with a view of converting her into a pirate ship. On December 1, 1842, Spencer, the boatswain's mate and a seaman were hanged on the yardarm of the brig-of-war while she was on her way from Liberia to New York by way of St. Thomas in the Virgin Islands. The execution took place about 525 miles from St. Thomas and the *Somers* arrived at the Brooklyn navy yard thirteen days later. Although Spencer was executed upon mere suspicion a naval court of inquiry decided that the commander of the vessel, Commodore Alexander Slidell Mackenzie, had simply performed his duty, a verdict which was later confirmed by a court-martial.

Who gave the Golden Rule its name?

In *Matthew 7:12* Jesus says, "All things whatsoever ye would that men should do to you, do ye even so to them." This, Jesus added, is the "law and the prophets." It is known as the Golden Rule of Life. "Do as you would be done by," is a homelier but more popular way of expressing the same thought. Who first called this precept the Golden Rule is not known for certain. The *London*

Encyclopædia, published in 1845, attributed it to Isaac Watts (1674–1748), the British theologian and hymn writer. Watts frequently employed the word *golden* when he desired to express quality or great value. In *Logick, or the Right Use of Reason in the Enquiry after Truth,* published in 1725, he said: "In matters of equity between man and man, our Saviour has taught us an effectual means of guarding against this prejudice, and that is ;—to put my neighbor in the place of myself, and myself in the place of my neighbor, rather than be bribed by the corrupt principle of self-love to do injury to my neighbors. Thence arises that Golden Rule of dealing with others as we would have others deal with us." This is the earliest known application of *Golden Rule* to the famous precept of Jesus. But Clement Ellis, an English churchman, indirectly applied *golden* to the rule fourteen years before Watts was born. In an address delivered in 1660 he said: "The Gentleman is too much a man to be without all passion, but he is not so much a beast as to be governed by it. In this moderation and empire over himself . . . the just rule he goes by, is not opinion, but knowledge; not that *leaden* one, which is so easily bent and made crooked, or melted and dissolved by the heat of passion . . . but that other *golden* one, which lies so close and firm, as it is made straight and even." Jesus, of course, did not originate the thought embodied in the Golden Rule. It had been previously taught, almost in the same words, by many great teachers in different parts of the world. Five centuries before the time of Jesus the great Chinese philosopher laid down a similar precept. In the 23rd chapter of the *Analects of Confucius* appears this passage: "Tsze-king asked, saying, Is there one word which may serve as a rule of practice for all one's life? The master said, Is not *reciprocity* such a word? What you do not want done to yourself, do not do to others."

What is the Staked Plain?

Staked Plain is a literal translation of Spanish *Llano Estacado* and is the name of an extensive plateau in northwestern Texas and eastern New Mexico. There are two theories as to how the region acquired its unusual name. According to one, the early Spanish explorers in that region called it the Staked Plain because they set stakes in the ground to mark their routes over this large stretch of almost level and woodless plain where watering places were few and far between. According to the other, the Spanish so named the plateau because of the tall, naked, stake-like boles of yucca plants, known as Spanish bayonets and Spanish daggers, which grew there in abundance. The area known as Llano Estacado, says the U. S. Geological Survey, is bounded in a general way on the north by the Canadian River, on the west, southwest and south by the valley of the Pecos, and on the east by the headwaters of the Red, Brazos, and the Colorado rivers. It is a high, isolated plateau or broad mesa, projecting above the surrounding plains in a nearly flat, island-like mass. The slope or escarpment of the Staked Plain is composed of limestone, which is more resistant to erosion than the underlying beds. It is remarkable in that it forms an abrupt, precipitous and nearly horizontal rim. This region, which has a rather light rainfall, was in its virgin condition practically devoid of trees and contained a sparse but uniform covering of grasses.

Did Mrs. O'Leary's cow start the Chicago fire?

Mrs. O'Leary's cow is a mythical animal. The great Chicago fire of 1871 started October 8 in a barn owned by Patrick O'Leary. It destroyed 250 lives, and about 17,500 buildings having an estimated value of nearly $200,000,000. The exact cause of the fire has never been determined. It is supposed, however, that the original flame was due either to spontaneous combustion in the O'Leary haymow, or to the carelessness of persons smoking in the barn. The story that the fire was started by a kerosene lantern kicked over by a cow which Mrs. O'Leary was milking was fabricated by a newspaper reporter. Michael Ahern, who died in 1927, admitted several years before his death that he had invented the story about Mrs. O'Leary and her cow to make his account of the conflagration more interesting.

Do Eskimos live in snow houses?

Snow houses or igloos are not very common among Eskimos. There are about 30,000 Eskimos in North America and Greenland. Perhaps not half of these have even seen a snow house, and only a fraction of the remainder have spent a winter in one.

Eskimo habitations vary considerably with the region, but in a general way they conform to three types. During the summer Eskimos usually live in tents made of skins stretched over poles. Their winter dwellings consist of shallow excavations covered with turf and earth laid on a framework of driftwood or whale ribs. Sometimes houses of snow are used as winter dwellings, but such dwellings are unknown among the Alaskan Eskimos, and in the Mackenzie delta region they are resorted to only in emergencies. The snow house, however, long has been and still is the customary winter habitation of a number of Eskimo groups scattered eastward from Coronation Gulf to Greenland. Even in that desolate region the snow house is regularly inhabited only when no other building materials are available. Some of the Eskimo hunters are very expert at constructing houses of snow for the temporary shelter of their families. The Labrador Eskimos do not live in snow houses, and out of the 15,000 Eskimos in Greenland only a few hundred living around Cape York ever use such structures as regular dwellings, and the more usual dwelling even among them consists of walls of earth and rafters of stone slabs or the large bones of animals or whales. It is supposed that the Eskimos are descended from American aborigines who gradually worked their way into the Arctic. Ancient ruins found throughout the region where snow houses are still regularly or occasionally used indicate that the house of stone, driftwood and whale bone is older than the igloo or hemispherical house built of blocks of snow laid in spiral courses. In fact the snow house appears to have been a later Eskimo invention necessitated by the absence of material suitable for house building in parts of the far north.

Who was the first European to smoke tobacco?

In Spain there is a tradition that Rodrigo de Jerez, a native of Ayamonte, was the first European known to have smoked tobacco. He went with Columbus on his first expedition to the New World in 1492 and learned to smoke from the natives of the West Indies. When he returned to his village in Spain he took some tobacco leaves with him and his fellow townsmen were greatly astonished when they saw smoke emerging from his mouth and nose. His wife denounced him to the Holy Inquisition as a man who "swallows fire, exhales smoke, and is surely possessed by the devil." The first recorded mention of tobacco is probably that found in Columbus's diary under date of November 29, 1492. The tobacco plant itself was introduced into Europe in 1558 by Francisco Fernandes, a physician, whom Philip II of Spain sent out to investigate and report upon the products of America. Jean Nicot, French ambassador at Lisbon, sent some tobacco seeds to Catherine de Medici, queen of France, and his connection with the early history of tobacco is commemorated in the scientific name of the genus —*Nicotiana*. But in France and Spain tobacco was at first regarded merely as a medicinal or curative plant. The smoking habit seems to have spread from England rather than Spain. Thomas Hariot, a mathematician sent by Sir Walter Raleigh to report on the commercial and colonization possibilities of Virginia, is credited with being the first Englishman to smoke tobacco. Be that as it may, Ralph Lane, first governor of Raleigh's colony in America, learned to smoke from the Indians and brought the habit to the attention of his eminent patron, Sir Walter, who, with Sir Francis Drake, popularized it at Queen Elizabeth's court. Raleigh continued to smoke the rest of his life, and it is recorded that he "tooke a pipe of tobacco a little before he went to the scaffolde." At first the habit was bitterly opposed. In his *Counterblast to Tobacco* King James I characterized smoking as "a custom loathsome to the eye, hateful to the nose, harmful to the brain, dangerous to the lungs, and in the black stinking fume thereof nearest resembling the horrible Stygian smoke of the pit that is bottomless." Sir John Hawkins made a voyage to Florida in 1565 and in his journal, published in 1589, he described smoking among the natives; from this circumstance many writers infer that Hawkins introduced tobacco smoking into England.

Why are Italians called wops?

Wop, like *dago,* is a contemptuous slang name often applied in America to the lower class of Italian immigrants. The appellation is keenly resented by those to whom it is applied and many efforts have been made to discourage its use. The term is of unknown derivation. "It is a vulgarism of the streets which probably originated in the underworld," said Dr. Frank H. Vizetelly

40

in a letter to the author dated July 2, 1924. *Wop* may have been borrowed from the Italian immigrants themselves. It is often stated that the slang word is a shortened and corrupted form of *wapparousa* (or *vapparousa,* since *w* does not occur in Italian except in foreign words), supposedly a Sicilian dialectical or colloquial term meaning "a good-for-nothing fellow." If true, this may account for the origin of the disagreeable and stinging connotation of *wop* as interpreted by the Italians themselves. But the author has been unable to find any positive evidence that such a word exists in the Sicilian dialect. There is, however, a Sicilian word *vappu,* meaning a bully or braggart, and according to Gaetano Ceraso's *Vocabolario Napoletano Italiano,* published in 1910, the term has a similar meaning in the Neapolitan dialect. Dino Bigongiari of the department of Italian at Columbia University thinks that possibly *wop* is derived from *vappu,* which, he says, has acquired a more recent meaning, namely, a member of the underworld who is not yet fully trained, a sort of *green thug.*

Are elephants afraid of mice?

It is often said that elephants are particularly afraid of mice. Such, it would seem, is not a fact. The director of the National Zoological Park informs the author that elephants in the park at Washington pay no attention whatever to the numerous mice running about the barns. Raymond L. Ditmars, curator of mammals at the New York Zoological Park, gives similar testimony. "I am inclined to think that elephants, generally, are not afraid of mice," he wrote to the author in 1928. "I have often noted both rats and mice in the hay in circuses and animal shows, and the elephants apparently pay no attention whatsoever to them." Nor is there any evidence that elephants in the wild state exhibit any particular fear of mice. Of course it is quite possible that individual elephants may have such a fear. A writer who had many years of experience with wild elephants in India states that their two greatest fears are dogs and human beings. Still the belief that elephants have an especial fear of mice is very persistent. A few years ago a popular writer asserted that elephants are afraid of mice because small mouse-like animals found in their wild haunts sometimes crawl up the trunks of the huge beasts when they are feeding and dig their claws into the flesh. The elephant becomes frantic and blows violently but is unable to dislodge the tiny crea ture, which, it is said, not only produces great pain but in some cases actually causes the death of its victim. This story, told to explain an imaginary phenomenon, is probably pure fiction.

What is the function of air spaces in eggs?

It is supposed that the air sac at the large end of an egg performs an important function in the development of the embryo chick. The chick makes use of the air in this pocket during the brief period between the time when it begins to breathe and the time when it is strong enough to break through the shell with its beak. This air sac enlarges materially during incubation, and in a normal egg the chick at hatching time always has its head pointing toward the large end of the egg and the air space. It is the opinion of the U. S. Bureau of Animal Industry that the air sac is formed by the contraction of the contents of the egg immediately after it is laid. The temperature of an ordinary hen's body is about 107° Fahrenheit, and it is reasonable to suppose that as soon as an egg is laid the yolk and white contract somewhat. Because of the peculiar shape of the egg the air space is nearly always formed at the large end. Now and then it occurs on the side, but never at the small end.

Does the exact center of a wheel turn?

Many people believe that the exact center of a solid wheel does not move when the wheel rotates on a stationary axis. This notion, which would apply to any other object rotating under the same conditions, is based on the following reasoning. Since both time and distance enter into motion the speed of any part of a moving wheel decreases as the center is approached. Theoretically the element of distance is totally lacking at the exact center and the motion at that point should be zero. In order to move at all the exact center would have to move in two directions at the same time, which is clearly impossible. This, however, is true only in theory. A wheel is a rigid object and when it turns every conceivable part of it moves, for the human mind cannot conceive of an ultimate particle. If you can conceive of any particle of matter whatever, be it ever so small, you can always conceive of that particle divided in half, and this process of division can be continued indefinitely. "The particles lying in the axis of rotation of a solid wheel must turn with the wheel," says the U. S. Bureau of Standards. "Otherwise these particles would have to slip with respect to adjacent particles off the axis. Of course no such slipping occurs."

What is meant by second wind?

Second wind is the name given to the return of normal breathing after a temporary loss of breath during sustained physical exertion, especially running. It is an adjustment of the heart rate to breathing. When a person begins to run he generally uses more energy than is necessary, which results in rapid breathing and so-called loss of breath; but after running some distance he may become adjusted to the gait and regain normal respiration. Horses and other animals are affected in the same manner. Physiologists state that when a person begins to run the sudden action produces large quantities of lactic acid in the muscles, and the heart is speeded up by the automatic impulses of the nervous system. Some time, however, is required for the entire system to adjust itself to the higher speed of operation. When the runner's heart and lung action is approximately fast enough to take care of the extra energy expended by the body he is said to have his second wind.

When is the longest day in the year?

About ninety-nine persons out of a hundred will answer this question by saying June 21. That, however, is only the approximate date of the longest day. Under our present calendar the longest day in the year may be either June 21 or June 22 in places using Standard Time. In each year preceding a leap year the longest day is June 22, while in all other years it is June 21. Likewise the shortest day in the year may be either December 21 or December 22. It is December 22 in all years except leap years, when it is December 21. The longest and shortest days in the year are determined by the summer and winter solstices, the exact time of which is determined by mathematical calculation. The solstices are the times of the year when the sun is at its greatest declination, either north or south. For instance, the summer solstice is the time at which the sun reaches its farthest point in its swing northward from the Equator and which accordingly marks the longest day in the year. The year consists of approximately 365¼ days, and the solstices fluctuate because of the fractional day of each year, which is adjusted by leap years. The longest and shortest days differ in length from the days immediately preceding and following them only by a fraction of a minute.

Is a foreign-born citizen eligible to the Presidency?

A foreign-born citizen of the United States is eligible to the Presidency in respect to citizenship if he is an American citizen by virtue of birth and not naturalization. The Constitution says: "No person except a *natural born* citizen of the United States . . . shall be eligible to the office of President." But *natural born* does not necessarily mean *native born*. Suppose, for instance, a person were born in the American embassy at Paris while his father was in the foreign service of the United States. There would be no question as to this person's qualification for the Presidency of the United States in respect to original citizenship. It is inferred that the same would be true of all persons born of American parents in foreign countries, even if the parents were in private business or merely traveling. That such was the understanding of the founders of the American Government is shown by an act of Congress approved March 26, 1790, which provided: "The children of citizens of the United States, that may be born beyond sea, or out of the limits of the United States, shall be considered as natural born citizens: Provided, That the right of citizenship shall not descend to persons whose fathers have never been resident in the United States." The provision in the Revised Statutes covering this subject, like the act of 1855 on which it was based, does not contain the words *natural born,* but it is presumed that the intent was the same. Section 1993 of the Revised Statutes says: "All children heretofore born or hereafter born out of the limits and jurisdiction of the United States, whose fathers were or may be at the time of their birth citizens thereof, are declared to be citizens of the United States; but the rights of citizenship shall not descend to children whose fathers never resided in the United States." The last clause prevents the perpetuation of a line of foreign-born citizens. But persons who are born of American parents outside the limits of the United States and who continue to reside outside the country must comply with certain requirements in order to receive the protection of the American Government. In 1907 it was enacted that such persons upon reaching the age of eighteen must record their intention to become residents and to remain citizens of the United States, and upon attaining their majority they must take the oath of allegiance.

When was ice cream first made?

Ice cream as it is known today was not the product of a single discovery or invention. Therefore it is impossible to assign a definite date to its origin. There is reason for supposing, however, that ice cream originated in Italy, perhaps before the discovery of America. A variety of frozen compound was a common delicacy in Florence during the sixteenth century, and when Catherine de Medici became queen of France in 1533 she took her outfit for making ice cream with her to Paris. The proprietors of Florin's Café in Naples maintain that ice cream was manufactured and sold there by a man named Florin nearly two hundred years ago. We have no means of determining what the nature of this early ice cream was. Records of the introduction of ice cream into England are equally meager. In 1769 Mrs. Elizabeth Raffald published a book in London entitled *The Experienced Housekeeper* in which she gave the recipe for making a kind of ice cream. Ice cream made by a man named Hall, of 75 Chatham Street, now Park Row, was advertised in New York June 8, 1786, and there is record that a Mrs. Johnson served ice cream at a ball given in New York December 12, 1789. In 1802 Samuel Latham Mitchill, a member of Congress from New York, wrote a letter to his wife in which he described a dinner given in Washington by President Jefferson. The dessert, wrote Mitchill, was of frozen fruit juices, well sweetened and shaped like a ball, inclosed in a steaming hot pastry, which was placed on a plate, the whole being covered with rich cream. The fact that Dolly Madison served ice cream in the White House at a New Year's reception during the Presidency of her husband is referred to in a letter written at the time by a Mrs.

Seaton. But ice cream did not become common until many years later. It was still an oddity when the widow of Alexander Hamilton served it at a dinner given in Washington in honor of President Jackson. The first factory for the manufacture of ice cream in commercial quantities was established in Maryland in 1851.

Why are June marriages considered lucky?

The belief that June marriages are likely to be lucky is a relic of Roman superstition and mythology. "Prosperity to the man and happiness to the maid when married in June," was a proverb of Rome. It was popularly supposed that the month of June was named in honor of Juno, whose festival was held on the first of that month. Juno was the wife of Jupiter and she was not only the guardian of the female sex from birth to death, but also the patroness of happy marriages. June is still the favorite month of the year for weddings. May, supposedly named after the Roman goddess Maia, is regarded by the superstitious as unpropitious for marriages. A gruesome but ancient Scotch proverb says:

> From the marriages in May
> All the bairns die and decay.

Whether the months of June and May were actually named after the goddesses Juno and Maia is an unsettled question. Ovid has Juno say that June was named expressly in her honor; but since June and May were dedicated respectively to youth and old age, some authorities derive the names from *juniores,* comparative plural of *juvenis,* meaning young, and *majores,* comparative plural of *magnus,* aged or old. Others suppose June to be derived from *Junius,* a Roman family name.

What man was both son and father of a President?

John Scott Harrison, who was born in 1804 at Vincennes, Indiana, was the son of William Henry Harrison, ninth President of the United States, and father of Benjamin Harrison, the twenty-third President. As a young man he studied medicine but he abandoned the medical profession and became a farmer. From 1853 to 1857 he was a Whig member of Congress from Ohio. His death occurred in 1878 on Point Farm, near North Bend, Ohio, where President Benjamin Harrison was born.

Do all whirling winds turn counterclockwise?

All cyclones, tornadoes or twisters, and those waterspouts that originate at cloud level and after the manner of tornadoes, turn counterclockwise in the Northern Hemisphere and clockwise in the Southern. *Cyclone* is here used in the technical sense of an extensive system of winds blowing around a center of relatively low atmospheric pressure. Waterspouts that originate at the surface, as well as small whirlwinds and dust whirls, which also originate at the surface, turn in either direction, some turning clockwise and some counterclockwise in both hemispheres. We do not have sufficient space here to give an intelligible explanation as to why these air whirls turn as they do. The rotation of the earth, of course, is an important factor; but how it acts, and why it is a determining factor in some cases and only a minor one in others, present highly intricate problems. It has often been stated that when water is released through a small hole, such as the outlet of a bathtub or wash basin, the whirlpool thus formed always turns clockwise south of the Equator and counterclockwise north of the Equator. That is not true. Such whirlpools may turn in either direction in both hemispheres. The U. S. Weather Bureau says that the phenomenon of whirling water running through a hole is due entirely to conditions which have nothing to do with location in reference to the Equator.

How many square feet of skin does the body contain?

It is estimated that there are from fourteen to eighteen square feet of skin on the average adult human body. One investigator placed the figure as high as twenty-four square feet. Of course the surface area of the body, which is practically equivalent to the number of square feet of skin, varies with the sex, age, height and weight of the individual. Obviously the body of a tall, thin person might have a much greater surface area than the body of a short, fat person who has the same weight. The most common method of obtaining the surface area of the body is complicated and involves many factors, but charts have been devised whereby it can be estimated with a high degree of accuracy if the individual's sex, age, height and weight are known. The Imperial State Institute for Nutrition at Tokyo, Japan, computes the number of square inches of skin by pasting over the nude body a special kind of very thin but strong paper that adheres closely to curved surfaces. The paper is first dried, then removed, cut into small pieces and measured.

Can eggs be boiled hard on Pike's Peak?

Eggs can be boiled hard on Pike's Peak in an open vessel, but more time is required for the process than at lower altitudes. The boiling point of water depends on atmospheric pressure as well as on temperature. At sea level water boils at 212° Fahrenheit at mean atmospheric pressure. But higher up the atmospheric pressure is less and water boils at a lower temperature. There is a difference of one degree in the boiling point of water for about every 538 feet of altitude. For instance, 1,076 feet above sea level water boils at 210° instead of 212°. On the other hand, below sea level the pressure increases and a higher temperature is required to bring water to the boiling point. Thus at 1,076 feet below sea level water boils at 214° instead of at 212°. Early travelers, ignorant of the fact that altitude lowers the boiling point, were greatly puzzled to find water boiling while food in it remained uncooked. Marco Polo, writing of his experiences in the Pamirs in 1271, said that at those altitudes "fire does not burn so brightly, nor gives out so much heat as usual, nor does it cook food so effectively." Darwin, in *The Voyage of the Beagle,* relates an experience in the "republic of Mendoza," South America, where "the elevation was probably not under 11,000 feet." "At the place where we slept," wrote the scientist, "water necessarily boiled, from diminished pressure of the atmosphere, at a lower temperature than it does in a less lofty country; the case being the converse of that of a Papin's digester. Hence the potatoes, after remaining for some hours in the boiling water, were nearly as hard as ever. The pot was left on the fire all night, and next morning it was boiled again, but yet the potatoes were not cooked. I found out this, by overhearing my two companions discussing the cause; they had come to the simple conclusion, 'that the cursed pot (which was a new one) did not choose to boil potatoes.' " Theoretically there is an altitude at which water would not boil at all, where it would instantly turn into vapor if released from a closed vessel, but that point is many miles higher than the highest mountain. Pike's Peak is 14,108 feet high, and, according to the U. S. Bureau of Standards, the boiling point of water at a pressure corresponding to that found on the top of a peak of such altitude is about 187° Fahrenheit. This means that the greatest temperature obtainable by a boiling process in free air on top of Pike's Peak is 187° as compared with 212° at sea level. Water does not reach the boiling point until it begins to roll and agitate, although it frequently steams at a much lower temperature. Boiling water at 187° is not as hot as boiling water at 212°. Both the heat and agitation operate to cook food. Most foods cook very slowly in water boiling at temperatures as low as 187°. Whether foods like eggs can be cooked in open vessels at such an altitude depends on their coagulation point, that is, the temperature at which they undergo the change commonly described as cooking. The coagulation point of eggs is lower than the boiling point of water on Pike's Peak and accordingly they can be hard-boiled at that altitude, but the process is greatly retarded by the reduced temperature. As a matter of fact, lunches consisting of eggs, coffee and other foods and drinks have been regularly prepared in the usual way near the summit of that mountain. Some people maintain that eggs boiled at high altitudes have a better flavor and are more digestible than those boiled more rapidly at lower altitudes. It would be very difficult, if not impossible, to hard-boil eggs in an open vessel on Mt. Everest, which is more than twice as high as Pike's Peak. Needless to say, conditions would be entirely different if a closed vessel were used. Eggs are composed chiefly of albumen. Heat causes a rearrangement of the molecules in the albumen and changes it into a substance which is harder and more solid. Most other foods are softened, not hardened, by the combined effect of heat and water. The U. S. Bureau of Home Economics states that peas become tender more quickly if the water in which they are being cooked is permitted merely to simmer and is kept below the boiling point. The agitation in rapid boiling tends to break up vegetables, although the temperature of rapidly boiling water is no higher than the temperature of slowly boiling water, assuming the atmospheric pressure to be the same.

Why are cows milked from the right side?

The custom of milking cows from the right side is almost universal. It probably originated in man's decided preference for the right hand. Most people are right-handed and they find it more natural and possibly somewhat easier to manage the receptacle with the left hand and to do the heavier part of the milking with the more developed and stronger right hand and arm. When the milker sits on the right side of the cow his right arm has more room than it would have if he sat on the left. The custom became general and persists, even among left-handed people, because it was found advisable to train all cows to be milked from the same side. Cows trained to be milked from one side often resent being milked from the other and not infrequently they make it uncomfortable for the milker under such circumstances. When a cow freshens she can be trained to be milked from the left side just as well as she can be trained to be milked from the right side, and some farmers do milk their cows from the left side, although the practice is not common. Dairymen who use mechanical milkers generally attach the pumps from either side of the animals, and occasionally one finds a farmer who milks his cows indiscriminately from either side. Sometimes a cow will have such a large udder that milkers find it more satisfactory to milk some of the teats from one side and some from the other. A rural correspondent suggests that cows may have been originally milked on the right side because their stomachs are somewhat to the left, causing that side to bulge out more and making it more difficult for the milker to reach the udder.

What President first left the United States during office?

Grover Cleveland was the first man to pass beyond the legal boundaries of his country while President of the United States. Upon one occasion he exceeded the three-mile limit while fishing off the Atlantic coast. Theodore Roosevelt was the first President to leave the jurisdiction of the United States and visit a foreign country during his administration. He went to the Panama Canal Zone in 1906 and on November 15 of that year visited the City of Panama. William Howard Taft left the country four times while he was Chief Executive. On October 16, 1909, he crossed the Mexican border and attended a banquet given by President Diaz at Ciudad Juarez. The following year he made a tour of inspection through the Canal Zone and made a visit to the Republic of Panama. He made two other inspection tours to Panama while he was President. Woodrow Wilson left the United States twice while he was President, both times to attend the Paris Peace Conference. President Harding passed through British Columbia, Canada, when he visited Alaska in 1923, and in 1928 President Coolidge went to Havana, Cuba, to open the Pan-American Congress. There never has been any statute prohibiting the Chief Executive from leaving the jurisdiction of the American flag, and it is presumed that the Constitution permits him to go wherever he assumes his duty requires his presence. Chief Justice Taft pointed out that the only part of the Constitution which could have any bearing on the subject is the paragraph providing that "the powers and duties" of the Presidency "shall devolve on the Vice President" when the President is unable to discharge them. Continued absence from the country might be interpreted as such a contingency.

How tall do elephants grow?

Elephants do not grow so tall as is generally supposed. They are so great in bulk that there is a tendency to overestimate their size, and in consequence many extravagant estimates of their height have been reported. The largest elephants are the adult males of the African species. A specimen more than ten feet tall at the shoulders would be regarded as an extremely tall animal. Herbert Lang and Carl E. Akeley measured two elephants in East Africa that were eleven feet four inches in height. They were probably the tallest elephants of which there is authentic record. Such a specimen in good physical condition would weigh four or five tons. Of course there is no reason why there may not be elephants in the jungles larger than any that have ever been measured, but it is not probable that any specimen belonging to a living species has grown much taller than twelve feet. It is very difficult to measure a wild elephant on the hoof. "When a big elephant is dead," says Dr. William Hornaday, "probably no man on earth could measure its shoulder height as it lies and hit upon the figure representing its standing height while alive. Nor is it likely that any two men could measure a dead elephant and find their figures for height in agreement. The position of the dead fore leg is a puzzle. As that member lies prone and relaxed in death, it would be almost impossible to know how much to push it up into the shoulder in order to place it just as in life." Jumbo, the famous African elephant exhibited first in the London Zoological Park and later by the Barnum and Bailey Circus, weighed six tons and was ten feet nine inches tall. He was killed in a railway accident at St. Thomas, Canada, in 1885. Indian elephants seldom exceed ten feet in height, and the average for adult males is about eight feet. In the British Museum there is the fossil of a prehistoric elephant which was fourteen feet in height.

What language did Jesus speak?

Scholars are not agreed on this subject. Four languages were in use in Palestine in the time of Christ—Hebrew, Aramaic, Latin and Greek. It is generally supposed that the native tongue of Jesus was the Galilean dialect of the Aramaic or Syriac language. *Aramaic* is derived from *Aram,* an old Semitic geographical term which was applied to Syria, Mesopotamia and adjacent regions, although it did not originally include Palestine. The Aramaic dialects were acquired to some extent during the captivity; they were a corrupted form of Hebrew proper and contained many words from that language. As one writer expresses it, Aramaic bore a relation to Hebrew somewhat similar to the relation that modern Yiddish bears to Hebrew. Several centuries before the birth of Jesus the Aramaic language, in one form or other, spread over Palestine; by the time of Augustus Cæsar it had supplanted Hebrew as the spoken language of the common people, who could no longer speak the language of the Old Testament. Even the books of the Old Testament itself were translated or paraphrased in the vulgar tongue, although Hebrew remained the learned and sacred language of the Jews. The inhabitants of Galilee probably spoke

Aramaic with a peculiar accent which distinguished them from the people in other parts of Palestine. In *Matthew 26: 73* we read, "And after a while came unto him they that stood by, and said to Peter, Surely thou also art one of them; for thy speech bewrayeth thee." There is no reason for supposing that Jesus spoke Latin, a language confined chiefly to the Romans. It is likely that he used the vernacular of the district and his mother tongue in speaking to his disciples and countrymen. In fact he would be obliged to do so in order to be understood. Some scholars suggest that Jesus may have spoken Greek, the original language of the New Testament. That language was in everyday use in the eastern part of the Roman Empire during the first century and it was the common means of communication between the different classes and nationalities. According to *Luke 23: 38,* the inscription on the cross was in Greek, Latin and Hebrew so that all could read. Whether *Hebrew* here refers to Hebrew proper or to the Aramaic is not clear, because the latter was generally referred to as Hebrew or the Hebrew vernacular and consequently writers often confused the two languages. It does not seem probable that the simple fishermen and village folk of Galilee were familiar with Greek or any language except Aramaic. Whether Jesus read the classical Hebrew is not known. He may have read the Scriptures in Hebrew, in Greek, or in the *Tragums* or Aramaic translations.

Is it illegal to mail chain letters?

Chain letter is the term commonly applied to a prayer or good luck message containing a threat of misfortune or bad luck to the recipient if he does not send copies to others. Since such messages contain threats they are not mailable if they appear on post or postal cards or on the outside of mail; but, according to the U. S. Post Office Department, they are mailable when sent in envelopes with the postage prepaid. Some chain letters are commercial in their nature and are designed to spread propaganda; those containing schemes for collecting money or selling merchandise violate the postal laws and regulations. There is no law prohibiting the starting of good luck chains, but the Post Office Department discourages such letters and advises the public to ignore them. Obviously it would be difficult to trace the originator of chain letters. They thrive on a species of superstition that is almost impossible to eradicate, and hundreds of thousands of chain letters are sent every year notwithstanding they are continually condemned by religious, educational and fraternal leaders. Some of these letters may be sent in a spirit of fun, but undoubtedly the majority of them are mailed because the senders actually fear that misfortune will befall them if they break the chain. Frequently the names of well known persons are attached to chain letters to give them an air of authenticity. One of the most famous of all chain letters purports to have been written by Jesus just before the crucifixion and deposited by him beneath a stone at the foot of the cross. The receiver of the letter is enjoined to send copies of it to others upon pain of misfortune and bad luck. Compliance promises good fortune. Perhaps the most widely circulated chain letter of recent origin is known as the Flanders Chain of Good Luck. It reads, in substance, as follows:

This letter was sent to me and I am sending it to you. Do not break the chain. Send this and three copies within twenty-four hours to three friends whom you wish good luck and see what happens to you on the fourth day. This chain was started June 20, 1920, in Flanders by an American Army officer and will go around the world three times. Whoever breaks this chain will have bad luck. It is wonderful how this prediction is fulfilled.

Were Evangeline and Gabriel married?

Evangeline and Gabriel, as portrayed in Longfellow's *Evangeline,* were never married. The actual marriage ceremony had not been performed when they were separated. One evening, the poem relates, René Leblanc, the notary public, went to the home of Benedict Bellefontaine with his paper and inkhorn and drew up the civil contract of betrothal between Gabriel and Evangeline. He wrote the date, the ages of the parties, the dower of the bride, and then set the seal of the law on the margin. Benedict gave the notary three times the usual fee for such service, after which Father Leblanc arose, blessed the bride and bridegroom, and drank a tankard of ale to their welfare. Many suppose that Gabriel and Evangeline were actually married because they are referred to as *bride* and *bridegroom,* but these terms may mean persons either newly married or about to be married. The text does not justify the conclusion that they were actually united in marriage before their separation. The day after the legal contract was made Benedict, Basil and their friends celebrated "the feast of betrothal," at which Father Felician, the village priest, René Leblanc, Michael the fiddler, and many others were present. It was not a wedding. While the company was feasting and dancing the men were summoned to the church and seized by the British. After they were placed on different vessels five days later, the betrothed pair never saw each other again until Evangeline in her old age found her lover dying of fever in an almshouse in Philadelphia. It should be borne in mind that Gabriel and Evangeline, so far as the details of the poem are concerned, are fictitious characters, although Longfellow obtained the general plot from a real incident and he gave the poem a historical setting. Whether the persons who suggested Gabriel and Evangeline were married is not known for certain. Hawthorne, who heard the story before Longfellow did, says merely that the young couple were separated on their "marriage day." Under date of October 24, 1838, we find the following memorandum in Hawthorne's *American Note-Books:* "H. L. C.— heard from a French Canadian a story of a young couple in Acadie. On their marriage day all the men of the province were summoned to assemble in the church to hear a proclamation. When they assembled they were seized and shipped off to be distributed through New England, among them the bridegroom. His bride set off in search of him, wandered about New England all her lifetime, and at last when she was old, she found her bridegroom on his deathbed. The shock was so great that it killed her likewise." H. L. C. was Horace Lorenzo Conolly, then a neighbor of Hawthorne at Salem. He had been rector of St. Matthew's Protestant Church in South Boston. Hawthorne was probably in error in stating that Conolly obtained the story directly from a French Canadian. Be that as it may, sometime later Hawthorne took Conolly to dine with Longfellow at Cambridge. During the dinner the clergyman told Longfellow that he had been trying in vain to get Hawthorne to write a story based on an incident told him by Mrs. George M. Haliburton, a former parishioner, who had once lived in Nova Scotia. Conolly then related the story in brief.

Longfellow said to Hawthorne: "If you really do not want this incident, let me have it for a poem." Hawthorne readily consented, and *Evangeline* was the result. According to an elaborate tradition among the French of Louisiana, Evangeline in real life was Emmaline Labiche, and Gabriel was Louis Arceneaux. Emmaline, according to the legend, searched many years for Louis and at last found him on the banks of the Teche. But, of course, there is no substantial evidence that the persons in question were the characters used by Longfellow.

Who was the first circumnavigator of the globe?

It is often said that Ferdinand Magellan did not actually circumnavigate the earth because he was killed in the Philippines before his famous voyage was completed, and that accordingly the honor of having been the first circumnavigator of the globe belongs to Juan Sebastian del Cano, who returned to Seville in the *Vittorio* with thirty-one of the survivors of the ill-fated expedition. When Magellan was killed in a battle with the natives on Mactan Island April 27, 1521, he had sailed west to a point 124° longitude east of Greenwich. In 1512, however, when he was still a subject of Portugal, Magellan sailed as far east as Banda Island, which is about 130° longitude east. Therefore he, and not his subordinate del Cano, deserves the honor of having been the first person to circumnavigate the globe, although he was not the first to perform the feat in a single voyage.

What was Henry Hudson's nationality?

Henry Hudson, the explorer, was English, not Dutch as many suppose. His early life is obscure, but historians are agreed that he was an Englishman by birth. The impression, which is quite general, that he was Dutch arose from the fact that his third voyage, in the *Half Moon,* was undertaken under the auspices of the Dutch East India Company, and Dutch writers usually spell his first name *Hendrik.* In *Knickerbocker's History of New York* Washington Irving wrote: "Henry (or, as the Dutch historians call him, Hendrik) Hudson, was a sea-faring man of renown, who had learned to smoke tobacco under Sir Walter Raleigh, and is said to have been the first to introduce it into Holland, which gained him much popularity in that country, and caused him to find great favor in the eyes of their High Mightinesses, the lords states general, and also of the honorable West [East?] India Company." Hudson's first two voyages of exploration were made under the auspices of a British association known as the Muscovy Company. He undertook his third voyage of exploration for the Dutch East India Company with a view of finding a passage to China. While on this voyage, made in 1609, he explored New York Bay and the river which bears his name, and on these explorations the Dutch based their claim to New Netherland. The next year Hudson sailed to the New World in the *Discovery,* this time again under the auspices of an English company. He spent the last winter of his life in James Bay, an arm of Hudson Bay. In the spring of 1611 most of the crew mutinied and the captain with several companions was placed in a small boat and set adrift. The *Discovery* returned safely to England, but Henry Hudson was never heard of again.

How did chop suey originate?

The concoction of foods known as chop suey originated in the United States and is not a typical Chinese dish. According to Arthur W. Hummel, chief of the Chinese Division of the Library of Congress, chop suey was popularized in 1896 while Li Hung-chang, the great Chinese statesman, was making a trip around the world. When in New York Li entertained many of his American friends at Chinese restaurants in Chinatown where special Chinese foods were prepared. An American lady was especially pleased with one of the dishes served at a dinner given by Li and she asked what it was. The chef, who was called, said in Chinese: "It is a creation of my own—it is a chop suey." Li, very much amused, explained in English: "It is a chop suey." *Chop suey* is Chinese and literally means miscellaneous pieces or bits, namely, a mixture or hash, although the term had not been applied to any particular dish known in the Orient. Chinese restaurant proprietors in New York seized the chance to capitalize Li's name and the incident at his dinner, and soon they were serving various mixtures under the names Li Hung-chang Chop Suey and Li Hung-chang Rice, which were made especially to suit the taste of their American patrons. Later such mixtures came to be known in America simply as chop suey. The chop suey served at the dinner in question consisted of various meats and vegetables—such as pork, beef, chicken, celery, onions, noodles, mushrooms, peppers, mung-bean sprouts and bamboo sprouts—which had been chopped into small bits, mixed together, seasoned with sesame oil, cooked slowly, and then served in their own juice with rice. Of course all these ingredients were well known to Chinese in China and undoubtedly similar but less elaborate mixtures had often been made before. Even now there is no set way of making chop suey. But chop suey as a special dish is practically unknown in China. The Chinese regard it as too rich. A chop suey restaurant established in Peking several years ago went out of business in 1928 because there were not enough Americans in the city to support it. Efforts to introduce chop suey farther south have been more successful.

How would you write it?

The words *to, too* and *two* are pronounced alike. The question is often asked: How can one write this fact in a direct statement —"There are three (*to, too, two*)'s in the English language"? In such a case it is necessary to use a phonetic combination to represent the common sound of the three words. *Too* is the phonetic combination generally employed to indicate the pronunciation of *to, too* and *two,* when diacritical marks are not used. Therefore it is correct to write, "There are three *too's* in the English language," the *too* here standing not for the word so spelled but for the sound of all three words. It is merely a poor way of saying that there are three words in the English language pronounced *too,* or like the figure 2. The same problem arises in connection with any two or more words that are the same in pronunciation but different in spelling.

Does the sap of trees freeze in the winter?

Sap in trees frequently freezes during the winter. The freezing point of water is lowered by the addition of substances in solution. Since sap contains various solutes its freezing point is considerably below 32° and accordingly it does not freeze in moderate freezing temperatures. Trees are further protected from freezing by the fact that the moisture content near the surface is not so great in winter as in summer. But the sap freezes during extremely cold spells and sometimes much damage is done to the trees. The U. S. Forest Service says that in the Canadian woods when the temperature is 40° or 50° below zero the ruptures of tissue in trees caused by freezing can often be heard as a sort of sharp report. As a rule freezing that produces sufficient pressure to rupture the tissue results in vertical cracks running up and down the trunk of the tree. In succeeding seasons of growth the tree attempts to heal over these cracks, but ridges of protruding scar tissue remain as evidence of the injury. Although the wood of trees is frequently frozen hard, generally no serious ruptures result because the moisture is evenly distributed through the tissue.

What are the tallest trees in the world?

It is not true, as often supposed, that the big trees of California are the tallest trees in the world. That distinction belongs to the eucalyptus trees of Australia. The giant eucalypt or peppermint tree, known scientifically as *Eucalyptus amygdalina,* is the tallest tree of which there is authentic record. In his *Eucalyptographia* Baron von Mueller mentions recorded heights among these trees of more than four hundred feet and diameters ranging from eighteen to thirty-five feet. Since then specimens four hundred and eighty feet in height have been found. The big tree of California, *Sequoia washingtoniana,* rarely exceeds a height of more than three hundred and fifty feet. But in diameter it may exceed thirty-five feet, and as a general rule the big tree of California is more bulky than the eucalypt of Australia. The redwood of California, *Sequoia sempervirens,* reaches about the same maximum heights as the big tree, but it is not so bulky, its diameter ranging from ten to fifteen feet. Individual Douglas firs, *Pseudotsuga taxifolia,* more than three hundred feet in height have been recorded in the Pacific Northwest, and the Sitka spruce, *Picea sitchensis,* grows almost as tall, some specimens being considerably more than two hundred and fifty feet in height. The diameters of these trees, however, do not compare with either the eucalypts or the sequoias. Some of the hardwoods attain great heights. According to the U. S. Forest Service, the yellow poplar, *Liriodendron tulipifera,* in the Appalachian Mountains reaches heights ranging from two hundred to two hundred and twenty-five feet, and cottonwoods, *Populus deltoides,* in the Mississippi Basin are known to grow at least one hundred and ninety feet high.

What are the clothing colors for baby boys and girls?

According to a traditional color scheme, which is of unknown origin, baby boys are properly dressed in pink clothing and baby girls in blue, although in some parts of the country, particularly in the Southern States, this symbolical color arrangement is reversed and baby boys are dressed in blue and girls in pink. One writer says that blue was assigned to girls because that was the color assigned to the Virgin Mary and the royal house of David to which she belonged. At any rate, blue and pink have become associated with babies. When friends are notified that the stork has paid a visit to a home the announcement cards are often decorated with blue ribbons if the baby is a girl, and with pink ribbons if it is a boy. Apparently, however, this traditional color arrangement based on the sex of the child is giving way to more practical considerations. In the issue of *Forecast* for May, 1927, Mollie Amos Polk says on this subject: "According to the buyer of one of the most famous shops pink and blue are now used interchangeably for boys and girls. Pink, however, since it is universally becoming and will stand frequent tubbings, is much more popular for both." Since time immemorial blue has been associated with youth.

Why is the engagement ring worn on the fourth finger?

The custom of wearing engagement and wedding rings on the fourth finger of the left hand originated in an ancient belief that a very delicate nerve runs directly from that finger to the heart. According to Aulus Gellius, this belief was mentioned in the Egyptian writings of Appianus, who wrote at Alexandria in the second century A. D. During the Middle Ages the connection was supposed to be a blood vessel instead of a nerve. Henry Swinburne, an English ecclesiastical lawyer who died in 1623, left a quaint observation on this subject in his *Treatise of Spousals or Matrimonial Contracts.* "The finger on which this ring [wedding ring] is to be worn," said Swinburne, "is the fourth finger of the left hand, next unto the little finger; because, by the received opinion of the learned and experienced in ripping up and anatomizing men's bodies, there is a vein of blood which passeth from that fourth finger unto the heart called *vena amoris,* love's vein."

What was the religion of the assassins of the Presidents?

There is a persistent legend that the men who assassinated Presidents Lincoln, Garfield and McKinley were all members of the Catholic Church. A French-Canadian ex-priest named Chiniquy (1809–1899) was largely responsible for the story that Lincoln was assassinated by the Jesuits, who employed John Wilkes Booth as their tool. This legend, often repeated by anti-Catholics, accounts for the rather common belief that Booth was a Catholic. Booth was born at Bel Air, Maryland, and was the son of an English actor named Junius Booth, who immigrated to the United States. The family had been Anglicans or Episcopalians for generations. There is no conclusive evidence, however, that the assassin was a communicant of any church. He was only twenty-six years old when he shot President Lincoln at Ford's Theater in Washington on April 14, 1865. Charles Julius Guiteau, who shot President Garfield in a railway station at Washington on July 2, 1881, was of French Huguenot ancestry. He was a disappointed office seeker and it is supposed was incensed at the President because of the latter's usage of Senator Roscoe Conkling and the Republican Stalwarts. Guiteau was religiously inclined and had adhered to various denominations. At one time he professed to be a firm believer in Seventh Day Adventism. For several years he was a member of the sect known as the Oneida Community, whose purpose was to reintroduce "primitive Christianity." Harold Emmons, a lawyer in whose office Guiteau once rented a desk, said: "He was a good deal at the Y.M.C.A. and took part in the weekly prayer meetings there." In 1913 Charles G. White, Guiteau's brother-in-law, wrote: "Charles Guiteau hated the Catholic Church with all the hate that was in him. He was a Protestant, converted by Moody. He told many a time that God inspired him to kill Garfield. He was insane on that one subject." Guiteau was hanged in the District of Columbia jail June 30, 1882. Leon Czolgosz, who shot President McKinley at Buffalo on September 6, 1901, was of Polish-German extraction. He was born at Detroit and was brought up a Catholic. According to his own testimony, he was an anarchist and was bitterly opposed to all religions. He declined to see a priest or minister of any denomination before his electrocution in the New York State prison at Auburn. John Schrank, who attempted to assassinate ex-President Roosevelt at Milwaukee during the Presidential campaign of 1912, was also born and brought up a Catholic, but, according to his testimony at the trial, he had not gone to confession for fifteen or sixteen years. He was born in Bavaria and came to America when he was about twelve years old. The court adjudged Schrank insane and he was committed to a State asylum in Wisconsin.

Why do kings and editors use *we* for *I*?

The royal *we* and *us* were probably adopted by sovereigns because they thought that the plural form of pronouns in the first person was more dignified and authoritative when acting and speaking officially for the whole nation. The sovereign, although one person, represents and speaks for many subjects. Lord Coke in his *Institutes* says that King John was the first English king to use the plural form for one person. He, according to Coke, introduced *nos* and *noster* into grants and other legal documents, while his predecessors were content with *ego* and *meus*. That is not quite correct. A survey of Rymer's *Fœdera* shows that the royal *we* was adopted by John's brother and predecessor, Richard the Lion-Hearted. It has been suggested that the royal *we* may be a survival of the time when there were two Roman rulers, who reigned at different capitals and issued identical decrees under their joint authority. Many modern sovereigns, including the king of Great Britain, have discontinued the use of *we* for *I*. Sometimes the plural form of the pronoun is used in the King James version of the Bible when God is quoted as speaking. For instance, *Genesis 1: 26* says: "And God said, Let *us* make man in *our* image, after *our* likeness." Writers frequently employ *we* and *us* instead of *I* and *me* in order to make their style appear more impersonal and to give their writings the stamp of greater authority. It is assumed that by alluding to himself as *we* and *us* an author avoids the appearance of egotism which would result from the frequent repetition of *I* and *me*. The editorial *we* used by editors is slightly different. It is intended to impress the reader with the fact that the writer is understood to be supported in his opinions and statements by the editorial staff collectively. In *Advice to a Young Reviewer*, published in 1807, Edward Coplestan thus ridiculed the practice: "There is a mysterious authority in the plural *we* which no single name, whatever may be its reputation, can acquire."

What is the swiftest four-footed animal?

The cheetah or hunting leopard of Asia and Africa has the reputation of being the fastest four-footed animal in the world. Although this species is not capable of great speed for prolonged periods, it can leave the fleetest horse, fox or greyhound far behind in a short race. The swiftest greyhounds are credited with a speed of more than sixty miles an hour; the fastest speed of a horse is about forty miles an hour. Whether the hunting leopard is actually the swiftest quadruped cannot be determined for certain, because of the difficulty in ascertaining the maximum speeds attainable by wild animals in their natural state. The cheetah possesses such a mixture of canine and feline characteristics that scientists regard it as a connecting link between the dogs and the cats. It is three or four feet in length, has long slender legs, and a long tail, somewhat bushy at the tip. Unlike true members of the cat family its head is short and round and its claws are only partially retractile, and it is free from the suspicious nature generally associated with felines. For thousands of years these dog-cats have been captured alive in central Asia and employed for hunting antelope and deer. They are given practically no training, but are merely permitted to do what they learned in the wild state. For that reason cheetahs raised in captivity are useless as hunters. The hunting leopard, after being reduced to submission by sheer cruelty, is taken to the field, hooded and chained, in a low cart without sides. About two hundred yards from the game the hood is slipped off and the cheetah, taking advantage of every bush and stone for concealment, creeps stealthily forward. When the antelopes, or whatever the game hunted may be, take fright the leopard rushes toward them in gigantic bounds. If it does not strike down an antelope with a single blow of its paw it makes no further effort to make a capture, but returns to the cart apparently crestfallen. If successful it seizes the victim by the throat and begins to suck its blood. The hunting leopard can be induced to release its prey only by offering it a piece of flesh or a draft of fresh blood.

How long is a generation?

The whole body of individuals born about the same period are called a generation; and, by extension, the term is applied to the time covered by their lives. It does not represent a definite period. Generally a generation is regarded as being from 30 to 33⅓ years in length, there being about three generations in a century. The basis of the generation as a period in chronology is the average interval of time between the birth of parents and that of children, although some chronologists base the generation upon the average lifetime of all persons of synchronous age who survive infancy. David Brewster makes the following interesting observation on this subject in his *Life of Sir Isaac Newton:* "M. Freret concludes that the Argonautic expedition took place 532 years earlier than Sir Isaac made it. His second objection to the new system of chronology relates to the length of generations, which he says is made only eighteen or twenty years. Sir Isaac, on the contrary, reckons a generation at thirty-three years, or three generations at 100; and it was the length of the reigns of kings that he made eighteen or twenty years. This deduction he founded on the reigns of sixty-four French kings. Now the ancient Greeks and Egyptians reckoned the length of a reign equal to that of a generation; and it was by correcting this mistake, and adopting a measure founded on fact, that Sir Isaac placed the Argonautic expedition forty-four years after the death of Solomon, and fixed some of the other points of his system." In the Old Testament the term *generation* apparently refers to a period of more than fifty years.

Do rattlesnakes and prairie dogs live together?

It is widely believed that rattlesnakes, burrowing owls and prairie dogs live together in peace and harmony. Such is not the case, according to the best informed naturalists. This belief arose from the fact that rattlesnakes and burrowing owls are often found in the dens of prairie dogs. The relationship, however, is by no means peaceful. In fact both the rattlers and the owls are fond of small mammals as an article of diet and they visit the prairie dog dens primarily to catch and eat young prairie dogs. The snakes prowl among the burrows and fill themselves with young prairie dogs, after which they frequently remain in the holes while the meal is being digested. It is not an uncommon thing to see rattlesnakes sunning themselves at the entrance of prairie dog burrows. Burrowing owls not only feed upon young prairie dogs but also use deserted burrows for building their nests and rearing their young. In *The Oregon Trail* Francis Parkman wrote: "Several times I passed through villages of prairie dogs, who sat, each at the mouth of his burrow, holding his paws before him in a supplicating attitude, and yelping away most vehemently, energetically whisking his little tail with every squeaking cry he uttered. Prairie dogs are not fastidious in their choice of companions; various long, checkered snakes were sunning themselves in the midst of the village, and demure little gray owls, with a large white ring around each eye, were perched side by side with the rightful inhabitants." And again: "The snakes are apparently the prairie dogs' worst enemies, at least I think too well of the latter to suppose that they associate on friendly terms with these slimy intruders, who may be seen at all times basking among their holes, into which they always retreat when disturbed. Small owls, with wise and grave countenances, also make their abode with the prairie dogs, though on what terms they live together I could never ascertain."

What animal was first domesticated?

It is impossible to arrange domestic animals in the chronological order of their subjugation and domestication. All of our more important domestic animals were already domesticated four or five thousand years ago and nobody has been able to determine with any degree of certainty which ones were tamed and used for domestic purposes first. "Dogs, horses and pigs," says the U. S. National Museum in a letter to the author, "appear to have been domesticated from the earliest time of which we have authentic record." At the dawn of history we also find oxen, humped-back cattle, sheep, goats, asses, camels, cats, pigeons and geese in a state of domestication. Even elephants were already tamed, and honeybees had been hived and made to gather honey for man. All are agreed that the dog was one of the earliest of human associates. It was domesticated at a very remote date in nearly all parts of the inhabited world. That the camel, ox, sheep and ass were domesticated very early is evident from the book of *Job,* one of the oldest portions of the Bible, in which these animals are listed as part of the wealth of the patriarch. Many people regard the sheep as the first domestic animal because in the book of *Genesis* we are told that Abel was "a keeper of sheep" and that he brought an offering unto the Lord "of the firstlings of his flock and of the fat thereof." It is interesting to note that no new species of animal of great economic importance has been domesticated in the last two thousand years.

Are brown eggs richer than white eggs?

Many people believe that brown eggs are richer and more nutritious than white ones and this popular belief is an important factor in the commercial distribution of eggs. There is, however, no good reason for supposing that the richness of the egg is related to the color of the shell. Analysis shows that eggs are practically the same in chemical composition regardless of the color of the shell and that there is no difference in the food or nutriment content of light-colored and dark-colored eggs. All eggs are designed by nature for the development of chicks and they contain a great amount of nourishment in a limited space. The young of birds or fowls which lay white eggs require as much food while in the shell as do the young of birds or fowls which lay dark eggs. Oddly enough, American poultrymen report that light-colored eggs are generally preferred by the public in New York while dark-colored ones are preferred in Boston.

What is the stamp language?

The stamp language is a system of playful or sentimental communication based on the positions of postage stamps on envelopes. It was invented a decade or two after the Civil War and became a fad during the latter part of the nineteenth century. Many sentimental people still carry on *stamp flirtations,* to the despair of post office clerks, who like to have the stamps placed on the envelopes in the extreme upper right-hand corner in order to facilitate canceling. In a letter to the author the U. S. Post Office Department says: "The so-called stamp language, namely, expressing ideas or sentiments by the position of postage stamps on envelopes, is objectionable to the postal service because it requires the placing of stamps in various positions on mail matter and interferes with the expeditious handling of the mails. For years the Department has waged a constant campaign to obtain the coöperation of the public in properly preparing their matter for dispatch, and one of the fundamental points stressed is to urge mailers to see that the stamps in payment of postage are affixed in the upper right-hand corner. This facilitates its handling, as letters are faced and run through the canceling machine at high speed, and if the stamps are placed in various odd positions on the envelopes it is obvious that confusion·and delay will result, with consequent increased cost of handling and possible loss of revenue through failure to cancel the stamp." There are many variations and refinements in the so-called stamp language. The following are the general positions with their respective meanings: Inverted in usual position in upper right-hand corner of envelope—Stop writing. At angle in same corner—Do you love me? Inverted in upper left-hand corner—I love you. At angle in same corner—I do not love you. Straight in same corner—Farewell. Straight in lower left-hand corner—I desire your friendship. Straight in lower right-hand corner—Be cautious. In center at top —in reply to question—Yes; in center at bottom—No. On line with surname—Accept my love. Inverted on line with surname—I am engaged. Same at angle—I want to see you.

Why is Hoover called the thirty-first President?

Although Herbert Hoover is referred to as the thirty-first President of the United States, he was only the thirtieth person to assume that office. This is due to the fact that Grover Cleveland was both the twenty-second and the twenty-fourth President. His two terms were separated by the term of Benjamin Harrison. Previous to Cleveland's second term no President had served two terms without serving them in succession. When Cleveland took the oath of office on March 4, 1885, he became the twenty-second President of the United States. Four years later Benjamin Harrison became the twenty-third President. When Cleveland became President again in 1893 it was hardly logical to regard him as the twenty-second President, after there had been a twenty-third, and so he was called the twenty-fourth.

Why was the first Tuesday after the first Monday chosen as National election day?

Several circumstances made it desirable to select the first Tuesday after the first Monday in November as National election day. The Constitution provides that "Congress may determine the *time of choosing the electors,* and the day on which they shall give their votes; which day shall be the same throughout the United States." A law approved March 1, 1792, provided that the "electors shall be appointed [we now say *elected*] in each State for the election of a President and Vice President of the United States, *within thirty-four days* preceding the first Wednesday in December in every fourth year succeeding the last election." This was done to give the States ample time, in those days of slow communication, to ascertain the choice of the electors. The same law also fixed the first Wednesday in December as the day for the electors to meet and cast their votes. Until about 1824 the Presidential electors were chosen by the legislatures of the various States; after that date the general party tickets were gradually introduced, and since about 1868 the electors have been chosen in all the States by the qualified voters. South Carolina was the last State to give up the old method of choosing electors by the legislature instead of by popular suffrage. Before 1845 there was no National election day and each State fixed its own election day within thirty-four days of the meeting of the electors. All the States elected in November, but the dates varied. New York held her election on the first Tuesday after the first Monday; New Jersey, on the first Tuesday and the day following. In two States the second Monday was election day; in fourteen, the first Monday; in two, the first Tuesday; in two, the second Tuesday; and in two the Friday nearest the first of November. This lack of uniformity led to grave consequences. In contiguous States *repeating* was easy and became common. Popular demand for a uniform National election day resulted in the act of 1845, which fixed the first Tuesday after the first Monday in November as the time for choosing Presidential electors in all States. The law of 1792 still required the electors to meet on the first Wednesday in December. In fixing a uniform day Congress wished to make the time as close as possible to thirty days before the meeting of the electors. It was desirable to have one day intervene between Sunday and election day. This excluded Monday. The first Tuesday was excluded because it might fall on the first of the month, which it was thought would be inconvenient for business men. The second Tuesday might fall on the 14th, which would leave only twenty-two days between election day and the meeting of the electors. It was discovered that the first Tuesday after the first Monday in November, which was the day already selected by New York, would always place election day not later than November 8 and always about thirty days before the meeting of the electors on the first Wednesday in December. Therefore that date was selected. It is still retained, although the original reason for that particular date no longer exists, the time of the meeting of the electors having been twice changed since then.

How did the teddy bear originate?

Most people know that the teddy bear received its name from Theodore ("Teddy") Roosevelt, but very few know what incident was responsible for the name. The toy bear that we now call the teddy bear was invented by Margarete Steiff, a crippled dressmaker living in a village in Germany. About 1888 she used some left-over material to make a toy bear for a neighbor's child. This bear was popular in the village and other children immediately wanted rag bears also. Margarete's brother, Richard Steiff, later saw the commercial possibilities in these toys and began to put them on the market. By the spring of 1902 they had become popular at the Leipzig toy markets, and in the fall of that year George Borgfeldt & Company of New York imported a batch of the bears to the United States. At that time, of course, they were not called teddy bears and nobody thought of associating them with Teddy Roosevelt. They were offered merely as toy bears for small children. It so happened, however, that President Roosevelt went on a hunting trip to Mississippi that same fall. The public was very much amused by a news dispatch from Smedes, Mississippi, which stated that President Roosevelt had refused to shoot a small bear brought into the camp for that purpose. This inspired Clifford K. Berryman, the cartoonist, to draw a cartoon picturing Colonel Roosevelt in his hunting outfit with his back to a man who is dragging in a small cub with a rope. Roosevelt has his left hand raised after the manner of a traffic cop to indicate that he objects to killing the bear. The cartoon, which was labeled *Drawing the Line in Mississippi,* made a popular hit and Berryman adopted the bear as his cartoon mascot. This original bear was quite like the teddy bear as it was later manufactured. People began to associate the toy bears on the market with Teddy Roosevelt's bear hunting exploits and within a short time teddy bears were known throughout the country.

What Catholic priest served in Congress?

There is only one instance of a Catholic priest serving in either branch of Congress. Father Gabriel Richard, of Detroit, was elected Delegate from the Territory of Michigan to the eighteenth Congress (March 4, 1823—March 3, 1825). He sought reëlection but was defeated. Father Richard was born at Saintes, France, in 1767 and emigrated to the United States in 1792. He was sent to Detroit as a missionary in 1798, and while there he wrote several books on religious subjects, and printed the first paper published in Michigan and the first Catholic paper printed in the United States. During the War of 1812 Father Richard was arrested by the British and held prisoner in Canada for the remainder of the conflict. He died at Detroit in 1832.

Does the motion of a bullet overcome gravity?

The motion of a bullet traveling horizontally does not interfere with the operation of gravity. Gravity acts on such a bullet precisely the same way that it acts on a bullet dropped from the hand. Before the time of the Italian mathematician Niccolo Tartaglia, who died in 1559, it was generally believed that a ball on leaving a gun proceeded for some distance in a straight path, but it is now known that a bullet discharged from a horizontal gun begins to fall just as soon as it leaves the muzzle and it continues to fall at the same rate regardless of its forward speed. At no time in its flight does the bullet rise above a line projected through the axis of the bore. There is no force resisting the pull of gravity and the bullet will reach the ground just as quickly as if it were dropped from the hand at the same height. For the sake of simplicity the problem may be stated as follows: Suppose a gun, held exactly horizontal and at any height whatever, is fired over a perfectly level surface. Further suppose another bullet of the same weight and size is dropped from the level of the muzzle at the same instant the gun is fired. If this experiment were made in a vacuum where there would be no atmospheric disturbances the two bullets would strike the surface simultaneously. A bullet fired over a level surface must do its forward traveling in less time than it takes it to fall from the gun to the ground. A rifle appears to shoot *point blank* or straight ahead because the line of sight is above the bore and the axis of the bore is pointed slightly upward. The high speed of the bullet permits it to cover a great distance in a short time.

Why do monkeys search through their hair?

It is generally supposed that monkeys continually search through their own hair and that of other monkeys for fleas, lice, and other body parasites. An expert associated with the London Zoological Park says that such is not the case. Monkeys, he says, are quite free from such parasites unless they are neglected or kept in dirty cages. Salt exudes from the pores of the skin of monkeys and remains on loose bits of skin, and it is for these that the animals are continually searching and picking. Dr. William M. Mann, director of the National Zoological Park at Washington, substantially confirms this statement. He says: "As to why monkeys search their own hair and that of other monkeys, it is usually for loose bits of skin and salty exhalations. Of course, when there are fleas and lice on the monkeys they try to get them too, but I believe that more often they are searching for these salty particles." Raymond L. Ditmars, curator of mammals and reptiles at the New York Zoological Park, makes the following observation on the subject in a letter to the author: "With newly arrived specimens of monkeys, the search through the hair is for a definite purpose, and that is the capture of body parasites, which are fairly abundant on specimens from the jungle. These, however, seem quickly to disappear in captivity, and many monkeys examined have been found to be absolutely free from vermin. The search goes on, however, with every manifestation of success, but we are inclined to believe that this is actuated by a certain stimulus on the part of the monkeys—that the search is imaginary or conducted by the monkeys as a friendly token, one to the other."

Do men who marry sisters become brothers-in-law?

Many authorities restrict the term *brother-in-law* to mean the brother of one's husband or wife, or the husband of one's sister. According to this definition, when two men marry sisters they do not thereby become brothers-in-law. Thus Ben Hardin Helm, who married a sister of Mary Todd, was not a brother-in-law of Abraham Lincoln, although Helm was Mrs. Lincoln's brother-in-law. Popular usage, however, ignores this restriction and in common parlance *brother-in-law* includes the husband of one's wife's or husband's sister. The same general principle applies to the use of *sister-in-law*. According to the restricted definition, a sister-in-law is the sister of one's husband or wife, or the wife of one's brother. Strictly speaking, two women who marry brothers do not thereby become sisters-in-law. But here again popular usage ignores the restricted definition and the term is extended to include the wife of one's wife's or husband's brother. It was so used by the translators of the King James version of the Bible. According to the book of *Ruth*, Orpah and Ruth, two Moabites who were probably not related by blood, married the two sons of Naomi, that is, they married brothers. In *Ruth 1: 15* Naomi says to Ruth: "Behold, thy sister-in-law is gone back unto her people, and unto her gods: return thou after thy sister-in-law."

What three brothers served in Congress at the same time?

Three sons of Israel Washburn, a shipbuilder and trader of Livermore, Maine, had the unique distinction of serving in the National House of Representatives at the same time from three different States. Cadwallader C. Washburn represented a Wisconsin district in the House from 1855 to 1861 and again from 1867 to 1871. From 1851 to 1861 Israel Washburn, Jr., sat as a member of Congress from Maine. Elihu Benjamin Washburne, who added an *e* to his surname, represented an Illinois district from 1853 to 1869. Thus all three of the brothers served in the 34th, 35th and 36th Congresses—from 1855 to 1861. Curiously enough, another brother, William Drew Washburn, was later a member of Congress from Minnesota, the fourth State to be represented in the Federal legislature by the sons of "the Father of Congressmen." He was a Representative from 1879 to 1885 and a Senator from 1889 to 1895.

Where do houseflies go in winter?

Scientists have not determined definitely whether any adult houseflies live throughout the winter in northern latitudes. It is popularly supposed that some flies survive the winter by hibernating in crevices and refuse heaps and that these individuals breed the next spring. The London health authorities, after three years of investigation, failed to find a single housefly that had lived through the winter. No fly, says the U. S. Department of Agriculture, has been known to live from fall to spring. Experiments show that temperatures below freezing, if continued very long, are invariably fatal to adult flies. The life of the housefly, naturally brief even during the warm seasons, is generally only a few weeks in length, although a few specimens have been known to live for about ninety days under favorable conditions. There is evidence that flies survive the winter in the larva and pupa state, which accounts for part of the flies seen in the late winter and early spring. The Department of Agriculture has come to the *tentative* conclusion that most of the early flies are the offspring, not the survivors, of adults which escaped Jack Frost in the fall. Flies emerge from manure heaps as late as December and some of these seek shelter in kitchens, stables and other warm places, where, if there is a good medium, they may continue to breed. Consequently adult flies emerge from time to time throughout the winter, although no individual fly may live from fall to spring. The scarcity of flies early in the spring confirms this theory. "There is also the possibility," wrote F. C. Bishopp of the Bureau of Entomology in 1928, "that many of the flies appearing in northern latitudes in the spring are introduced from more southern latitudes by normal dissemination or by transportation in vehicles and trains." Benjamin Franklin made some observations which are particularly interesting in this connection. One day at dinner, while he was representing the American Colonies in London, a bottle of wine which had been prepared in Virginia many months before was opened. In the first glass poured there were three drowned houseflies. Franklin had heard that drowned flies could be revived by placing them in the rays of the sun, and accordingly he exposed these to the sun in the sieve with which he strained them from the wine. "In less than three hours," wrote the philosopher, "two of them began by degrees to recover life. They commenced by some convulsive motions of the thighs, and at length they raised themselves upon their legs, wiped their eyes with their fore feet, beat and brushed their wings with their hind feet, and soon after began to fly, finding themselves in Old England without knowing how they came thither." Franklin added that the third fly continued lifeless till sunset when he lost all hope of its recovery and threw it away. "I wish it were possible, from this instance," concluded Franklin, "to invent a method of embalming drowned persons in such a manner that they may be recalled to life at any period however distant; for having a very ardent desire to see and observe the state of America a hundred years hence, I should prefer to any ordinary death the being immersed in a cask of Madeira wine, with a few friends, till that time, to be then recalled to life by the solar warmth of my dear country!" This account cannot be accepted as scientific evidence. There is no assurance that Franklin was absolutely certain that the flies were ever inside the bottle of wine; they may have been in the cup before the wine was poured into it. Besides the moral leads us to suspect that Franklin may have invented at least part of the story.

Do the inner car wheels slip in making curves?

When two car wheels of equal size are fastened rigidly to the same axle one wheel, according to the U. S. Bureau of Standards, must slip in going around a curve. The difference in the length of the two rails in a curve may be several feet. Part of this difference is made up by *coning* the treads of the wheels of railway cars. When such a car goes around a curve the centrifugal force throws it over as far as the flange on the outside wheels will permit. This slightly increases the diameter of the outside wheels where they come in contact with the rails, and it likewise decreases the diameter of the opposite wheels to the same extent. Coning, however, compensates for only a small part of the greater distance that the outside wheels must travel around a curve. That the difference is made up by the slipping of the inside wheels is indicated by the greater wear on the inside rails.

Who was the first Catholic nominated for President?

Charles O'Conor, a prominent New York lawyer, was the first Catholic to be nominated for the Presidency of the United States. He was nominated in 1872 by a portion of the Democratic Party opposed to the election of Horace Greeley. He ran as an Independent Democrat and received 29,408 popular votes, although he did not carry a single State. John Quincy Adams, grandson of the President of the same name, ran with O'Conor as the candidate for Vice President. Governor Alfred E. Smith of New York, who was nominated by the Democratic Party in 1928, was the first member of the Catholic Church nominated for the Presidency by a major political party.

Which is heavier, wet or dry sand?

Dry sand is heavier, measure for measure, than wet sand—up to a certain percentage of moisture. A cubic foot of average wet river sand will weigh from twelve to fifteen pounds less than a cubic foot of the same sand in a dry condition. The man who buys a cubic yard of damp sand by measure will get less than the man who buys an equal volume of dry sand. When a certain standard of concrete is required contractors fill a barrow level with dry sand, but they are permitted to heap the barrow with wet sand. When sand is dampened moderately its volume increases out of all proportion to the amount of water added. Consequently any given measure of moist sand will weigh less than the same measure of dry sand. This bulking or piling of sand is due to a film of water which forms around the individual grains and prevents them from flowing together. As a general rule fine sand bulks more with the addition of water than coarse sand does. From a dry condition to about five per cent of moisture sand bulks greatly. This bulking, however, is governed by the percentage of moisture and does not continue indefinitely with the addition of water. According to the U. S. Bureau of Public Roads, if sand is thoroughly saturated so that all the voids are filled with water, it again approximates its original weight, measure for measure. A cubic foot of sand having a moisture content of about fourteen per cent weighs about the same as an equal measure of dry sand. In other words, when sufficient water is incorporated the saturated sand is equivalent in weight to the same bulk of dry sand. To illustrate: suppose a cubic yard measure is filled with dry sand and then water is poured slowly into it until the sand reaches the saturation point; or, suppose the measure is first filled about one-third full of water and the sand is then added slowly until the measure is full: the measure will weigh about the same as if it were full of dry sand. This process is known to engineers as inundation.

What is the origin of Mother's Day?

Mother's Day became a legal public holiday in 1914, largely as the result of the efforts of Miss Anna Jarvis, of Philadelphia. On May 8 of that year President Wilson approved a joint resolution of Congress providing that "the second Sunday in May shall hereafter be designated and known as Mother's Day." This resolution was introduced in the House of Representatives by J. Thomas Heflin of Alabama upon the request of Miss Jarvis. The following day the President complied with a further provision of the resolution by issuing the first annual proclamation directing "Government officials to display the United States flag on all Government buildings" and inviting "the people of the United States to display the flag at their homes or other suitable places on the second Sunday in May as a public expression of our love and reverence for the mothers of our country." The idea of a public holiday in tribute to motherhood was conceived by Miss Jarvis in 1908, three years after the death of her own mother, Mrs. Anna M. Jarvis. Miss Jarvis adopted the second Sunday in May because it fell nearest the anniversary of her mother's birth. It was also Miss Jarvis who suggested the wearing of the white carnation on Mother's Day. "This flower was chosen," she said, "because it typifies the beauty, truth and fidelity of mother love." Later usage introduced the practice, quite common, of wearing a white carnation in memory of a deceased mother and a red one in tribute to a living mother. Miss Jarvis promoted her plan for a national Mother's Day through the

Mother's Day International Association, which she organized. It should not be supposed that the idea of a mother's day was original with her. Before 1890 Miss Mary Towles Sasseen of Kentucky suggested such an observance to the teachers of her State. She suggested April 20, the anniversary of her mother's birth, or the Sunday nearest that date. In 1902 Frank E. Hering, of South Bend, Indiana, began to agitate for a national mother's day through the Fraternal Order of the Eagles. The Universalist Church of Our Father in Baltimore has held an annual service for motherhood since 1892. On May 22 of that year the death of Mrs. Emily C. Pullman, the mother of the pastor and of George M. Pullman, inventor of the Pullman sleeping car, was announced, and Robert K. Cummins, superintendent of the Sunday-school, suggested that the service be made a memorial one for her. Later he proposed that the service be held each year, not in memory of Mrs. Pullman in particular, but in tribute to mothers in general. For many years the Sunday nearest May 22 was observed, but after Congress designated a different date the local service was changed to conform to it. A question has been raised as to the correct form of the name of this holiday. *Mother's Day,* with the singular possessive of *mother,* is the accepted form. It is employed in the act of Congress and the executive proclamations, as well as in the name of the *Mother's Day International Association.* Some authorities, usage notwithstanding, think that the plural possessive, *Mothers' Day,* would be more accurate.

Does the body weigh the same immediately after death?

There is no appreciable decrease or increase in the weight of the human body at the instant death occurs. If a body is weighed immediately before and immediately after death the scales will register the same in each case. Charles II of England, who was an amateur anatomist, attempted to determine whether the human soul had weight by having the body of a prisoner weighed before and after execution. Those in charge of the experiment reported that the body actually weighed less after the departure of the spirit. The experiment, of course, is merely a curiosity without scientific value. Strangely enough, there is a popular belief that the body *increases* in weight immediately after death. "One reason that a dead body is thought to be heavier than a living one," wrote Dr. J. B. Harrison, a British surgeon, "is probably this, that in carrying a living person we have the center of gravity adapted by the person carried to suit the convenience of the carrier and maintained in a position as far as possible to fall within the base of his body. Again, the elasticity of the structures of the body, especially the cartilages, though not in reality diminishing in weight, gives an appearance of lightness, as we see in the beautiful movements of the stag, and this would seem to corroborate the notion of living creatures being lighter than dead ones." *Dead weight,* meaning the unrelieved weight of an inert object, may have been suggested by this belief.

Can underground water be located with a witching stick?

There is no known scientific basis for the popular belief that underground water, oil, mineral deposits or hidden treasures can be located by means of a forked twig carried over the surface in a certain manner. The belief is probably a relic of ancient methods of divination. Early in the fifteenth century miners in the Harz Mountains of Germany prospected with witch hazel twigs, and this practice, which was introduced among the Cornwall miners in the time of Queen Elizabeth, was later adopted for finding water. It should not be confused with modern scientific methods of prospecting with instruments based on gravitational, magnetic, seismic, electrical, radioactive, or geothermal principles. Water witches are generally more or less illiterate persons who maintain that they have a special gift for finding water with the witching stick, dowser, divining rod, or doodiebug, as it is variously called. Some of them even go so far as to say that the gift of finding water with a crotched stick is peculiar to persons born under certain signs of the zodiac. As a rule, water witches insist on a twig of witch hazel, willow, ash, peach or elder, although occasionally a piece of wire is employed instead. The diviner holds the two prongs of the twig in his hands in accordance with definite rules and walks over the ground slowly. When he passes over a vein of flowing water under the surface the part of the twig projecting upward is said to bend toward the ground. Water witches frequently state that the mysterious pull upon the twig is so great at times that those parts held in the hand will break if they are held too firmly. The U. S. Bureau of Mines investigated this subject and came to the conclusion that the so-called divining rod is not rational or scientific and is not based on any physical principles that are understood or even known. "That is to say," stated the Bureau in a report, "the divining rod is either a fraud (whether deliberate or unintentional) or is based on some physiological principles of which at present we know little or nothing—like the sense of direction in migrating birds and fishes." Water witches almost invariably fail when they attempt to exercise their art under conditions satisfactory to scientists. If in some cases they are successful in locating water in a higher percentage of the tests than can be accounted for by mere chance, it is not, in all probability, because of any mysterious power acting upon the crotched stick, but because the person holding it is a quick observer and has had considerable experience in finding water.

When was the Declaration of Independence signed?

The Declaration of Independence was not signed by the members of the Continental Congress on July 4, 1776. That it was is one of the most curious misconceptions of American history. The Congress on July 2, 1776, adopted a resolution declaring the Colonies free and independent of the British crown, and on July 4 it adopted the formal document known as the Declaration of Independence, which was prepared by a committee consisting of Jefferson, Adams, Franklin, Livingston and Sherman. No signatures were attached to the document on the 4th, except perhaps those of Hancock, the president, and Thomson, the clerk, whose names would appear on any official act. Either on the evening of the 4th or the morning of the 5th a Philadelphia printer named John Dunlap printed a broadside of the Declaration under the supervision of the committee that prepared it. This printed copy, which was pasted in the *rough* Journal, contains no signatures, but closes with the printed words, "Signed by order and in behalf of Congress, John Hancock, President." Oddly enough the manuscript copy later prepared for the *corrected* Journal is not as accurate as the printed copy in the rough Journal. Nobody knows what became of the original manuscript copy which was used officially by the Congress on the 4th and from which Dunlap printed his broadside. It seems to have disappeared mysteriously and all search for it has been in vain. Perhaps Dunlap tore it up after setting the type and having the proofs corrected by the committee, or possibly it was officially destroyed later. This document, the original *official* draft of the Declaration of Independence, would now be priceless. Such a copy must have existed, because Jefferson referred to a *fair* copy made from his draft, and it is hard to believe that the copy in his handwriting would have been submitted as the report of the committee. Jefferson's draft, now in the Library of Congress, was found among his papers after his death and is believed to be the copy submitted to the committee after being corrected by Franklin and Adams. It contains changes not only in the hands of Franklin and Adams, but also alterations apparently made by the Congress. This document, with the changes mentioned, became the Declaration of Independence. It is so filled with erasures and interlineations that in certain places no one but the author could have read it without a magnifying glass. The first page alone contains nineteen erasures and additions besides those indicated in the margin by Jefferson as being in the hands of Franklin and Adams, and in many cases it is difficult to determine whether the changes were made by the Congress or by the author in process of composition. That this was not the copy submitted to the Congress by the committee, officially adopted and ordered printed, is further confirmed by the absence of Hancock's signature, which it certainly would have borne if it had been the official copy. Be that as it may, on July 19, 1776, it was resolved that the Declaration adopted on the 4th be "fairly engrossed on parchment" and signed by every member of the Congress. Accordingly, on August 2, 1776, an engrossed copy was signed by every member then present. However, all those who voted for the Declaration did not sign it, nor did all those who signed it vote for it. The name of George Wythe, for instance, appears on the document signed August 2, yet it is positively known that he was in Virginia and not at Philadelphia July 4, 1776. Although most of the signatures were attached August 2, several were attached later. Matthew Thornton of New Hampshire did not sign until November 4 of the same year. It was not until January, 1777, that printed copies containing the signatures were authorized by the Congress for public circulation. Thomas M'Kean of Delaware, who voted for the Declaration on July 4, did not attach his signature to the document until sometime in the year 1781. The engrossed parchment signed August 2 reads, "In Congress, July 4, 1776. The unanimous Declaration of the 13 united States of America." As a matter of fact, New York did not vote her adhesion until July 9 and the fact was not announced to the Congress until more than a week later. The formal signing was postponed largely to give some of the delegates an opportunity to receive instructions from their States. Jefferson, in his notes alleged to have been taken at the time but evidently rewritten in his old age, says that on July 4 "the declaration was reported by the committee, agreed to by the house, and signed by every member present, except Mr. Dickinson." If this statement were true there must have been two formal signings of the historic document. When Jefferson was shown the actual records of the Continental Congress, proving that the resolution providing for the signatures was not adopted until July 19, he replied that he did not refer to the engrossed copy, but to another copy. All the evidence, however, indicates that Jefferson's memory was at fault and that there was only one signing. The engrossed parchment signed August 2, though dated July 4, is generally referred to as the *original copy* of the Declaration of Independence. This copy, which is now on exhibition in the Library of Congress, is not the original copy, although it is the original copy bearing the signatures of the signers. So far as known it was made from the printed broadside of Dunlap.

What is spontaneous combustion?

Spontaneous combustion is the ignition of a combustible material without the application of external heat or flame. The self-generated heat produced by cotton soaked in oil and confined in a poorly ventilated room sometimes becomes sufficient to ignite the cotton. Fires started by spontaneous combustion are common in coal mines, due chiefly to the rapid oxidation of coal dust when it comes in contact with air. Damp or improperly cured hay, especially of the legume variety, is particularly subject to self-generated heat. If the pile is large enough to afford the necessary insulation the self-generated heat will proceed to such a temperature that a small amount of air filtering into the pile will produce self-ignition. It is generally believed that the initial heat is generated by the fermentation of micro-organisms, such as bacteria, yeasts and molds, which multiply rapidly in damp hay, grain, manure or other agricultural products, and which are killed by their own heat at a temperature somewhere in the neighborhood of 160° Fahrenheit. The subsequent higher temperatures required to ignite the substance may be the result of purely chemical processes. Although the theories seeking to explain spontaneous combustion in damp vegetable matter are legion, very little is actually known of the exact cause of this phenomenon.

Did the pre-Columbian Indians practice kissing?

Kissing between the sexes as it is known among Caucasian peoples was probably never practiced by the American Indians of pre-Columbian times. Even at present this manner of showing affection is not indulged in to any considerable extent by the aborigines of North America. Kissing is a product of Western civilization and is practically unknown among primitive tribes and among the Orientals. Richard Steele, the British essayist, speaking of the kiss, declared that "nature was its author and it began with the first courtship." But the fact that kissing is unknown to millions of the inhabitants of the earth disproves the theory that it is the natural way of expressing physical love and kindred emotions. Cato, according to Pliny, believed that husbands started kissing in order to determine whether their wives had been imbibing wine! Apparently kissing on the lips began in the early stages of Caucasian civilization and developed very slowly. Some peoples, including the Eskimos and Polynesians, practice what is known as pressing or rubbing noses, but this practice, while it may be related to the kiss of salutation, bears no relationship to the kiss of affection between the sexes.

Who made the first flight across the Atlantic?

The first aircraft to fly across the Atlantic Ocean was the United States Navy seaplane NC-4. In May, 1919, it flew from Rockaway, New York, to Plymouth, England, a distance of 3,925 nautical miles, in fifty-seven hours and sixteen minutes. Stops were made at Chatham, Massachusetts; Halifax, Nova Scotia; Trepassy, Newfoundland; Horta and Ponta Delgada, Azore Islands; Lisbon, Portugal; and Ferrol, Spain. The principal ocean flight was from

Trepassy Bay to Horta, a distance of 1,200 miles, which required fifteen hours and eighteen minutes. Lieutenant Commander Albert C. Read was in command. His crew consisted of Lieutenants Elmer E. Stone, Walter K. Hinton and J. L. Breese, Ensign H. C. Rodd, and Chief Machinist's Mate E. S. Rhoads. The first *nonstop* flight across the Atlantic was made by Captain John Alcock and Lieutenant Arthur Whitton Brown of the British Royal Air Force. In a biplane they left St. Johns, Newfoundland, June 14, 1919, and landed at Clifden, Ireland, sixteen hours and twelve minutes later, having covered a total distance of 1,960 miles. Both Alcock and Brown were knighted for their achievement. The first transatlantic flight made by a dirigible was made in July, 1919, by the British dirigible R-34. With thirty-one men on board she flew from East Fortune, Scotland, to Mineola, New York, a distance of 3,130 miles, in one hundred and eight hours and twelve minutes. She also made a return trip from Mineola to Pulham, England. The Zeppelin dirigible ZR-3 (afterwards renamed *Los Angeles*) left Friedrichshafen, Germany, October 12, 1924, and arrived at Lakehurst, New Jersey, eighty-one hours and seventeen minutes later, with thirty-three men on board. Due to the great publicity given to his flight, a legend is growing up that Charles A. Lindbergh was the first person to make a nonstop flight across the Atlantic. He was the third man to make a nonstop flight across the Atlantic in a heavier-than-air machine, and the sixty-seventh to make a nonstop transatlantic flight in aircraft of any kind. Lindbergh made his spectacular flight from New York to Paris in May, 1927. His flight was remarkable in that it was the first nonstop flight in an airplane from the mainland of America to the mainland of Europe, and he made the flight alone. Miss Amelia Earhart, of Boston, was the first *woman* to make a nonstop flight across the Atlantic. In 1928 she, with Wilmer Stultz and Louis Gordon, flew from Trepassy, Newfoundland, to Burry Port, Wales.

Is perpetual motion possible?

Mechanical perpetual motion is impossible according to all known laws of nature. As the term is generally understood, perpetual motion refers to a mechanical device or arrangement which, once set in motion, would continue to run until its parts wore out, without drawing on any external source of energy. For instance, a clock or other machine that would run by weights and would wind itself up and thus run indefinitely until worn out would be a perpetual motion machine. But nobody has ever constructed a machine that in each complete cycle of its operation will supply more energy than it has absorbed. No machine will do more work than the equivalent of the energy put into it, minus that lost by friction, whether the original energy is in the form of heat, chemical reaction, electricity or human labor. In the transmission of energy some of it is always lost as the result of friction. A self-generating, self-perpetuating motive power which overcomes friction would be contrary to the best-established of all physical laws, namely, the principle of the conservation of energy, which is that energy is uncreatable and indestructible in the regular course of nature. Therefore, in the light of modern scientific knowledge, it is absurd to suppose that energy can be created or multiplied by a mere arrangement of wheels, levers, cranks, weights, or other devices. One of the most common of all proposals for the mechanical creation of energy is an overbalancing wheel turned by the pull of gravity on attached mallets or on quicksilver. A perpetual motion device of this type was suggested as early as the thirteenth century. The quest for mechanical perpetual motion is now regarded as an unpromising enterprise, and the U. S. Patent Office, annoyed by numerous cranks on the subject and convinced that perpetual motion is a physical impossibility, stipulates that no application for a patent on such a device will be even considered unless the inventor submits a working model that demonstrates beyond question that the machine, after being started, will run indefinitely without receiving energy from any outside source whatever. Needless to say, no such working model has ever been submitted. Perpetual motion should not be confused with machinery which merely converts energy from one form into another.

Does it take more posts to fence over a hill?

It depends on how the fence is built. Suppose a fence is built along one side of a piece of land one mile square. When rolling or mountainous land is surveyed for division purposes it is treated as a plane surface and the surveys are made exactly as if the hills or mountains did not exist. Although there are more actual square rods of surface area in a section of hilly or mountainous land than there are in a section of level land, both contain the same acreage from the standpoint of the surveyor. Therefore in the case supposed the fence is one mile long regardless of hills and valleys. No more posts or pickets are required to build the fence if the line traverses hills than if it traverses only level land, provided the posts are placed parallel to one another and the same horizontal distance apart. The ground distance between two posts is greater than the horizontal distance and forms the hypotenuse of a right-angled triangle one side of which is equal to the ground distance between the posts on level land. Accordingly, if only ground distance is considered, fewer posts are required to build a mile of fence over a hill than are required to build a mile of similar fence on level land, because on the hill the posts are not placed at right angles to the ground. When horizontal distance across the field is considered the number of posts is the same whether the ground is level or hilly. However, when a fence is so constructed it is often necessary to use longer posts on the hillsides, especially if the decline is decided. Sometimes in building fences over rolling ground the posts are set more or less perpendicular to the surface, in which case the posts are not parallel but are slightly closer together at the bottom than at the top. More posts or pickets are required to build such a fence over a hill than are required to build it on level land. With the wire it is different. In both cases more wire is required to go over a hill because it follows the actual curvature of the ground and a curved line connecting two points is longer than a straight line between the same two points.

How did Sunday become the Christian Sabbath?

Adoption of Sunday as the Christian Sabbath was gradual. The word *Sunday,* which occurs nowhere in the Bible, is derived from Anglo-Saxon *sunnandaeg,* day of the sun, the first day of the week having been dedicated to the sun by the pagans. The fourth commandment—"Remember the Sabbath day, to keep it holy"—referred to the ancient Jewish Sabbath, which was the seventh day of the week. That the New Testament writers clearly distinguished between the Sabbath and the first day of the week is shown by several passages in which the first day is mentioned as following the Sabbath. Although Jesus himself observed the Sabbath, St. Paul seems to have placed observance of this day among the customs not obligatory on Christians. "Let no man therefore," he says in *Colossians 2: 16,* "judge you in meat, or in drink, or in respect of an holy day, or of the new moon, or of the Sabbath days." This passage indicates that the question of the Christian's relation to the Jewish Sabbath was raised at an early date, although it is not certain that the passage refers to the weekly Sabbath. Be that as it may, from the beginning many of the Christians commemorated the first day of the week as Resurrection day, the day on which Jesus rose from the dead. *Lord's day* first occurs in *Revelation 1: 10. I Corinthians 16: 2* seems to imply some sort of observance of the first day of the week. There is no evidence that the first day was originally intended as a substitute for the Jewish Sabbath. In fact it seems that most of the early Christians observed both the Sabbath and the Lord's day, and this was the tendency as long as the Christians were composed chiefly of former adherents of Judaism. Neither is there any evidence that the first day was regarded in Apostolic times as a day for general rest from secular pursuits. On the other hand, it is probable that the first Christians held special worship on the Lord's day, for, according to *Acts 20: 7,* Paul preached at Troas "upon the first day of the week when the disciples came together to break bread" and the apostle continued to speak "till the break of day." This, however, may have been only a special meeting. The association of Sunday with the true Sabbath and its development as a day of rest came later. In the first century St. Ignatius wrote that Christians no longer observed the Sabbath but the Lord's day instead. St. Justin, writing in the second century, was probably the first Christian writer to refer to the Lord's day as Sunday. "On the Lord's day," wrote Tertullian in 202 A. D., "we ought to abstain from all habit and labor of anxiety, putting off even our business." This tendency to observe the first day of the week as a day of general cessation from work was further confirmed in 321 A. D., when the Roman emperor Constantine issued a civil decree that "all the judges and townspeople, and the occupation of all traders," should "rest on the venerable day of the sun." The decree excepted farmers. This edict was a good stroke of policy, because the pagan "day of the sun" and the Christian "Lord's day" both fell on the first day of the week and both Christians and pagans were pleased. Later the Roman Church prescribed the hearing of mass and rest from work on Sunday. It was not pretended that Sunday observance was based upon any specific passages in the Bible. As centuries passed and the Church grew in strength the majority of Christians paid less and less attention to the Sabbath and more and more to the Lord's day. In time the Lord's day or Sunday supplanted the Sabbath in their eyes, and many began to take the position that the first day of the week had some kind of divine sanction and that the fourth commandment was applicable to it instead of to the Scriptural Sabbath of the Hebrews. In his *History of the English People* John Richard Green says: "A more galling means of annoyance was found in the different views of the two religious parties on the subject of Sunday. The Puritans identified the Lord's day with the Jewish Sabbath, and transferred to the one the strict observances which were required for the other. The Laudian clergy, on the other hand, regarded it simply as one among the holidays of the church, and encouraged their flocks in the pastimes and recreations after service which had been common before the Reformation." Macaulay says on the same subject: "In defiance of the express and reiterated declarations of Luther and Calvin, they [the Puritans] turned the weekly festival by which the church had, from the primitive times, commemorated the resurrection of her Lord, into a Jewish Sabbath."

What two ex-Presidents served in Congress?

Andrew Johnson has been the only ex-President of the United States thus far to sit as a member of the American Senate. He was elected to the Senate by the legislature of Tennessee January 26, 1875, nearly six years after his retirement from the White House. Ordinarily Johnson would not have begun his duties as a Senator until December of the same year, but President Grant called a special session of the Senate to act on a treaty which the United States had negotiated with the king of the Sandwich Islands, and accordingly the ex-President took the oath as a Senator March 6, 1875. On March 22 Johnson made a speech opposing a resolution approving Grant's conduct in reference to Louisiana. It was his only speech in the Senate after being President. He died July 31, 1875. Johnson had previously served as a Senator from Tennessee from October 8, 1857, to March 4, 1862. John Quincy Adams has been the only ex-President to serve as a member of the House of Representatives. He served in that body from March 4, 1831, until his death February 23, 1848. Adams had never previously served in the House, but he had been a Senator from Massachusetts from March 4, 1803, to June 8, 1808.

Is the hide of the rhinoceros bullet-proof?

It is not true, as generally supposed, that a bullet will not penetrate the thick skin of a rhinoceros except between the deep folds. In his book entitled *In the Zoo* Dr. W. Reid Blair, director of the New York Zoological Park, says: "From the immense thickness and apparent toughness of its great folds, it was long considered that the hide of the Indian rhinoceros was bullet-proof, except at the joints of the armor-like shield plates. As a matter of fact, the skin of the animal is quite soft and can readily be penetrated in any place by a bullet or pierced by a hunting knife. When dried, however, it becomes exceedingly hard and it was formerly employed by the Indian princes in the manufacture of shields for their soldiers." Big-game hunters generally use large-caliber rifles when hunting the rhinoceros—.45 being a popular size in East Africa. Sometimes the animals are hunted and killed with guns of small caliber. "The two favorite shots," according to Dr. William M. Mann, director of the National Zoological Park, "are the heart shot, back of the right foreleg and into the heart, and the neck shot, about eight inches back of the ear and somewhat below so as to break the neck bone."

How does a person change his name?

Although it is customary for a person to bear the name of his parents, he is under no legal obligation to do so. In the United States anybody may change part or all of his name at will, provided he does it in good faith and for an honest purpose. If he desires he may change his name simply by adopting a different one, without any legal process whatever. Most of the States have statutes covering the subject. These statutes generally do not repeal the common-law privilege of changing one's name at will without legal formality. They merely supply an additional method, which consists of applying to a court to authorize the change. This procedure is recommended because such applications are granted as a matter of course and the order of the court serves as a public record and furnishes a means of future identification. In a few cases courts have held that after an individual has changed his name by legal process he is not entitled to the privilege of changing it at will. The Naturalization Act of 1906 provides: "It shall be lawful, at the time and as part of the naturalization of any alien, to make a decree changing the name of said alien, and his certificate of naturalization shall be issued to him in accordance therewith." Should the alien not have his name changed when he is naturalized he may do so later like any other citizen.

How are rainbows formed?

The secret of the rainbow lies in the individual raindrops. Drops of falling water act like a glass prism in splitting light into its primary colors. A rainbow is produced by the refraction and reflection of light rays by drops of rain, mist or spray. The most perfect rainbows are seen when the sun is shining brightly behind the observer and rain is falling in large drops in front of him. Sometimes several bows are seen simultaneously when the sun is shining on a sheet of rain. This is due to the fact that the drops refract and reflect light differently at different angles from the observer. The principal bow is known as the primary rainbow; it exhibits by far the finest display of the colors of the spectrum, being red on the outside and violet on the inside. To form such a rainbow each ray of light is refracted twice and reflected once; refracted on entering the drop, reflected from its interior surface, and then refracted as it emerges on its way to the observer's eye. What is known as the secondary rainbow, often seen outside the primary, is larger and fainter and differs from the other in that the order of the colors is reversed. In this case two internal reflections instead of one occur in each drop of water. The angular radius of the primary bow is about 42°; that is, if lines were drawn from the observer to each end of the bow the angle thus formed would be about 42°. That formed by the secondary bow would be about 52°. The concentric bands composing a rainbow have their common center on a straight line passing through the sun and the eye of the observer, and accordingly this center is always the same angular distance below the horizon as the angular distance of the sun above it. Two persons standing near each other do not see exactly the same rainbow. The sky is full of rainbows when the necessary conditions are present, but a person focuses only one, or one series; if he takes a step forward or backward his eyes focus a slightly different bow. Many people have a notion that a rainbow is semicircular because the earth is round or because the sun is round; the explanation given above shows that the shape of the bow is due to the refraction and reflection of light by the individual raindrops and consequently the spherical form of the earth has nothing to do with it. The rainbow is invariably curved because each color is formed by rays which reach the observer at a given angle, and this angle remains constant for the same color.

What are the names of the wedding anniversaries?

The practice of giving peculiar gifts on various wedding anniversaries originated in Germany. Among the medieval Germans it was customary for friends to present a wife with a wreath of silver when she had lived with her husband twenty-five years. The silver symbolized the harmony which was assumed to be necessary to make so many years of matrimony possible. On the fiftieth anniversary of a wedding the wife was presented with a wreath of gold. Hence arose the names silver and golden wedding. This idea, originally borrowed from the Germans, has been elaborated upon in modern times and we now have a long list of wedding anniversaries which many people think should be observed with peculiar gifts. Thus we have the cotton wedding, the wooden wedding, the tin wedding, and many others. There is some difference of opinion and practice as to the proper names and the appropriate materials of the gifts for the various wedding anniversaries, but the following are the most widely accepted:

First—Cotton.
Second—Paper.
Third—Leather.
Fourth—Fruit and Flower.
Fifth—Wooden.
Sixth—Candy.
Seventh—Woolen.
Eighth—Rubber.
Ninth—Willow.
Tenth—Tin.
Eleventh—Steel.
Twelfth—Silk and Linen.

Thirteenth—Lace.
Fourteenth—Ivory.
Fifteenth—Crystal.
Twentieth—China.
Twenty-fifth—Silver.
Thirtieth—Pearl.
Thirty-fifth—Coral (or Sapphire).
Fortieth—Ruby (or Emerald).
Fiftieth—Golden.
Seventy-fifth—Diamond.

Does dew rise or fall?

Three different sources of dew are recognized by meteorologists. In many cases a large part of the dew, and in some cases probably all of it, is produced after nightfall when moisture already in the air before sunset comes in contact with and condenses on bodies cooler than the atmosphere. During the day the earth receives heat from the sun; after sundown this heat is rapidly radiated into the air, and the ground and objects near it become cool; if this cooling goes below a certain point—known as the dewpoint—any moisture that happens to be in the air will condense on objects near the ground in the form of dew. Such dew may be said to fall. It is formed in the same manner as the moisture which gathers on the outside of a vessel of cold water. However, in other cases much of the dew, and in some cases probably all of it, is produced by the evaporation of water from the soil during the night. Considerable moisture is always ascending from the earth; during the day it passes off as invisible vapor, but during the night the chilled air may cause it to condense as dew. Such dew may be said to rise. No doubt in many cases the dew is derived partly from one of these sources and partly from the other. Frequently in the morning *sparkling dewdrops* are seen on the tips of growing grass and other live vegetation. This is known as *false dew* and consists of exhalations from the plants themselves.

Water comes up the sap tubes of the leaves and exudes at the tips where the tubes are open. Such dew, of course, does not consist of any part of the dew seen on roofs, fences, and other *dead* objects. Thus it will be seen that the dew on any given morning may be derived from any one or from all of three different sources.

What is the most northern point of land in the world?

The most northern point of land in the world, according to the American Geographical Society, is Cape Morris K. Jesup on the northeastern extremity of Greenland, which is under the sovereignty of Denmark. It is at 83° and 39″ North. In 1901 Commander Robert E. Peary, the arctic explorer, killed a musk-ox within half a mile of this point. The cape was named after Morris K. Jesup, a New York banker and philanthropist, who helped finance several of Peary's expeditions into the far north.

Do bananas grow pointing up or down?

The stem or spike bearing bananas projects from the top of the main stalk of the plant. When the fruit is small the individual bananas point outward and somewhat downward from the spike, but as they grow larger the spike bends over from its own weight and the bananas then point upward. Thus bunches of bananas seen hanging in stores are usually upside down in reference to their position on the plant when removed, but right side up in reference to their position on the plant at an earlier stage of their growth. In other words, when bananas are hung up in markets to ripen the string is attached to what was the free end of the spike on the plant, and not to the end which was cut, as one unacquainted with the growing plants would naturally suppose.

Why is it considered unlucky for a black cat to cross one's path?

That it is a sign of bad luck for a black cat to cross one's path a short distance ahead is one of the most prevalent of all superstitions, especially among women. It is probably a survival of the medieval belief that Satan often assumed the form of a black tom-cat when he sallied out upon an excursion of mischief. The ancient Egyptians regarded the cat as sacred, but during the

Middle Ages this animal fell into bad repute among Europeans, who associated black specimens especially with the devil and darkness. In some countries it was believed that all black cats were transformed into evil spirits at the end of seven years. Up until a few hundred years ago all witches were supposed to have black cats as familiars, and in popular representations at Halloween time witches are still shown accompanied by black cats while on their nocturnal journeys. Strangely enough, the appearance of a stray cat of any color into a home has always been regarded as a sign of good luck, especially if it remains.

Does a horse pull or push a wagon?

Pull, according to *Webster's International Dictionary,* means "to exert force upon so as to cause, or tend to cause, motion toward the force." The same authority defines *push* as pressing "against with force in order to drive or impel." These definitions imply that a pulling force is applied in advance of the object moved, while a pushing force is applied behind the thing moved. Both of these actions are involved when a horse draws a load. If the animal is hitched to a vehicle in the usual manner it presses or pushes against the collar or breast strap of the harness for the purpose of pulling the vehicle. But the collar is not the load; it is merely the mechanical equipment by which the horse draws the load. Part of the animal is even in front of the collar. Therefore it is more logical to say that the vehicle is pulled and not pushed by the horse. This is also supported by accepted usage, although some people insist on saying that a horse pushes the wagon because it pushes against the collar or harness. Perhaps *draw* expresses the idea better. According to the authority just quoted, *draw* means "to cause to move continuously by force applied in advance of the thing moved."

Does fright actually raise the hair?

Hair-raising by fright is a reality and not a mere figure of speech. Each hair on the bodies of mammals, including human beings, is equipped with a tiny muscle capable when properly stimulated of pulling the hair erect. The muscles are all connected with the sympathetic nervous system by means of nerve fibers and they can act simultaneously in response to a single stimulus. They are especially well developed on the backs of cats and certain other animals. When a cat is suddenly frightened or infuriated the hair on its back rises with an explosive-like rapidity. Perhaps this ability to make the hair stand on end was originally a protective feature in all animals, similar to the porcupine's ability to raise its quills for defense. Be that as it may, the hair muscles in the human race have been dormant so long that they will respond only to an extraordinary stimulus such as a severe fright. These vestigial muscles of the hair have been cited as corroborative evidence of man's evolution from a lower form of life.

What is meant by finding a pot of gold at the end of the rainbow?

According to an ancient legend, if a person were to dig at the spot where a rainbow touches the ground he would find a pot of gold. The source of the legend is unknown. Visionaries and dreamers who try to achieve the impossible are sometimes called "rainbow chasers," because they are said to be seeking the fabled pot of gold at the foot of the rainbow.

Will gasoline freeze?

Gasoline, according to the U. S. Bureau of Standards, has no definite freezing point. It slowly stiffens up like wax at temperatures much lower than those commonly encountered in the Arctic, and as the temperature is lowered it gradually becomes more and more viscous until it is a solid mass. The temperature at which ordinary gasoline solidifies ranges from 180° to 240° Fahrenheit below zero. Gasoline containing benzol will solidify at higher temperatures in proportion to the percentage of benzol.

Why wasn't President Monroe reëlected unanimously?

The second time James Monroe was elected President of the United States he received all the electoral votes except one—231 out of 232. It had been expected that he would be elected unanimously. Historians often state that one elector withheld his vote from Monroe in order to prevent him from sharing an honor previously granted only to George Washington. This is a myth.

William Plumer, of New Hampshire, was the elector who refused to vote for Monroe. He explained the reason for his action in a letter to his son, William Plumer, Jr., dated January 8, 1821. "I was," he wrote, "obliged from a sense of duty and a regard to my own reputation to withhold my vote from Monroe and Tompkins; from the first because he had discovered a want of foresight and from the second because he had grossly neglected his duty." Plumer voted for John Quincy Adams for President and Richard Rush for Vice President.

How many times has Congress declared war?

Congress has passed and the President has approved only five acts formally declaring the existence of a state of war between the United States and a foreign nation. It was enacted June 18, 1812, "That war be and the same is hereby declared to exist between the United Kingdom of Great Britain and Ireland and the dependencies thereof, and the United States of America and their territories." The Federal Government never formally declared war against Mexico, but on May 12, 1846, the Senate passed and the President approved a House bill entitled "An Act Providing for the Prosecution of the Existing War between the United States and the Republic of Mexico." This act carried the following preamble: "Whereas, by the act of the Republic of Mexico, a state of war exists between that Government and the United States." Nevertheless the act was equivalent to a formal declaration of war, because Mexico did not formally declare war against the United States until May 23 of the same year. On April 25, 1898, it was enacted, "That war be, and the same is hereby, declared to exist and that war has existed since the 21st day of April, anno Domini 1898, including said day, between the United States of America and the kingdom of Spain." A bill approved April 6, 1917, after relating that Germany was actually waging war against the United States, provided, "That the state of war between the United States and the Imperial German Government which has thus been thrust upon the United States is hereby formally declared." Eight months later, December 7, 1917, it was enacted, "That a state of war is hereby declared to exist between the United States of America and the Imperial and Royal Austro-Hungarian Government." The

United States, of course, has been engaged in more than these wars since the adoption of the present Constitution. There were no formal declarations of war in the cases of the war with the Barbary States, the numerous Indian wars within our borders, and the other minor conflicts in which the Army and Navy have taken an active part. Nor was war formally declared against the Confederate States at the outbreak of the Civil War. That war, which did not begin and close at the same time in all the States, was regarded by the Federal Government as a domestic conflict.

How do snakes travel?

Two general principles are involved in the movement of snakes over a surface. Locomotion in terrestrial snakes is effected for the most part by undulating movements of the body. These undulations are popularly supposed to be vertical and they are frequently so pictured in conventional representations of snakes in motion. They are, however, always lateral. A series of waves is passed from the front end of the body to the rear and each wave in passing presses against the surrounding medium and forces the snake forward. Small banks of dust pushed up in this manner may be seen where a snake has crossed a dusty road. The undulations are produced by the repeated contraction and expansion of the muscles between the ribs on alternate sides of the body. But snakes do not depend on these undulating movements alone for locomotion. This method is efficient only when the surrounding medium is dense enough to offer resistance to the passage of the undulation. Snakes are provided with an additional mechanism, consisting of transverse scales or shields, overlapping with the free edges pointing backwards, which cover the entire lower surface of their bodies. To each of these plate-like scales, called scutes by zoologists, is attached a pair of movable ribs. The scutes slip easily over irregularities on the surface when they are carried forward by the ribs, but they catch on the slightest projections when moved backward. Thus the snake is able to propel itself. Snakes, of course, cannot travel over a surface that is absolutely smooth, but there are two or three hundred scutes on the ventral surface of the average snake and each scute is ready to take advantage of even the smallest irregularity or projection. "In gliding," says the U. S.

Biological Survey, "the fore part of the snake's body is first advanced; the ventral transverse scales on this part are then partially erected, the weight of this part of the body thrown on these erected transverse scales, and a rather firm hold obtained on the surface; the rest of the body is then drawn forward by the contraction of muscles. This process is rapidly repeated, and as the ribs are active agents in this peculiar method of propulsion, snakes are sometimes referred to as *rib-walkers.*" Although they seldom remain long in motion, some species can travel with great rapidity. In swimming, snakes depend on the undulating movements of the body and on short strokes of the tail. Undoubtedly all snakes at one time walked on four legs. It is believed that they lost their limbs at a time when they lived in dense vegetation where locomotion by lateral undulations was especially advantageous. All snakes have vestigial hind limbs and in the pythons and boa constrictors these rudimentary legs are still used to some extent. Snakes are really lizards that have lost their legs and undergone other modifications. The so-called *glass snake,* which is classified as a legless lizard, is an example of a lizard in the process of becoming a snake. It is a connecting link between the true snakes and the true lizards.

Which is correct, *Fort* or *Fortress* Monroe?

The military post in Virginia on Hampton Roads is officially and correctly called *Fort* Monroe, not *Fortress* Monroe. This post is often erroneously referred to as Fortress Monroe even by careful writers. The post office at the same place, however, is officially listed by the Post Office Department as Fortress Monroe. In 1821, when James Monroe was President, the Federal Government acquired from Virginia a tract of land at Old Point Comfort for a military post. The first detachment of troops was stationed there in 1823. A question as to the proper form of the name arose soon after the post was established, and on February 8, 1832, Secretary of War Lewis Cass ordered "that the work at Old Point Comfort be called Fort Monroe, and not Fortress Monroe." Before this order was issued by the Secretary of War the post was sometimes referred to as Fortress Monroe in official correspondence. The U. S. Geographic Board affirmed the name *Fort* Monroe in a decision rendered May 25, 1891. Notwithstanding these orders and decisions relative to the name of the military post, the U. S. Post Office Department continues to use *Fortress* Monroe as the official name of the post office at Old Point Comfort. The terms *fort* and *fortress* are often used interchangeably. Both refer to a military fortification designed to defend an important position. *Fort* is applied to almost any detached fortification, while *fortress* is more frequently applied to a larger, more durable and extensive fortification, especially one with water batteries. A fortress may consist of a chain of forts.

When does Indian summer begin and how long does it last?

Indian summer is the name given in America to a type of mild, calm, hazy weather usually occurring in the fall and corresponding to St. Martin's summer in Europe. According to the U. S. Weather Bureau, the popular belief that Indian summer is a definite period which occurs more or less regularly each autumn is not based on accurate meteorological data. Indian summer is extremely erratic in the time of its occurrence and it varies greatly in duration. It may occur once or several times during the fall and early winter or it may not occur at all, and if it does occur it may last a day or two or several weeks. There is no truth in the common notion that Indian summer always follows a spell of wintry weather known as squaw winter. Attempts to trace the origin of the term *Indian summer* have not been very successful, and none of the numerous theories advanced are supported by evidence. One of the earliest known uses of the term occurs in St. John De Crèvecœur's *A Snow Storm as It Affects the American Farmer,* supposedly written between 1770 and 1774. "Then," De Crèvecœur wrote, "a severe frost succeeds which prepares it [the ground] to receive the voluminous coat of snow which is soon to follow; though it is often preceded by a short interval of smoke and mildness, called *Indian summer.* This in general is the invariable rule: winter is not said properly to begin until these few moderate days and the rising of the waters announce it to man." Horace Walpole used the term in 1778, apparently in reference to the intensely warm weather of India and the tropics. A note in James Freeman's *Sermons,* published in 1812, contains the following observation: "Two or three weeks of fair weather, in which the air is perfectly transparent, and the clouds, which float in a sky of the purest azure, are adorned with brilliant colors . . . This charming season is called Indian summer, a name which is derived from the natives, who believe that it is caused by a wind, which comes immediately from the court of their great and benevolent god Cautantowwit, or the South-western god." Dr. Joseph Doddridge, writing in 1824, advanced a theory which is still often repeated as the true origin of the term. "The smokey time commenced," Doddridge wrote, "and lasted for a considerable number of days. This was the Indian summer, because it afforded the Indians another opportunity of visiting the settlements with their destructive warfare." The theory is based on the assumption that the Indians were interrupted in their campaigns against the whites by the approach of cold weather, but were able to resume them again for a brief time should there be a period of pleasant weather in the late autumn or early winter. According to another theory, Indian summer was so called because the settlers supposed the smokiness to be produced by Indian fires, and Charles Brockden Brown, the early American novelist, stated in a note in *Volney* that "its American name it probably owes to its being predicted by the natives to the first immigrants who took the early frost as the signal for winter." At one time such a spell of mild weather in the fall was known as "second summer."

Why are shoes thrown at newly married couples?

The custom of throwing a shoe at a newly married couple is very old and may be a relic of the ancient practice of giving a shoe to another to symbolize the transfer of possession. Sometimes new ownership was symbolized by throwing the shoe on the property in question. "Over Edom will I cast out my shoe," says *Psalm 60: 8,* meaning that the country will be subdued. "Now this," we read in *Ruth 4: 7,* "was the manner in former time in Israel concerning redeeming and concerning changing, for to confirm all things; a man plucked off his shoe, and gave it to his neighbor: and this was a testimony in Israel." Accordingly, when Boaz's kinsman relinquished his rights in Ruth and her inheritance he "drew off his shoe" in the presence of witnesses. Among the Anglo-Saxons it was customary for the father to give one of his daughter's shoes to the bridegroom, who touched her on the head with it, the ceremony signifying the passage of authority and dominion over the daughter from parent to husband. Later, it is supposed, the custom degenerated and the shoe was thrown after the couple as they departed for their new home. Some writers, however, believe that throwing shoes at newly married pairs represents missile-throwing and is a savage survival of the days when the bride was often carried away by force from her people who attempted to drive off her abductor. This theory seems to be partially confirmed by the present practice in Turkey and other parts of the Near East, where the bridegroom alone is chased by the guests and pelted with slippers. The custom of throwing rice, grain, nuts and fruit at a newly wedded pair had a different origin and probably symbolized originally the wish that they might be blessed with children.

How did the willow pattern on chinaware originate?

The first chinaware bearing the popular design known as the willow pattern was made about 1780 by Thomas Turner in the Caughley porcelain factory near Brosely, Shropshire, England. It is supposed that Turner got the design from old blue chinaware imported from Canton and that the pattern illustrated a well known Chinese romance. The designs vary considerably, but the typical plate pattern shows a house near a river on which there is a boat. An orange tree is shown beyond the house, which is inclosed on the land side by a wall and a fence. In the foreground is a bridge, with a willow tree at one end and a cottage at the other. A cottage on an island is shown in the upper left-hand corner. Two turtledoves are also conspicuous in the design. According to the legend, as generally accepted, the large house was occupied by a wealthy mandarin whose only daughter, Koong-se, fell in love with Chang, the mandarin's former secretary, who frequently met his lover clandestinely under the orange trees. When the father discovered the secret affair he warned Chang never to come near the house again and built a fence across the path between the wall and the water to prevent him from entering. Koong-se was shut up in the house and betrothed to a ta-jin or nobleman, a wealthy friend of the mandarin who was much older than she. This was when the willow was in bloom, and the marriage was to take place when the peach tree blossomed. The ingenious Chang, however, contrived to communicate with Koong-se by means of a tiny boat which he let drift down the river with a message. While the mandarin and the ta-jin were arranging the preliminaries of the marriage they got drunk with wine, and Chang, disguised as a servant, entered the house and eloped with his sweetheart. The drunken mandarin pursued, but the pair gained the bridge and made good their escape. This pursuit is represented in the design by three figures on the bridge—first Koong-se bearing a distaff, then Chang carrying a box of jewels which the ta-jin had given Koong-se and which they took with them to defray their expenses, and last of all the mandarin with a whip. For a time the refugees concealed themselves in the gardener's cottage, but later Chang swam across the river for a boat in which he transported his bride to a distant island, where they lived happily for many years in a cozy cottage. Finally, however, the ta-jin learned of their whereabouts and obtained permission to have Chang arrested for carrying away the jewels. Accordingly, he and an armed force made their way to the island and attacked Chang, who was killed in the struggle. Koong-se immediately committed suicide by rushing into the burning cottage. But the gods of old China were not asleep. They cursed the ta-jin and made the remainder of his life miserable, and Chang and Koong-se were transformed into two turtledoves, symbol of eternal love and union. As one would expect, the story, like the pattern itself, has many refinements and variations. Nobody apparently has been able to trace the legend farther back than 1849, when it appeared as an elaborate story in an English magazine known as *The Family Friend*. There is no proof that it is of actual Chinese origin, and it may be pure fiction, suggested by the pattern rather than the pattern by it.

How should a widow write her name?

There is no rule, as many people seem to think, that a widow's name should invariably consist of *Mrs.* followed by her Christian name and her husband's surname—Mrs. Mary Jones, for instance. According to a common notion, Mrs. John Jones becomes Mrs. Mary Jones when her husband dies. No such distinction is recognized by the most approved usage. A widow continues to use the same name she used when her husband was alive. On social stationery and visiting cards the name of John Jones's wife or widow is written Mrs. John Jones. She herself would write her signature Mary Jones or (Mrs.) Mary Jones, but it would be improper for another to so address her socially. In legal and business matters she would be addressed as Mary Jones, that being her signature, and on business and professional stationery and cards she might use Mrs. Mary Jones. A divorced woman, if her maiden name is not restored, may continue to use her former husband's full name, or she may substitute her maiden surname for his Christian name. If Nellie Brown, for example, is married to John Jones and later divorced, she may use the name Mrs. John Jones on her social stationery and visiting cards, or she may prefer Mrs. Brown Jones. Her signature would be either Nellie Jones or Nellie Brown Jones.

Does the top of a wheel move faster than the bottom?

This question gives many people trouble because they confuse the two motions of a wheel on a moving vehicle—its rotation on its axis and its motion forward. In relation to the road the highest point on the wheel moves forward with a much greater speed than does the lowest point. At any given moment the highest point and the lowest point are even, one being as far advanced as the other. As the carriage moves both points move forward, leaving the top and bottom positions respectively; but at the end of a quarter of a revolution the point that was at the top is the length of the diameter of the wheel farther forward than is the point that was at the bottom. The point on the wheel on the ground directly under the axle may be said to be momentarily stationary with respect to the road, because the road is stationary and the wheel does not slip. It marks the point between the downward and upward motion of the revolution of the wheel—the end of the cycloid curve—and is neutralized between the forward movement of the carriage and the backward motion of part of the turning wheel. Thus, as the U. S. Bureau of Standards points out, with respect to the road the highest point of the wheel moves forward twice as fast as the center of the wheel, or any point on the vehicle itself, while, on the other hand, the lowest point momentarily stops. Of course with respect to the center of the wheel all of its parts rotate at the same rate. The wheel is a rigid object and obviously one part of it cannot revolve faster than another with respect to the center. It is because of the double motion of a wheel that any given point on its circumference travels considerably more than a mile while the vehicle travels that distance. The route of a point on the circumference of a carriage wheel is represented by what is known as the cycloid curve.

What causes corrugated surfaces on gravel roads?

It is commonly supposed that the washboard effect frequently found on gravel roads is due either to the hoofs of horses or to poor dragging. The rhythmic corrugations, however, are too widespread and uniform to be attributed to maintenance methods, except perhaps in a few individual cases. They occur on gravel roads in all parts of the country and are remarkably uniform. The distance from crest to crest averages about thirty-one inches and is rarely less than twenty-five or more than thirty-five. People traveling over such stretches of road almost invariably estimate the distance at eight to twelve inches. Even many highway engineers fall into this error. Similar but less uniform corrugations occur on bituminous and cinder roads. This corduroy-like condition often becomes a real annoyance to motorists and accordingly the subject was thoroughly investigated by the U. S. Bureau of Public Roads. That Bureau concluded that rhythmic corrugations in gravel roads are generally produced by the vertical oscillations of rapidly moving motor vehicles. When a rear wheel of a car descends with accelerated rotation after bouncing on a bump or depression it kicks back some of the loose surface material. The rebound causes a repetition of the action and small mounds of loose material are thus formed. Continued traffic transfers the action to the other rear wheel and a parallel set of little mounds is the result. The weaving in and out of cars connects the pairs of mounds into ridges which in time become continuous across the track. Apparently the shifting of cars across the center of the road extends the corrugations until they are picked up by traffic going in the opposite direction. Finally a series of crests and troughs is formed from one side of the road to the other. Corrugations formed in this manner are seldom very compact, and after weeks of heavy traffic they can sometimes be scraped away with the hand. The theory is supported by the fact that the corrugations do not occur on steep hillsides. When going up a steep grade the wheels hug the road more closely and when going down they coast or are controlled by the brakes. Further corroboration of the theory is found in the fact that one investigator was able to make a corrugated surface experimentally by having heavy traffic pass over a rope stretched across a smooth gravel road. Corrugations of a more firm nature are sometimes produced by the rhythmic impact of both front and rear wheels of cars over roadbeds which are slightly plastic, as when clay is mixed in the gravel. Sometimes the corrugations may be formed by a combination of these two methods.

How did Pershing get the nickname Black Jack?

The nickname Black Jack was given to John J. Pershing by the cadets while he was tactical instructor at West Point in 1897. Since 1892 Pershing had been an officer in the Tenth U. S. Cavalry, the famous colored regiment which later distinguished itself in the Spanish-American War by coming to the support of Colonel Theodore Roosevelt and the Rough Riders. It was only natural that *Jack* Pershing's long service with this unit of Negro troops should give birth to a nickname. At first he was called Nigger Jack, which was gradually supplanted by Black Jack. This nickname, however, was not new in the American Army. Major General John A. Logan of Civil War fame was known as Black Jack because of his swarthy complexion and black hair and mustache.

Was Robert E. Lee's mother buried alive?

Apparently there is no truth in the oft-repeated story that Robert E. Lee's mother was buried alive about fifteen months before the birth of her distinguished son. The Confederate chieftain's father, Henry Lee, known in Washington's army as Light-Horse Harry, was married twice, first to his second cousin, Matilda Lee, by whom he had four children, and second in 1793 to Anne Carter, who was for many years an invalid and by whom he had six children—Algernon, Charles, Anne, Sydney, Robert and Catharine. According to the story in question, the second Mrs. Lee was subject to cataleptic spells during which she would suddenly lose consciousness and become rigid, and in 1806, being in this state, she was pronounced dead by her physicians and was buried in the family vault at Stratford, the ancestral home of the Lees in Virginia. Later a member of the household, accidentally hearing a noise in the tomb, investigated and found Mrs. Lee alive in her coffin. She not only completely recovered and lived until 1829, but about a year after the incident she gave birth to her fourth son, who was to become the most famous of all the Lees. Such is the story which is frequently cited as a remarkable instance of reviviscence and which has been told so many times that it is acquiring the characteristics of a legend. It is in all probability pure fiction. There is no contemporaneous record of the alleged incident, and it is not even so much as alluded to by the early biographers of Henry Lee and his more distinguished son. Dr. Lyon Gardiner Tyler, the Virginia historian, informed the author that he had often heard the story but attached no importance to it.

What is the difference between ale and beer?

Ale is a kind of beer. All ale is beer but all beer is not ale. Originally the terms were synonymous. Now beer is a general name for all malt liquors, while ale is applied specifically to the paler kinds, the malt of which has not been roasted or burnt. Ale differs from ordinary beer in having a lighter color, a smaller proportion of hops and a higher alcoholic content. It is generally sweeter than beer because it contains more or less unfermented saccharine matter. Of course the application of *ale* and *beer* varies considerably in different countries and localities. Before the adoption of prohibition American ale was a malt liquor made by *top fermentation,* in which the newly formed yeast went to the top and was removed.

Why is *q* always followed by *u?*

This is a holdover from ancient times. We borrowed it from the Latin along with most of the letters of our alphabet. Q in English is always pronounced like *k* and in regularly formed words it is never used except when followed by *u,* plus another vowel, the combination *qu* being practically a single letter. Therefore *q* could be eliminated without any loss whatever to our language.

It corresponds to Kappa in the most ancient Greek alphabets. Apparently it was borrowed from the Phœnicians, who in turn got it from the Egyptians. We find it only in the earliest Greek inscriptions. Being always pronounced the same as Kappa or K it disappeared from most of the dialects at an early date and was retained only in the Ionic alphabet where it degenerated into a mere numerical symbol for 90. As a regular letter it survived longest when followed by Omicron or Upsilon, as at the beginning of the place name *Corinth*. Thus it is seen that even in the time of the earliest Greeks there was already a tendency to use *q* only when combined with *u*. In Latin *q* was regularly used in combination with *u* or *v* (originally the same letter) to represent the sound *kw*. The Normans were responsible for the introduction of *qu* into English, for *q* did not occur in Anglo-Saxon, the sound of *qu* being represented by *cw* or *cu*. Most of the English words containing *qu* are of Latin or French origin, although in some cases the combination was substituted for *cw* in Saxon words. Thus, apparently, we have *q* as a superfluous letter in English simply because it existed in the Phœnician and Egyptian alphabets with a real office. *Q* is used without *u* only in the case of a few foreign names and terms; as, Qadirlyah, a member of a Moslem ascetic order; Iraq, an Arab kingdom in Asia, and Qaisari-Hind, meaning Cæsar of India, the official title of the British sovereign as ruler of that country. Scholars sometimes use *q* without *u* to transliterate the Hebrew Kôph in such words as Qabbala for Cabbala.

Is the silver fox a distinct species?

The silver fox is not a separate species. It is merely a phase of the red fox. The black fox and the so-called cross fox also belong to the red fox species. Typical silver foxes have a silvery appearance, due to the white tips on many of the hairs. The bushy tail is black with the exception of a white tip. Black, silver and cross foxes are found in the northern part of North America and in Siberia. Totally black specimens of this species are seldom found except in the far north. As a rule, the fur of the cross fox has a yellowish or orange tone with some silver points and dark cross markings on the shoulders. Pelts of silver foxes vary in color from black with a slight dusting of silver on the head and shoulders to half black and half silver. All these phases are rare in the wild state and it is believed that they are usually born in litters of normally red cubs.

How does a sanitarium differ from a sanatorium?

Many people apply the words *sanitarium* and *sanatorium* interchangeably to any hospital or institution in which sick and injured persons are given medical and surgical treatment. In this sense *sanitarium* is the more common. Some authorities, however, attempt to distinguish between the two terms in modern usage. *Sanitarium* is derived from Latin *sanitas,* health, while *sanatorium* comes from *sanatorius,* curing or health-giving. Accordingly, it is maintained, a sanitarium is a health resort where people go to keep well and a sanatorium is a hospital where sick people go to get well. A sanitarium might be a retreat in the mountains or on the seashore where people in a run-down condition go to recuperate and to build up their health by means of natural therapeutic agents such as rest, sunlight, diet and a beneficial climate. If treatment is given in such a sanitarium it is chiefly prophylactic or preventive. A sanatorium, on the other hand, is an establishment where healing is performed by active and artificial means, such as medicine and surgery. A person with indigestion or a broken leg would go to a sanatorium for treatment. Often the term is restricted to mean a hospital in which persons with a particular disease are treated by the application of a specific remedy. For instance, institutions for the treatment of tuberculosis patients are almost invariably called sanatoriums. Usage does not always bear out these distinctions and not infrequently the definitions in dictionaries are unsatisfactory. Sometimes *sanatorium* is erroneously spelled *sanitorium,* due to confusion with *sanitarium,* and *sanitarium* is incorrectly spelled *sanatarium,* due to a similar confusion with *sanatorium.*

Why are the inhabitants of Kansas called Jayhawkers?

The people of Kansas received their nickname during the guerrilla warfare waged between bands of free-soil and pro-slavery men just before and during the Civil War. Previously *jayhawker* seems to have been used in the sense of a bandit, freebooter or irregular soldier. At first it was applied alike to the border ruffians and the anti-slavery men, but gradually it became fixed on the latter. In 1858 A. D. Richardson wrote as follows in *Beyond the Mississippi:* "Found all the settlers justifying the *Jayhawkers,* a name universally applied to [James] Montgomery's men, from the celerity of their movements and their habit of suddenly pouncing upon an enemy." Montgomery was one of the anti-slavery leaders. In September, 1861, Charles R. Jennison was commissioned lieutenant colonel of the Seventh Kansas Cavalry, a regiment which soon became famous as *Jennison's Jayhawkers.* Gradually the term was extended to embrace all inhabitants of Kansas. Just how *jayhawker* acquired its earlier meaning—one who plunders—is not definitely known. The Kansas Historical Society mentions the fact that the term is supposed to have been used by Houston's troops during the war for Texan independence, but there is no confirmatory evidence. M. Schele de Vere in 1871 thought *jayhawker* had been coined by convicts in Australia and imported by way of California. Alexander Majors in *Seventy Years on the Frontier* says the name *Jayhawkers* was adopted playfully by a party which started for California in 1849 from Galesburg, Illinois, and his statement is supported by the recollections of others. The New York *World* discussed the origin of the term as early as January 8, 1862. That paper, quoting the Leavenworth *Conservative,* stated that the term was first applied to Colonel Jennison himself, who was from New York. He was called the *Gay Yorker* because of his festive habits. His men were called *Gay Yorkers* and as the word traveled it underwent many changes, finally crystallizing as *Jayhawker.* This theory is disposed of by the fact that the term was previously applied to Montgomery's men. A curious story, sometimes referred to as a *tradition,* is often told by Kansas writers. In 1856, according to the story, an Irishman named Pat Devlin rode into Osawatomie with his horse heavily laden with booty. When his neighbors asked him how he had obtained the goods, Pat replied: "I jayhawked them." Upon being asked to explain what he meant, the Irishman said that he obtained the booty in the same manner that the jayhawk made its living. The jayhawk, he explained, was a fierce bird of prey in Ireland. Pat became known in the community as the *Jayhawker,* and upon the outbreak of the Civil War enlisted in Jennison's regiment, which became known as the Jayhawkers. There are several obvious objections to this story, aside from the fact that it lacks authenticity and smacks of pure fiction. The word *jayhawker,* it is quite well established, was in use before 1856. There is not now and never has been a bird known as the jayhawk, either in this country or in Ireland, although the name has since been given to a Western spider or tarantula. There are jays and hawks in Ireland, but no jayhawks. In a letter to the author the director of the National Museum of Ireland says: "I have never heard the word *jayhawk,* nor can I find any record of it, and there is certainly no hawk in Ireland at the present time known by that name. I have referred the matter to Mr. C. B. Moffat, our leading ornithologist, and the word is unknown to him also." Notwithstanding these facts, many people have a strong feeling that the word was suggested by the habits of some predatory bird. The assertion of Richardson, in the excerpt quoted above, that jayhawkers were so called from their quick movements and their habit of "suddenly pouncing upon an enemy," implies a comparison between the anti-slavery band and a predatory creature capturing its victim. Cartoonists generally assume that the name was suggested by a bird, either imaginary or real, and have invented a grotesque representation to supply the public demand. *Jayhawker,* it has been suggested, may have been derived from a combination of the names of the blue jay and the sparrow hawk, both of which are plunderers.

How often does the Dipper move around the North Star?

To observers in the Northern Hemisphere the constellation known as the Great Dipper or Ursa Major seems to move around the North Star or Polaris once every sidereal day, which is 23 hours and about 56 minutes in length—a few minutes shorter than the solar day. This motion, of course, is merely apparent, as it is the earth that is actually moving. The same apparent journey is made each sidereal day by all other stars within a circle which has for its radius the distance of the North Star above the horizon. Stars within this circle never set to observers in the Northern Hemisphere. This is because the axis on which the earth rotates points very nearly to Polaris, which therefore seems to be almost stationary and is known as the pole star. Although it is not exactly at the true pole of the heavens, it is at the present time only about a degree from that point and the circle which it seems to describe is so small that the unaided eye can see no change without making exact observations. Polaris is gradually moving but it will remain the approximate pole star for several centuries.

Why are artificial limbs called cork legs?

Artificial limbs are called cork legs because such limbs were formerly made of steel or other solid material covered with layers of cork to give them the necessary resilience. In 1901 an elderly manufacturer of artificial limbs at Exeter, England, stated that limbs constructed partly of cork were still used in the time of his youth. This explains why many reference works contain misleading statements to the effect that cork is used in the manufacture of artificial limbs. Because no cork is used for this purpose now many curious theories attempting to account for the popular name have been advanced by persons who did not know that cork was formerly so employed. Cork legs, according to one writer, were so called after their inventor, Dr. Richard Cork; and according to another the name arose from the alleged fact that the great manufacturers of such articles were established in Cork Street, London. Still another derives the name from the supposed fact that these limbs were first made in Cork, Ireland. These theories are not confirmed by any evidence whatever and they are, in all probability, pure fiction. Artificial limbs were not invented by a doctor named Cork and they were not first made in Cork, Ireland. Neither was Cork Street, London, ever noted for establishments engaged in the manufacture of cork legs.

What kind of fur is Hudson seal?

Hudson seal is not the name of any species of animal. It is merely a trade name for common muskrat fur dressed and dyed to resemble seal. The U. S. Federal Trade Commission regards *Hudson seal* as an "improper name for seal-dyed sheared-muskrat." That Commission has ruled, "That in order to describe a fur, in every case the correct name of the fur must be the last name of the description; and if any dye or blend is used, simulating another fur, the word *dyed* or *blended* must be inserted between the name signifying the fur that is simulated, and the true name of the fur; as, *seal-dyed muskrat* or *mink-dyed marmot.*" Hudson Bay seal as the trade name of seal-dyed rabbit is a similar misleading designation.

Is a bullet's greatest penetrating power near the muzzle?

A bullet does not necessarily have its greatest power of penetration close to the muzzle of the gun from which it is fired. It depends on the type of bullet and the composition of the object which it strikes. Penetration is not the measure of striking energy. A bullet has its greatest striking energy where it has its maximum speed, which is generally near the muzzle. But it does not always have its greatest penetrating power at that point. Full metal patch bullets which are not supposed to upset upon impact give the greatest penetration at or near the muzzle of the gun. On the other hand, bullets which are supposed to upset or *mushroom* upon impact give the greatest penetration at their extreme ranges, or at the point where the velocity is decreased to such an extent that the expansion does not occur upon impact. For instance, the .30 Winchester center fire cartridge, with the soft point bullet, has a penetration of eleven boards, whereas the same cartridge with the full patch bullet will penetrate fifty boards, the energy of both being the same. All other things being equal, the bullet which resists deformation most will generally give the maximum penetration. According to the U. S. War Department, the bullets used in the Army service rifles usually give the greatest penetration at fifty to fifty-five yards from the muzzle. Tests show, says the Winchester Repeating Arms Company, that pointed bullets fired into sawdust, sand, loam and materials of similar description have an increased penetration at long ranges. When pointed bullets were fired into moist sand the penetration was ten inches at fifty feet, fourteen inches at one hundred yards, and sixteen inches at five hundred yards. When the same type of bullet was fired with equal force into boiler plate the penetration was .5 of an inch at fifty feet, .4 at one hundred yards, and .1 at five hundred yards. Some materials offer less frictional resistance to soft bullets than they do to hard ones. The penetration of wax bullets might be greater in some substances than lead bullets of the same shape and size fired with the same force.

What is meant by the tonnage of a ship?

Tonnage may refer to either the capacity or weight of a vessel. The word itself is derived from *tun*, a large cask or barrel in which wine, ale and other liquids were formerly transported. In the fifteenth and sixteenth centuries *tunnage* or *tonnage* was the number of *tuns* of wine a merchant ship could carry. Later tonnage was estimated by measurements which gave approximately the actual cubic content of the vessel. As now applied to American merchant ships tonnage is classified under *space* or *statutory* tons and *weight* tons. A space or statutory ton is 100 cubic feet of space. Gross tonnage is the capacity of the spaces within the frames or ceiling of the hull and the capacity of the closed-in spaces above the deck available for cargo, stores, passengers, crew, etc. Net or register tonnage is what remains after the spaces occupied by the propelling machinery, fuel supply, crew quarters, master's cabin and navigation spaces have been deducted from the gross tonnage. This is the usual basis for tonnage taxes and port charges. A weight ton is a unit of weight, not capacity. The dead-weight tonnage of a vessel, as applied to merchant ships, is the weight in avoirdupois tons of 2,240 pounds required to depress it from the light water line, when only machinery and equipment are on board, to the load line. It is, therefore, the weight in tons of the cargo, fuel, stores, water, crew, etc., which the vessel is designed to carry with safety. The tonnage of a warship is the total weight of the vessel measured by the weight of the water displaced. A warship with a tonnage of 30,000 displaces 30,000 long tons of water.

Do turkey buzzards find carrion by sight or smell?

This subject has long been debated by naturalists and has not yet been definitely settled. A preponderance of evidence supports the view that turkey buzzards and other carrion vultures are guided to their food largely by sight. Although it has been demonstrated that their olfactory organs are well developed physically, they do not have a very acute sense of smell. Their sense of sight, on the other hand, is exceptionally keen. Nearly a century ago Charles Darwin experimented with condors in South America and concluded that their sense of smell was comparatively dull. Audubon, Owen, Bachman and others performed experiments of various kinds, all of which indicate that the turkey buzzard does not locate its food by smell. Bachman covered highly offensive offal with a thin cloth on which pieces of meat were placed. Buzzards ate the meat and then stood quietly on the cloth with their beaks within an eighth of an inch of the putrid mass below without discovering it. But the birds immediately discovered the offal when a small rent was made in the cloth. This experiment was repeated several times with similar results. According to Dr. Charles W. Richmond, an ornithologist of the U. S. National Museum, one observer saw a number of buzzards tugging vigorously at an old inner tube of an automobile tire. In that case the birds appeared to depend on the sense of sight entirely. Evidently these birds frequently find carrion not by seeing it but by seeing evidences of its presence. It is quite certain that the actions of animals and other creatures sometimes lead buzzards to their prey, and the sudden descent of one bird is a signal to others of the species in the district. There is, however, some evidence that turkey buzzards are occasionally guided to carrion by smell. Dr. Richmond speaks of a writer who saw dozens of buzzards coming *up the wind* to a field freshly fertilized with fish guano, which indicates that the sense of smell may sometimes be employed when the wind is in the right direction. Darwin gives another case. In *The Voyage of the Beagle* he says a man told the Zoological Society of London that he had seen "the carrion-hawks in the West Indies on two occasions collect on the roof of a house, when a corpse had become offensive from not having been buried; in this case, the intelligence could hardly have been acquired by sight."

Who was the oldest President of the United States?

Andrew Jackson was the oldest man who has occupied the Presidency thus far. He was born March 15, 1767, and lacked only eleven days of being seventy years of age when he retired from the White House March 4, 1837. James Buchanan lacked fifty days of being seventy when on March 4, 1861, he yielded the Presidency to Abraham Lincoln. William Henry Harrison, who was born February 9, 1773, was the oldest President at the time of his election and inauguration. He was sixty-eight when elected and sixty-nine when inaugurated March 4, 1841. Harrison died a month later. Theodore Roosevelt was the youngest man who has occupied the Presidency. He was born October 27, 1858, and lacked forty-two days of being forty-three years of age when he became President as the result of McKinley's death September 14, 1901. Roosevelt was also the youngest man who has been *elected* to the Presidency, being only a few days past forty-six when he was elected in 1904. Ulysses S. Grant, his nearest competitor in respect to youth, was also forty-six, but a few months older, at the time of his election the first time.

How can a person blow both hot and cold?

If a person blows forcefully upon his hand with lips nearly closed the effect is decidedly cooling; but if he blows gently with the mouth open the effect is decidedly warming. Moisture in the skin is responsible for this difference in effect. Heat, like time, is measured only by its loss. In the first case the breath is expelled so rapidly that it cools the skin by evaporating the moisture, while in the second case the skin comes in contact with the warm air without losing much of its moisture. If a person blows upon a thermometer instead of the skin the effect in both cases is the same, or rather reversed, because the instrument registers only the actual temperature. The cooling effect of an electric fan is due to the fact that each puff of air absorbs heat and moisture as it passes over the skin. In reality the fan raises the temperature of a room by setting the air in rapid motion. The collection of fables attributed to Æsop contains one on the subject of blowing hot and cold. A man who lost his way in the woods on a winter night was invited to take shelter and food in the cell of a satyr. The stranger, as he entered the cell, held his hands near his mouth and blew on them. Upon being asked by the satyr why he did this, he replied: "My hands are cold and my breath warms them." Later when a dish of hot porridge was placed before him the man raised a spoonful of it to his mouth and blew upon it. Again the satyr demanded an explanation. "The porridge is hot," replied the guest, "and my breath cools it." This was too much for the host. "Get out," exclaimed the satyr. "I will have nothing to do with a man who blows hot and cold with the same breath."

Does a bullet fired vertically descend at the same speed?

It is not true, as often supposed, that a bullet fired vertically into the air will return to earth at the same speed with which it left the gun. Such, however, would be the case if the bullet were traveling through a vacuum. Gravity does not pull a bullet through the air as fast as a charge of powder drives it. Even if the bullet were fired by an aviator straight down from a great altitude the atmospheric resistance would at first retard its velocity. Whether a bullet fired vertically has sufficient force in its descent to kill a person on the ground depends on the size of the bullet and the distance it falls. Rather exhaustive vertical firings have been made to determine this point. "It has been demonstrated," says the Winchester Repeating Arms Company, "that a pointed bullet, such as the .303 British mark VIII, takes approximately fifty seconds to ascend and descend when fired vertically. The initial velocity when leaving the gun is approximately 2,400 feet per second and the velocity upon return to the earth is 475 feet per second. The returning velocity is equivalent to a striking energy of eighty-six foot pounds and it is considered that a striking energy of sixty foot pounds is sufficient to put a soldier out of action." Barring unusual circumstances, an ordinary rifle or pistol bullet fired vertically would hardly descend with enough force to kill or seriously injure the gunner.

Do dogs endanger large suspension bridges?

According to a popular notion the even tread of a small animal walking over a large suspension bridge will sometimes cause sufficient vibration to endanger the bridge. Many people believe that cats and dogs are not permitted to cross long bridges of this type. It is a fact that a comparatively small force, applied at regular intervals under favorable circumstances, will occasionally set up considerable oscillation in such a structure, but it is improbable that a modern suspension bridge would be affected to a dangerous extent by a cat or dog, although the vibration so produced might be appreciable. Experts testify that a few soldiers marching over a long bridge in regular step might produce more vibration than a whole regiment out of step. That is why troops are usually ordered to *rout step* before starting over a bridge. Two hundred and twenty-six men lost their lives in 1850 when a suspension bridge over the Maine at Angers, France, broke down under 487 marching soldiers. The crash was caused by the vibration of the men in step, combined with their great weight.

What river is said to reverse the direction of its current?

There is a common belief that the Casiquiare River or Canal in southern Venezuela sometimes flows north into the Orinoco, sometimes south into the Negro, and sometimes it is so sluggish that there is no current at all. That this stream reverses the direction of its current is stated by many writers. On some maps the direction of the current of the stream is indicated by arrows pointing both ways. A few writers go so far as to say that the Casiquiare flows into the Orinoco half of the year and into the Rio Negro the other half. The fact is, says the U. S. Geological Survey, that "the Casiquiare carries water at all times from the Orinoco to the Rio Negro, a tributary of the Amazon, and does not carry water in the opposite direction. The volume of discharge to the Rio Negro is largely from streams tributary to the Casiquiare, although the latter is described by different authorities as diverting from one-sixth to one-third of the flow of the Orinoco at their bifurcation." On September 12, 1928, the Venezuelan Bureau of Cartography at Caracas made the following statement in a letter to the author: "The amount of water in the Casiquiare is considerably different in wet and dry seasons, but the current is always in the same direction." Father Acuna, who in 1639 first reported the freakish stream, called it a canal and it is still generally so described. Dr. A. Hamilton Rice, whose report on the subject was published in 1921 in the journal of the Royal Geographical Society of London, says this remarkable stream is the only example of its kind in the world. In reality it is a branch of the Negro and its waters are discharged into that stream. Scientists suppose that it connected with the Orinoco at a later geological period by cutting back. It joins the Orinoco about nine miles below Esmeraldas and the Rio Negro near San Carlos, thus linking the vast Orinoco and Amazon systems far from their source. Neither the Negro nor the Orinoco has completely succeeded in capturing the Casiquiare. Rice estimated the length of the latter stream at 227 miles. The angle of slope from the Orinoco to the Negro is very gradual and slight. At its mouth in the Orinoco the average water-level of the Casiquiare is 283 feet above sea level; at its mouth in the Negro it is 212 feet. This accounts for the fact that during the dry season there is no perceptible current in the Casiquiare. One writer states that the belief that this stream reverses the direction of its current arose from the fact that when heavy rains fall in the Amazon basin the waters of the Rio Negro back up into the Casiquiare and cause the latter to flow into the Orinoco. Such is not the case, according to several eminent investigators. However, such a condition does occasionally occur in small streams. For instance, the Crossing, a small stream in Penobscot County, Maine, sometimes flows south and sometimes north, depending on the flood conditions in the Souadabscoot and Kenduskeag rivers, which it connects.

Why were forests absent from the great plains?

Scientists are not agreed as to the cause of the absence of trees from the great plains and prairies of the western and central part of the United States. Insufficient rainfall, according to the U. S. Forest Service, is the most commonly accepted explanation of this treeless condition. "In addition to this major cause," says that Bureau, "other contributing causes are the fineness of the soil, which causes what rainfall there is to run off rapidly instead of seeping into the soil; periodic drouths that kill tree seedlings that may have started in the more favorable seasons; the competition of grass against the young tree seedlings for available moisture; and frequent fires, caused by lightning, which burn tree seedlings along with the dry grass. The so-called prairies of Illinois, Iowa, eastern Nebraska and other States are probably primarily the result of fire, as there is sufficient rainfall in those regions to permit tree growth." Perhaps many centuries ago large stands of timber were removed from the region in question by frequent fires ignited in swamp lands during the dry seasons. Such fires, repeated often enough, might be able to establish a type of prairie vegetation able to hold its own against the encroachments of timber. That such changes can be brought about by fires is proved by the brush fields on the slopes of Mt. Shasta, where a solid stand of timber must have once existed, judging from the numerous charred stumps and snags on every hand. Nevertheless the surrounding forests make practically no inroads upon the chaparral, which consists of some twenty species of brush. However, this explanation of the treeless condition of the great prairies is not entirely adequate. It is by no means certain that the great prairies were covered with forests in our geological age except along the river bottoms and on certain isolated highlands. A type of prairie vegetation seems to have always prevailed there. That portions of these vast prairies were covered with forests in past geological ages is proved by the presence of coal beds beneath the soil.

Can a fire started by lightning be put out with water?

That a fire caused by lightning cannot be extinguished with water is an old popular belief which still survives in many localities. Fire is fire no matter how started, whether by a match, spontaneous combustion, or a flash of lightning. A fire produced by lightning has the same physical properties that other fire has and can be extinguished in the same manner. Another odd belief is that there are two kinds of lightning, hot and cold, and that a flash of hot lightning will start a fire while a streak of cold lightning will not. Needless to say all lightning is composed of electricity and will start a fire under proper conditions.

How do the Protestant and Catholic Bibles differ?

The Protestant and the Catholic Bibles differ considerably in the contents of the Old Testament. At the Council of Trent (1545–1563) the Roman Catholic Church enumerated the books which should be regarded as "sacred and canonical" and consequently as parts of the Bible. This list comprises the present Catholic Bible and includes all but three—*Esdras I, Esdras II* and the *Prayer of Manasses*—of the books and portions of books which are not found in the Jewish editions of the Old Testament and which Protestants denominate the Apocrypha. Accordingly the Catholic Bible comprises all of the Old Testament books accepted as canonical by

118

Protestants, and in addition *Tobias, Judith, Wisdom of Solomon, Ecclesiasticus, Baruch, Maccabees I, Maccabees II,* and certain fragments of *Esther* and *Daniel.* Strictly speaking, the Apocryphal books are not an essential part of the Protestant Bible, although they were formerly printed between the Testaments in nearly all Protestant editions, and the Bibles on the lecterns of the Anglican Church and the Protestant Episcopal Church of the United States contain these books, and lessons are taken from them on certain days of the Church Year. Thus, it will be seen that the chief difference between the Protestant and the Catholic Bibles is that the Catholics regard all but three of the so-called Apocryphal books and parts of books as canonical and essential parts of the Scriptures, while Protestants read them merely for inspiration and edification and do not use them to establish points of doctrine. The Council of Nicaea in 325 A. D. rejected all of the books and fragments of the Apocrypha as uninspired. In the Septuagint version employed by the Eastern Church these books are interspersed among the other books of the Old Testament and are regarded by that church as of equal authority in every respect. Of course, since different translations are used by Protestants and Catholics, there are many minor differences in the texts of their Bibles.

Why are firecrackers used at Christmas time in the South?

In the Northern States firecrackers and other fireworks are used almost exclusively on the Fourth of July; in the South they are used almost exclusively at Christmas time. There are several reasons for this difference in practice. Firecrackers originated in the Orient. The Chinese use them at social, military and religious functions, as well as at births and funerals. During the fourteenth century, it is supposed, they were introduced into Italy, where they were used from the first on Saints' days, Christmas and other religious festivals. This custom survives not only in Italy but also in France, Spain and other Latin countries. The Southern States borrowed the practice of shooting firecrackers on Christmas and New Year from the inhabitants of Louisiana, Florida, the West Indies, Mexico and other regions to the south formerly in the possession of France and Spain. The fact that the Puritans of New England frowned on the practice while the Cavaliers of Virginia did not object to it had much to do with establishing the custom in the South and prohibiting its introduction in the North, where firecrackers and other fireworks were used only on patriotic and military occasions. After the Revolution they came to be used chiefly on the Fourth of July, which is usually regarded by Northerners as the most important holiday on the calendar. In the South Christmas is regarded as a far more important holiday than the Fourth of July, which has never been celebrated much in that section of this country. Even before the Civil War the South paid little attention to Independence Day as a holiday. The result has been that in the South firecrackers are peculiarly associated with Christmas, while in the North they are associated with the Fourth of July. Of course in both sections their use is largely restricted to children. According to the U. S. Department of Commerce, duties were assessed on firecrackers from the Orient as early as 1859.

Can a moving object reverse its course without stopping?

Suppose a rifle bullet is traveling in one direction and that it meets and is carried back by a cannon ball traveling in the opposite direction. Does the rifle bullet stop completely in reversing its course to travel back with the cannon ball? The fact is the rifle ball will have to stop a theoretical instant before starting in the opposite direction, notwithstanding the cannon ball continues on its original course. No moving object can completely reverse its course without first coming to a standstill. Theoretically the cannon ball would be slowed up slightly.

Why are condemned persons executed just before sunrise?

It is impossible to say just how dawn became the favorite time for executions. The custom of putting condemned persons to death early in the morning has been prevalent since ancient times and one writer suggests that it may be a survival of the practices of prehistoric sunworshippers who offered human sacrifices to the sun as it rose in the east. Another thinks the practice is of military origin; persons condemned in the military are generally shot as early as possible on the specified day, that is, just as soon as it is light enough for the firing squad to see to take aim. Be this as it may, there are several good reasons for following the custom at the present time. The day on which an execution is to take place is set by the court; the exact hour is left to the discretion of prison officials. Usually the unpleasant task is performed when it will interfere least with the routine of prison life, which is as early as possible in the day, when the prisoners are in their cells and most of them are asleep. An execution has an unfavorable influence on all the inmates of a prison and if the condemned prisoner were electrocuted or hanged during the day or early in the night his fellow prisoners might be incited to riot. Where executions are public the number of morbid spectators is reduced by having them at dawn.

What is collective bargaining?

Collective bargaining is a labor-union term and refers to a method of determining wages, hours and working conditions by direct negotiation between the representatives of a labor union on one hand and an employer on the other. Instead of acting individually, as in the case of individual bargaining, the employees act as a group in presenting their demands and their representatives hold conferences with the representatives of the employers in order to adjust matters of dispute. The individual employee subordinates himself to the common interest of his fellows and in return receives benefits which he could not obtain alone. Labor compelled capital to recognize the principle of collective bargaining only after a long struggle. The exact origin of *collective bargaining* is not a matter of record. "The term," says the U. S. Department of Labor in a letter to the author, "correctly describes the act performed and doubtless came into use when labor agreements began to be generally made. The expression was but occasionally used until after the opening of the present century. It became very common during the World War and has been in general use since the Industrial Conference called by President Wilson in the fall of 1919."

How did *horselaugh* originate?

A horselaugh is a loud, coarse, boisterous laugh. The term dates back to the early part of the eighteenth century, if not much further. In 1713 Richard Steele wrote in No. 29 of the *Guardian:* "The Horse-Laugh is a distinguishing characteristick of the rural hoyden." Thomas Carlyle, in his life of Frederick the Great, says of

Prince Leopold of Anhalt-Dessau: "He plays rough pranks, too, on occasion; and has a big horse-laugh in him, where there is a fop to be roasted, or the like." A few authorities are of the opinion that *horselaugh* was suggested by the loud, laughing-like noise frequently made by horses. One etymologist believes that *horse* in this connection is merely a corruption of *coarse*. Be that as it may, *horse* is widely used attributively to denote anything large, inferior, coarse, or unrefined. That was probably its original application in *horselaugh,* just as it probably was in many plant names, such as horse-chestnut, horse-radish, horse beans, horse balm, horse bane, horse cassia, etc. Likewise, rude, boisterous play is called horseplay, and a person with a long, coarse face is said to be horse-faced. In view of this common usage it is not probable, as sometimes stated, that *horse-chestnut* was suggested by the horseshoe-shaped scars left on the twigs of this tree when the leaves fall.

Where did Logan deliver his famous speech?

The celebrated speech attributed to the Indian leader Logan, whose native name was Tah-gah-jute, was not delivered in person. Thomas Jefferson, who first called public attention to this piece of Indian eloquence, says in his *Notes on Virginia:* "I may challenge the whole orations of Demosthenes and Cicero, and of any more eminent orator, if Europe has furnished more eminent, to produce a single passage superior to the speech of Logan, a Mingo chief, to Lord Dunmore, when governor of this State." In Colonial times *Mingo* was a common name for those Iroquois Indians who lived beyond their proper boundaries, especially in Ohio. Logan, who was often called John, was not a chief in the technical sense. His father, Shikellamy, was supposedly a white man who had been captured by the Indians when a child and who became a chief among them. In the spring of 1774 two Shawnees murdered some settlers on the frontiers of Virginia. The whites, in accordance with frontier practice, retaliated by waylaying and massacring several Indians who were in a canoe near the mouth of Yellow Creek. Some of those killed were relatives of Logan, who had long been known as the white man's friend and who was then living peacefully at Old Chillicothe on the Sciota River in Ohio. In the so-called speech Logan says that all his relatives were murdered.

The evidence indicates that his sister and possibly another relative were killed, but not his wife; and he had no children. He firmly believed that Colonel Michael Cresap committed the murders, although it is pretty well established now that Cresap was not present and the party of settlers was led by a man named Greathouse. Be that as it may, Logan took up the tomahawk and for several months perpetrated fearful barbarities upon the isolated settlers, sparing neither man nor woman, nor child. He boasts of these killings in his speech. In the fall of the same year the Indian allies were defeated at Point Pleasant by the Virginia militia in what is known as Lord Dunmore's War. The Indians sued for peace and the governor of Virginia invited their chiefs to attend a peace meeting at Chillicothe. Logan refused to be present, but, according to tradition, he sent a message to Lord Dunmore. This message is now known as Logan's speech. Inaccuracies in it are explained by the fact that it was only a memorandum written down from the chief's verbal statement and read before the meeting at Chillicothe. The message, as preserved by Jefferson, reads as follows:

I appeal to any white man to say, if ever he entered Logan's cabin hungry, and he gave him not meat; if ever he came cold and naked, and he clothed him not. During the course of the last long and bloody war, Logan remained idle in his cabin, an advocate of peace. Such was my love for the whites, that my countrymen pointed as they passed, and said, "Logan is the friend of the white man." I had even thought to have lived with you, but for the injuries of one man. Colonel Cresap, the last spring, in cold blood, and unprovoked, murdered all the relations of Logan, not sparing even my women and children. There runs not a drop of my blood in the veins of any living creature. This called on me for revenge. I have sought it: I have killed many: I have fully glutted my vengeance. For my country, I rejoice at the beams of peace. But do not harbor a thought that mine is the joy of fear. Logan never felt fear. He will not turn on his heel to save his life. Who is there to mourn for Logan? Not one.

Are bulls excited more by red than by other colors?

Bulls are proverbially supposed to become particularly infuriated when they see a red object, especially a piece of red cloth in motion. This is a myth. Dr. George M. Stratton, an American psychologist, investigated this subject and came to the conclusion that all cattle arc practically color blind. Experiments made by Dr. Stratton at the University of California indicate that bulls and steers are unable to distinguish red from pink, green, purple or white. The bulls reacted to red just the same as they reacted to other bright colors. According to the U. S. Department of Agriculture, a bull's attention can be attracted with a bright-colored object more readily than with one dull in color. One investigator came to the conclusion that, if there is any difference at all, white is the most effective color for infuriating a bull. Bullfighters dress in bright colors and wave pieces of bright-colored cloth in the arena not only to infuriate the animals but also to attract the spectators. Red is naturally a favorite color for this purpose because it is bright, the color of blood, and it reacts most quickly on the human optic nerve. But it is the brightness of the cloth in motion rather than the particular color that excites and maddens the bull.

Does the wind ever shift directly from east to north?

Many people believe that the wind never shifts from north to east and back to the north again without veering around by way of the south and west. It is a fact well known to meteorologists that the wind very seldom veers from the north to the east and then, without further shift, back from east to north. But, according to the U. S. Weather Bureau, such changes can, and sometimes do occur. "In fact," asserts that Bureau, "such are the necessary changes in wind direction whenever the center of a barometric *high* or *anticyclone* passes on its eastward course north of the observer, followed by a barometric *low* or *cyclone* passing eastward with its center south of the observer. This is because winds always flow spirally clockwise out from the center of an anticyclone, and spirally counterclockwise in towards the center of a cyclone."

Why are English walnuts so called?

A species of walnut which is native only to Asia and southeastern Europe is known in the United States as the English walnut. This name arose from the fact that these nuts were first introduced into America from England, where they have been grown since 1562, if not since the Roman occupation. Among the Ro-

mans they were called Persian nuts, a name by which they are
still sometimes known. The so-called English walnut is indigenous
to Jugoslavia, Greece, Turkey, Persia and the region eastward to
China. Scientifically it is *Juglans regia*. Jove's nut, royal nut, French
walnut, and Madeira walnut are other popular names for the same
species.

Do the phases of the moon govern crops?

Many rural people practice what is known as moon-farming;
that is, they plant seeds, shear sheep, prune trees, butcher animals,
lay shingles, and do other farm work according to the phases of the
moon. They believe, for instance, that pork from hogs killed in
the dark of the moon will shrink when cooked; animals born during
the new moon thrive better; fleeces sheared in the wane of the
moon weigh more; the seeds of corn and other crops that grow
above the ground rot when planted in the light of the moon; crops
that grow under the ground, like potatoes and beets, grow near
the surface and produce a light yield when planted in the dark
of the moon; and shingles laid during the new moon curl up and pull
the nails out. In a sentence, nothing should be done except "when
the moon is right." Darwin wrote that the Gauchos of the Argentine
think that "nothing can succeed without it be begun when the
moon is on the increase." Before the Revolution the French government directed its foresters to cut timber only "in the wane of
the moon," on the theory that wood cut during that phase would
not rot so quickly. Belief in the moon's influence over such activities
dates back thousands of years and is probably a survival of moon
worship among the ancients. Only two centuries ago many people
still believed that the lunar orb was an active agent in controlling
human affairs. Scientists have sought in vain for a relation between
the phases of the moon and activities on the earth. Repeated experiments indicate that the phases of the earth's satellite have no
effect whatever on the germination of seeds, the warping of shingles,
the weight of wool, or the shrinkage of pork. Moon-farming, says
the U. S. Department of Agriculture, has no support from any
scientific point of view. Most of the beliefs associated with moon-
farming are not based on the assumption that direct moonlight is
especially potent, but rather that the moon exercises some mysteri-

ous and occult power over mundane affairs. Even the light and heat from the moon are not sufficient to affect plant growth materially. The moon does not govern agriculture because it has no appreciable influence on any of the major conditions affecting the growth of plants. Moonlight is merely reflected sunlight. Experiments show that full daylight is about 600,000 times brighter than full moonlight. Plants so shadowed that they receive only $\frac{1}{100}$ part as much light as normal daylight grow little better than they do when in total darkness. But light $\frac{1}{100}$ as strong as daylight, which is too feeble to stimulate plant activity appreciably, is still 6,000 times brighter than full moonlight. Therefore the stimulus of moonlight on plants must be negligible. From time to time some pseudo-scientist revives the theory that moonlight, being reflected light, is *polarized* and therefore particularly potent in affecting plants. There is no evidence that such is the case.

Are plants in bedrooms unhealthful?

According to a popular belief, dating back many centuries, plants and flowers give off a mysterious night-time emanation that is injurious to the human body and accordingly they should never be left in sleeping rooms over night. In many hospitals the nurses regularly remove all plants and flowers from the sick room at sundown with a view of preventing injury to the patients while sleeping. The U. S. Public Health Service says there is no scientific basis for the belief that plants are especially injurious to the human body during the night. Non-poisonous plants are beneficial rather than harmful in sleeping rooms, according to the director of scientific work in the U. S. Department of Agriculture. During the day plants absorb carbon dioxide from the atmosphere and after assimilating the carbon they return most of the oxygen to the air. This process slows up during the night. Plants *breathe* much as animals do; that is, they at all times, day and night, absorb oxygen and give off carbon dioxide. Thus there are two processes at work, and while plants give off more oxygen than carbon dioxide during the day, at night they may give off more carbon dioxide, but a whole greenhouse of plants would hardly give off enough of this gas to affect unfavorably the healthfulness of the air in a ventilated room. However, there may be practical reasons for removing plants and flowers from bedrooms at night. When the windows are opened during certain seasons of the year the atmosphere in the rooms is likely to get too cold for growing plants. In most hospitals cut flowers are removed from the rooms each day as a matter of course in order to change the water. Then, too, from the psychological point of view it may be good nursing practice to remove plants and flowers from sick rooms at night and return them in the morning. It relieves the monotony of the environment and gives the patient a fresh interest in the flowers.

Why is the speed of ships reckoned in knots?

The knot is a unit of speed equivalent to one nautical mile an hour. When a ship goes eight nautical miles an hour her speed is said to be eight knots. The knot is a survival of the earliest practical method of ascertaining the speed of vessels. This method consisted of casting out a log-line with a triangular piece of wood weighted with lead attached to the end to keep it upright and to retard its passage through the water. When the line was permitted to pass freely from a reel on board the ship the weighted piece of wood remained stationary for all practical purposes. The line itself was divided into sections, called knots because they were marked by pieces of cord worked in between the strands of the line. The distance between these knots bore the same ratio to a nautical mile as twenty-eight seconds does to an hour (3,600 seconds); that is, they were forty-seven feet three inches apart. A nautical or geographical mile is one-sixtieth of a degree on the earth's equator, or about 6,080 feet. Therefore the number of knots that ran off the reel in twenty-eight seconds by a sandglass showed with fair accuracy the number of nautical miles the vessel was traveling an hour. Six nautical miles are equal to about seven English statute miles, so a ship traveling twelve knots is actually traveling at the rate of almost fourteen statute miles an hour. Strictly speaking, the knot is not a unit of distance and it is loose usage to employ the term as a synonym of *nautical mile*. It is a unit of speed, and instead of saying a ship is traveling eight knots an hour we should say simply that it is traveling eight knots, or that it is traveling eight nautical miles an hour. Although knot as a unit of speed is still used, the old method of measuring the speed of vessels has been superseded almost entirely by automatic logs which register on dials. There is no etymological relation between the words *knot* and *nautical,* as many people suppose. The former is derived from the Anglo-Saxon *cnotta,* meaning knot in the sense of intertwined cord, while the latter comes to us through the Latin from the Greek *nautikos,* an adjective formed from *naus,* ship.

Was there ever a woman Pope?

During the Middle Ages it was almost universally believed that a woman disguised as a man occupied the papal chair between the reigns of Leo IV (847–855) and Benedict III (855–858). The story of a woman Pope apparently was first alluded to by Marianus Scotus, an Irish recluse, in a chronicle compiled between 1069 and 1082. In 1243 the story was related by Jean de Mailly, a Dominican chronicler ; and Stephen of Bourbon, another Dominican, incorporated it in his *Seven Gifts of the Holy Spirit,* written a few years later. Stephen gives the alleged popess no name and says she reigned about the year 1100. Her history remained in a nebulous state until about 1250 when it was related in a circumstantial manner by Martin of Troppau in his epitome of the history of the world, an uncritical work containing many fables and popular legends, which received a wide circulation because it was written at the request of Pope Clement IV. For the first time the popess was given a name—Joan or Joanna. She was an English girl, educated in Germany, says Martin, and she fell in love with a monk with whom she went to Athens disguised in man's apparel. The monk died and Joan, still in male attire, went to Rome where, as Joannes Anglicus —John of England—she entered the priesthood, became a cardinal, and upon the death of Leo IV in 855 was unanimously elected pope under the title of John VIII. After occupying the papal chair for more than two years her death and disgrace came when she gave birth to a child during a papal procession. This tale was retold by numerous writers who made alterations and amplifications to suit their fancy. It is open to several objections. There was no vacancy between Leo IV and Benedict III, as shown by coins issued during the reign of the latter ; and the title John VIII is assigned to a pope who reigned from 872 to 882. Nevertheless the story was accepted as fact by Bartholomew of Lucca, a prolific church historian who died in 1327; and when John Hus referred to the female Pope before the Council of Constance in 1413 nobody questioned the fact of her existence. During the fourteenth and fifteenth centuries the popess was regarded as a historical character, and a carved bust of her was placed in the cathedral at Siena, Italy. In the fifteenth century a few scholars began to doubt the story, and after the sixteenth century nearly all Catholic historians, as well as many Protestant writers, began to deny the existence of Pope Joan or any other popess. From the standpoint of modern research there is not a particle of evidence that such a person ever occupied the papal chair, and Pope Joan is undoubtedly a mythical character, although the legend is still a favorite weapon of attack on the papacy by anti-Catholics; in fact it is so often told for this purpose that many erroneously suppose it to be an invention of the Protestants. David Blondel, a French Calvinist, undertook to explode the myth, a task which was finally accomplished by Johann Dollinger, an eminent German theologian and historian who was excommunicated from the Roman Church. Several theories have been advanced as to how the legend originated. It may be the survival of an ancient Roman folk-tale, or it may have been started as a satire on some of the effeminate and licentious Popes of the tenth century, several of whom were named John. Possibly it was the corruption of an earlier tale about Byzantium, for in 1055 Pope Leo IX said in a letter that he had heard that eunuchs and even a woman had occupied the episcopal chair at Constantinople.

Do cats actually sharpen their claws on trees?

Domestic cats frequently arch their backs and claw at the bark of a tree or the leg of a table. It is commonly supposed that the animals do this to "sharpen their claws." How merely scratching wood or bark would sharpen the claws is difficult to understand. According to another popular notion, the cat goes through these characteristic motions to stretch and to exercise the small toe muscles on which it largely depends for a livelihood. Scientists, however, believe that members of the feline family scratch trees and other objects to rid themselves of loose pieces of toenail. Often bits of broken claws are found sticking in the bark of trees where cats make a practice of clawing. In the forests of southeastern

Asia certain trees are worn smooth by cheetahs or hunting leopards which regularly go there to "sharpen their claws." Darwin observed the same thing in South America. In *The Voyage of the Beagle* he wrote:

One day, when hunting on the banks of the Uruguay, I was shown certain trees, to which these animals [jaguars] constantly recur for the purpose, as it is said, of sharpening their claws. I saw three well known trees; in front, the bark was worn smooth, as if by the breast of the animal, and on each side there were deep scratches, or rather grooves, extending in an oblique line, nearly a yard in length. The scars were of different ages. A common method of ascertaining whether a jaguar is in the neighborhood is to examine these trees. I imagine this habit of the jaguar is exactly similar to one which may any day be seen in the common cat, as with outstretched legs and exserted claws it scrapes the leg of a chair; and I have heard of young fruit trees in an orchard in England having been thus much injured. Some such habit must also be common to the puma, for on the bare hard soil of Patagonia I have frequently seen scores so deep that no other animal could have made them. The object of this practice is, I believe, to tear off the ragged points of their claws, and not, as the Gauchos think, to sharpen them.

Why are fish eaten on Friday?

Fish became associated with Friday in a roundabout way. Friday corresponds to the day of the week on which Jesus was crucified and many of the early Christians observed it as a weekly fast day, that is, a day on which they abstained from eating flesh meats. Pope Nicholas (858–867) declared that abstinence on Friday was obligatory on all communicants of the Roman Church. Fish is the principal non-flesh meat and accordingly it became the favorite food for those days when flesh meats were forbidden. Nowadays many Protestants and other non-Catholics follow the Catholic practice of serving fish almost exclusively on Friday. This is partly out of respect for the numerous Catholics found in most communities; but fish dealers report that many housewives buy fish to be served on Friday because they feel that they can obtain fish of better quality at that time of the week because of the prevailing custom. The fish was one of the earliest symbols of the Savior and Christianity in general. There were several reasons for this. Fish and fishing played an important part in the daily lives of Jesus and his disciples. Peter and several of the other disciples were fishermen by trade and Jesus told them that if they would follow him he would make them "fishers of men"; and the reader will recall the miraculous multiplication of the loaves and fishes, as well as the repast after the Resurrection on the shores of the Sea of Galilee, when some of the disciples ate fish caught by following the instructions of the Lord. The fish as an emblem of Christianity was further popularized by the coincidence that the Greek word for fish, which we render *ichthys,* is spelled in Greek with five letters, corresponding to *I-CH-TH-U-S,* which form what is known as an acrostic; that is, the component letters of the word for fish are the initial letters of *Iesous CHristos, THeou Uios, Soter,* meaning Jesus Christ, Son of God, Savior.

Why is *Jno.* used as the abbreviation of *John?*

Jno. as the abbreviation of *John* originated when this proper name was still in the process of formation. The English form of the name is derived from *Johannes,* which was first contracted to *Johan;* in time the *a* was either dropped or an *o* was substituted for it and the name was written *John* or *Johon.* Sometimes, however, it was spelled *Jhon,* due either to the omission of the first instead of the second *o* in *Johon,* or to the transposition of *h* and *o* in *John.* In early times the name was probably pronounced in two syllables. Be that as it may, centuries ago it was a common practice to use *n* for *h* and *John* was abbreviated either *Jho.* or *Jno.* The latter form prevailed and is still the favorite abbreviation.

What queen of England was never in England?

Queen Berengaria, wife of Richard the Lion-Hearted, was never in England. Richard left England in 1190 to take part in the third crusade. Berengaria, the beautiful daughter of Sancho VI of Navarre, was brought to him by his mother Eleanor while he and his troops were wintering in southern Italy, and the marriage took place in Cyprus on May 12, 1191. Later in the same year the English queen joined the king at Acre on the coast of Palestine. During Richard's imprisonment on the continent Berengaria lived in Italy and France. Upon his release early in 1194 he proceeded immediately to England, where he remained less than two months, after which he left for his foreign dominions never to return. It is said that he met his wife only once again, sometime in 1195. However that may be, they became estranged, and the queen's later years were spent chiefly at Le Mans in France, where she died about 1230 without ever having set foot on English soil. Richard died in France in 1199 of a wound received while besieging the castle of Châlus.

What causes the ascent of sap in trees?

How sap rises in trees is a question that has never been definitely settled. The water absorbed from the soil by the roots ultimately escapes from the leaves in the form of vapor. This water in the living plant, with certain substances in solution, is popularly known as sap. Some trees grow more than three hundred feet high, and a single specimen may lose many gallons of water daily through transpiration. What mechanism in the tree is capable of raising that much water to so great a height? Several theories have been advanced to explain this apparent contradiction of the law of gravity. It was formerly believed that water was raised in trees by the force of capillarity; the sap, it was supposed, rose in a stem much as oil rises in a wick through the natural tendency of liquids to climb up in narrow tubes and crevices. It is now known, however, that capillary attraction cannot raise water high enough or fast enough to account for the rapid loss of water through evaporation. The theory of atmospheric pressure is open to a similar objection; this force can raise water to heights of only about thirty feet. Nor is there sufficient root pressure for the purpose; besides, root pressure is most active in the spring while transpiration is most active in the summer, and experiments show that water will rise in tall trees even after being severed at the base. According to another theory, certain cells in the wood exert a continuous pumping action, taking water from a lower vessel and forcing it into a higher one. But experimental data and the known structure of wood have compelled the abandonment of this so-called *vital* theory of the ascent of sap. Obviously, if there is no pumping mechanism in the wood itself, and the sap is not pushed from below, the liquid must be pulled from above. Therefore the cohesive theory, which is comparatively new, is now accepted as the best explanation of the phenomenon. This theory holds that the water is drawn up by a pulling force exerted by evaporation on the leaves. Experiments prove that a leafy shoot will exert a considerable pull even after being cut. Ordinarily we think of a stream of water as being as unstable as a rope of sand. But it is known that a liquid like water in a tube where it cannot change its form has a peculiar tensile strength or cohesive property, due to the attraction of one particle for another. When air is excluded from the tube the water can support a remarkably heavy tensile strain. The fine fibers in the living wood are really a connected system of slender tubes in which water is carried, but from which air is excluded. Thus it is supposed that the water threads in the tissues are able to transmit any pull exerted on them from above and that their tensile strength is sufficient to raise water to the tops of the tallest trees. Subsidiary factors may also contribute toward the elevation of the sap. The dendrograph proves that the trunk of a tree contracts when the leaves are transpiring and expands when the leaves are closed at night. Any change in pressure in one part is quickly transmitted to others. Fifteen minutes after the sun strikes the leaves the trunk begins to contract.

How much is the curvature of the earth to the mile?

The curvature of the earth is about eight inches to the mile and varies as the square of the distance. For two miles the curvature is four times eight inches; for half a mile it is one fourth of eight inches, and so on. By curvature of the earth is meant the distance that a great circle departs from a line tangent to the earth at its point of contact. Suppose, for instance, that a man whose eye is five feet from the ground stands on a perfectly level section of the earth. If there were no refraction of the atmosphere the line of the horizon would be 2.74 miles away. Because of refraction the distance is actually greater than this. In order to determine the distance at which a vessel of given height can be seen at sea both curvature of the earth's surface and the refraction of the atmosphere must be taken into consideration. The curvature of the earth, making allowances for refraction, is about 229.5 feet for twenty miles. Therefore a ship 200 feet high would be completely out of sight at a distance of twenty miles, assuming the eye to be near the level of the sea. A person would have to be 358.6 feet above the surface in order to see a target on the surface of the sea twenty-five miles away. The following table, prepared by the U. S. Coast and Geodetic Survey, gives the various corrections for curvature and refraction:

Distance Miles	Correction Feet	Distance Miles	Correction Feet	Distance Miles	Correction Feet
1	0.6	21	253.1	41	964.7
2	2.3	22	277.7	42	1012.2
3	5.2	23	303.6	43	1061.0
4	9.2	24	330.5	44	1111.0
5	14.4	25	358.6	45	1162.0
6	20.6	26	388.0	46	1214.2
7	28.1	27	418.3	47	1267.7
8	36.7	28	449.9	48	1322.1
9	46.4	29	482.6	49	1377.7
10	57.4	30	516.4	50	1434.6
11	69.4	31	551.4	51	1492.5
12	82.7	32	587.6	52	1551.6
13	97.0	33	624.9	53	1611.9
14	112.5	34	663.3	54	1673.3
15	129.1	35	703.0	55	1735.8
16	146.9	36	743.7	56	1799.6
17	165.8	37	785.6	57	1864.4
18	185.9	38	828.6	58	1930.4
19	207.2	39	872.8	59	1997.5
20	229.5	40	918.1	60	2065.8

Do rainbows ever appear as complete circles?

Rainbows due to showers of rain, says the U. S. Weather Bureau, are never seen as complete circles by observers at ordinary elevations. Such bows, however, do sometimes appear from points well up in the air, as from a balloon, airplane or mountain top. Aviators see the phenomenon most frequently at a considerable altitude when the sun is near the horizon. The peculiarly colored circles which occasionally appear around the sun and moon are not true rainbows. Occasionally a circular rainbow produced by mist or spray is seen at ordinary elevations. In *The Voyage of the Beagle* Darwin describes such a rainbow seen during a storm at sunset off the coast of Chile. "During a few minutes there was a bright rainbow," writes the naturalist, "and it was curious to observe the effect of the spray, which being carried along the surface of the water, changed the ordinary semicircle into a circle—a band of prismatic colors being continued, from both feet of the common arch across the bay, close to the vessel's side: thus forming a distorted, but very nearly entire ring."

What are sea serpents?

This is the name given to monstrous snakelike creatures believed by many to live in the ocean. Sea serpents are now regarded as mythical. There is no scientific evidence that such creatures exist. The only actual serpents found in the sea are certain snakes which live in tropical waters. These snakes do not grow large compared with some other snakes and they are distinguished by the compressed, rudder-shaped tail. Their chief food consists of fish and they are unable to move on land. Speaking of the sea snakes found near the coast of northwestern Australia the National Geographic Society says: "Sea snakes are frequently seen curled up asleep on the surface of the water. These reptiles are poisonous and grow to about twelve feet in length." Belief in enormous serpents of the sea dates from ancient times. The accounts left by early Norsemen abound in stories of sea serpents several hundred feet in length and twenty feet in circumference. Olaus Magnus, writing in 1555, described such a monster which, he said, not only ate calves, sheep and swine, but also "disturbs ships, rising up like a mast, and sometimes snaps some of the men from the deck." These stories were generally believed during the seventeenth century, according to Erick Pontoppidan. That such creatures lived in American waters was vouched for by many eminent persons as late as the nineteenth century. Literature on the subject is full of affadavits made by mariners who claimed to have seen the monsters. Even at the present time the sight of sea serpents is occasionally reported. As one would expect, the descriptions vary widely. Modern ships, says Austin H. Clark, a Smithsonian Institution scientist, have done much to destroy fables about sea serpents. Inaccurate observation and optical illusions probably are responsible for many of the reports in question. Some of the alleged sea serpents were undoubtedly squids or other well known marine animals. The squid, often fifty feet long and a foot thick, has branching arms that might easily be taken for serpents. Sometimes several creatures seen together may mislead unwary observers. For instance, a number of porpoises swimming one behind the other, half emerging and then sinking, might at a distance create the illusion of a large animal showing a succession of snakelike undulations. Masses of seaweed have been cautiously approached and harpooned under the impression that they were sea monsters. Even a flock of birds in flight has created the illusion of a monster swimming on the surface. There may still be enormous creatures in the ocean which are unknown to scientists, but the sea serpent stories are highly improbable.

Why does salt melt snow?

Salt melts snow and ice by physical rather than chemical action. The freezing point of a solution is always lower than that of its solvent. When Gabriel Fahrenheit, the German physicist, was experimenting with varying degrees of temperatures he found that the lowest temperature he could obtain was producd with a mixture of salt and ice. Salt mixed with snow or ice at a temperature not too far below the freezing point forms a solution with a lower freezing point than water, snow or ice. That is why salt causes snow and ice to melt. If salt is mixed with snow in extremely cold weather little change is noticed, because the resultant liquid freezes as fast as it is formed. Ice and salt make an excellent mixture for freezing ice cream. The cream is not frozen by taking cold from the ice, as popularly supposed; it is frozen because its temperature is lowered by the absorption of heat by the melting ice. It is impossible for ice to melt without absorbing heat and a freezing temperature cannot be obtained inside an ice-cream freezer unless the ice is melted. Salt is added merely to hasten the melting of the ice and to speed up the freezing of the cream by taking heat away from it.

How many of our Presidents were slave-owners?

Ten men who have occupied the Presidency were owners of slaves at one time or another during their lives. They were Washington, Jefferson, Madison, Monroe, Jackson, Tyler, Polk, Taylor, Johnson, and Grant. The first eight of these were slave-owners in the full sense of the term and most of them had slaves while holding the office of President. Andrew Johnson bought a few slaves whom he kept as personal servants, but he never sold one of them. Ulysses

S. Grant was at one time joint owner of at least one slave and accordingly was technically a slave-owner. After his marriage his father-in-law presented him and his wife with a slave boy.

What officials have the franking privilege?

The franking privilege is the privilege of sending mail without paying postage. *Frank* is from Old French *franc,* meaning free. Two distinct Federal laws govern the transmission of franked or free mail. Members of the executive and judicial branches of the Government, including the President and the justices of the Supreme Court, do not have the franking privilege proper. They enjoy what is commonly known as the *penalty privilege,* so named from the style of envelopes and labels required. In order to send mail free by this method the sender must use penalty envelopes or tags on which "Penalty for Private Use, To Avoid Payment of Postage, $300" or words to that effect are printed. Members of the legislative branch have the regular franking privilege and may send mail free simply by franking or signing it. Officials may legally exercise the franking and penalty privileges only for official mail and are not supposed to frank personal letters. The wives of officials, including the President's wife, are not recognized as officials and do not have the privilege of sending mail free. Lawrence Richey, secretary to President Hoover, wrote as follows to the author May 6, 1930: "There is no authority of law permitting the wife of the President to send mail free of postage. Stamps are placed on all mail dealing with social affairs." Congress may and does sometimes, as a mark of honor, confer the franking privilege on private citizens for private correspondence. In 1800 it was enacted, "That all letters and packages to and from Martha Washington, relict of the late General George Washington, shall be received and conveyed by post free of postage, for and during life." Free postage on mail both to and from Mrs. Washington was granted because in those days postage was usually paid on receipt of the mail. It has since become customary to confer the franking privilege on all the widows of men who have been President. In order to exercise the privilege all that is necessary is for the sender to write his autograph signature in the upper right-hand corner of the envelope or wrapper, preferably but not necessarily under the word *Free.* Such mail is carried free only to places where domestic posttage rates apply.

Is *anthracite coal* correct?

The word *anthracite* is derived directly from the Greek *anthrax,* meaning coal. It is a noun and is applied to hard coal, that is, coal consisting of nearly pure carbon. Accordingly we should correctly say simply *anthracite,* not *anthracite coal;* the latter is tautological and equivalent to *coal-like coal. Bituminous,* on the other hand, is an adjective and should properly be followed by the word *coal.* Bituminous coal is soft coal, that is, coal that yields considerable volatile bituminous matter when heated.

Why is ice cream and syrup called a sundae?

Sundae is of unknown origin. Several unauthenticated stories supposed to account for it have been widely circulated. Most of them are based on the assumption that the term was originally *Sunday* and became *sundae* through error or a process of evolution. In *American English,* published in 1921, Gilbert M. Tucker says *sundae* originated "about 1897, at Red Cross Pharmacy, State Street, Ithaca, N. Y., directly opposite to barroom of Ithaca Hotel, which was closed on Sunday, suggesting to the pharmacy people to offer a distinctively Sunday drink." The sundae is not a drink and the story is probably the figment of somebody's imagination. There are three or four similar stories, differing chiefly in the time and place of the alleged event. According to one, a druggist at Shreveport, Louisiana, about 1908 served fruit juices with ice cream to avoid violating a law forbidding the sale of carbonated soda waters on Sunday. His clerk was a poor speller and wrote "Sundae Special" instead of "Sunday Special" on the window. Another has it that a customer in a Connecticut confectioner's shop on Sunday ordered the usual ice-cream soda. The clerk, being out of soda water, filled a glass with ice cream and poured the syrup over it. This dish so appealed to the customer that he advertised it through the town and the shop was flooded with requests for what "So-and-so had Sunday." None of these theories are acceptable to the etymologist because there is not a particle of evidence to support them. One writer goes so far as to say, without any evidence whatever, that the dish was first called Friday, then Sunday, and finally sundae. It may be that *sundae* was deliberately invented for advertising purposes. There is a story, also unconfirmed, that the dish in question was invented and named after a New Orleans druggist named Sundae.

Does the House of Representatives have a permanent Speaker pro tempore?

The House of Representatives does not have a permanent Speaker pro tempore. The Constitution specifically provides that the Senate shall choose a President pro tempore to preside in the absence of the Vice President, but it simply says that "the House of Representatives shall choose their Speaker and other officers." House Rule I, Section 7 is as follows: "He [the Speaker] shall have the right to name any member to perform the duties of the Chair, but such substitution shall not extend beyond three legislative days: *Provided, however,* That in case of illness, he may make such appointment for a period not exceeding ten days, with the approval of the House at the time the same is made: and in his absence and omission to make such appointment, the House shall proceed to elect a Speaker pro tempore to act during his absence."

What is the freedom of the city?

When a distinguished person is officially welcomed to a city he is said to receive the freedom of the city. Nowadays conferring the freedom of the city amounts to little more than an expression of esteem, but during the Middle Ages in Europe the ceremony had a greater significance. *Freedom* was the name given to the privileges of certain cities, usually known as free cities, and by extension the term was applied to the municipal privileges of the citizens themselves. Hence the freedom of the city meant the privileges of citizenship. A citizen was called a freeman. In those days the ordinary person could become a freeman or citizen only by a long apprenticeship to a recognized guild. Occasionally, however, the customary requirements were dispensed with and a person of great wealth or renown was granted citizenship or the freedom of the city in recognition of his position or his services to the community. His name was placed on the list of burghers or freemen and he was entitled to all the privileges of municipal citizenship, including those of voting and holding office. In view of the difficulties involved in becoming a citizen it was a substantial favor as well as a great honor to be granted the freedom of the city. Accordingly the phrase became associated in the popular mind with honor and esteem. Later honorary citizenship was sometimes conferred; that is, the freedom of the city, carrying only nominal privileges, was conferred on eminent non-residents purely as a mark of honor. Many European cities still welcome distinguished persons by granting them the freedom of the city and the documents presented are modeled after those employed on similar occasions during the Middle Ages. In America *freedom of the city,* like *keys of the city,* is merely a figurative expression and is seldom employed in the language of the scroll presented to a visitor of distinction when he is given an official reception.

Who built the first steamboat?

Robert Fulton did not build the first boat propelled by steam power, as commonly supposed. He made the first really practical application of steam to navigation and accordingly is known as the "Father of the Steamboat," but before he began his experiments several men had succeeded in propelling boats by the application of steam power through various crude and rather impractical devices. It is not definitely known who first propelled a boat by steam power. In 1543 a Spanish sea captain named Blasco de Garay demonstrated a crude steam craft in the harbor of Barcelona, and there are records of several similar attempts to apply steam to navigation during the next 250 years. In October, 1783, James Rumsey, a native of Maryland, successfully demonstrated a steamboat on the Potomac River near Sir John's Run. This boat was driven by means of a steam-operated pump which took up water near the front of the boat and forced it out at the stern. John Fitch launched a steamboat on the Delaware River about 1786. His craft was propelled by means of a series of paddles operated by a steam engine. These pioneers were confronted with a double difficulty—the development of a practical steam engine and the invention of a satisfactory method by which the steam power could be applied to propel a boat. Although their crude devices actually propelled boats through the water, none of them proved very practical, and it was the method of propulsion devised by Robert Fulton which led to the application of steam to commercial navigation. Fulton's first steam-driven boat was demonstrated at Paris in 1803, and in 1807 he launched on the Hudson River the *Clermont,* known as the first practical steamboat.

What is the principle of the thermos bottle?

The thermos bottle or vacuum flask consists essentially of a glass container with double walls inclosing a partial vacuum. Heat escapes from or enters into ordinary closed vessels by means of conductivity and radiation and it is conducted through the air by the movements of the molecules. When the space between the walls of the vessel, especially when the vessel is composed of a substance like glass, is partially exhausted of air the conductivity is greatly reduced. In fact an approximate vacuum between the walls of glass becomes practically a non-conductor of heat. The only place where the inner and the outer walls of the thermos flask join and provide a path for the communication of heat from one to the other is at the neck, which is therefore made as small as practical. Highly reflecting surfaces are poor radiators of heat. That is why the walls of the thermos bottle are silvered. The silvered walls and the partial vacuum combined retard the inflow and outflow of heat to such an extent that the contents of the vessel remain either cold or hot for a considerable period irrespective of the temperature of the surrounding atmosphere. The principle of the thermos bottle was discovered about 1892 by Sir James Dewar (pronounced *Dew-ar*), an eminent British chemist and physicist, who designed vacuum-jacketed vessels for storing gases after he had liquefied them. These flasks, known at first as Dewar bulbs, proved to be very effective for preserving liquefied gases by preventing the influx of external heat.

Why do cats always land on their feet?

Nearly everybody has at some time turned a cat upside down and dropped it to see the animal right itself while falling and then land on all fours. Cats do not seem to mind the experiment much. They apparently are conscious of their remarkable ability to turn their bodies while falling. This facility in landing right side up, coupled with well padded feet, occasionally saves the life of a cat. In 1880, while the Washington Monument was under construction, a cat fell from the top of the unfinished shaft to the ground 160 feet below without serious injury. The ability of the cat to light on its feet is due to a reflex action which it performs as unconsciously as a person closes his eyes when somebody suddenly makes a pass at him. A Dutch scientist proved this by performing an operation on a cat's brain and depriving the animal of the ability of doing any conscious act whatever. When the cat was tossed in the air it fell on its feet with the same unerring accuracy that it did before the operation. Slow motion pictures show how a cat manages to right itself during a fall. It first extends both hind legs perpendicular to the axis of its body and simultaneously draws the forelegs close in toward the body. A twisting motion through the body then causes the closely held forequarters to rotate nearly 90 degrees in advance of the hindquarters, that is, the thorax turns while the rear part of the body remains almost immobile. Next the front legs are quickly extended and the hind legs drawn in while the rear part of the body is turned by another body motion. The cat's body is so muscular and supple that this entire operation requires only an instant and the animal is ready to land on its feet when it reaches the ground even though it may fall only a short distance. From the standpoint of physics, the secret of the cat's action is that its muscles enable it to modify the moment of inertia of certain parts of its body, causing one part to turn a little farther than the other and in the desired direction.

How long is a Sabbath day's journey?

Under the rabbinical law a Sabbath day's journey was the distance that the Jews were permitted to go on the Sabbath. In *Exodus 16:29* it says, "let no man go out of his place on the seventh day." It is evident, however, that the people were allowed to go a certain distance on that day. For instance, they could go to the Ark from the tents in the remote part of the camp—2,000 cubits. The cubit was an ancient linear measure corresponding to eighteen or twenty inches; therefore many Bible commentators infer that a Sabbath day's journey was from 3,000 to 3,300 feet, that is, the distance between the Ark and the extreme end of the camp or city. Of course, after going to the Ark the people would be permitted to return to their tents or homes. In *Acts 1:12* it says, "Then returned they unto Jerusalem from the mount called Olivet, which is from Jerusalem a Sabbath day's journey." According to Josephus, the Mount of Olives was five *stadia* or about 3,033 feet from Jerusalem. Thus it will be seen that a Sabbath day's journey was considerably less than one statute mile. Perhaps the last quotation should be construed, "which is within a Sabbath day's journey of Jerusalem." Under an old Puritan law it was permissible in case of necessity to make a journey of ten miles on Sunday. That distance, according to medieval legal practice, was one half of an ordinary or week-day journey, namely, twenty miles.

Does it ever get too cold to snow?

The saying that it is sometimes too cold to snow has some scientific basis, but it should not be interpreted literally. It is true in the literal sense, says the U. S. Weather Bureau, only when the temperature approximates 40° or 50° below zero and when the moisture content of the air is inappreciable. It never gets too cold to snow if there is sufficient moisture in the atmosphere. Snow is formed by the freezing of the water vapor in the air and when the temperature drops to zero or lower the atmosphere can carry very little vapor; consequently heavy snowfall from such air is impossible. Light snows, however, occasionally occur at exceedingly low temperatures, and sometimes even heavy snows fall when the surface air is quite cold. In the latter case the upper atmosphere where the snow is formed is comparatively warm at the time. Great amounts of snow accumulate in the polar regions where temperatures are generally below the freezing point throughout the winter season. But it is not probable that the common expression "too cold to snow" originally had reference to extreme temperatures. In more or less temperate latitudes the greater part of the snow falls when the temperature is very little below the freezing point rather than when it approximates zero. This is because precipitation of any kind is most likely to come with southerly to easterly winds, that is, in what meteorologists call the rainy part of the cyclonic or storm area. As a rule these winds are comparatively warm. The winds generally shift to a northwesterly direction as the storm passes and become colder. In other words, the precipitation is likely to be followed by a clearing-up condition, accompanied by a decided drop in temperature. Therefore when the winter wind is from the northwest it is usually cold and from the wrong direction to produce snow. Those unfamiliar with meteorology then say that it is "too cold to snow." But the absence of snow is not due entirely to the coldness. It is due, rather, to the absence of other conditions necessary to produce precipitation.

What is the official name of the National Capital?

Several experiments were made in naming the Capital of the United States and the tract of land on which it is situated before the present names became fixed. From the beginning the legislative and executive branches of the Federal Government failed to discriminate carefully between the City of Washington and the District of Columbia. Frequently these two names, along with several others, were used indiscriminately in acts of Congress and in other official documents. At first it was customary to refer to the National Capital as "The Federal City," but on September 9, 1791, the three commissioners appointed by President Washington named the city "The City of Washington" and the district "The *Territory* of Columbia." These names were used in the original laws for the district approved December 15, 1800, by the Sixth Congress. But this precedent was not followed. February 25, 1801, "City of Washington, *District* of Columbia," was employed instead. A short time later, however, "City of Washington, *Territory* of Columbia" was used again. A proclamation dated September 6, 1800, has "City of Washington" without reference to the district, while a reply of the President to the House of Representatives, November 27, 1800, has simply "Washington." Jefferson's first inaugural address, March 4, 1801, has "Washington, D. C." After that we find "District of Columbia," "City of Washington," "Washington, D. C.," and "Washington" used more or less indiscriminately in official documents issued by all branches of the Federal Government. In 1871 the municipal charters of Washington and Georgetown were revoked by Congress and there ceased to be any difference between Washington and the District of Columbia so far as government and laws are concerned. President Harding's Thanksgiving proclamation of 1921 was "done in the Capital of the United States." This unusual designation raised the question as to what the official name of the National Capital should be. Accordingly an Executive Order was issued designating "The City of Washington" as the official name of the Capital of the United States.

Who was the tallest President?

Abraham Lincoln was about six feet four inches in height and was the tallest man who has been President of the United States. George Washington, who was about six feet two inches in height, was the second tallest. In a letter to Jesse W. Fell in 1859 Lincoln wrote: "If any personal description is thought desirable, I am in height six feet four inches, nearly." The records of the Black Hawk War, in which Lincoln served as a captain, gave his height as six feet four and a half inches. Henry C. Whitney, who traveled with Lincoln on the circuit in Illinois and often slept with him, wrote the following description: "He was six feet and four inches in height, his legs and arms were disproportionately long, his feet and hands were abnormally large, he was awkward in his gait and actions." There is also ample evidence of Washington's approximate height. In 1760 George Mercer, his friend and companion in arms, gave the following description of Washington: "He may be described as being as straight as an Indian, measuring six feet two inches in his stockings, and weighing 175 pounds, when he took his seat in the House of Burgesses in 1759." Later David Ackerson, of Alexandria, Virginia, recorded that "Washington's exact height was six feet two inches in his boots." James Madison, who was only five feet four inches in height, was the shortest President.

Can a person be punished twice for the same offense?

There is no provision in the Constitution of the United States which makes it illegal for a person to be tried and punished for the same offense by both a State and a Federal court. Amendment V of the Constitution says in part: "Nor shall any person be subject for the same offense to be twice put in jeopardy of life or limb." This provision, however, merely prohibits the Federal Government from punishing a person twice for the same offense. Five men were convicted in a Federal court in the State of Washington on charges of manufacturing intoxicating liquor in violation of the Federal statutes. Later these five men were convicted for the same offense in a State court on charges of violating the State statutes prohibiting the manufacture of intoxicating beverages. In 1922 the Supreme Court of the United States sustained this double conviction, Chief Justice Taft declaring that the "double jeopardy" clause in the Constitution applies solely to dual punishment by the Federal Government for the same offense. Many people do not seem to be aware of the fact that the first ten Constitutional Amendments, popularly called the American Bill of Rights, have always been construed as applying only to the Federal Government. They were intended not to restrain the States, but to protect them against the Federal power. It frequently happens that a person by a single act violates both a Federal and a State law.

What does the Lion of Lucerne commemorate?

The Lion of Lucerne is a sculptured lion hewn from living sandstone in a niche near Lucerne, Switzerland. It was made from a model designed by the Danish sculptor Albert Thorwaldsen. The statue was dedicated in 1821 and is a memorial commemorating the tragic fate of the twenty-six officers and seven hundred and sixty privates of the Swiss Guard who sacrificed their lives in defense of Louis XVI and Marie Antoinette after the French guards had deserted during the attack of the mob on the Tuileries in Paris August 10, 1792. The lion is represented as being transfixed with a broken spear; and, although dying, it is still trying to protect with its paw a shield bearing the Lilies of France. In the rock below are carved the names of the Swiss heroes.

How would the vacancy be filled if a nominee for President should die during the campaign?

The national committee of each major political party has power to fill vacancies on the ticket from any cause. That power is usually conferred on the committee by the national convention which makes the nominations. For instance, the Republican national convention which met in 1928 and nominated Herbert Hoover for President and Charles Curtis for Vice President passed the following resolution granting the Republican National Committee the power to fill vacancies on the ticket:

Resolved: That the Republican National Committee be and is hereby authorized and empowered to fill any and all vacancies which may occur by reason of death, declination or otherwise in the ticket nominated by the convention and that, in voting in said committee, the committee members representing any State, Territory, Territorial Possession or the District of Columbia, shall be entitled to cast the same number of votes as said State, Territory, Territorial Possession or the District of Columbia was entitled to cast in the national convention; or, that the National Committee in its judgment may call the national convention for the purpose of filling such vacancy.

Therefore if the party nominee for President or Vice President should die or resign before the November election the national committee of that party would designate another person to fill the vacancy or would call the national convention into session again for that purpose. Only once has the national committee of a major political party had occasion to act in such an emergency. On October 30, 1912, a few days before the national election, Vice President James S. Sherman died. He was at the time running for reëlection on the Taft ticket. The Republican National Committee, acting under the power conferred on it by the national convention which had met at Chicago and made the nominations, designated Nicholas Murray Butler of New York to fill the vacancy caused by Sherman's death. Only eight electors pledged to Taft and Butler were elected—four from Vermont and four from Utah.

Who would become President if the President-elect and the Vice President-elect should both die just before March 4?

There is no Constitutional or statutory provision for such a contingency. What would take place in that event can be only a matter of conjecture, for thus far the contingency has never arisen and apparently it was never contemplated by the framers of the

Constitution. Congress would have to provide a method for choosing a chief magistrate after the emergency arose. If only the President-elect died the Vice President-elect could be sworn in on March 4 as usual and he would then automatically become President by operation of the Constitution. The people do not vote directly for President and Vice President, but for electors who elect those officers. Strictly speaking, it is not correct to speak of the *winning* candidates after the general election as President-elect and Vice President-elect. They are merely President-designate and Vice President-designate until they are actually chosen by the electoral college and declared elected by Congress. If the President-designate and the Vice President-designate should die or resign after the election in November and before the meeting of the electors in their respective States, the electors would still have an opportunity to elect a President and Vice President. The electors are morally but not legally obliged to vote for the nominees of their parties. Political parties are completely ignored by the Constitution, and there are no statutory restrictions on the electors in that respect. They can vote for whom they please. They do, however, invariably vote for their party nominees, because they are pledged to do so. But if a nominee died the electors would be at liberty to vote for somebody else. Only once in American history has a Presidential nominee died between the November election and the meeting of the electors. In that case the nominee who died had lost in the general election and the result was not affected. Horace Greeley, who was nominated by both Liberal Republicans and the Democrats in 1872, died a few weeks after the popular election, that is, the election of Presidential electors. The electors pledged to him hardly knew what to do. Three of them voted for the dead man, and the remainder scattered their ballots among four men. The death of the head of the successful ticket would create a more serious situation, and it is not difficult to see how the decision of the nation at the polls might be nullified. Perhaps most of the electors pledged to vote for the dead President-designate would cast their votes for the Vice President-designate, unless he were also eliminated by death or resignation. The natural thing would be for the electors to vote for men designated by their party committees. It is doubtful, however, whether it would be Constitutional for a party committee to undertake to influence the action of the electors after they were chosen. It would be a dangerous precedent. No great harm is done by having the candidates for electors pledge themselves in advance—apparently no provision of the Constitution is violated, at least technically. But for a national party committee to attempt to dictate to the electors after their choice by the voters would be a different matter. If both the President-elect and the Vice President-elect should die or resign *after their election by the electors* and before March 4 a still more serious situation would be created. The electors meet in their respective States in pursuance to law and the votes are then canvassed by Congress according to a prescribed method. After this function is discharged the electoral college, which never meets as a whole, ceases to exist legally, and there is no provision for reconvening it. No legal provision is made for altering the verdict of the electors after the returns have been canvassed by Congress. The so-called Presidential Succession Act of 1886 was intended to apply only to cases where vacancies occur as the result of removal, death, resignation or inability of both President and Vice President. In the case supposed no such vacancy occurs. Nevertheless some authorities hold that recourse might be had to the act of 1886 in such an emergency. No tenure of office is fixed for Cabinet officers, and though a President may automatically become a private citizen March 4, the members of his Cabinet remain in office until they resign or are superseded. Thus in the event both President-elect and Vice President-elect died, or no President and Vice President were chosen either by the electors or by Congress, the Secretary of State in the outgoing administration might act as President in accordance with the provisions of the Presidential Succession Act.

Who would become President if both the President and Vice President died in office?

Article II of the Constitution says in part that "the Congress may by law, provide for the case of removal, death, resignation or inability, both of the President and Vice President, declaring what officer shall then act as President, and such officer shall act accordingly, until the disability be removed, or a President shall be elected." In 1886 Congress passed what is popularly known as the Presidential Succession Act, thereby repealing part of an act approved in 1792. The later statute provides that in case of the removal, death, resignation or inability of both the President and Vice President, the Secretary of State "shall act as President until the disability of the President or Vice President is removed or a President shall be elected." There are, however, certain conditions. The Secretary of State cannot act as chief executive unless he is Constitutionally qualified for the Presidency in respect to age and citizenship. If there is no Secretary of State, or if the Secretary of State is not qualified, or if he has not been confirmed by the Senate, or if he is under impeachment, then the Secretary of the Treasury shall act as President, provided he is qualified to act. If there is no Secretary of the Treasury, or if for some reason he is not qualified for the Presidency, the Secretary of War shall act as President, and in like manner the succession passes to the Attorney-General, Postmaster-General, Secretary of the Navy and the Secretary of the Interior in the order that their Departments were created. The same qualifications are required for each Cabinet officer before he may act as President. Thus it will be seen that an alien-born Cabinet official, such as Carl Shurz or Albert Gallatin, could not act as President in the emergency contemplated. The Secretaries of Agriculture, Commerce, and Labor were not mentioned in the law for the simple reason that their Departments had not yet been created when the statute was enacted. The statute further provides that whenever the functions of the office of President shall temporarily devolve upon a Cabinet official, if Congress is not in session and will not meet in accordance with law within twenty days thereafter, it shall be the duty of the Cabinet officer acting as President to call an extraordinary session of Congress, giving twenty days notice of the meeting. It is not clear whether the Cabinet officer thus designated to act as President would serve out the unexpired term or would merely discharge the duties of chief executive until Congress could choose a President or provide for a special election. It is not probable that the framers of the Constitution ever contemplated that any person should actually become President or Vice President without being chosen either by electors or by Congress. The fact that the acting President is required to call Congress in extraordinary session if it is not already in session indicates that, in the contemplation of the statute, he would serve only until a President could be chosen. Nobody can say definitely just what the status of the acting President would be. It is presumed that the Cabinet officer acting as President would retain his Cabinet portfolio, because it is by virtue of his holding such office that he is entitled to act as chief executive. If that is correct he would not draw the salary of President, but merely his salary as head of his Department, unless Congress made special provision to the contrary. He would still probably be no more than Secretary of State acting as President and could not give up his Cabinet position without ceasing to be acting President. But the brevity and general character of the statute make this question purely speculative. Should the emergency arise under the present law the Congress then in existence would have to decide the point. The fact that the phrase *act as President* is used in the Constitution is not conclusive, as some writers have supposed. The same words are used in Amendment XII in reference to the Vice President. "If the House of Representatives," says that Amendment in part, "shall not choose a President whenever the right of choice shall devolve upon them, before the fourth day of March next following, then the *Vice President shall act as President,* as in the case of the death or other Constitutional disability of the President." When President Harrison died in 1841 many public men insisted that Vice President Tyler did not become actual President, but merely acting President, in view of the language employed in Amendment XII. Tyler, taking the position that he had been specifically elected to become President in such an emergency, settled the question by promptly assuming all the powers and duties of President. Undoubtedly that was the intent of the framers of the Constitution, because the Vice President is elected in the same manner as the President, and Article III, Section 1, Clause 6 says that, "In case of the removal of the President from office, or of his death, resignation, or inability to discharge the powers and duties of the said office, the same shall *devolve on* the Vice President." But the status of a Cabinet officer acting as President would be more difficult to determine. Who is to decide when a President is disabled, or when his disability ceases? James Madison, in the course of the debates on the adoption of the Constitution, pointed out that the officer acting as President could not become actual President, for if he could there might be two Presidents, one exercising the functions of the office and a disabled one, a line of reasoning which might be followed in the case of a Vice President acting during the disability of a President. On the other hand, Congress would be under no Constitutional obligation to choose a new President or to provide a special election. Should such an emergency ever arise circumstances would probably determine the course taken. If the time for a regular election were near, and if the person acting as President were popular, Congress might permit him to continue to act as President for the remainder of the unexpired term. Presumably the acting President would have the power to approve and veto acts of Congress, including acts dealing with his own status. Should the acting President declare himself actual President and appoint a Secretary of State in his place, he would have full control of the administration and could be ousted only by the cumbersome process of impeachment. Whether such a coup could succeed would depend entirely upon the acting President's influence in Congress.

What is the meaning of and/or in legal documents?

The phrase *and/or* frequently found in legal and commercial documents means that the idea expressed is both distributive and inclusive. "John Brown *and/or* Paul Jones" signifies the same as "John Brown and Paul Jones or either of them"; that is, these two men are responsible individually as well as collectively. The conjunctions are so written to avoid using them side by side—*and or*—which would be awkward as well as confusing.

Which is the mother of the chick, the hen that lays the egg or the one that hatches it?

This old question has the habit of bobbing up at frequent intervals. The fact that a hen incubates an egg which she did not lay gives her no blood relationship to the chick. The hen that lays the egg is the blood mother of the chick regardless of how it is incubated. A hen that incubates an egg laid by another hen, although she contributes materially to the hatching process, is merely a foster mother to the chick. Her relationship to the chick would be the same physiologically as that of a goose, duck, or even mechanical incubator that happened to incubate the egg. The term *mother* usually indicates actual parentage, and in that sense, which certainly is the most general, the hen that lays the egg is the chick's mother. But most people are not particularly interested in the actual maternity of their chicks, and therefore the hen that incubates the egg and cares for the chick is popularly regarded as the mother of the chick irrespective of the source of the egg.

Why does one's reflection in a spoon appear upside down?

When a person looks into the bowl of a brightly polished spoon he always sees his reflection upside down. This is because the concave part of the spoon acts like a lens. If the spoon were flat it would reflect like an ordinary mirror. To illustrate: in focusing a plate camera images are thrown on the ground glass upside down. When rays of light are passed through a lens they converge on each other until they all meet at a single point. At this point the rays cross and when they continue their journey toward the eye their positions are reversed. That is why stereopticon slides and motion picture films must be put in the projecting machine upside down in order to make the pictures appear right side up on the screen. Any hollow reflecting object, like the polished bowl of a spoon, acts in the same manner. The rays that strike in its exact center are reflected straight back, while those that fall on the curved sides are turned inward. Hence all the rays cross at a point and the reflection appears upside down. A flat reflecting surface, like a mirror, does not reflect the light rays toward a converging point and the rays do not meet. Accordingly the reflection is right side up.

Who invented radio?

It cannot be said that any one person invented or discovered radio. Modern wireless is the result of a long series of inventions and discoveries in several fields of physical science. Radio, as the term is now used, is the transmission and reception of sound by means of electromagnetic waves radiated through space. The theory of radio was understood long before anybody was able to devise a practical means for using it as the basis of a new method of telegraphic communication. Wireless was the next logical step after electrical communication by wire had been perfected. As early as 1864 a Scotch physicist, James Clerk Maxwell, foresaw electromagnetic waves from the standpoint of a mathematician. Later Heinrich Hertz (1857–1894), a German physicist, and several others investigated these waves experimentally. Hertz, after showing that electromagnetic waves correspond to light and heat waves, advanced the general theory upon which all radio devices are based. Numerous inventors in different parts of the world worked simultaneously to perfect apparatus for putting the theory into practice. Without detracting from the many others who contributed toward the commercial development of radio and who were not far behind him, probably Guglielmo Marconi is entitled to the honor of being called the father of radio. At any rate he was the first to build practical equipment for the transmission of radio signals. He began his experiments in 1895 at his father's country home near Bologna, Italy. Before the close of the year he had established successful wireless communication over a distance of more than a mile. The following year he went to England where he continued his experiments and where he obtained the first patent ever granted for wireless telegraphy by means of electric waves. In 1897 Marconi, now known as "the wireless wizard," established radio communication between a shore station and a ship eighteen miles away. The word *radio* is from Latin *radius,* meaning ray or radiation. When wireless telegraphy was first developed it was called *radio-telegraphy* to distinguish it from ordinary telegraphy by wire. Later the last part of the cumbersome name was dropped and it became simply *radio.* What may be termed as the second revolutionary step in the development of commercial radio came in 1906 when Lee De Forest, an American, patented the vacuum rectifier, commonly known as the audion.

What is the value of German notes issued before 1924?

German mark notes issued before 1924 are without value. Due to the inflation during and immediately after the World War the German paper mark decreased in value until it became practically worthless for purposes of exchange. Before the war the legal rate of exchange was about 4.20 marks for one dollar. In November, 1923, one dollar could be exchanged for about four trillion paper marks. Accordingly it became necessary for the·German government to reorganize its currency. By a law enacted in October, 1924, a new bank was established under the Dawes plan. Paper marks of the old Reichsbank were made exchangeable at the rate of one trillion old marks for one of the marks of the new Reichsbank until July 5, 1925, when the old paper money ceased to be exchangeable and when it ceased to be legal tender. In a similar manner the old paper-mark bonds of the German national government, as well as German state, municipal and private bonds, of whatever date, came under the operation of the revaluation and redemption acts passed by the Reichstag July 16, 1925. A time limit was fixed for the presentation of such bonds for redemption or revaluation. The general rate of revaluation for public loans was 2½% of the indebtedness, but the actual percentage offered to the holders of such bonds depended on various circumstances. In some cases the bonds were redeemed; in others they were revaluated and reissued. The gold mark, of course, continues to be the monetary unit of Germany and still has its pre-war exchange value of about 23.8 cents in American money.

Which is correct, *sitting* or *setting* hen?

Set is generally a transitive verb, while *sit* is intransitive. According to the usual grammatical construction of these verbs, a hen sits, not sets, on eggs. That is the construction approved by nearly all dictionaries. In language, however, good usage rather than logic should be the guide. The lexicographer must be behind the times by the very nature of his work, which is to record words and indicate their standing in the language. When William of Orange was king of England he had a road cut through Hyde Park to Kensington Palace. French was then the court language—even William spoke English poorly—and the new road was called *Route du Roi,* that is, King's Road. But the majority of Londoners could not pronounce the French name and they called the road Rotten Row, and this corrupted form, in spite of the court, became the accepted name of the fashionable bridle path and promenade. It is an excellent example of how usage determines the ultimate form of a name or word. Something similar is taking place in America in respect to *set* and *setting* when they refer to chickens. Probably the majority of people, including the educated classes, use *set* as an intransitive verb when applied to a hen, and as such the verb may be said to have acquired a separate meaning. All farmers know that a hen may sit without setting, and that a setting hen does not sit all the time. A setting hen is not merely a hen that sits; she is a hen which undergoes certain biological and temperamental changes, such as an increase in body temperature, preparatory to the act of incubating eggs. Both hens and roosters may and do perform the simple act of sitting, but it is customary for only hens to set. Therefore *sitting* hen not only sounds affected, but fails to discriminate between the simple act of sitting and the process of incubation known as setting. *Setting hen* has taken its place as a trade term and those who employ it are in good company even if the dictionaries still pronounce it a "dialectic corruption" which is not "approved in serious writing." There is an analogy for using *set* as an intransitive verb in such expressions as the sun sets, plaster sets, and fruit sets. Why should we say the sun sets instead of *sits?* We do not say it raises, but rises in the morning. At one time, no doubt, grammarians would have argued that the sun properly sits, but usage settled the question long ago.

How do huckleberries differ from blueberries?

Huckleberries and blueberries belong to entirely different plant families, although many people erroneously apply the name *huckleberry* indiscriminately to both berries. It is not uncommon for a person who asks for huckleberry pie in a public restaurant to receive blueberry pie, and vice versa, with no explanation offered as to why the substitution is made. A huckleberry contains ten large seeds or nutlets and is more acid than a blueberry, which contains numerous tiny seeds. On this subject the U. S. Bureau of Plant Industry says: "In the southern United States and in the Middle West blueberries are not ordinarily distinguished from huckleberries, but in New England the distinction is very clearly drawn. The name *huckleberry* is there restricted to plants of the genus *Gaylussacia,* the berries of which contain ten large seeds with bony coverings like minute peach pits, which crackle between the teeth. The name *blueberry* is applied in New England to the various species of the genus *Vaccinium,* in which the seeds, though numerous, are so small that they are barely noticeable when the berries are eaten. It is probable that the comparatively low estimation in which this fruit is held in the South is largely due to the lack of a distinctive popular name and the consequent confusion of the delicious small-seeded southern *Vacciniums* with the coarse large-seeded *Gaylussacias*." The blueberry, which is blue in color, is a softer, richer berry and usually grows on smaller bushes than the huckleberry, which is blue-black in color.

How does wood alcohol differ from denatured alcohol?

The common names for alcohol in its various forms are confusing. Pure alcohol—C_2H_5OH—is properly called ethyl alcohol or ethanol. Such alcohol acquired the name *grain* alcohol because formerly it was made largely by fermenting grain; at the present time it is made chiefly from blackstrap molasses. So-called wood alcohol—CH_3OH—is of a different chemical composition and is properly called methyl alcohol or methanol. It received its common name because it is obtained principally by distilling wood. Wood alcohol has some of the properties of ordinary ethyl alcohol, but unless purified it has a foul odor, and when drunk it may cause not only intoxication, but also blindness, vertigo, coma, or even death. To denature means to change the nature of. Denatured alcohol is ethyl or pure alcohol which has been treated to make it unfit for bodily consumption without impairing its industrial qualities. Sometimes wood alcohol or methanol is put in ethyl alcohol to denature it and for that reason any denatured alcohol is often incorrectly called wood alcohol.

Who invented rayon?

No one person deserves the entire credit for inventing rayon, which is now the recognized trade name in the United States for all synthetic fibers formerly known as artificial or imitation silk, regardless of the process of manufacture. The lustrous filaments of the fiber are made from various solutions of modified cellulose, such as wood pulp in a proper solvent, which is pressed or drawn through orifices and solidified by means of a precipitating medium. In 1664 Robert Hooke, an English experimental physicist, published a book in which he described a microscopic examination of natural silk and suggested the possibility of producing a similar thread artificially. René Réaumur, the French scientist, made a similar suggestion in 1734. Perhaps the first patent for the use of nitro-cellulose for the specific purpose of manufacturing imitation silk was that taken out in 1855 by Georges Audemars of Lausanne. The modern rayon industry, however, did not really begin until after 1884, when Count Hilaire Chardonnet of France patented his method of imitating the silkworm in the production of a filament of cellulose.

What State has the greatest coast line?

Florida has a longer coast line than any other State in the Union. California is second in the extent of its coast. It should be borne in mind that unless the scale of the maps employed and the method of measurement are given, a numerical statement of the length of the coast line of a body of land conveys no definite information, because the results will vary so widely that there will be no common basis of comparison. The smaller the unit of measurement the greater will be the number of indentations included. No matter what method is adopted the scale of the maps will be an important factor. According to the method employed by the U. S. Coast and Geodetic Survey, the general coast line of Florida, exclusive of islands, is 1,197 statute miles—399 on the Atlantic and 798 on the Gulf of Mexico—while that of California is 913 miles. Lake shore line is not regarded as coast line by the Coast and Geodetic Survey. If it were Michigan would have the second longest coast line. The coast of Maine is so indented that if a small unit of measurement were employed that State would have a coast line of about 3,000 miles.

Who wrote the Negro spirituals?

The spirituals are sacred folk songs created by Negroes in America. Their individual authorship is not known. Many of the spirituals apparently grew up in Negro communities and are the expression of group rather than individual experiences. The songs have several distinctive features. They combine Christian sentiments with rhythm and music possessing African characteristics. Most of them are based on Biblical stories, which are frequently told dramatically and vividly. We have no means of determining when the Negroes began to create these beautiful folk songs. Some pieces undoubtedly date back nearly two centuries. The Negro has always had a tendency to put his experiences into song and it is probable that Negro bards began to create the spirituals soon after their subjection to slavery and their conversion to Christianity. These songs are remarkable in that, though born in slavery, they contain not a single note of bitterness. No effort was made to record the spirituals until after the Civil War and they were not fully appreciated by music critics until after they were introduced to the public in 1871 by the Fisk Jubilee Singers. Professor N. G. Balanta, a native of West Africa, spent many years in an endeavor to trace the source and history of the Negro spirituals. "Christianity," he wrote in 1930, "was the force that breathed life into the innate musical talent of the African in his new environment. Far from his native land, despised by those among whom he lived, knowing the hard taskmaster, feeling the lash, the Negro seized Christianity, the religion of compensations in the life to come for the ills suffered in the present existence. The result was a body of songs voicing all the cardinal virtues of Christianity—patience, forbearance, love, faith and hope—through a modified form of primitive African music."

How many Americans were killed in the Revolution?

No official compilation of the number of American soldiers killed during the Revolutionary War has been made. Many of the original records have been lost and some of those preserved are imperfect. The problem is made more difficult by the fact that the militia of the various Colonies frequently fought side by side with the Continental troops without officially becoming a part of the regular force. Statistics based on the incomplete records in the State and War Departments at Washington show that at least 4,044 American soldiers were killed in action during the Revolution. The Adjutant General of the Army states that the actual number of battle deaths probably exceeded this figure considerably. According to the same records, 6,004 men were wounded, 6,642 were captured by the enemy, and 2,124 were reported missing in action and unaccounted for. It is estimated that a total of 230,000 Continentals and 164,000 militiamen enlisted in the American armies in the course of the Revolutionary War. Of course the number of men in service at any one time was only a small fraction of these figures. No statistics are available relative to the number of British killed. The original returns in the British record office show that the British troops in America attained their greatest numerical strength about December 1, 1780. On that date there were 42,267 British soldiers in the United Colonies, Canada, Florida and the Bahama Islands. It is probable that more than 10,000 British troops were killed in action or died of wounds received in action during the American Revolution.

Which is colder, the North or the South Pole?

Most people in our latitudes are so accustomed to associating cold with the north and warmth with the south that it is hard for them to realize that similar climatic conditions prevail at both of the poles of the earth. There is reason for supposing, from the fragmentary data available, that both the average and the extreme temperatures reached at the South Pole are lower than those reached at the North Pole. Other things being equal, temperature falls with altitude, and the South Pole is on an elevated plateau while the North Pole is at sea level in the Arctic Ocean. Peary reported temperatures ranging from 11° to 30° below zero Fahrenheit at the North Pole. Amundsen reported 18° below zero at the South Pole, and Admiral Byrd's thermometer registered about 15° below when he flew over that point. All these temperatures were taken in the summer time. Temperatures of 73° and 77° below zero have been recorded on the Antarctic ice barrier during the winter, but no winter figures are available for the high plateau around the South Pole. In May, 1903, a temperature of 67° below zero was registered on board the *Discovery* in the Antarctic, and in August, 1911, Amundsen reported 74.2° in the same region. The lowest temperature experienced in the Arctic by Nares was 74° below zero, while De Long encountered 72° and General Greely 62° below zero. It is a common mistake to suppose that it gets colder at the North Pole than at any other spot in the world. The temperature drops lower in parts of Siberia, Tierra del Fuego and other regions than it does at either pole. On February 5 and 7, 1892, 90.4° below zero was recorded at Verkhoyansk, Siberia, which is at 67° 34′ north latitude and 134° 20′ east longitude. Although there is some doubt as to whether the instruments were properly exposed, the U. S. Weather

Bureau says that figure is generally accepted as the lowest temperature ever recorded under natural conditions. Undoubtedly the temperature frequently drops to more than 80° below zero in parts of Siberia. The lowest known average monthly temperature is also that of Verkhoyansk—56° below zero for January. The next lowest monthly average is that of Fort Conger, Grinnell Land—40° for February. However, the year's average for Fort Conger—4° below zero—is much lower than that of Verkhoyansk. The lowest temperature ever authentically recorded in the United States proper was 65° below zero, which occurred at Ft. Keough, near Miles City, Montana, in January, 1888. It is not probable that it ever gets much colder than that at the North Pole, although, of course, the average temperature at the pole is much lower than at any place in the United States.

How did Jimson weed get its name?

Jimson in this connection is a corruption of *Jamestown.* Jamestown weed, known botanically as *Datura stramonium,* belongs to the nightshade family. It received its name from the fact that it was found growing in abundance around Jamestown in Virginia. Early in the spring the weed sprang up in the rich ground under the very shadows of the buildings that the colonists had erected on the tiny island in the river. The narcotic properties of this plant were known to the Algonquin Indians as well as to the Mexicans, both of whom used it as a ceremonial intoxicant. In his *History and Present State of Virginia,* published in 1705, Robert Beverly tells an interesting story of the effect that eating Jamestown weed had on some of the British soldiers sent over to subdue Bacon's rebellion in 1676. "The James-Town Weed . . . is supposed to be one of the greatest Coolers in the World," wrote Beverly. "This being an early Plant, was gather'd very young for a boil'd salad, by some of the Soldiers sent thither, to pacifie the troubles of Bacon; and some of them eat plentifully of it, the Effect of which was a very pleasant Comedy; for they turn'd natural Fools upon it for several Days: One would blow up a Feather in the Air; another wou'd dart Straws at it with much Fury; and another stark naked was sitting up in a Corner, like a Monkey, grinning and making Mows at them; a Fourth would fondly kiss, and paw his Companions, and snear in their Faces, with

a Countenance more antick, than any in a *Dutch Droll*. In this fran-
tick Condition they were confined, lest they should in their Folly destroy themselves; though it was observed, that all their Actions were
full of Innocence and good Nature. Indeed, they were not very
cleanly; for they would have wallow'd in their own Excrements, if
they had not been prevented. A Thousand such simple Tricks they
play'd, and after Eleven Days, return'd themselves again, not re-
membring anything that had pass'd." In his *Notes on Virginia*
Thomas Jefferson referred to the "singular quality" of the Jamestown weed. "The late Dr. Bond informed me," wrote the Sage of
Monticello, "that he had under his care a patient, a young girl, who
had put the seeds of this plant into her eye, which dilated the pupil
to such a degree, that she could see in the dark, but in the light was
almost blind."

Who receives the resignation of a member of Congress?

A member of the Senate or of the House of Representatives
may resign by transmitting a letter of resignation either directly to
the executive of his State or to the presiding officer of the house of
Congress of which he is a member. In the House the usual practice
is to transmit the letter of resignation directly to the Governor, at
the same time notifying the Speaker of the House of the action.
When a member resigns directly to the Senate or to the House of
Representatives the body to which the resigning member belongs
orders its presiding officer to inform the Governor of the State of
the resignation.

Was Cleopatra a blonde or a brunette?

There is just as much reason for supposing that Cleopatra was
a blonde as there is for supposing that she was a brunette. According to the popular conception, she was a decided brunette, with
dark skin, dark eyes and dark hair, and she is frequently referred
to as "the dark queen of Egypt." But historical sources supply us
with no evidence as to her actual complexion. It should be borne in
mind that Cleopatra was Greek by ancestry, and Egyptian only by
birth. So far as known she did not have a single drop of Egyptian
blood in her veins. The Ptolemies, it is supposed, remained pure
Macedonian Greeks, and their capital, Alexandria, was the center

of Greek rather than Egyptian culture. They even dressed as Greeks except on certain ceremonial occasions. Therefore Cleopatra must be regarded as a Macedonian type, and the dark skin and black hair of the native Egyptian afford no clue as to her complexion. Many Greeks were dark-complexioned, but among the Macedonians white skin, fair hair and blue eyes were not uncommon, and one of Cleopatra's ancestors, Ptolemy Philadelphus, is described by Theocritus as having light hair and a fair complexion. When the American actress Jane Cowl played the rôle of Cleopatra in Shakespeare's tragedy she portrayed the Egyptian queen with red hair. Shakespeare himself alluded to Cleopatra as *tawny*.

Which is correct, *"spic* and span" or *"spick* and span"?

"Spick and span" is the correct spelling of this common phrase. It is frequently but erroneously written *"spic* and span," due apparently to a mistaken notion of its derivation. The original phrase was simply "span new," *span* being an old word for a chip or splinter of wood. "Span new" meant bright and new as a chip just cut. In Icelandic it is *spannyr,* from *spann,* chip, and *nyr,* new. "Spick and span new" was merely an emphatic extension of the earlier phrase, *spick* being an old provincial or colloquial form of *spike,* a large nail. When a thing was particularly fresh in appearance it was said to be spick and span new, that is, bright and new as a new spike and a freshly cut splinter. Those who write the phrase *"spic* and span" do so on the assumption that the obsolete word for *spike* was spelled *spic.* There is no evidence that such was the case and the examples given in the Oxford dictionary indicate that it was always spelled *spick.* There was, however, an old word *spic,* meaning bacon or fat meat.

What became of the Ark of the Covenant?

It is not known for certain what became of the Ark of the Covenant after the Babylonians captured and destroyed Jerusalem about 600 B. C. There are several traditions as to its final disposition. The Ark was an oblong chest, made of acacia wood overlaid with gold, and in it were placed the tables of the law, a gold pot of manna and the rod of Aaron. It was taken from Jerusalem by David when he made that city his capital and later it was placed in the Holy of Holies of Solomon's temple. The books comprising the Protestant Bible are silent on the fate of the Ark, but a tradition on the subject is recorded in *II Maccabees,* one of the sacred books of the Catholic Bible. The passage is quoted from a writing of Jeremiah and is as follows: "The prophet [Jeremiah], being warned by God, commanded that the tabernacle and the Ark should accompany him, till he came forth to the mountain where Moses went up and saw the inheritance of God. And when Jeremiah came thither he found a hollow cave and he carried in thither the tabernacle and the Ark and the altar of incense, and so stopped the door. Then some of them that followed him, came up to mark the place; but they could not find it. And when Jeremiah perceived it, he blamed them, saying: the place shall be unknown, till God gather together the congregation of the people and receive them to mercy." This story dates back at least two centuries B. C. It was widely believed among the rabbis of old that the Ark would be found when the Messiah appeared. In 1927 Dr. A. F. Futterer, a Jewish-American, obtained permission from the Palestine government to search for the lost Ark on a mountain identified by him as Mt. Nebo, from which Moses surveyed the Promised Land and where Jeremiah is supposed to have concealed the sacred chest in a cave. In the *Apocalypse of Esdras,* which is regarded as apocryphal by both Catholics and Protestants, it is related that the Ark of the Covenant was carried away by the Babylonians. This seems probable, because the troops of Nebuchadrezzar stripped the temple of its brass, silver and gold. The Jewish editors of the *Talmud* state that the sacred chest was hidden by King Josiah in a secret place which had been prepared by Solomon himself in case the temple should be captured and destroyed.

Is Great Britain a part of Europe?

Great Britain, although an island, is so close to the continent of Europe that it is generally regarded as being a part of it. Scientists are of the opinion that the British Isles, which are on what is known as the continental shelf, were formerly joined to the mainland and were not separated from it until comparatively recent times, geologically speaking. The rest of the world regards Great Britain as a European nation, although the British people themselves refer to continental Europe as *the continent* to distinguish it from the British Isles. Europe itself, strictly speaking, is not a continent, but merely part of the continent of Eurasia.

Did Lincoln originate, "Government of the people, by the people, for the people"?

Neither the thought nor the phraseology was original with Lincoln. He borrowed both from Theodore Parker, a noted minister and abolitionist, who on several occasions employed nearly the same words which Lincoln later used in the last sentence of the Gettysburg address. Parker used the following expression on May 29, 1850, in a speech on *The American Idea* before the New England Anti-Slavery Convention in Boston: "A democracy,—that is a *government of all the people, by all the people, for all the people.*" On Sunday, September 22, of the same year he repeated the identical expression in a sermon. William Herndon, Lincoln's law partner at Springfield, was in the habit of procuring copies of speeches made by the leading anti-slavery men of the time. In 1858 Herndon returned from a trip to New York and Boston. "I brought with me additional sermons and lectures by Theodore Parker, who was warm in his commendation of Lincoln," wrote Herndon in his life of Lincoln. "One of these was a lecture on *The Effect of Slavery on the American People,* which was delivered in the Music Hall in Boston, and which I gave to Lincoln, who read and returned it. He liked especially the following expression, which he marked with a pencil, and which he in substance afterwards used in his Gettysburg address: *Democracy is direct self-government, over all the people, for all the people, by all the people.*" More than two years before the Gettysburg address was delivered—July 4, 1861—President Lincoln himself said in a message to Congress: "It presents to the whole family of man the question whether a constitutional republic or democracy—*a government of the people by the same people*—can, or cannot, maintain its territorial integrity against its own domestic foes." The concluding sentence of the Gettysburg address is often misquoted. There is no *and* before the preposition *for* in the famous expression, which reads simply, "Government of the people, by the people, for the people." It should not be supposed, however, that Parker was the author of the idea merely because he several times expressed the same thought in nearly the same language. The thought, variously expressed, was already old. Daniel Webster said January 26, 1830: "The people's government, made for the people, made by the people, and answerable to the people." John Marshall used the expression, "Government over all, by all and for the sake of all," and William Wirt and others had expressed the idea in similar words. In 1795 Thomas Cooper published in London *Some Information Respecting Americans,* in which he said that "the government is a government of the people, and for the people." There is a tradition that in the fourteenth century John Wyclif wrote: "This Bible is for the government of the people, by the people, and for the people," and a similar statement is attributed to John Hus. As a matter of fact, the idea was expressed by Cleon of Athens, who lived about 400 B. C. The Duke of Wellington used the same scheme of expression as Lincoln when he called the government of France a "government of politicians, by politicians, for politicians." Lincoln improved and refined the expression, and by uttering it on a historic occasion and in a proper phrase setting he gave it to the world in a finished form. It belongs to him because it bears the stamp of his genius. As Lowell so aptly said:

> Though old the thought and oft expressed,
> 'Tis his at last who says it best.

What is goldbeaters' skin?

Goldbeaters' skin is a fine membrane made of the outer coat of the blind gut in cattle and is used by goldbeaters to separate the leaves of metal during the last and most difficult stages of hammering out goldleaf. The intestine, after being put through several processes, is cut into pieces about five inches square. Its tenacity and powers of resistance are so great that it will resist the continuous pounding of a heavy hammer for several months. Goldbeaters still do their work by hand as they did in ancient times. A large number of leaves are beaten at the same time and hammers ranging in weight from seven to twenty pounds are used. Gold is the most malleable of all metals and the minimum thickness to which it can be beaten with patience and skill is not known for certain.

A single grain of gold has been beaten into a leaf having an area of seventy-five square inches and a thickness of less than 1/368,000 of an inch. Commercial goldleaf ranges from 1/200,000 to 1/250,000 of an inch in thickness.

Who owns the Ohio River?

Rivers are the property of the States in which they are located. The limited jurisdiction of the Federal Government over navigable streams is merely incidental to its Constitutional power to regulate and improve navigation for interstate and foreign commerce. When a river forms the boundary between two States the title of each State is presumed to extend to the middle of the main channel, provided there is no legal arrangement to the contrary. Sometimes two States agree, for police purposes, to exercise concurrent jurisdiction over a river which forms the boundary between them. The Ohio, Chattahoochee and Potomac rivers are notable exceptions to the general rule. Kentucky and West Virginia have absolute jurisdiction over the entire Ohio River along their shores as far as the low-water mark on the Ohio, Indiana and Illinois banks. If a person commits a crime on that river near the Illinois, Indiana or Ohio shore he is amenable to the laws of Kentucky or West Virginia, and the game and fishing laws of the latter States are enforced to the northern bank of the stream. Thus it is possible for a person to violate a Kentucky law by fishing on the Ohio side of the river. This boundary line has been judicially recognized many times by the Supreme Court of the United States and the supreme courts of the various States involved. The Northwest Territory, from which Illinois, Indiana and Ohio were carved, was ceded to the Federal Government in 1784 by the Commonwealth of Virginia. The resolution of cession retained title and jurisdiction over the Ohio River to the low-water mark on the northern bank, and these rights were transmitted to Kentucky and West Virginia when they were later formed from Virginian territory. Likewise the western boundary of Georgia extends to the high-water mark on the Alabama side of the Chattahoochee River. A similar but more complicated situation exists in regard to the Potomac between Maryland on the one hand and Virginia and West Virginia on the other. When King Charles I granted Maryland to Cecilius Calvert in 1632 "the farther bank" of the Potomac was fixed as the western boundary of the province. This was interpreted as meaning the high water mark on the western side of the river, but in 1877 arbitrators fixed the low-water mark as the boundary, giving as their reason Virginia's long occupation of the land between that line and the high-water mark. Although Maryland and Virginia exercise concurrent jurisdiction over the Potomac on tidewater, the former State exercises absolute jurisdiction over the entire river above tidewater except where the District of Columbia adjoins the stream. The territory composing the District was ceded to the Federal Government by Maryland and accordingly the boundary of the District on the Potomac is the high-water mark on the Virginia shore. The decision of the arbitrators of 1877 did not shift this portion of the boundary from the high to the low-water mark. District of Columbia courts have held that persons fishing below the high-water mark on the Virginia side of the Potomac opposite Washington are amenable to the fishing laws of the District of Columbia and not those of Virginia.

Who said he would rather live in Hell than Texas?

"If I owned Texas and Hell I would rent out Texas and live in Hell," is attributed to General Philip H. Sheridan. One would naturally suppose that the remark was made after Sheridan was famous as a military commander. Such, apparently, was not the case. Soon after his graduation from West Point in 1853 Sheridan, then a second lieutenant, was sent to Fort Duncan, a frontier post on the Rio Grande near Eagle Pass. The weight of evidence indicates that the statement in question was made in 1855 while Sheridan was either on a visit to or on duty at Fort Clark, in what is now Kinney County, Texas. Somebody at the officers' mess asked Sheridan how he liked Texas, and the now celebrated saying was the reply. In those days Texas, as well as the Southwest generally, was sparsely populated and was the butt of much crude humor. We have it on the authority of Judge Richard B. Levy, of Texarkana, that Albert Sidney Johnston told General Webster Flanagan that he heard about the incident in 1856 while in Texas as a colonel of infantry. Judge Levy himself was stationed at Fort Clark during the Spanish-American War and he states that he frequently heard that the famous remark was made by Sheridan while at that army post in 1855. The saying, of course, was not generally quoted until after the Civil War. It should be mentioned here, however, that there is an oft-repeated story that General Sheridan gave utterance to the remark while on an inspection tour when he was commander of the Southwestern military department.

How did the custom of half-masting the flag originate?

Half-masting the national flag in token of mourning originated at sea, as the use of the term *mast* instead of *staff* indicates. "Hoise your Sailes half mast high," said Captain Smith in his *Seaman's Grammar,* published in 1627. The custom dates back several centuries and probably grew out of the earlier custom of lowering the flag on vessels at sea as a sign of submission to a foe. The flag is also lowered to half-mast as a signal of distress, a practice followed by the Spanish as early as the seventeenth century. According to flag etiquette, when a national flag is placed at half-mast as a tribute of respect to the dead it is first raised to the top, of the staff or flag-pole and then slowly lowered to a position at or near the middle of the staff.

What is the Maelstrom?

Maelstrom, pronounced *mail-strom* with the accent on the first syllable, is the name of a famous whirlpool between islands of the Lofoden group lying in the Arctic Ocean off the northwest coast of Norway. There are many legends concerning the dangers of this whirlpool. Centuries ago navigators believed that the Maelstrom would engulf and destroy any vessel that came within its reach. Anthony Jenkinson, the English sea captain and traveler, wrote of it in 1560 as follows: "There is between the said Rost Islands, and Lofoote, a whirle poole, called Malestrand [Maelstrom], which . . . maketh such a terrible noise, that it shaketh the rings in the doores of the inhabitants houses of the said Islands, ten miles of." The Maelstrom, however, is no longer regarded as very dangerous. Only in winter or when the wind blows from the northwest is there any danger to ships, and then only to small vessels. Ordinarily it can be navigated with safety at both high and low tide. The whirlpool is produced by the union of several currents from the great West Fiord between the Lofoden Islands and the mainland. *Maelstrom* is used figuratively as a common noun to describe other whirlpools or any overpowering movement or wide-reaching influence. The name is believed to be derived from Dutch *malen,* to grind, and *stroom,* stream; thus it literally means current or stream that grinds.

Who was David's mother?

"Who was David's mother?" is often quoted as an unanswerable question, like "How old was Ann?" and "Who hit Billy Patterson?" King David, who reigned over Israel about 1000 b. c., was the son of Jesse of Bethlehem and had several brothers and sisters. The name of his mother is nowhere recorded in the Bible. It is supposed that David alludes to his mother in *Psalms 86: 16:* "O turn unto me, and have mercy upon me; give thy strength unto thy servant, and save the son of thine handmaid." Also in *Psalms 116: 16:* "O Lord, truly I am thy servant; I am thy servant, and the son of thy handmaid: thou hast loosed my bonds."

How did the wedding ring originate?

Many writers state that the wedding ring is a survival of savage servitude, being a symbol of the bondage pledged to their husbands by primitive women. But it seems more probable that the wedding ring, which in its form is a symbol of eternity, had a later and nobler origin and grew out of the use of signet rings, which are rings bearing seals. In time it became customary for a man to authorize important transactions by merely stamping the necessary papers with his seal instead of giving the ring to the agent. "And Pharaoh took off his ring from his hand," says *Genesis 41: 42,* "and put it upon Joseph's hand." In *Esther 3: 10* we read that Ahasuerus took his ring from his hand and gave it to Haman, an act which gave the latter full authority to carry out his wicked design of destroying the Hebrews within the empire. Thus entrusting another with one's signet ring was a token of complete confidence in him. A woman could issue commands in her lord's name after she received his ring. Possession of his ring made an Egyptian woman in every respect her husband's representative. If this theory is correct, the wedding ring was not originally a badge of slavery, but the symbol of common authority over the household. The giving of an engagement ring was a later elaboration and at first was intended merely as a pledge that authority over the household would be given in due time.

What is the gold standard?

The gold standard is a monetary system in which gold alone is used to measure value. When a country has its prices adjusted to a gold standard it is said to be on a gold basis. The type of gold standard varies somewhat in different countries. A complete gold standard is characterized by no restrictions on gold imports and exports, full redemption in gold of notes in any amount, and unlimited obligation on the part of the government to purchase gold at a fixed price. The complete gold standard was adopted in the United States in 1900, although the country had been practically on a gold basis since 1873. Bimetallism is the name given to the monetary system in which gold and silver stand precisely on the same footing in regard to mintage and legal tender. This system prevailed in the United States until the outbreak of the Civil War. The price of gold is now fixed by the government at $20.671835 a troy ounce, and the gold dollar, weighing 25.8 grains 900 fine, is the monetary unit.

Do animals think?

Whether animals think and reason has long been a moot question. Most naturalists now are of the opinion that the so-called lower animals have a limited capacity to think and reason and that their minds differ from those of human beings merely in degree and not in kind. It is the high development of man's brain that separates it from that of the ape, the horse, and the dog. Many animals exercise considerable intelligence in certain matters, especially in obtaining food and in escaping from danger. Instinct, which acts blindly and which is probably the result of inherited experiences through many generations, plays a much larger part in animals than it does in human beings, and reasoning capacity varies in different animals and different species of animals just as it does in different individuals and different races of mankind. That the dog possesses an imagination and has the ability to picture absent objects mentally is indicated by his capacity to dream and his grief over the loss of a master. When the baboon throws a missile at an intruder and when the elephant breaks off a twig and uses it for a flybrush they are exercising an intelligence which is undoubtedly capable of simple deductions. Recent experiments indicate that crows in the wild state have the ability to count to three or four. Nevertheless it is very difficult to demonstrate that animals reason from an observed cause to its probable effect.

What is the philosopher's stone?

A person looking for a short cut to riches is said to be searching for the philosopher's stone. The ancient alchemists believed that somewhere in nature there existed a substance which would convert ordinary metals into gold. This imaginary substance was called the philosopher's stone because it was supposed to have a philosophic basis and was linked with the theories of matter advanced by the philosophers. The idea of transmuting base metals into noble ones seems to have originated among the Greeks at Alexandria in the early centuries of the Christian era. In medieval times the philosopher's stone was reputed not only to have the property of transmuting the baser metals into gold but also the power of curing most of the ills that the body is heir to.

Is Newfoundland a part of Canada?

Newfoundland is neither geographically nor politically a part of the Dominion of Canada. It is a self-governing dominion with its own governor-general, premier and parliament, and is a full-fledged member of the sisterhood of British commonwealths, having a status in the empire similar to that of the Dominion of Canada itself. When the Dominion of Canada was created in 1867 provision was made for the admission of Newfoundland into the federation, but that commonwealth has never availed itself of the privilege, being satisfied with its separate dominion status. Newfoundland is often called "the senior British colony" because it antedates in discovery, though not in continuous settlement, all the other overseas dominions of Great Britain. John Cabot discovered the island in 1497, at least a year before Columbus saw the mainland of South America, and the following entry in the accounts of the privy-purse expenditures is supposed to refer to the discovery: "1497, Aug. 10. To hym that found the New Isle, £10." The name, of course, alludes to the fact that the island had just been found. Newfoundland's first governor-general was appointed in 1728 when Canada was still in the possession of France. It is a common mistake to suppose that Newfoundland is a part of the Dominion of Canada, and Newfoundland business men are continually being referred by American firms to their Canadian distributors.

What is free verse?

Free verse is a literal translation of the French *vers libre* and is the name given to a form of poetry written without meter or rime and usually without regular stanzas. Sir Robert Bridges, poet laureate of England from 1913 to 1930, defined free verse as "cadenced prose arranged in sections resembling stanzas or verses." It is based on the assumption that true poetry depends on the substance rather than the form, and the composer of free verse deliberately discards customary meter and rime, attempting to isolate his essential thought and convey it to the reader unhampered by form. Although free verse did not become common in any country until after the World War, Matthew Arnold wrote such poetry during the Victorian period, and *The Song of Solomon,* whether intentionally or accidentally, meets the essential requirements of free verse. The writer of free verse is an imagist; he claims absolute liberty in choosing his subject matter and attempts to express his ideas and emotions through a unified series of precise images.

How did *honeymoon* originate?

Many writers suppose that *honeymoon* originally referred to the moon or month after marriage when the ancient Teutons celebrated by drinking a liquor made of honey. In his *Etymological Compendium,* published in 1828, William Pulleyn says: "It was the custom of the higher order of the Teutones, an ancient people who inhabited the northern parts of Germany, to drink mead, or metheglin, a beverage made with honey, for thirty days after every wedding. From this custom, comes the expression, *to spend the honey moon.*" Attila the Hun died suddenly in 453 during the night following a banquet celebrating his marriage to a damsel named Ildico, and since the king was notorious for his intemperance it is supposed that his death was due to over-indulgence in honey mead at his wedding feast. Dr. Samuel Johnson apparently had some such theory in mind when he defined *honeymoon* as "the first month after marriage, when there is nothing but tenderness and pleasure." However, the early examples given by the Oxford dictionary indicate that the term originally had no reference to the period of a moon or month, but rather compared the mutual love of newly married people to the changeable character of the moon, which is no sooner full than it begins to wane. Richard Huloet, in 1552, said in his dictionary: "Honey moon, a term proverbially applied to such as be new married, which will not fall out at the first, but the one loveth the other at the beginning exceedingly, the likelihood of their exceeding love appearing to assuage, the which time the vulgar people call the honey moon." The custom of the honeymoon probably symbolizes the primitive practice of stealing the bride and concealing her from her people. Nowadays the honeymoon is merely a vacation which newly married couples take before settling down.

Who decides when and where a world's fair shall be held?

World's fair is merely a convenient term to denote any large international industrial exhibition. The name was suggested by the local fairs held at regular intervals to stimulate industry by bringing together the buyers and the sellers of a district. Although similar expositions had been previously held on a small scale, the term *world's fair* was first applied—popularly but not officially—to the London industrial exposition held in 1851 in the Crystal Palace, a magnificent structure of iron and glass built especially for the purpose. A royal commission managed the exhibition and the British government guaranteed the expenses in case of financial failure. In 1853 a similar universal industrial exhibition was held in New York in a structure of iron and glass also called the Crystal Palace. Two years later France held its first *Exposition Universelle* in the Champs Elysées. Since then products and articles from the majority of civilized countries have been displayed at numerous similar expositions. A world's fair or exposition is promoted by a nation, state or city, and other nations, states and cities are invited to take part in it. A national, state or city commission is usually appointed officially to supervise the exposition, and local citizens generally subscribe to a fund guaranteeing any expenses which may not be covered by admission fees and charges for concessions and the like. Needless to say there is no particular method by which it is determined when and where such an exposition shall be held. It depends on the desire of those promoting it. Frequently the anniversary of an important historical event is selected. The most famous and successful world's fair held in America was the World's Columbian Exposition at Chicago in 1893, although the exposition held at St. Louis in 1904 to celebrate the Louisiana Purchase was the first to be officially styled a world's fair.

What is meant by *feet of clay*?

Feet of clay comes from Biblical usage. Figuratively it is applied to the more earthly and baser side of human nature. "He has learned that his idol has feet of clay" is said of a person who is disappointed or disillusioned. *Daniel 2: 32, 33* and *34* says: "This image's head was of fine gold, his breast and his arms of silver, his belly and his thighs of brass, his legs of iron, his feet part of iron and part of clay. Thou sawest till that a stone was cut out without hands, which smote the image upon his feet that were of iron and clay, and brake them to pieces." In the holy city of Benares, India, there is a god whose feet of clay are replaced each year by the priests after being washed away by the Ganges.

How long is a light year?

A light year is the distance traversed by light in one year, which is more than 63,000 times the distance between the earth and the sun. It is a linear unit used especially in measuring the vast distances between fixed stars and our planet. All astronomers, however, do not use the same year as a basis for such computations, although the Julian year is generally taken as the basis of the light year, since it is somewhat simpler than the others, being exactly 365 days and six hours in length. "Round numbers only," says the U. S. Naval Observatory, "are used in dealing with the light year. The Julian year of 365.25 days is in common use among astronomers and may be very safely employed in computing stellar distances." The U. S. Bureau of Standards says: "The term *light year* is used in astronomy to designate an approximate order of distance, and not as an exact unit of length. The year used in reckoning is the tropical or calendar year, and were the velocity of light accurately known, it would be possible to calculate the light year exactly in miles, kilometers, or other familiar units of length." On November 13, 1928, Edwin B. Frost, director of the Yerkes Observatory, wrote to the author on this subject as follows: "The light year is a perfectly definite unit of distance. It may be determined by multiplying the number of seconds in a year by the velocity of light, for which the latest value (by Prof. Albert A. Michelson of the University of Chicago) is 186,227 miles per second. This equals 5,876,746,000,-000. Speaking roughly, the light year is therefore a little less than six million million miles."

Why are the dead buried with heads pointing west?

In all early Christian cemeteries in Great Britain and northern Europe the graves were carefully orientated, the body being almost invariably laid with the feet pointing toward the east. This custom prevailed until a century or two ago and is still widely observed. Even in the family burying grounds on the Colonial estates of Maryland and Virginia the bodies usually lie with the head pointing west. The custom arose from medieval legends and pagan practices. Christ, according to legend, was interred in the sepulchre with his head to the west. Many suppose that *Matthew 24: 27* means that when Jesus comes in judgment he will appear in the east. That verse reads: "For as the lightning cometh out of the east, and shineth even unto the west; so shall also the coming of the Son of man be." Bodies, therefore, were buried with the feet toward the east, so that when they arise on the morning of resurrection they will face the east and can hurry in that direction to meet the Lord. Because of this custom, the east wind is known in Wales as "the wind of the dead man's feet." Orientation of the dead, however, is older than Christianity. The pagan Franks placed their dead in the tombs with the feet to the east; and Walter Johnson, in *Byways in British Archæology,* describes a cemetery at Charvaise dating back to the earliest iron age, in which all but two or three of the more than seventy graves were so orientated that the head lay at the west end. In fact there was a surprising uniformity among primitive peoples who buried their dead lying east and west, although sometimes the head pointed west and sometimes east. Such orientation is believed to be a relic of the rites of the ancient sun worshippers and their solar symbolism. The head of the corpse is laid pointing to the east or to the west, depending on whether the dead are thought of in relation to the sunrise, the home of the sun god, or in relation to the sunset, the destination of departed souls. According to Francis LaFlesche, an American ethnologist, some of the Osage Indians of the present time bury their dead with the head to the west so that when they rise they will face the rising sun. Likewise, some primitive tribes, such as the Samoans, Fijians, Guarayos and some American Indians, inter their dead with the feet and face toward the region in which their future will be spent. Dr. J. Walter Fewkes, of the Bureau of American Ethnology, found the graves similarly orientated in the ancient cemeteries excavated at Elden Pueblo near Flagstaff, Arizona. "A key to the religious beliefs of the builders of this pueblo," he wrote in 1928, "is found in the orientation of the walls—north to south, and east to west. This is almost universal in ancient rectangular pueblos where sun worship was the prevailing cultus. Also the prevailing habit of burying the dead with the head to the east confirms this evidence." Moslems of the present day carefully orientate their dead.

How is *Eyre* pronounced in *Jane Eyre?*

Eyre in *Jane Eyre,* Charlotte Brontë's famous novel, is correctly pronounced as if spelled *air*. It is frequently mispronounced *ire*. The proper pronounciation of the heroine's surname is indicated in Chapter XI of the book in the following dialogue between Jane Eyre and her pupil, little Adèle Varens:

> "And Mademoiselle—what is your name?"
> "Eyre—Jane Eyre."
> "*Aire?* Bah! I cannot say it."

The name *Eyre* occurs in the Hundred Rolls (*Rotuli Hundredorum*) of 1274, and is the Middle English form of Old French *Heir,* which was also pronounced *air*. Edward John Eyre (1815-

1901), the English explorer and colonial governor, pronounced his name *air,* and Lake Eyre in South Australia, which was named after him, is pronounced in the same way. The old word *eyre,* meaning a circuit or a court of circuit judges, is also correctly pronounced *air.*

Can bees sting a person while he holds his breath?

Many people believe that bees, wasps and other stinging insects cannot sting a person while he holds his breath, clenches his fists tightly or grasps one wrist firmly with the opposite hand. According to the popular notion, the insect is physically unable to penetrate the human skin under such circumstances, no matter how hard it may ply its stinger, because the pores are then closed. The U. S. Bureau of Entomology investigated this question and reported that the belief has no foundation in fact. The stinger of a bee does enter the skin through the pores, and these tiny openings may be slightly affected by breathing, but the difference is not sufficient to interfere with the operation of the bee's stinger. If bees do not sting a person while he holds his breath or clenches his fists it is not because they cannot sting under such conditions, but because the person is then likely to be more quiet. Bees seem to be able to detect the slightest sign of fear in a human being and are stimulated to sting by any quick, nervous movements. A person who remains quiet and who shows no fear is not in great danger of being stung. Bees, however, are repelled by certain body odors, and some persons do not excite and anger bees as others do. It is absurd to suppose that a person tampering with bees would be immune from their stings merely because he held his breath or clenched his fists. Some have tested the popular belief to their sorrow.

Why are fractional votes cast in political conventions?

Fractional votes in American political conventions may result from several causes. The national political parties generally allot their adherents in each State a number of votes based on the number of representatives the State has in Congress. For instance, the Democratic Party gives its adherents in each State twice as many votes in the national nominating convention as the State has Representatives and Senators in Congress. Thus a State with twelve members of Congress is entitled to twenty-four votes in the convention. But the parties do not generally restrict the number of delegates that a State may send to the convention; they restrict only the number of votes they may cast. In 1924 the Democratic Party of Connecticut sent twenty delegates to the Democratic convention held in New York and they were permitted to cast only fourteen votes. Accordingly each delegate had only 0.7 of a vote and the result was that on many ballots William G. McAdoo received 4.9 votes and Alfred E. Smith 9.1 from the Connecticut delegation. Sometimes delegates at large are given half a vote each while district delegates are given full votes. It depends entirely on the party organization in each State. Not infrequently delegations from rival factions of the same party in a State are admitted to a national nominating convention and the total vote allotted to the State is divided equally between the two delegations. This practice accounts for many of the half votes. At the Democratic convention held in Baltimore in 1912 Champ Clark received 440½ votes on the first ballot while Woodrow Wilson received 324.

How did the thistle become the emblem of Scotland?

The thistle became the Scotch national emblem as the result of a traditional incident during the wars between the Scots and the Danes. Just when the incident occurred is not authentically recorded. Some writers place it in the eighth century, while others place it about 1010 during the reign of Malcolm II. The Danes, it is believed, were finally driven out of Scotland in 1040, about the time that Duncan I was murdered by his kinsman Macbeth, who seized the throne and reigned about sixteen years. Be that as it may, according to the most usual version of the legend, the Danes planned a surprise attack by night on Sterling or some other castle. The sleeping Scots within the castle were suddenly aroused when a member of the Danish advance guard, creeping along noiselessly because barefooted, stepped on a thistle in the moat and uttered a howl of pain. Whether the legend is true or not, the thistle as the heraldic emblem and seal of Scotland is very ancient. *Nemo me impune lacessit* is the Scottish national motto; freely translated it means, "Nobody attacks me with impunity." Although there is a prickly plant known as the Scotch thistle, the species of plant represented on the emblem has never been positively identified. Archius, king of the Scots, created the Order of the Thistle in the early part of the tenth century after his victory over Athelstan, and this order was revived in 1687 by James II as a distinctively Scottish order of knighthood.

Why are so many companies incorporated in Delaware?

A large number of firms doing business on a national or interstate scale are incorporated under the laws of Delaware because the corporation laws of that State are more liberal than similar laws in other States, with the possible exception of two or three. Delaware requires a smaller percentage of subscribed stock, and she grants many privileges to corporations not granted by other States. The State derives a large revenue from the several thousand charters issued annually, and *Incorporated in Delaware* and *This is a Delaware Corporation* are bywords throughout the business world.

Who are the White Russians?

Strictly speaking, the term *White Russian* does not refer to the color of the skin of the people whom it designates; nor does it contrast their political doctrines with those of the Reds or Socialists, as many people suppose. As constituted before the revolution of 1917 European Russia proper consisted of three grand divisions—Great Russia, Little Russia and White Russia—and the emperor styled himself the Czar of All the *Russias*. Three racial groups corresponding to these geographical divisions can be distinguished among the Russians from the dawn of their history. Great Russia consisted of the central and northeastern provinces, and the language of its inhabitants, particularly the Moscow dialect, was the literary and official language of the empire. Little Russia was the name given to the southern provinces inhabited by the Ukrainians and the Cossacks. White Russia was a comparatively small group of western provinces bordering on Poland and the Baltic states. The White Russians intermingled to some extent with the Great and Little Russians, but they were influenced most by the Poles and Lithuanians. Just why they were called White Russians has never been determined. Perhaps the designation originally contrasted the Caucasian inhabitants of this region with the Mongolians

in eastern Russia. Their language, which is spoken by about 10,-
000,000 people living chiefly in the old provinces of Vitebsk, Mo-
hilev, Minsk and parts of Pskov, Smolensk, Chernigov and Vilna,
resembles Polish more than it does literary Russian and it has a very
meager literature. After the dismemberment of the Russian empire
White Russia established a soviet government and federated with
the union of soviet republics. Popularly, however, the term *White
Russian* is now used to distinguish the anti-Bolshevik Russians
from the Reds.

What battle and kingdom were lost for want of a nail?

The story of a battle and kingdom being lost for want of a
horseshoe nail is merely an elaboration of an observation made by
Benjamin Franklin. In the preface of *Poor Richard's Almanack
for 1758* Richard Saunders, the fictitious author of the almanac,
quotes a man known as Father Abraham as saying: "And again,
he Richard adviseth to circumspection and care, even in the smallest
matters, because sometimes *a little neglect may breed great mischief,* adding, for want of a nail, the shoe was lost; for want of a
shoe the horse was lost; and for want of a horse the rider was lost,
being overtaken and slain by the enemy, all for want of care about
a horseshoe nail." It is not probable that Franklin alluded to any
particular historical incident. He no doubt merely drew upon his
imagination for an illustration for his precept. A more elaborate
version of the Franklin story is as follows: "For the want of a nail
the shoe was lost; for the want of a shoe the horse was lost; for
the want of a horse the rider was lost; for the want of a rider the
battle was lost; for the want of a battle the kingdom was lost—and
all for the want of a horseshoe nail."

Why does Maine elect Congressmen in September?

Maine is popularly regarded as a political barometer because
National Senators and Representatives from that State are elected
in September instead of November. The Federal Constitution provides that unless Congress directs otherwise the time of holding
elections for Senators and Representatives "shall be prescribed in
each State by the legislature thereof." During the early days of the
Federal Government no law on the subject was passed. In 1845

Congress fixed the first Tuesday after the first Monday in November as the day for choosing Presidential electors, and that day is still National or general election day. The same day was designated for the election of Representatives and Senators, but an exception was made in the case of those States in whose constitutions a different day was specified. Accordingly, for many years three States— Arkansas, Oregon and Maine—elected their Congressional representatives earlier than November. Arkansas and Oregon, deeming it more convenient and practical to hold State and Congressional elections every fourth year on the same day as the Presidential election, changed their constitutions to conform with the act of 1845. Maine is the only State in the Union which continues to hold these elections on a different day. Election day in Maine was placed in September during the early days of the Republic when traveling facilities were poor and when bad roads and cold weather frequently would have prevented the rural inhabitants from going to the polls late in the fall. Even at the present time climatic conditions in Maine no doubt contribute toward the retention of the earlier date for State and Congressional elections. All the States, including Maine, elect Presidential electors on the first Tuesday after the first Monday in November.

How long after desertion is a deserter free from arrest?

The laws governing punishment for desertion are different for the Army and the Navy. If a person deserts from the American Army when the United States is at war or in a technical state of war he is always liable to arrest, trial and punishment for the offense. Trials for desertion occurring between April 6, 1917, and March 3, 1921, are not infrequent at the present time. A statute of limitation, that is, a law limiting the time within which an action can be brought against an offender, protects peace-time deserters. According to the Articles of War, if a person deserts from the Army in time of peace the statute of limitations becomes effective three years after the date of desertion, provided the deserter has been within the reach of the military court. Any period of time that the deserter is absent from the jurisdiction of the military court is deducted from the three-year period. The U. S. Navy Department says that if a person deserts from the American naval service when

182

the country is actually or technically at war the statute of limitations becomes effective two years after the date on which he was declared a deserter, that is, he is immune from trial and punishment two years after his desertion, provided he was where the military court could reach him by reasonable diligence. If he is classed as a peace-time deserter from the Navy the statute becomes an effective bar to trial two years after the date of the expiration of the enlistment. Desertion from the Army or the Navy in time of war is a very serious offense, and may bring a sentence of death. Peace-time deserters are usually given a dishonorable discharge and sentenced to a term of penal servitude.

How did *son of a gun* originate?

This expression is used daily in conversation by thousands of persons who would never think of using it if they even so much as suspected its unsavory origin. It formerly expressed the utmost contempt for the person to whom it was applied. William Pulleyn, in his *Etymological Compendium* published in 1828, probably gave the correct origin of the phrase. *Son of a gun,* he wrote, "is derived from *gong,* an old word for the temple of Cloacina—of course it implies bastard, or born in a necessary." *Gong* and *gong man,* though still recorded by unabridged dictionaries, are obsolete. Dr. Frank Vizetelly gives a different theory. "It is an epithet of contempt in slight degree," he says, "and was applied originally to boys born afloat, when wives accompanied their husbands to sea. One admiral declared that he was actually thus cradled—under the breast of a gun-carriage." The phrase *son of a gun* was used as early as 1708 in the *British Apollo*.

Did Uncle Sam coin any liberty-head nickels in 1913?

Whether the American Government minted any liberty-head nickels bearing the date 1913 has been a subject of considerable controversy, due to the fact that a coin dealer offered a large sum of money for such coins. According to the official report of the mint no such coins were struck off. In a statement prepared for the author the Director of the Mint says: "The only nickels authorized to be coined at the mints in 1913 were those of the current design, known as buffalo nickels, having on one side the Indian head and on the other the buffalo. This design took the place of the five-cent piece bearing the female head of liberty on the obverse, the last of which were coined in 1912." Notwithstanding this statement, it is stated upon what is believed to be reliable authority that several liberty-head nickels bearing the date 1913 were minted. The coin dealer explained the rarity of the coins as follows: At the close of 1912 the mint authorities, not having yet received proper orders to use the dies of the buffalo nickel at the beginning of 1913, prepared a master die of the liberty-head coin, and from this die several pieces were struck. Consequently a few 1913 liberty-head nickels are in existence, although the Government never authorized them. None of these coins, however, passed into public circulation, but five pieces were obtained from the mint by a man who showed them at the convention of the American Numismatic Society held in Detroit in August, 1913. It was pointed out that this was not the first time that the official report of the mint omitted to mention coins that were struck off. For instance, there was no mention in the official report that $2.50 gold pieces were minted at Philadelphia in 1841, yet specimens are known to exist. Likewise the records omit to state that similar pieces were coined in New Orleans in 1845, when in fact such coins are comparatively plentiful.

Why is *controller* sometimes spelled *comptroller?*

The spelling *comptroller* was introduced about 1500 and arose from a mistaken derivation of the word from *compt,* an obsolete form of *count* suggested by the French *compte.* Since a controller's business was to examine and verify accounts it was supposed that the word should be spelled *comptroller.* The erroneous form now survives only in certain official usage; as, Comptroller General of the United States, Comptroller of the Currency, and Comptroller of the Post Office Department. *Controller* is the correct spelling for ordinary purposes. In both cases the word is pronounced the same—*kon-trol-er.*

How can a watch be used as a compass?

An ordinary watch, if it is keeping correct time, makes a fairly accurate compass when the sun is shining. All that is necessary is to let the timepiece lie flat with the face up and the hour hand pointing as nearly as possible toward the sun. A line running from the center of the dial to a point half way between the hour hand and the point indicating 12 : 00 o'clock will point due south in the Northern Hemisphere and due north in the Southern Hemisphere. For example, suppose it is 3 : 00 in the afternoon and the hour hand is pointed toward the sun. A line running from the center of the dial to a point midway between XII and III—the point indicating 1 :30— will point due north in the Southern Hemisphere and due south in the Northern Hemisphere. The process may be reversed by turn ing one's back to the sun and pointing the hour hand in the direction one's shadow takes. In that case a line running from the center of the watch through a point half way between the hour hand and 12 : 00 o'clock will point due north in the Northern Hemisphere and due south in the Southern Hemisphere. This is true because when a perpendicular object casts a shadow by the sun the shadow always extends due north and south at 12 : 00 o'clock noon, local apparent time. Standard time, owing to our system of dividing the continent into time zones, does not always correspond to solar time. Nevertheless, the visible path of the sun itself is the primary dial, of which those in clocks and watches, with one major difference, are mere mechanical reproductions. The difference is that the sun's circuit is a twenty-four hour dial, while the ordinary timepiece has a twelve hour dial. That is why the half-way point instead of the 12 : 00 o'clock point, must be taken as indicating the direction when a watch is used as a compass.

What determined the width of standard gauge railroads?

The standard gauge railroad is four feet eight and one half inches wide, measured from the inside of one rail to the inside of the other. This width was determined largely by chance. When tramways were first built in the English coal districts their width was made to conform to the gauge of the common road wagons to be used on them. It happened that the gauge between the wheels of these wagons was about four feet eight and one half inches. When later rails were laid for steam railroads the same gauge was adopted in many cases. In fact nearly all the early English railways were standard gauge. William Jessop is often credited with being the author of the standard gauge for steam railways. About 1800 he designed a track between Loughborough and Nanpantan in which the rails were four feet eight and one half inches apart, or five feet minus the width of two of the rails. Many years afterwards railway builders and operators differed widely on the most desirable width for the tracks. The dispute reached its zenith about 1833. George Stephenson threw the weight of his influence in favor of the standard gauge. He believed it was "most economical in construction, not only as regards the engines and carriages, but more particularly of the railway itself." The standard gauge was fixed by Parliament in 1840. The act was applicable to all railways in England and Scotland except the Great Western and certain branches, which had adopted a broad or six-foot gauge. Not until 1874 did this railway conform to the almost universal practice by substituting standard gauge track. In the United States, as well as in many other countries, the standard gauge prevailed after many broader and narrower gauges had been tried.

Why are poppies associated with the World War?

In Roman mythology the red poppy was the symbol of death and as such was dedicated to Somnus, the god of sleep. For hundreds of years this flower has been associated with the battlefields of western Europe, especially in Flanders, where it grows as a pest in the wheat and in uncultivated fields. Poppies grew luxuriantly on the famous battlefields of this region simply because such fields were torn up and then neglected for a season or two. Superstitious people believed that the red flowers symbolized the blood of those that had been slain. Contemporary writers refer to the profusion of poppies which sprang up on the battlefields of Landen, Ramillies, Malplaquet, Fontenoy and Waterloo. William of Orange and Luxemburg fought the sanguinary battle of Landen in the summer of 1693. In his history of England Macaulay says of this famous battlefield: "During many months the ground was strewn with skulls and bones of men and horses, and with fragments of hats and shoes, saddles and holsters. The next summer the soil, fertilized by twenty thousand corpses, broke forth into millions of poppies. The traveler, who, on the road from Saint Tron to Tirlemont, saw that vast sheet of rich scarlet spreading from Landen to Neerwinden, could hardly help fancying that the figurative prediction of the Hebrew prophet was literally accomplished, that the earth was disclosing her blood, and refusing to cover the slain." The poppy was adopted as the official memorial flower of the American Legion and it is widely worn on Memorial Day—May 30—which by reason of this fact is frequently called Poppy Day. In 1922 the Veterans of Foreign Wars inaugurated the custom of selling *Buddy Poppies,* artificial flowers made exclusively by the disabled veterans. The peculiar association of the poppy with the battlefields of the World War is largely the result of the popular poem by John McCrae, Canadian physician, soldier and poet, who died of pneumonia in 1918 while still in France. *In Flanders Fields* was written during the second battle of Ypres and was originally published in the issue of London *Punch* dated December 9, 1915. The complete poem follows:

> In Flanders fields the poppies blow
> Between the crosses, row on row,
>   That mark our place; and in the sky
>   The larks, still bravely singing, fly
> Scarce heard amid the guns below.
>
> We are the Dead. Short days ago
> We lived, felt dawn, saw sunset glow,
>   Loved and were loved, and now we lie,
>   In Flanders fields.
>
> Take up our quarrel with the foe:
> To you from failing hands we throw
>   The torch; be yours to hold it high.
>   If ye break faith with us who die
> We shall not sleep, though poppies grow
>   In Flanders fields.

Do snakes have voices?

Snakes do not have larynges or vocal chords and consequently they do not have true voices in the generally accepted sense of that term as applied to animals and human beings. Naturalists do not credit the reports of snakes that bleat like deer, purr like cats, cough like monkeys, or make other vocal sounds. Most species of snake are capable of making a hissing noise, which is produced by the air rushing from the throat when the lungs are deflated. This, according to the Smithsonian Institution, is the only *voice* possessed by snakes. The hissing of some species, such as the boa constrictors, pythons and the little American puffing adders, can be heard at a considerable distance. Rattlesnakes make the rattling noise by vibrating the tips of their tails, and other species make a swishing sound by the movement of the scales one over another.

What is meant by the freedom of the seas?

Freedom of the seas is merely a popular term without definite meaning in international law. In a general way, however, it is the converse of the *command of the seas* and is applied to the principle that all nations have equal rights on the high seas at all times. This principle is at present accepted only in time of peace. Complete freedom of the seas would mean that when two nations are at war neutral nations would have the right to carry on unrestricted commerce with either or both of them unless prevented from doing so by a complete and effective blockade of the ports. There would be no contraband of war, all articles of commerce, even weapons and munitions, being exempt from seizure on the high seas by the belligerents. But nations engaged in war claim the right to curtail the freedom of the seas by paper blockades and by searching vessels on the high seas and seizing articles which they deem contraband of war. In fact the freedom of the seas in time of war is restricted by numerous treaties and principles of international law. The second of President Wilson's *fourteen points* provided: "Absolute freedom of navigation upon the seas outside territorial waters alike in peace and in war, except as the seas may be closed in whole or in part by international action for the enforcement of international covenants."

Do canaries live in the wild state?

Domestic canaries have been altered to such an extent by hundreds of years of selective breeding that their wild progenitors cannot be positively identified. Their early history as cage birds is obscure. It is generally supposed, however, that they sprang from a species of finch still found in the wild state in the Canary Islands and Madeira, off the northwestern coast of Africa. The wild birds in the Canary

Islands are grayish brown, sometimes varied with other hues, but they never have the beautifully colored plumage so common in domestic varieties. According to the usual story, specimens of these birds were captured in the Canaries during the sixteenth century and domesticated in Italy, whence they were carried to other parts of the world. Canaries breed freely with European finches and certain other birds, a fact which leads some authorities to believe that the domestic canary is the product of interbreeding as well as selective breeding and consequently not the descendant of any one species. In the United States common American goldfinches or thistle birds are sometimes called "wild canaries." These birds, of course, are not canaries at all. *Canary* is derived from Latin *canis,* dog, and according to the elder Pliny, these islands were called Canaria "from the multitude of dogs of great size" found there by King Juba of Mauretania when he visited the islands about 40 B. C.

How many Presidents have died in the White House?

Only two Presidents of the United States have died in the Executive Mansion, although six have died in office. William Henry Harrison and Zachary Taylor both died in the White House, the former April 4, 1841, one month after his inauguration, and the latter July 9, 1850, about sixteen months after he assumed office.

When is a person's first birthday?

Birthday has two distinct meanings. It may mean the day a person is born, that is, the day of his birth, in which sense he has only one birthday—it is his first and last; or, the term may mean the anniversary or annual observance of a person's birth, in which sense a person's first birthday is the day he is a year old—he has a birthday each year after that as long as he lives. Thus when a person reaches his eightieth birthday he is eighty years of age. Many people confuse these two meanings of the word *birthday* and they regard one's first anniversary as his second birthday. *Birthday* in the sense of the anniversary of a person's birth is very old in English literature. In 1382 John Wyclif used it in his translation of *Mark 6: 21:* "Eroude in his birthe-day made a soper to the princes." Shakespeare, in *Julius Cæsar,* makes Cassius say to Messala on the plains of Philippi: "This is my birth-day; as this very day was Cassius born."

The custom of observing birthdays dates back thousands of years. In *Genesis 40: 20* it is stated: "And it came to pass the third day, which was Pharaoh's birthday, that he made a feast unto all his servants."

Why does a star precede the number on some bills?

On certain currency notes or bills issued by the U. S. Bureau of Engraving and Printing an asterisk or a small star precedes the serial number instead of the customary letter of the alphabet. The Treasurer of the United States says that these stars are put only on substitute bills used to replace those which are defective or spoiled in the process of printing. Paper money is printed and finished in sheets and the finishing process includes printing the serial numbers. Although all currency is subjected to several examinations before the numbering and sealing is done, it sometimes happens that after a serial number is printed the bill must be discarded because of some imperfection in it. A special bill is prepared to take the place of the discarded one and its number is not in the regular series. The asterisk before the number identifies it as a substitute bill. Naturally the percentage of spoiled bills is very small and only a few are so numbered.

Were Catholic priests ever permitted to marry?

In the early days of the Roman Church the clergy were permitted to marry. St. Peter, who is regarded by Catholics as the first Pope, was married according to *Matthew 7:14,* where his "wife's mother" is referred to. Even at the present time some Eastern.churches under the jurisdiction of Rome have a married priesthood. The growth of celibacy, first as a custom and then as a rule of discipline, was gradual. Many bishops and priests voluntarily began to practice celibacy at an early date. Second marriages of priests began to be questioned; then marriage of priests was restricted to virgins. The first church council which definitely forbade marriage to the higher clergy was the local synod of Elvira in 305 A. D. Eighty years later—385 A. D.—Pope Siricius issued a decretal enjoining strict celibacy upon all bishops, priests and deacons. He insisted on the immediate separation of those who were married and prescribed expulsion as the penalty for disobedience. This may be regarded as the real beginning of universal compulsory sacerdotal celibacy in the Catholic Church as a rule of discipline. This rule was later extended to subdeacons. For several centuries, however, the rules against the marriage of clerics in sacred orders were widely violated both openly and secretly. Even many bishops had wives. In the eleventh century several Popes turned their attention to the question and took stringent measures to enforce the injunctions against marriage among the clergy. Gregory VII, who was Pope from 1073 to 1085, especially distinguished himself in this respect. He enforced the celibacy rules so stringently that he is still often erroneously credited with being their author.

Why is the heir to the British throne called the Prince of Wales?

Prince Edward, fourth son of Edward I and afterward Edward II, was the first heir to the English throne to bear the title *Prince of Wales*. The title itself was borrowed from the Welsh princes, who ruled Wales from the tenth to the thirteenth century, and was conferred on Edward by the Lincoln parliament in 1301 to commemorate his father's conquest of Wales and to soothe the national pride of the Welsh. Henry III recognized Llewelyn ap Jorwerth as *Prince of North Wales,* but withdrew the title in 1229. Llewelyn ap Gryffydd in 1256 assumed the more pretentious title *Prince of Wales,* which the English government sanctioned in 1267 along with the privilege of receiving homage from the other nobles of his principality. In 1277, however, this prince was compelled to submit to Edward I, who decreed that the title *Prince of Wales* should cease at Llewelyn's death. Llewelyn took up arms against the English again in 1282. According to an old prophecy of Merlin, a Prince of Wales would be crowned in London when English money became round. This prophecy, Llewelyn convinced his credulous subjects, was at last fulfilled when the English issued new copper coins and enacted a prohibition against the common practice of breaking silver pennies into halves and quarters. But Edward I promptly crushed the rebellion and reconquered Wales. Llewelyn fell in battle, and thus perished the last Prince of Wales who could speak Welsh. There is a legend that Edward promised the Welsh that if they would cease resistance he would place over them a native-born prince who could not speak a word of English. It so happened that two years after Llewelyn's death Queen Eleanor gave birth to a son at Carnarvon in Wales. The king, according to the legend, kept his promise by conferring the title *Prince of Wales* on his fourth son, who later became heir by the death of his brother and finally ascended the throne as Edward II. This story is undoubtedly fiction. Edward was the first to bear the title *Prince of Wales* as heir to the throne, but it was not conferred on him until 1301. Later Edward the Black Prince bore the same title. He did not survive his father, Edward III, and consequently never became king. Since his time the title has been conferred on most of the heirs apparent to the English crown. It is not inherited, although any sovereign may make the heir apparent Prince of Wales by letters patent. If a Prince of Wales dies before his father the title is extinguished, as it is when the prince becomes king, and it has no further existence except by fresh creation.

What did George III say about the loss of America?

On November 10, 1782, during the peace negotiations between Great Britain and the United States at the close of the Revolution, King George III wrote as follows to the prime minister, the earl of Shelburne: "I cannot conclude without mentioning how sensibly I feel the dismemberment of America from this empire, and that I should be miserable indeed if I did not feel that no blame on that account can be laid at my door, and did I not also know that knavery seems to be so much the striking feature of its inhabitants that it may not in the end be an evil that they will become aliens to this kingdom." The earl of Shelburne had consented to take office under the marquess of Rockingham only on condition that the king would recognize the United States. Rockingham died soon afterwards and Shelburne became premier.

Is it unlawful to write a check for less than a dollar?

It is not unlawful, as many suppose, to write a check for less than one dollar. The belief that it is arose from a misinterpretation of Section 178 of the Federal Criminal Code. This section, which was approved March 4, 1909, reads as follows: "No person shall make, issue, circulate, or pay out any note, check, memorandum, token, or other obligation for a less sum than one dollar, intended to circulate as money or to be received or used in lieu of lawful money of the United States; and every person so offending shall be fined not more than $500, or imprisoned not more than six months, or both." A bank check is not intended to circulate as money or to be received and used in lieu of lawful money. It is merely an order to pay money. In a statement prepared for the author the Department of Justice says: "The statute is aimed against such checks as are 'intended to circulate as lawful money or to be received or used in lieu of lawful money of the United States' and does not apparently have any reference to an ordinary individual bank check, and it has always been the view of the Department that the statute does not apply to such a check." In some countries tokens and checks issued by private firms and associations are used for money. For instance, in France tokens issued by Chambers of Commerce are everywhere employed for small change. The section of the criminal code in question was designed to forbid the circulation of such private money. Certain banks are permitted to issue currency in the form of bank notes, but under this section such notes cannot be issued for sums less than one dollar.

Why is selling a dog considered wrong?

Many people have a decided prejudice against selling dogs. Some go so far as to regard the sale of a dog as positively sinful. We know of an elderly woman who severely condemned a man who engaged in the business of raising shepherd dogs for sale. She branded his business as sinful and protested against her church accepting contributions of his money, which she said was *tainted*. The origin of this prejudice is not known for certain. It may be based on the old Hebraic Scriptural teachings. *Deuteronomy 23: 18* says in part: "Thou shalt not bring . . . the price of a dog into the house of the Lord thy God for any vow." Many commentators, accepting *dog* in this passage in the literal sense, state that Moses declared dogs unclean and prohibited traffic in them. Others take a different view of the passage, although they do not deny that the Hebrews regarded the dog as unclean. They say that *dog* here does not refer to the animal, but to a person who has prostituted himself by committing any abominable action, such as sodomy.

This opinion receives some confirmation from the context, especially the preceding verse. In Palestine the dog was regarded as filthy and was looked upon with loathing and aversion. With few exceptions, whenever the dog is mentioned in the Bible (more than forty times altogether) it is referred to with contempt. *Dog* was the most contemptuous term in the old Hebrew vocabulary. Mohammedans still speak of *Christian dogs.*

What is the difference between cocoa and chocolate?

The common beverages known as cocoa and chocolate are both prepared from the seeds or beans of a tropical tree, *Theobroma cacao.* In making chocolate the cacao beans are roasted, shelled and ground into a smooth, fine-grained paste, which is run into molds and cooled in the form of cakes or bars. These cakes, which contain fifty per cent or more of the fat called *cocoa butter,* constitute the chocolate of commerce. Sometimes, however, instead of cooling the chocolate paste and molding it into cakes it is subjected to pressure and part of the cocoa butter is extracted. The partially defatted press cake is pulverized and sifted, and the fine powder resulting is put in packages and sold as cocoa. Chocolate, then, is the ground and caked cacao beans which have not had their fat extracted; cocoa is the ground and powdered beans deprived of a large part of their fat. Accordingly, chocolate is richer and more nutritious than cocoa and the beverage is somewhat harder to prepare properly. Frequently no sharp distinction is drawn between the beverages made from chocolate cakes and cocoa powder. In many restaurants a customer will get the same beverage no matter whether he orders cocoa or chocolate.

How did T. B. in Maryland get its name?

Perhaps one of the oddest names on the map of the United States is T. B., a small village in the southern part of Prince Georges County, Maryland. Because *T. B.* is the slang abbreviation of *tuberculosis,* many people mistakenly suppose that the Maryland village received its name from a sanatorium for the treatment of tuberculosis patients. The letters composing the name are the initials of Thomas Brooke (or Brookes), who acquired several thousand acres of land in that neighborhood in colonial days. There is a tradition that when the village grew up one of the original Brooke boundary stones was found within the village limits. This stone bore the initials of Thomas Brooke and from that circumstance the inhabitants fell into the habit of calling their village T. B.

Why is Indiana called the Hoosier State?

Hoosier, variously spelled, was previously used in parts of the South in the sense of a green, gawky and uncouth countryman, and it was first applied in ridicule to the early settlers of southern Indiana. In time the term lost its contemptuous connotation and became the accepted nickname of the State and its inhabitants. This, at least, seems to be the most probable theory of the origin of *Hoosier* as applied to Indiana, and it is supported by early usage. The first recorded use of the nickname occurs in John Finley's poem entitled *The Hoosier's Nest.* In a volume issued in 1860 Finley says this poem was written in 1830, but apparently it was not published until January 1, 1833, when it appeared as the *Address of the Carrier of the Indianapolis Journal,* probably on a separate sheet. Even at that time *Hoosier* had an accepted meaning. Finley stated that he heard it in current use and had no knowledge of its origin. His poem immediately attracted considerable attention and was largely responsible for the general adoption of the word in reference to Indiana. At that time the spelling was not yet fixed. In the original version of Finley's poem it was spelled *Hoosher* and inclosed in quotation marks, indicating its newness in print. Later the author spelled it *Hoosier.* The spirit of *The Hoosier's Nest* and the original application of the nickname may be gathered from the following excerpts:

> Blest Indiana! In whose soil
> Men seek the sure rewards of toil,
> And honest poverty and worth
> Find here the best retreat on earth,
> While hosts of Preachers, Doctors, Lawyers,
> All independent as wood-sawyers,
> With men of every hue and fashion,
> Flock to the rising "Hoosher" nation.
> Men who can legislate or plow,
> Wage politics or milk a cow—
> So plastic are their various parts,

Within the circle of their arts,
With equal tack the "Hoosher" loons,
Hunt offices or hunt raccoons.

* * *

But having gone so far, 'twould seem
(Since "Hoosher" manners is the theme)
That I, lest strangers should take exception,
Should give a more minute description,
And if my strains be not seraphic
I trust you'll find them somewhat graphic.

* * *

Suppose in riding somewhere West
A stranger found a "Hoosher's" nest,
In other words, a buckeye cabin
Just big enough to hold Queen Mab in,
Its situation low but airy
Was on the borders of a prairie,
And fearing he might be benighted
He hailed the house and then alighted.
The "Hoosher" met him at the door,
Their salutations soon were o'er;
He took the stranger's horse aside
And to a sturdy sapling tied;
Then, having stripped the saddle off,
He fed him in a sugar trough.
The stranger stooped to enter in,
The entrance closing with a pin,
And manifested strong desire
To seat him by the log heap fire,
Where half a dozen Hoosheroons,
With mush and milk, tincups and spoons,
White heads, bare feet and dirty faces,
Seemed much inclined to keep their places,
But Madam, anxious to display
Her rough and undisputed sway,
Her offspring to the ladder led
And cuffed the youngsters up to bed.
Invited shortly to partake
Of Venison, milk and Johnny-cake
The stranger made a hearty meal
And glances around the room would steal;

One side was lined with skins of "varments",
The other spread with divers garments,
Dried pumpkins overhead were strung
Where venison hams in plenty hung,
Two rifles placed above the door,
Three dogs lay stretched upon the floor,
In short, the domicile was rife
With specimens of "Hoosher" life.

*   *   *

One more subject I'll barely mention
To which I ask your kind attention,
My pockets are so shrunk of late
I can not nibble "Hoosher" bait.

Only a week after the appearance of this poem John W. Davis, a member of the Indiana legislature, gave "The *Hooshier* State of Indiana" as a toast at the Jackson dinner in Indianapolis, and in the following August a weekly paper called *The Hoosier* was established at Greencastle. "I am now in the land of the *Hooshiers* and find that long-haired race much more civilized than some of their Western neighbors are willing to represent them," wrote C. F. Hoffman in *A Winter in the West* under date of December 29, 1833. "The term *Hooshier,* like that of Yankee, or Buckeye, first applied contemptuously, has now become a soubriquet that bears nothing invidious with it to the ear of an Indianian." In September, 1834, the Indianapolis *Democrat* referred to Finley as "the poet laureate of Hoosierland" who immortalized "our State in verse, by that justly celebrated epic the *Hoosier's Nest.*" Almost immediately the origin of *Hoosier* was discussed publicly. Many curious theories, some of them ludicrous, were advanced and still comprise part of the literature on the subject. The term was variously derived from *husher,* a bully who hushes or stills his opponent; from a contractor named Hoosier who employed many settlers on a canal in southern Indiana; from *Who's yere,* the gruff inquiry with which the settlers are alleged to have replied to a knock on the door; and from *hooshar,* which is said to represent the peculiar noise made by Indiana woodchoppers as they expelled the air from their lungs with each stroke of the ax. Still another theory held that the word is a corruption of *hussar* and that it was introduced as the result of an incident in connection with Colonel John Jacob Lehmanowsky, a Polish officer who had served under Napoleon. This theory is disproved by the fact that the Polish hussar did not visit Indiana and Kentucky until after *Hoosier* was in common use. James Whitcomb Riley, the poet, ridiculed these theories in the following manner: "These stories commonly told about the origin of the word *Hoosier* are all nonsense. The real origin is found in the pugnacious habits of the early settlers. They were very vicious fighters, and not only gouged and scratched, but frequently bit off noses and ears. This was so ordinary an affair that a settler coming in to a bar on a morning after a fight, and seeing an ear on the floor, would merely push it aside with his foot and carelessly ask, *Who's year?*"

What kind of wood was the true cross made of?

There is no authentic information as to the composition of the cross on which Jesus was crucified. Most of the alleged fragments of the cross preserved as sacred relics are composed of pine. Legends on the subject are legion. According to one, the original Christian cross was made of four kinds of wood—palm, cedar, olive and cypress—representing the four quarters of the earth. A poetic legend has it that the true cross was made of aspen, which accounts for the almost constant quivering of the leaves of that species of tree.

How did *dun* originate?

Dun in the sense of requesting payment of a bill is believed to have been derived from the surname of Joseph Dun, an English petty official, who was noted for his success in collecting debts. Many stories have been published about Joe Dun's unusual and picturesque methods of making debtors pay. In 1708 the following explanation of the term was printed in the *British Apollo:* "The word *Dun* owes its birth to one Joe Dun, a famous Bailif of the Town of Lincoln. It became a Proverb . . . when a man refused to pay his debts, Why don't you *Dun* him? That is why don't you send Dun to arrest him? . . . It is now as old as since the days of King Henry the Seventh." The monarch mentioned reigned from 1485 to 1509. Whether this was the true origin of the term cannot be stated positively, because there is no contemporary evidence.

The earliest known use of the word occurs in *Microcosmographie, or a Peece of the World discovered in Essayes and Characters,* published in 1628 by John Earle (1601?–1665), afterwards bishop of Salisbury. Earle wrote: "An Vniversitie Dunne . . . Hee is an inferiour Creditor of some ten shillings or downwards. He is a sore beleaguer of Chambers." This quotation definitely disposes of the theory, advanced by Maitland in his *American Slang Dictionary,* that *dun* is an Americanism derived from *din,* meaning noise. Dr. Samuel Johnson derived the word from Saxon *donon,* meaning to clamor. It is possible that *dun* is from French *donne,* a familiar imperative form of *donner,* meaning to give.

Do the northern lights make a noise?

Many scientists believe that a faint but characteristic swishing sound accompanies displays of the northern lights when they are close to the ground and when great stillness prevails. Whether the noise is actually produced by the aurora borealis is a disputed question. Popular writers frequently refer to this phenomenon. For instance, in *Kazan,* which was published in 1914, James Oliver Curwood says: "The stars began to glow white and metallic, and from far in the north there came faintly a crisping moaning sound, like steel sleigh-runners running over frosty snow—the mysterious monotone of the northern lights." Elsewhere in the same book Curwood describes this sound as a "hissing crackling monotone, like the creaking of steel sledge-runners on frost-filled snow." The issue of the *Journal* of the Royal Astronomical Society of Canada for July and August, 1928, contains the following statement on the subject by W. E. Harper, president of the society: "It has often been said that, in brilliant displays, sounds are heard like the rustling of silk or the crash of breaking glass. Some people stoutly declare they have heard such sounds, while others are equally emphatic that such are never heard. While I have never heard them myself, I am prepared to accept the idea that noises do accompany brilliant auroræ. I have talked with our surveyors in the Yukon who undertook to test out a certain one of their number who stated he could hear such sounds. During a brilliant display they blindfolded him perfectly, but with each brilliant flash he would exclaim instantly, 'There it is; don't you hear it?' It would seem as if some people have ears attuned to catch these sounds better than others." The U. S. Coast and Geodetic Survey is inclined to believe that Mr. Harper states the matter correctly. This conclusion is confirmed by the report of Captain H. P. Dawson, who in 1882 and 1883 was in charge of the British Polar Station at Fort Rae in northwestern Canada. "There can be no doubt," reported Captain Dawson, "that distinct sound does occasionally accompany certain displays of aurora." He asserted that Indians and *voyageurs* of the Hudson Bay Company, who often pass their nights in the open, report that such sounds are quite common. On one occasion, Captain Dawson says, he heard the northern lights himself. "The sound," he said, "was like the swishing of a whip or the noise produced by a sharp squall of wind in the upper rigging of a ship, and as the aurora brightened and faded so did the sound which accompanied it." Nevertheless the evidence is not conclusive. The Carnegie Institution of Washington expressed the opinion that the testimony of the majority of experienced observers is to the effect that displays of the northern lights are not accompanied by a faint rustling or any other characteristic noise.

How did Westminster Abbey get its name?

Minster is an old name for a monastery or Christian religious house. In Anglo-Saxon it was *mynster*. Strictly speaking, the word *abbey* is superfluous in *Westminster Abbey* because *minster* means an abbey church and is still used in that sense in York Minster, Beverley Minster, and similar names. It is often stated that Westminster was so called to distinguish it from Eastminster, the Abbey of Grace on Tower Hill in London. This is disproved by the fact that a charter of sanctuary was granted to *Westminster* by Edward the Confessor, who died in 1066, while Eastminster was not founded until the fourteenth century. Westminster was probably so called because it was west of the Cathedral of St. Paul's, or because it originally referred to a monastery on the west side of London. In later years a church connected with a monastery or one which had its origin in a monastic establishment was called a minster. When the Abbey of St. Peter was built on the north bank of the Thames, on the site of the old *west minster*, it became popularly known as Westminster Abbey, and under that name it is now the most famous church in Great Britain. Many people habitually misspell and mis-

pronounce *Westminster* under the mistaken impression that the
second part of the compound name is *minister*. It is *minster,* with
only one *i*. Westminster Abbey is best known as the burial place
of British sovereigns and notables. There are no specific requirements for burial in Westminster. When a person of distinction dies
the deans of Westminster may or may not invite his relatives to
have his remains interred in the Abbey.

Where is Podunk?

Podunk is a derisive name for any small, out-of-the-way country town or village. In other words, Podunk is a jerk-water town.
It is not known just how the name acquired its odd meaning. No
such post office is listed in the U. S. Postal Guide, although the
name is applied to a neighborhood in Connecticut. As early as
1877 John R. Bartlett defined Podunk as " a term applied to an
imaginary place in burlesque writing or speaking." The name is of
Indian origin. The Podunk Indians were a small tribe who lived
in South Windsor, Hartford County, Connecticut, and Podunk,
their chief village, was at the mouth of the small stream which
still bears the name Podunk. At the close of King Philip's War
in 1676 the Podunks, or Windsor Indians as they were also called,
disappeared with the hostile tribes and never returned. There is a
Podunk Pond in North Brookfield, Worcester County, Massachusetts, and a local historian gives the Indian meaning of the name
as "place of burning." It seems more probable, however, that
Podunk is related to *Potunk,* a place name on Long Island, which is
supposed to be derived from *P'tuk-ohke,* an Algonquian word meaning "a neck or corner of land."

How did *mad as a hatter* originate?

There has been much speculation as to the original application
of *hatter* in *mad as a hatter*. It is probably merely a corruption of
adder in the older phrase *mad as an adder,* which obviously alludes
to the ostentatious manner in which the adder shows anger or irritation. In Anglo-Saxon and Old English *mad* was used in the sense
of furious, angry, and even venomous; it is still widely used as a
synonym for angry in English and American dialect. Originally
mad as a hatter meant very angry or furious; now it more frequently

means violently insane. There is probably no truth in the oft-told story that the phrase originally referred to a crazy hat-maker, William Henry Miller, who was elected to the British parliament in 1830. According to the story, Miller suffered sunstroke while being carried through the street bareheaded by his enthusiastic supporters after his election was announced. Miller may have been known as "the Mad Hatter," but there is reason for believing that *mad as a hatter* was proverbial long before his time. Many authorities state that *mad as a hatter* was popularized in 1863 by Charles Lutwidge Dodgson in *Alice's Adventures in Wonderland*. That is incorrect. The phrase had been used in numerous popular works before the publication of Dodgson's famous book. Thomas Chandler Haliburton had used it in *The Clockmaker: or The Sayings and Doings of Samuel Slick of Slickville*, which was published between 1837 and 1840. Haliburton wrote: "Sister Sall . . . walked out of the room, as mad as a hatter." In 1849 William Makepeace Thackeray wrote in *Pendennis:* "We were . . . chaffing Derby Oaks—until he was mad as a hatter." "He's a very good fellow, but mad as a hatter," wrote Thomas Hughes in 1857 in *Tom Brown's School Days*.

What snake ejects a poisonous spray?

The spitting snake, which is found in South Africa from Senegambia to the Transvaal, received its name from the fact that it sometimes ejects a venomous spray from its mouth when annoyed or irritated. It is related to the cobras and is scientifically known as *Sepedon hæmachates*. Members of this species attain a length of only about two or three feet. Besides *spue slang,* meaning spitting snake, the Boers of South Africa call the species *ringhals,* that is, banded neck, a name which is also applied to the cobra proper. Whether the spitting cobra actually aims its venom at the eyes of its enemies in order to blind them, as continually reported, is a disputed question. Placards on the cage of a spitting cobra in the Reptile House of the New York Zoological Park state that the species "ejects its poison a distance of fifteen feet" and that "the venom is sprayed towards the eyes in an effort to blind the intruder." Dr. W. Reid Blair, director of the Park, says in his book entitled *In the Zoo* that the African spitting cobra when aroused "can eject its venom in a fine spray for a distance of eight to ten feet, aiming apparently for the eyes of its victim. The poison is quickly absorbed wherever it strikes mucous membranes. The skin is unaffected but the moist eye allows of an absorption so rapid that sharp pain and temporary blindness instantly result from the contact." The official guide to the London Zoological Park says that the ringhals "sprays or spits its venom in a steady jet at the eyes of its enemy, causing total blindness even in man. Crystallized venom can usually be detected on the glass of the ringhals' cage." This snake also injects its venom with its fangs. The poison sprayed in the air is not particularly dangerous to human beings unless it gets in the eyes. Often the ringhals shams death like an opossum in order to escape or gain an opportune time to strike. Spitting snakes are very ferocious in confinement and they frequently open their mouths and erect their fangs when approached. Sometimes the poison can be seen flowing from their fangs in drops. It is possible that the ejection of the poison from the mouth is due merely to the hissing and that the venom is not deliberately directed at the intruder. In *Reptiles of the World* Raymond L. Ditmars says: "Occasionally, the writer has witnessed the ability of cobras to eject their venom when in a coiled and defensive position. It seems that in striking the snake simultaneously compresses the poison glands by a contraction of the jaw and muscles and ejects the poison, though quite accidentally, in the direction of its annoyance. If the fluid should enter the eyes, blindness or death are the probable consequences. The habit is common with the South African hooded snake, *Sepedon,* and with the latter species seems quite voluntary." The Javanese black cobra, as well as certain other cobras, eject poison in a similar manner.

Does odor have weight?

Odor is the name of the sensation produced when certain substances come in contact with the olfactory region. The term is also applied to the collective particles which produce this sensation. Very little is known about the sense of smell and it is a disputed question whether it depends on a chemical or a physical process. The substances which produce the sensation are either in a gaseous condition or they are infinitesimal in size. They certainly must have weight, although nobody has been able to weigh them. "A nonvolatile substance," says the U. S. Bureau of Standards, "cannot have an odor, because none of it can get to the nose. As the sensation of odor is caused by minute amounts of the odorous substance reaching the nose, obviously the substance must be evaporating. In other words, it is losing weight, and what reaches the nose has some weight, however little." The remarkable fineness of the particles producing odor is demonstrated by a simple experiment. Air conveying odor is filtered through a tube packed with cotton wool and inserted into the nose. Notwithstanding the packed cotton wool, the smell is discernible. One scientist estimates that the particles must be less than 1/100,000 of an inch in diameter in order to pass through the cotton wool packed in the tube. A grain of musk will scent a room for years, and if it is then weighed no appreciable loss of weight can be detected. The smell of camphor can be detected when mixed with water in a proportion of one part of camphor to 400,000 of water. Vanilla is also very pungent and can be recognized when mixed in water in the proportion of one to 10,000,000.

Did Columbus die in prison?

Christopher Columbus did not die in prison, as many seem to suppose. Neither did he die in extreme poverty. The oft-repeated story that he died in utter destitution is a legend which has no foundation in fact. His will and other evidence indicate that he possessed considerable wealth at the time of his death at Valladolid in 1506. The great explorer was disappointed because he was neglected by the court, but he was not destitute.

How did April-fooling originate?

April 1 is peculiar in that it is a day consecrated to practical joking. It has long been customary to fool friends and acquaintances on this day by playing practical jokes on them and sending them on foolish errands. The victim of such jokes is called an April Fool and the day is known as All Fools' Day or April Fools' Day. Numerous theories have been suggested to account for the origin of the custom, none of them, however, being very satisfactory. April-fooling, it would seem, is of considerable antiquity. Similar festivities in the springtime have been popular in different parts of the world since the dawn of history. The Romans played burlesque tricks on February 17, the Feast of Fools, known as *festum stultorium* in Latin. This burlesque festival was revived during the Middle Ages and often celebrated even in the churches on New Year's Day. Similar practical jokes are played on friends by the Hindus during the celebration of the Huli festival, which ends March 31. One writer supposes that the Huli festival was started in memory of Noah's mistake in sending forth the dove before the waters of the flood had subsided. Be that as it may, one of the chief features of the Huli is the sending of persons on fools' errands. But, assuming that April-fooling is related to the fun-making at these once almost universal festivals held near the spring equinox, the exact origin of our April Fools' Day still remains inadequately explained. April Fool practices in England did not acquire their present form until about the beginning of the seventeenth century. It is commonly supposed that the English and Germans borrowed the custom from the French, who call an April Fool *un poisson d'avril,* an April fish, which may allude to the general voraciousness of fish in the spring, the fact that an April fish would be young and therefore easily caught, or to the fact that in that month the sun leaves the zodiacal sign of the Fish. This has led many to suppose that April Fools' Day originated with the change of calendar in France in 1564. When the Gregorian was substituted for the Julian calendar New Year's Day was changed from March 25 to January 1. Formerly the new year festivities lasted eight days, beginning March 25 and reaching their highest point April 1, which was set apart especially for giving presents and making calls. Possibly, it is argued, the celebration on the old date was converted into burlesque after the new date was adopted. No importance is attached to the theory that April Fool was originally suggested by the medieval miracle plays, many of which showed Jesus being sent from Annas to Caiaphas, from Caiaphas to Pilate, from Pilate to Herod, and from Herod back to Pilate.

What is the Domesday Book?

Domesday Book is a digest of a survey of England ordered by William the Conqueror in 1085 to ascertain and record the fiscal rights of the king. This survey, it is supposed, was modeled after a similar one made by Alfred the Great. Domesday Book is in Latin and consists of two volumes, one considerably larger than the other. The smaller deals with the three eastern counties and the other with the rest of England minus the more northern counties. Commissioners visited each county and used the hundred as a unit in gathering information. Each entry in the register was made upon the verdict of a jury of twelve men, six Normans and six English. When digested and written down in Domesday Book the data were arranged according to the names of the landowners. Most of the work deals with the valuation of rural estates, the chief source of national wealth at that time. The acreage of pasture, timber and arable land is generally indicated. In some counties the number of tenants, cottagers and slaves is included, and often water-mills, salt-pans and fisheries are enumerated. Livestock is listed only in the smaller volume. Although the reckoning is rather crude and confused, the volumes incidentally contain a great store of personal, political, ecclesiastical and social history of that period. They supply the basis for many land deeds, and in tracing genealogies Domesday Book is to England what the Mayflower Log is to America. Originally the book was called "the Book of Winchester," after the city where it was kept, but in the twelfth century, during the reign of Henry II, it was already referred to as Domesday or Doomsday Book, supposedly because, like the day of judgment, there was no appeal from the arbitrament of its record.

Can horses sleep while standing?

Horses have the power of sleeping while standing. Their legs are provided with muscular mechanisms which cause them to lock, as it were, and permit the animals to rest somewhat as if they were standing on stilts. When a standing horse is unconscious there is no direct brain control over the muscles essential to the maintenance of an erect posture. The muscles in the legs, back and chest are controlled by the reflex actions of the spinal cord. In a similar manner a bird sleeping on a swaying limb maintains a reflex balance while its consciousness is in abeyance. Horses sleeping while standing occasionally, though rarely, fall down. More often certain muscles in the forelegs relax suddenly and the horse knuckles over on to the fetlocks and then immediately catches itself. Horses sometimes go for months without lying down. It is astonishing how little sleep they require. This is true also of other Herbivora, including elephants. An Indian elephant will feed eighteen or twenty hours and then rest and sleep only one or two. It is said that they have been known to remain standing even after they were dead. When horses lie down to sleep their eyes usually remain open or partly open and they sleep so lightly that they are awakened by the faintest sound. They seldom lie long in the same position because their great weight cramps their muscles and prevents the under lung from functioning.

What does *Amerind* mean?

Amerind is a telescopic word composed of the first syllables of *American* and *Indian* and is a general term employed to designate the races of man who inhabited the New World before the arrival of Europeans. It was suggested in 1899 by J. W. Powell, director of the Bureau of American Ethnology, who advocated it as a convenient substitute for the numerous awkward and inappropriate names usually applied to the aborigines of America. In 1900 Dr. W. J. McGee published an article in the journal of the Anthropological Institute of Great Britain in which he made a plea for the general adoption of *Amerind*. Delegates who attended the International Congress of Americanists at New York in 1902 discussed the merits of the new term at considerable length. Since then *Amerind* has won its way into both scientific and popular literature. It is pronounced *am-er-ind*, with the accent on the first syllable. *American Indian* is regarded as too cumbersome by many writers, while simply *Indian* leads to confusion with the name of the inhabitants of the East Indies.

How did Coney Island get its name?

Coney Island, which is noted for its amusement resorts, is a strip of land on Long Island about nine miles southeast of the Battery. It is about five miles in length and ranges in width from a few hundred feet to three-fourths of a mile. The island is separated from the mainland by Gravesend Bay, Sheepshead Bay and a narrow tidal inlet known as Coney Island Creek. How the island received its present name is not known for certain. In his *History of the State of New York*, published in 1853, John Romeyn Brodhead says that "Coney Island was patented to Gysbert op Dyck on the 24th of May, 1644." For more than two centuries it was considered a worthless waste and produced nothing but weeds and brush. For this reason many suppose that the name of the island arose from the fact that it once abounded in rabbits, *coney* being an old English name for rabbit. In the Indian release of 1650 the island is called *Narioch,* which is a Massachuset Indian word meaning a point of land. With reference to Dutch place names in New York, Judge Egbert Benson made the following statement in a *Memoir* read before the New York Historical Society in 1816: "To an island immediately westward of it [Barren Island] they gave the name of Conyn's Island; Coney Island; *Conyn,* a Dutch surname still remaining among us; from the name *Coney,* there are already symptoms of the beginning of a tradition that it once abounded in rabbits." *The Origin of Certain Place Names in the United States,* prepared for the U. S. Geological Survey by Henry Gannett and printed in 1905 by the Government Printing Office, contains the following: *"Coney;* island at the extremity of Long Island, New York, which is said by some to have been so named because of the numbers of rabbits there. Another theory ascribes it to the winds having driven the sand into truncated cones. It appears, however, to have been originally called Congu, which suggests another derivation." *Congu,* in Gannett's statement, seems to be an error for Conyn. The U. S. Geographic Board investigated the subject and prepared the following statement for the author: "The Board has ascertained from Dutch publications that the name Coney Island, as applied to an island at the entrance to New York Harbor, was given to it because of the finding of rabbits on the island in the early days. In a *Sea Atlas of Nieu Nederland,* written by J. van Keilen and published in Amsterdam in 1682 this island is marked *Konyen Eyland.* On a map of *Manatus Gelegen op de noot Rivier,* 1639, the name is spelled *Conyni Eyland.* The Dutch word for rabbit is *konijn* or *konyen.* Therefore, Henry Gannett's theory that it means rabbit island may be literally correct." These citations, however, do not disprove Benson's statement that the name of the island is derived from the family name Conyn. There appears to be no foundation to the theory, advanced by some authorities, that the name of the island is derived from *konooh,* an Indian word meaning bear. Nor is there any etymological evidence to support the theory that Coney Island was originally called Coleman's Island, from the fact that John Coleman, or Colman, one of Henry Hudson's men, was killed in that vicinity by an Indian arrow.

Do Catholics kiss the Pope's foot?

Formerly Catholics who were presented to the Pope regularly saluted him by kissing a cross embroidered on his slipper. At present Catholics usually salute the Pope by kneeling and kissing the ring on his right hand. Kissing the Pontiff's foot is reserved for special occasions. According to the *New Catholic Dictionary,* published in 1929, it is "a salute of respect in solemn papal Mass, at the *veneration* of the Pope by cardinals, and in a private audience." The *Catholic Encyclopedia* says that the custom of kissing the Pope's foot existed as early as the eighth century and is the characteristic act of reverence by which the faithful do honor to his holiness as the vicar of Christ. Non-Catholics are received as they would be by a temporal sovereign. When President Wilson paid a visit of courtesy to the Vatican in 1919 he neither knelt nor kissed the Pope's ring. The President of the United States simply advanced toward the Pope with body and head erect, and the Pope, with both hands extended, came forward to greet him. Even Catholic sovereigns and Catholics of high rank may be received in this manner unless they desire to express their devotion to the Roman see in a particular manner by kissing the Pope's ring.

What is the oldest institution of higher learning under the American flag?

The University of Santo Tomás at Manila, Philippine Islands, is the oldest institution of learning situated on territory under the jurisdiction of the American flag. It was established in 1611 by Dominican missionaries and has been operated continuously ever since under Catholic auspices. Harvard University, founded in 1636, has been operated continuously longer than any other institution of learning in the continental United States. The College of William and Mary, founded at Williamsburg, Virginia, in 1693, is regarded as the second oldest institution of learning in the United States proper and the third on soil under the jurisdiction of the

United States, although college activities at William and Mary were suspended for several years during the Revolutionary and Civil wars. Yale University, established in 1701, comes next in point of age.

Is Amsterdam or The Hague capital of The Netherlands?

Amsterdam is the *legal* capital of The Netherlands; The Hague is the *actual* capital. Most American reference works give The Hague as the capital of Holland. It is the seat of the national government and the regular residence of the sovereign, as well as of all foreign diplomats accredited to the government of The Netherlands. The Dutch constitution, however, recognizes only Amsterdam as the legal capital of the nation and formerly it was the seat of government. Under the constitution the sovereign must spend at least eight days each year in Amsterdam and all royal baptisms, marriages and coronations must take place in that city. The Dutch have no difficulty in regarding Amsterdam as the capital of their country because it is their chief commercial city. In the United States *capital* is applied to a seat of government irrespective of its relative size, while in many European countries the term is applied to the metropolis or most important city, whether or not it is the seat of government. The Dutch point of view is illustrated by the following comment made by the counselor of the Royal Netherland Legation at Washington in a letter to the author : "Amsterdam is the capital of The Netherlands. The Hague is the sovereign's residence as well as the seat of government." In America The Hague is called the capital of The Netherlands because it is the seat of government, just as Albany is called the capital of New York State and Washington the capital of the United States. Many Europeans regard New York City as the American capital.

What causes the London fogs?

The famous London fogs, like most inland fogs, are caused by the cooling of humid surface air to a relatively low temperature. This occurs on clear nights and when there is practically no wind. Ordinary fog consists of tiny drops of water like fine spray and is precisely the same thing as cloud except it is near the ground instead of high in the air. Town fogs, such as those over London, are denser because they consist of a mixture of moisture, dust, smoke, soot and chimney gases. Clear nights and the absence of wind are atmospheric conditions which have the double effect of producing fog and causing smoke to hover over the city. The millions of particles in the air serve as centers upon which droplets of moisture condense, just as invisible moisture in the atmosphere condenses on the sides of a pitcher of cold water in hot weather. Some of the tiny drops may condense on invisible electrified atoms of the gases of the air. That the formation of all fog is some kind of electrical phenomenon has long been suspected by many scientists, and it may be that all the nuclei and particles are somewhat electrified. Many investigators believe that the fog particles are prevented from evaporating by an oily film produced by smoke; but, according to the U. S. Weather Bureau, the existence of this film has not been definitely established. The London fogs have been decreasing in number in recent years, due undoubtedly to the introduction of electric and gas stoves and heating plants. Now the dense fogs that enshroud London a day or two in late November or early December may not be repeated during the remainder of the winter. These fogs, however, are still a serious problem. Often they are so dense that objects are indistinguishable only a few feet away. Automobile and bus drivers are compelled to proceed slowly behind men carrying lanterns. Such a fog is said to be a *pea-souper*.

Does the United States send diplomats to all nations?

The United States exchanges diplomatic representatives with all important independent nations, unless there is some specific reason for not doing so. In the early days of the Federal Government we exchanged diplomatic agents with only a few nations; now nearly every country of the world is represented at Washington. "The policy of this Government," says the Department of State in a letter to the author, "has been to establish diplomatic representation in foreign countries commensurate with the needs of international intercourse and promotion and protection of American interests. The growth of diplomatic representation throughout the world is due largely to the closer relations among nations." It sometimes happens, however, that we are at peace with a country whose government we do not officially *recognize,* and consequently there is no exchange of diplomatic agents. At present we have more than fifty ambassadors and ministers stationed at the various capitals of the world. Of course some countries are not politically or commercially important enough to justify the maintenance of resident ministers or even consuls. For instance, the American ambassador to Belgium is also minister to the grand duchy of Luxemburg, and the American consul at Florence, Italy, is also consul at San Marino, capital of the tiny republic of the same name. The practice of exchanging resident diplomats grew out of the commercial dealings between European countries during the fifteenth and sixteenth centuries. It was unknown to ancient nations, who sent ambassadors to foreign countries only upon special missions.

Which is correct, *Serbia* or *Servia*?

Serbia is now the accepted English form of the name of the Balkan kingdom which became part of Jugoslavia after the World War. Before the outbreak of the war *Servia* was the favorite spelling of this name in America. In fact on February 2, 1897, the U. S. Geographic Board adopted that spelling and it was followed by the Department of State. But *Servia* was objectionable to the inhabitants of that country because of its analogy with Latin *servus*, meaning slave, and because the Slavic spelling of the name in Latin characters is *Srba* or *Srbija*. Accordingly, on March 3, 1915, the Geographic Board reversed its earlier decision in favor of *Serbia*.

Where is Columbus buried?

There is a controversy as to the present location of the remains of Christopher Columbus. He was originally buried at Valladolid, Spain, where he died May 20, 1506. Several years later his remains were removed to a convent in Seville. But in his will Columbus had asked to be buried at Santo Domingo, the oldest city in the New World founded by Europeans, and accordingly, sometime between 1536 and 1541, his body was transferred to the cathedral in that city. Santo Domingo was threatened with British invasion in 1655 and the archbishop of the island ordered every external trace of Columbus's tomb effaced, lest it should be desecrated by the enemy. Only twenty-eight years later the synod of Santo Domingo declared that the exact location of the grave was already a matter of tradition. When Spain ceded the island to France in 1795 the Spanish authorities ordered the remains of Columbus taken to Havana in order to keep them under the Spanish flag. The next year bones believed to be those of Columbus were exhumed and entombed in Cuba. Those who had charge of the work found no inscription, tablet or other mark of identification on the casket and their only guide was the local tradition. There was a rumor at the time that the remains removed from the cathedral were not those of the great navigator. Spain lost Cuba in the Spanish-American War and the supposed remains of Columbus in the Cuban capital were taken up and transferred to the cathedral in Seville, where they still rest. Many investigators, however, maintain that a mistake was made in 1796 and that the remains of Columbus were never removed from Santo Domingo. In 1877, while the cathedral in that city was being repaired, excavations made under the direction of Father Francisco Bellini revealed a lead casket containing inscriptions and other evidence tending to prove that it contained the remains of Columbus. This casket had not been disturbed in 1796. Those who believe that it contained the remains of the First Admiral hold that the bones previously removed were those of Columbus's son Diego, or some other member of the family. The evidence is of such nature that the question will probably never be conclusively settled and both Spain and Santo Domingo will no doubt continue to claim to be the last resting place of the remains of the great discoverer.

Did the Supreme Court ever decide that the United States is a Christian nation?

The statement is often made that the Supreme Court of the United States once rendered a decision that this is a Christian nation. Strictly speaking, the Supreme Court never made such a decision. Whether the United States was a Christian nation was not the point at issue, and the declaration in the opinion that "this is a Christian nation" was merely dictum incidentally given in deciding the main point. The case in question was *Trinity Church v. United States.* E. Walpole Warren, a subject and resident of England was employed by the Church of the Holy Trinity in New York City to come to the United States as its rector and pastor. The point was raised that this was a violation of the alien contract labor act of 1885, which prohibited the importation or migration of aliens under contract to perform labor in the United States. The Federal Circuit Court held that the contract was in violation of the statute and rendered judgment accordingly. This decision was reversed by the Supreme Court, which admitted that the case came within the letter of the statute, but denied that it came within its spirit and the intent of the framers. Associate Justice David J. Brewer rendered the opinion on February 29, 1892. "No purpose of action against religion," declared Justice Brewer, "can be imputed to any legislation, State or National, because this is a religious people." After citing many declarations in our Federal and State laws to bear out his assertion, the justice said:

If we pass beyond these matters to a view of American life as expressed by its laws, its business, its customs and its society, we find everywhere a clear recognition of the same truth. Among other matters note the following: The form of oath universally prevailing, concluding with an appeal to the Almighty; the custom of opening sessions of all deliberative bodies and most conventions with prayer; the prefatory words of all wills, "In the name of God, amen;" the laws respecting the observance of the Sabbath, with the general cessation of all secular business, and the closing of courts, legislatures, and other similar public assemblies on that day; the churches and church organizations which abound in every city, town, and hamlet; the multitude of charitable organizations existing everywhere under Christian auspices; the gigantic missionary associations with general support, and aiming to establish Christian missions in every quarter of the globe. These, and many other matters which might be noticed, add a volume of unofficial declarations to the mass of organic utterances that *this is a Christian nation*. In the face of all these, shall it be believed that a Congress of the United States intended to make it a misdemeanor for a church of this country to contract for the services of a Christian minister residing in another nation?

The United States is a Christian nation only in the sense that Christianity is the prevailing faith of its citizens and its public opinion is influenced to a considerable extent by the teachings of that religion. Neither God nor Christianity is mentioned in the Federal Constitution, and Amendment I of that document provides that "Congress shall make no law respecting an establishment of religion, or prohibiting the free exercise thereof." Clause 3, Article

VI of the same document says: "No religious test shall ever be required as a qualification to any office or public trust under the United States." Accordingly, a Mohammedan, Hindu, Jew or other non-Christian is Constitutionally eligible to any Federal office, including the Presidency, provided he is otherwise qualified. In 1796 President Washington negotiated and the Senate presided over by Vice President Adams confirmed a treaty with Tripoli which explicitly declared that "The Government of the United States is not in any sense founded on the Christian religion." This was intended to give the Mohammedans of northern Africa assurance that the United States was not prejudiced against them on religious grounds.

What State touches only one other State?

Maine is the only State in the Union that adjoins only one other State. It is cut off entirely from the rest of the Union by New Hampshire. The honor of being bounded by the greatest number of other States is divided between Tennessee and Missouri, each being touched by eight other States. Tennessee is bounded by Missouri, Arkansas, Mississippi, Alabama, Georgia, North Carolina, Virginia, and Kentucky. Missouri is bounded by Tennessee, Kentucky, Illinois, Iowa, Nebraska, Kansas, Oklahoma, and Arkansas.

What was Patrick Henry's religion?

There is a general impression that Patrick Henry was Irish in nationality and Roman Catholic in religion. He was neither. The Virginia orator and statesman was of Scotch and Welsh descent; he was baptized in the Established Church of England and he adhered to the Episcopal faith throughout life. His mother was a convert to Presbyterianism, while his father, a native of Scotland, was a member of the Established Church. The notion that Henry was of Irish extraction is no doubt due to his first name.

How did *hobo* originate?

Hobo is believed to have originated in the Western part of the United States a decade or two after the Civil War. The term became common in everyday speech after 1890. In the *Contemporary Review* for August, 1891, a writer said: "The tramp's name for himself is Hobo, plural Hoboes." Now, however, *hobos* is regarded as the preferable plural form. *The Popular Science Journal* contained the following sentence in 1896: "The tramp can scarcely be distinguished from the dyed-in-the-wool hoboe." How the term originated is one of the unsolved puzzles of American etymology. The following explanation was offered in 1928 by Herman Gaul, a Chicago delegate to the International Convention of Hobos at Minneapolis: "In the old days when most of the boys were working in the agricultural sections of the West they were referred to as just *boys*. Then, to distinguish them from other workers, the name of one of their tools, the hoe, was applied to them and they became *hoe-boys*. From that it was only one step to *hoboes*." This theory is improbable. It is more likely that the term arose from the familiar and friendly salutation of the road, *Ho, Boy*, which is a corruption of *Hello, Boy*. The following statement by H. R. Jeffrey, of Delhi, Iowa, was published in *Dialect Notes*, the organ of the American Dialect Society, in 1920: "The word [Hobo] is entered in the dictionaries as of uncertain etymology. The following story of its origin is vouched for by a relative of mine who was working on the Oregon Short Line railroad in the 1880's. The mail carriers on the Oregon Short Line used the call *Ho, boy*, when they were delivering mail. Gradually these men came to be called *Hoboys*. Then those who traveled along the tracks, not carrying mail, came to be so called. In its final stage of development the *y* was dropped and the word used indiscriminately to designate vagrants." This is a fair sample of dozens of similar theories on record, all of which are unsupported by etymological evidence. But it is quite probable that *hobo* did originate among the migratory workers in the West and that it was suggested by the salutation *Ho, boy*. Another theory deserves brief mention here. One writer suggests that *hobo* may have sprung from *Ho-Boy* or *Haut Boy*, which was defined by John Farmer in 1889 as "a New York night scavenger." John Russell Bartlett defined this term as "a nightman, New York." Needless to say, evidence is lacking to establish a real relationship between the terms. Even the meaning of *hobo* is the subject of controversy. The term seems to connote more of romance and a good time and less of poverty and hardship than *tramp* does. The *New Standard Dictionary* defines *hobo* as "an idle, shiftless, wandering workman, ranking scarcely above the tramp." *Webster's New International*

Dictionary says a hobo is "a professional tramp; one who spends his life traveling from place to place, especially by stealing rides on trains and begging for a living." James Eads How, the "millionaire hobo," described members of his order as "migratory workers looking for employment." George Rothwell Brown, the Washington columnist, defined *hobo* as "a migratory worker looking for employment and praying to God he won't find it."

What is the oldest city in the United States?

St. Augustine, Florida, is the oldest city in the United States proper founded by Europeans. The Spanish settled on the site in 1565 and it has been continuously occupied ever since. Santa Fe, New Mexico, is the second oldest city. It was founded by the Spanish about 1605 on the site of a deserted Indian pueblo. Santo Domingo, capital of the Dominican Republic, is the oldest existing settlement of white people in the New World. It was founded in 1496. Panama, capital of the Republic of Panama, was founded in 1519 and is the oldest settlement of white people on the mainland of the Americas. Of course there are older cities of native origin. It is believed that Cuzco, Peru, was founded in the tenth century A. D. and has been inhabited continuously ever since. Mexico City is probably the oldest city on the North American mainland. According to Aztec tradition, it was founded in 1325.

How did Mother Goose originate?

The name Mother Goose became associated with nursery rimes and jingles in a roundabout way. In 1697 Charles Perrault, noted French author, published a collection of fairy tales entitled *Histoires ou contes du temps passé avec des moralités*. On the frontispiece was pictured an old woman engaged in spinning and telling stories to a man, a girl, a boy, and a cat. A placard near the picture says *Contes de ma Mère l'Oye*, which translated means "Tales of My Mother Goose." This book did not contain nursery rimes at all, but was a collection of wonder and folk tales for children, including *Little Red Riding Hood*. Only three of the contributions were original with Perrault. He probably selected Mother Goose as the imaginary relater of the tales because she was already at that time proverbial in French folklore for incredible tales. The term

Mother Goose, according to Andrew Lang, was employed in 1650 in Lorret's *La Muse Historique*. Perrault's book was very popular at the court of Louis XIV, and apparently a translation in English was published in London by Robert Samber in 1729. Ten years later—November 12, 1739—an advertisement in a bookseller's catalogue stated: "Mother Goose's Stories of Past Times, writ purposely for the Innocent Intertainment of Children, and yet are so contrived by the Author, that not only children, but those of Maturity have found in them uncommon Pleasure and Delight: As an Instance of which the famous Perault [sic] was so taken with them that he made the Morals to them himself, knowing they tended to the Incouragement of virtue, and the Depression of vice; the former of which is ever rewarded in them, and the latter ever punished." Mother Goose in connection with collections of English nursery rimes was undoubtedly borrowed from Perrault's book. According to a common story which has never been positively proved, a book of nursery rimes entitled *Songs for the Nursery, or Mother Goose's Melodies for Children* was published in Boston by Thomas Fleet in 1719, ten years before Perrault's book was published in English. Fleet in 1715 had married Elizabeth, daughter of Isaac and Elizabeth Foster Vergoose, or Goose as the name was generally simplified. The book published by Fleet, according to the story, was a collection of rimes and jingles which his widowed mother-in-law was in the habit of singing to his oldest child, and *Mother Goose* in the title referred to Mrs. Isaac Goose or Vergoose. There is positive proof that Thomas Fleet printed *Verses for Children* in 1719, although no known copy of the work is extant and we have no means of knowing the exact nature of its contents. If *Mother Goose* appeared in the subtitle of Fleet's book, as it may have, it was in all probability borrowed from Perrault, whose work was then famous in France. Still it is possible that the fact that his mother-in-law's name was Goose may have induced him to make use of it in his subtitle. Be that as it may, some English or American publisher undoubtedly brought out a book of nursery rimes early in the eighteenth century with *Mother Goose* in the title. It has been suggested that a Boston printer would hardly bring out a book of such trivial rimes in 1719. We do know, however, that in 1780 John Newberry of London published a little book entitled

Mother Goose's Melody, Solace for the Cradle, in Two Parts. "Part One," said the title, "contains the celebrated songs and lullabies of the good old nurses calculated to amuse children and to incite them to sleep." The material in this Mother Goose book was entirely different from that in Perrault's fairy-tale book, of which it was not a translation, as often carelessly stated, although translations of Perrault's work were then on sale. The name *Mother Goose* is not native to English folklore, but most of the original Mother Goose rimes were derived from that source, such, for instance, as those about Old King Cole, Simple Simon, and Little Jack Horner. Like the fables attributed to Æsop, the rimes were gathered from widely scattered sources.

Is the bat a bird or an animal?

Bats are animals, not birds. They suckle their young at the breast and are classed by zoologists as flying mammals. There was a time, however, before the habits of these creatures were understood, when bats were actually classified as birds. There are more than two hundred and fifty species and subspecies of bats in North America alone. Some of the tropical species are blood-sucking vampires, and others are fruit-eaters, but nearly all the bats of the United States and farther north are insectivorous. Usually the female gives birth to one young, although cases of twins are not uncommon. The young bats cling about their mother's breast where they are nourished by milk from two nipples. "Bats never make any nests or even attempt to fix over the crannies where they hide and where the little bats are born," says one writer. "These helpless little things are not left at home at the mercy of foraging rats and mice. When the old bat flits off into the twilight the youngsters often go with her, clinging about her neck. At times she deposits them on the branch of a tree where they hang, sheltered by the leaves."

What is a common-law marriage?

A common-law marriage is a marriage by mutual consent alone, without license or ceremony of any kind, either ecclesiastical or civil. Unions of this kind are said to be consensual, that is, existing merely by virtue of consent or acquiescence. Common-law mar-

219

riages, without either license or ceremony, are validated by the courts in most jurisdictions if proper proof is submitted, or if children and property are involved. For instance, Chapter 199, Section 12, of the New Jersey act of 1912 concerning marriages provides: "Nothing in this act contained shall be deemed or taken to render any common-law or other marriage, otherwise lawful, invalid by reason of the failure to take out a license as herein provided." It is erroneous to suppose, however, that the law recognizes a common-law wife or husband as distinguished from a legal one. The term *common-law* in this relation is employed merely to distinguish what is known as a *simple contract marriage* from a ceremonial marriage. For instance, in many States if a man and woman live together for one day under an agreement to be man and wife, they are legally married, although they may obtain no license and have no ceremony performed. On the other hand, if they live together for forty years without such an agreement, they are lover and mistress in the eyes of the law and as such are subject to the penalties provided. Whether a man and woman are to be regarded as common-law husband and wife depends on their ability to produce evidence that the necessary agreement existed. The evidence may consist of writings, declarations, or merely the conduct of the parties.

Do trees die of old age?

No close parallel exists between trees and animals in respect to maturity and longevity. Trees do not die of old age in the same sense that human beings do. Some authorities are inclined to believe that death of trees results only from accidents, disease or other *unnatural* causes. Few trees are permitted to die of "old age." They are generally killed by storms, insects, blights or other enemies. Most trees die of disease, and the disease usually takes the form of decay in the trunk, which shuts off the water and food supply from the soil. Still there is some reason for believing that trees do have a sort of life cycle or longevity period and that they would grow old and die as the result of the ravages of time even if not destroyed by unnatural or artificial means. Of course this life cycle, which is much longer in some species than in others, is very indefinite and cannot be calculated with any degree of accuracy.

A human being reaches his maximum height at a comparatively early age. In fact in later years his height often decreases somewhat. But a tree continues to grow as long as it is alive, although after it reaches a certain size, depending on the species and other factors, the rate of growth slows down. Some trees live and continue to grow for thousands of years.

Does the Bible say that angels have wings?

Nowhere in the New Testament are angels spoken of as having wings, although in his vision on Patmos John the Apostle "heard an angel flying through the midst of heaven" (*Revelation 8: 13; 14: 6*). The popular notion that faithful Christians after death are transformed into angels with two wings is hardly justified by any passage in the Bible. Isaiah describes seraphim with six wings each (*Isaiah 6: 2*), and the cherubim which Ezekiel saw had four wings (*Ezekiel 1: 11*). The cherubs of gold at the ends of the mercy seat in the Ark of the Covenant (*Exodus 25: 20*), as well as those of olive wood in Solomon's temple (*I Kings 6: 24*), had two wings each. These latter references to images of cherubs are the only instances in which angels of any order are referred to in the Bible as two-winged creatures. Some scholars suppose that the Hebrews borrowed their conceptions of winged seraphim and cherubim from the Assyrians, who depicted winged men with the heads of hawks on the walls of their buildings, and whose palaces were guarded by winged bulls and lions.

What is the Australian ballot?

Australian ballot is the name given to the ballot used in a common system of secret voting. The name arose from the fact that the essential features of the system were first introduced in 1858 in South Australia, one of the states of the Australian Commonwealth. A system modeled after that used in South Australia was adopted in England in 1872. In the United States the Australian ballot was first employed in local elections at Louisville, Kentucky, in 1888, and in the same year Massachusetts adopted it for all State elections, beginning in 1889. The Australian ballot, in one form or other, was in time adopted by nearly all the States in the Union, and it is still widely employed, although in many places it has been supplanted by voting machines, which retain the essential features of the Australian system. According to the original system used in South Australia, the names of all candidates appeared on the same ballot, which was strictly official, that is, it was compiled, printed and distributed at the polls under the direction of public officials and at public expense. This ballot had a fourfold purpose: to insure absolute secrecy, to protect the voter from outside influence while voting, to facilitate counting the ballots, and to prevent dishonesty in tabulating them. These ends were accomplished to a large extent by giving each voter a separate ballot and compelling him to go alone into a booth where he indicated his choice by making a mark opposite the names of the candidates whom he preferred. The ballot was then folded and dropped into a locked box which was not opened until the ballots were officially counted.

Why do lost persons travel in circles?

It has been noted since ancient times that a lost person almost invariably travels in a circle or spiral. According to the traditional explanation, the legs of an individual vary in length or strength and he takes a slightly longer step with the stronger or longer one. Biologists have measured the legs of numerous persons and have found that one leg is longer and stronger in the average human being. But experiments made in 1928 by Asa A. Schaeffer, professor of zoology at the University of Kansas, indicate that there is no connection between the length and strength of one's legs and the direction he takes when lost. After observing the motions of a single-celled amoeba in the water, Prof. Schaeffer set out to determine why men and animals travel in spiral paths when their senses fail them. He was not entirely successful, but he came to the conclusion that spiral movement is a universal property of living matter in motion. The scientist made hundreds of tests with persons blindfolded. Anybody who has tried to pin the tail on the donkey at parties knows how hard it is for a blindfolded person to find his way. Blindfolded individuals who attempt to walk straight ahead in an open field invariably make a path forming a clock-spring spiral. Some will circle to the right, others to the left, and occasionally one will change from right to left or vice versa, but usually the person will continue in the direction first taken. Further experiments revealed that swimmers and automobile drivers travel in similar spirals when blindfolded. There is a direct relationship, Professor Schaeffer concluded, between the small spirals made by blindfolded persons and the large ones made by lost persons. In both cases the eyes become useless as orientating organs, and the individual is guided in spirals by some steering mechanism, a sort of sixth sense, which takes control when the senses fail. The blind mouse, the single-celled amœba, the lost traveler, the blindfolded swimmer, all seem to be guided by the same spiraling instinct. A wild animal when hard pressed by pursuers runs in circles, probably because fear has paralyzed the orientating power of its senses. Even aviators when blindfolded or lost in a fog have a tendency to fly in circles.

Is food cooked in aluminum utensils injurious to health?

This question, raised soon after cooking utensils were first made of aluminum in 1892, has never been definitely settled. There appears to be no positive evidence that food cooked in aluminum vessels is more injurious to the health than food cooked in vessels of iron or copper. The U. S. Public Health Service, the American Medical Association and several other medical and health organizations have issued statements expressing the opinion that aluminum is not harmful in the minute quantities taken into the stomach with food cooked in aluminum ware. Foods cooked in aluminum vessels, like foods cooked in vessels of iron or copper, undoubtedly dissolve small quantities of the metal. If pure water is boiled in an aluminum kettle for half an hour and then is allowed to stand a sediment is formed. Many people accept this as evidence that the chemical activity of aluminum is very great. As a matter of fact the experiment is no indication that aluminum is particularly soluble, unless the water used is absolutely soft, which is very seldom the case. Mineral compounds in hard water are held in solution by carbonic acid. When the water is boiled the carbonic acid escapes and the minerals precipitate and form the sediment. It is this same process which causes the formation of scale in teakettles and it is independent of the material of which the utensil is composed. A trace of aluminum may dissolve from a freshly scoured utensil and appear in the form of aluminum hydroxide or some other aluminum compound. But it has not been established that these compounds are deleterious to the health. Numerous experiments tend to prove that aluminum salts and other compounds in food do not pass through the walls of the stomach or into the blood. Apparently all aluminum taken into the body is carried off with the fæces. None of the metal was found in the organs of animals used in the experiments, and none of it occurred in the urine. Aluminum, like iron and other metals, is slightly poisonous when injected into the blood, and it is probable that large quantities of aluminum salts would be injurious to the health. But in the ordinary process of cooking the metal does not seem to be attacked sufficiently by food acids to produce an objectionable amount of soluble salts. Delicate chemical tests are necessary to detect the presence of aluminum even in the juices of acid fruits and vegetables cooked for several hours in aluminum utensils. It should be borne in mind that aluminum regularly occurs in many common foods, and frequently it is present in drinking water. The popular charge that there is a direct relation between cooking in aluminum utensils and the prevalence of cancer is also rejected by the Public Health Service as being without proof. "Aluminum," says that Bureau in a letter to the author, "is considered a metal of low toxicity, and we are not acquainted with trustworthy data which indicate that any disease bears a relation to the use of cooking utensils." It may be safely said that at the present time the weight of evidence supports the opinion that health is not adversely affected by eating food cooked in aluminum ware.

Who is Mrs. Grundy?

Mrs. Grundy is an imaginary person who represents the composite opinion of our neighbors. She personifies social propriety and is a very proper and conventional lady who turns up her nose at the slightest violation of etiquette. Those who make a practice of "keeping up with the Joneses" are especially careful to observe her dictates. Mrs. Grundy (she has no first name), was created by Thomas Morton in a play entitled *Speed the Plough,* originally produced in 1798 at Covent Garden, London. She does not appear bodily in the play, but Farmer Ashfield's wife continually refers to the social pretensions of the Grundy family. Dame Ashfield's conversation is interlarded with cattish comments such as the following: "Farmer Grundy's wheat brought five shillings a quarter more than ours did." "Dame Grundy's butter was quite the crack of the market." "I wonder, Tummas [her husband], what Mrs. Grundy will say?" "Now Tummas is gone, I'll tell you such a story about Mrs. Grundy." "The Miss Grundys, genteel as they think themselves, would be glad to snap at him." "I'll go to church in a stuff one—and let Mrs. Grundy turn up her nose as much as she please." This continual harping on Mrs. Grundy and her affairs gets on Farmer Ashfield's nerves. "Be quiet, woolye?" he growls, "aleways ding, dinging Dame Grundy into my ears—what will Mrs. Grundy zay? What will Mrs. Grundy think?" His spouse denies that she envies Mrs. Grundy. "What d'ant thee let her aloane then?" the farmer demands. "I do verily think when thee goest to t'other world, the virst question thee't ax'il be, if Mrs. Grundy's there." But Dame Ashfield brings the subject up again: "Oh, Tummas, had you seen how Mrs. Grundy looked!" "Dom Mrs. Grundy," snaps the exasperated husband.

Where did Senator Vest make his dog speech?

The famous tribute to the dog by George Graham Vest was delivered, not in Congress as often supposed, but in a courtroom at Warrensburg, Johnson County, Missouri, in the fall of 1870, more than eight years before Vest was elected to the United States Senate. Charles Burden owned a foxhound named Old Drum, a hunting dog famed throughout the County for his speed and reliability. One morning Old Drum was found dead near the house of Leonidas Hornsby. Circumstantial evidence pointed to Hornsby as the slayer of the foxhound and Burden sued him in the justice of peace court for $150, the maximum sum recoverable under the law in such a case. After considerable delay the case, officially docketed as *Burden vs. Hornsby,* was appealed to the State Circuit Court. Burden was represented at the final trial by Colonel Wells Blodgett, a lawyer of distinction. The man charged with having shot Old Drum was represented by Thomas Crittenden, afterwards Governor of Missouri, and Francis Cockrell, later Vest's colleague in the United States Senate. It so happened that Vest, then practicing law at the neighboring county seat of Sedalia, was attending court in connection with another case. Blodgett persuaded his client to employ the distinguished ex-Confederate Senator as special counsel. Judge Foster Wright insisted that the case should go to the jury that day, and a recess was taken until after supper. Meanwhile word went out that George Vest was going to speak in a dog case. The courtroom was packed with people when the kerosene lamps were lighted and the judge took his seat on the bench. Blodgett made the opening speech. He was followed by Crittenden and Cockrell, who knew every man on the jury personally and were confident of victory. They spoke lightly of Old Drum and said it was ridiculous to make so much ado about a dog of small value. It was a fatal mistake. When Vest arose he made no reference whatever to the evidence or law involved, but concentrated his entire oratorical artillery upon a vindication of the slandered dog. He said:

Gentlemen of the jury, the best friend a man has in this world may turn against him and become his enemy. His son or daughter whom he has reared with loving care may prove ungrateful. Those who are nearest and dearest to us—those whom we trust with our happiness and good name—may become traitors in their faith. The money that a man has he may lose. It flies away from him, perhaps when he needs it most. A man's reputation may be sacrificed in a moment of ill-considered action. The people who are prone to fall on their knees to do us honor when success is with us may be the first to throw the stone of malice when failure settles its cloud upon our heads. The one absolute, unselfish friend that man can have in this selfish world—the one that never proves ungrateful or treacherous—is his dog.

Gentlemen of the jury, a man's dog stands by him in prosperity and poverty, in health and sickness. He will sleep on the cold ground, where the wintry winds blow, and the snow drives fiercely, if only he can be near his master's side. He will kiss the hand that has no food to offer; he will lick the wounds and sores that come in encounter with the roughness of the world. He guards the sleep of his pauper master as if he were a prince. When all other friends desert, he remains. When riches take wings and reputation falls to pieces, he is as constant in his love as the sun in its journey through the heavens. If fortune drives the master forth an outcast in the world, friendless and homeless, the faithful dog asks no higher privilege than that of accompanying him to guard against danger, to fight against his enemies. And when the last scene of all comes, and death takes the master in its embrace, and his body is laid away in the cold ground, no matter if all other friends pursue their way, there by his graveside will the noble dog be found, his head between his paws, his eyes sad but open in alert watchfulness, faithful and true even to death.

Unfortunately the rest of the speech was not preserved. "I have often heard him," said Governor Crittenden long afterwards, "but never have I heard from his lips, nor from the lips of any other man, so graceful, so impetuous and so eloquent a speech as this before the jury in that dog case. He seemed to recall from history all the instances where dogs had displayed intelligence and fidelity to man. He quoted more lines of history and poetry about dogs than I had supposed had been written. He capped the monument he had erected by quoting from the Bible about the dog which soothed the sores of the beggar Lazarus as he sat at the rich man's gate, and by giving Motley's graphic description of how the fidelity of a dog kept William of Orange from falling into the hands of the Duke of Alva. It was as perfect a piece of oratory as was ever heard from pulpit or bar. Court, jury, lawyers and audience were entranced. I looked at the jury and saw all were in tears. The foreman wept like one who had just lost his dearest friend. The victory for the other side was complete. I said to Cockrell that we were defeated; that the dog, though dead, had won, and that we had better get out of the courthouse with our client or we would be hanged." No riot followed, but the jury were swept from their feet and returned a verdict for $500, although the plaintiff had asked for only $150. The court reduced the amount to legal limitations and the Drum case was closed.

Whom was Pennsylvania named after?

Strictly speaking, Pennsylvania was not named after its Quaker founder, William Penn, as most people suppose. It was named after his father, Admiral Sir William Penn, who died in 1670. Admiral Penn lent Charles II £16,000 and his son inherited this claim against the crown. In repayment William Penn asked for "a tract of land in America north of Maryland," and in March,

1681, the grant received the king's signature. Penn explained in a personal letter at the time how the name originated. "This day," he wrote to his friend Robert Turner, "my country was confirmed to me under the great seal of England, with large powers and privileges, by the name of Pennsylvania; *a name the King would give it in honor of my father.* I chose *New Wales,* being, as this, a pretty hilly country, but Penn being Welsh for *a head,* as Penmaumoire in Wales, and Penrith in Cumberland, and Penn in Buckinghamshire, the highest land in England, called this Pennsylvania, which is, the high or head woodlands, for I proposed, when the secretary, a Welshman, refused to have it called New Wales, *Sylvania,* and they added *Penn* to it, and though I much opposed it, and went to the King to have it struck out and altered, he said it was past, and would take it upon him; nor could twenty guineas move the under-secretary to vary the name, for fear least it be looked on as vanity in me, and not as a respect in the King, as it truly was, to my father, whom he often mentions with praise." *Silva* is the Latin word meaning a wood or grove. On the Liberty Bell the name of the province is spelled *Pensylvania,* with only one *n* in the first syllable. This was due to a mistake originally made by the English casters of the first Liberty Bell, and the error was perpetuated for sentimental reasons when the bell was recast.

What two Presidents were bachelors when elected?

Two Presidents of the United States were bachelors when elected—James Buchanan and Grover Cleveland. During his first term, however, the latter was married to Frances Folsom, daughter of his former law partner at Buffalo. Therefore Buchanan, the only President who was never married, is known as the Bachelor President. He was the fifteenth President and was Lincoln's predecessor in the White House.

How did *printer's devil* originate?

The newest apprentice in a printing shop is called the printer's devil. He helps the printers, runs errands and does chores around the shop. It is supposed that the name arose from the fact that he frequently became blackened with ink in the days of hand presses. "The Press-man," wrote Joseph Moxon in 1683 in *Me-*

chanical Exercises, "sometimes has a Week-Boy to Take Sheets, as they are Printed off the Tympan: These Boys do in a Printing-House, commonly black and Dawb themselves: whence the workmen do jocosely call them Devils; and sometimes Spirits, and sometimes Flies." Some authorities, however, believe that the name was suggested by a traditional incident at Venice. According to a legend, Aldus Manutius, who became celebrated as a printer in the latter part of the fifteenth and the first part of the sixteenth century, employed a Negro boy as a helper in his shop. The Venetians were not familiar with the colored race and in those days belief in witchcraft was common. Many devout people in the city suspected the Negro boy was an imp or evil genius and began to clamor for an investigation. When the matter came to the attention of Manutius he not only let many citizens examine the boy, but issued a statement to the following effect: "I, Aldus Manutius, printer to the Doge and the Holy Church, have this day made public exposure of the printer's devil. All who think he is not flesh and blood are invited to come and pinch him." There is no evidence that the incident, if it actually happened, was responsible for *printer's devil* as the name for a printer's helper.

Are any two things exactly alike?

So far as science has been able to discover, there are no two objects in the world just exactly alike, no matter whether they are natural or artificial. No two leaves or snowflakes, no two objects manufactured by man, are exactly alike. Scientists believe that even each infinitesimal atom composing the elements differs from all the rest.

Why are maps made with north at the top?

Almost all modern maps and geographical charts are so orientated that north is at the top. Maps with other directions at the top are exceptional. This is a convenient practice based merely on centuries of usage. No scientific principle makes this particular orientation essential. It is probable, says the American Geographical Society, that most of the ancient Greek and Roman map-makers placed east at the top of their maps, that being the direction of the rising sun. As a rule the medieval cartographers of Christendom followed the same custom. Their belief that the original Garden of Eden lay on the eastern borders of the known world supplied a further incentive toward this orientation. Geographers who made maps with east at the top were guided by the same principle that guided architects who planned churches with the altar at the east end. There were occasional exceptions. A map exhibited at the British Museum during the International Geographical Congress in 1921 was orientated with west at the top. It was published at Rome in 1546 and was probably planned by George Lily. However that may be, the draughtsman apparently drew it west and east because he wished to fit the British Isles into an atlas which was wider than it was high. Another map in the same collection was orientated with south at the top. It was made in 1492, before the convention was well established that maps should be made with north up and south down, and it was the natural orientation for a German cartographer to adopt in preparing a map showing the way to Rome from Germany. Strangely enough, orientation toward the south was the general custom among the Arab map-makers of the Middle Ages. The modern custom of orientation toward the north was undoubtedly suggested by Ptolemy, the Greek geographer who lived at Alexandria in the second century. He made his maps with north up and south down. With the revival of Ptolemy's geography during the Renaissance the orientation adopted by him gradually became an established custom in Europe. The custom was further confirmed by the increasing use of meridians and parallels in cartography. North is at the top of the maps of the British Isles made by Matthew Paris in the thirteenth century, and the same orientation was used in sailors' charts dating from about 1300. It was natural that the globe-makers of the sixteenth century should observe the same custom and place the north pole on the upper hemisphere, because that hemisphere contained most of the known land area of the earth.

Are waterspouts composed of fresh or salt water?

Waterspouts at sea are composed chiefly of fresh water, not salt water, as commonly supposed. According to the U. S. Weather Bureau, there are at least two different kinds of waterspouts. One kind starts at the surface of the water, somewhat like dust whirls on hot, dry plains. The other kind, the typical waterspout, starts at a cloud level and burrows down; it is essentially a tornado over water, although it is usually less violent than the average tornado over land. Such a waterspout occurs as a rapidly whirling, funnel-shaped column of air, extending from a storm cloud to a water surface. The axis is visible as a column of water or water vapor. A strong upward indraft beneath the base of the cloud produces the formation, and the air supplying the indraft acquires a rapid rotary motion as it ascends. This produces a decided low pressure in the central axis of the eddy, and the rising air flowing into the column expands as it passes into places of low pressure. This in turn causes the air to cool and become visible by condensation of part of the moisture. Waterspouts usually agitate the water surface violently and appear to draw columns of water to meet the clouds above. This, however, is an illusion. The principal part of the column is not composed of sea water, but moisture from the cloud and from the atmosphere. As a rule, the sea water does not rise more than a few feet from the surface. That such is the case is demonstrated by the fact that when a vessel runs into a waterspout over salt water the ship is drenched with fresh, not salt water. "It is believed," says the Weather Bureau, "that most of the water that falls in a typical waterspout—and in most cases nearly all—is fresh. There is also some salt spray, but this is important in quantity only near the surface." It is popularly supposed that the water of waterspouts is dangerous to large vessels, but it is dangerous only to boats and small craft. The chief danger lies in the wind, the "column of water" being largely imaginary.

How did "All is quiet along the Potomac" originate?

"All is quiet along the Potomac" originated during the first few months of the Civil War and in those days referred to the state of military affairs in the vicinity of Washington. This and similar expressions frequently occur in the official dispatches and newspaper articles of the time. "All is quiet," "All is quiet today," and "All is quiet tonight" were favorite expressions in the telegrams sent to the Secretary of War by General George B. McClellan in 1861 and 1862 while he was in command of the Army of the Potomac. For that reason McClellan is sometimes given as the author of "All is quiet along the Potomac." It is also often attributed to Simon Cameron, Lincoln's first Secretary of War. The expression was further popularized by Ethelinda Eliot Beers ("Ethel Lynn") whose poem entitled *The Picket Guard* was published in the issue of *Harper's Weekly* dated November 30, 1861. This poem was so popular that several persons claimed the authorship. Mrs. Beers republished it in 1879 in a volume entitled *All Quiet Along the Potomac and Other Poems*. The first two stanzas and the last stanza of *The Picket Guard* are as follows:

"All quiet along the Potomac," they say,
    "Except, now and then, a stray picket
Is shot as he walks on his beat to and fro,
    By a rifleman hid in the thicket.
'Tis nothing—a private or two, now and then,
    Will not count in the news of the battle;
Not an officer lost—only one of the men
    Moaning out, all alone, the death-rattle."

All quiet along the Potomac tonight,
    Where the soldiers lie peacefully dreaming;
Their tents, in the rays of the clear autumn moon
    Or the light of the watch-fire, are gleaming.
A tremulous sigh, as the gentle night-wind
    Through the forest leaves softly is creeping;
While stars up above, with their glittering eyes,
    Keep guard—for the army is sleeping.

* * *

All quiet along the Potomac tonight,
    No sound save the rush of the river;
While soft falls the dew on the face of the dead—
    The picket's off duty forever.

What are deeds of derring do?

Feats of derring do are feats of daring and acts of bravery. In this sense *derring do* is largely the result of an error made by Edmund Spenser and copied by Sir Walter Scott and other writers of the romantic school. Literally *derring do* means *daring to do*. Chaucer and other early English writers used the phrase in various forms. In *The Hystory, Sege, and Destruccyon of Troye,* which was written between 1412 and 1420, John Lydgate spelled the phrase *dorryng do*. In the printed edition of 1513, as well as in the edition of 1555, it was spelled *derrynge do*. This apparently misled Spenser, who picked it up and misconstrued it as a noun phrase in his *Shepherd's Calendar,* published in 1579. A note in the glossary explained that the phrase meant "manhood and chevalrie." Later Spenser employed it again in the *Faërie Queene.* In Book II, Canto IV, section 42, the poet wrote:

> So from immortall race he does proceede,
> That mortall hands may not withstand his might,
> Drad for his derring doe and bloody deed;
> For all in blood and spoile is his delight.

Sir Walter Scott revived and accentuated this erroneous usage in *Ivanhoe,* which was published in 1820. In Chapter 29 is this passage: " 'Singular,' he [Ivanhoe] muttered to himself, 'if there be two who can do a deed of such derring-do.' " Scott, in a footnote, gave the meaning of *derring-do* as "desperate courage." Thus, says the Oxford dictionary, by a chain of misunderstandings and errors *derring do* has come to be regarded as a kind of substantive combination, meaning daring feats.

What is the difference between the Great Divide and the Continental Divide?

Divide is a precise geographical term which describes the line, ridge or watershed separating the waters of two drainage systems. The Continental Divide of North America consists of a continuous line extending north and south from the Arctic seas to the boundary between Panama and Colombia. As a general rule, in the United States it follows the most elevated portions of the Rocky Mountains. Water which falls east of this line flows into the Atlantic Ocean, and that which falls west of it flows into the Pacific. *The Great Divide* is merely a popular term, more or less indefinite in meaning, which is applied to a vast region in Wyoming, Colorado, Montana and Idaho traversed by the Continental Divide. The term is employed in somewhat different senses in different sections of the country. In 1928 John G. Marzel, State geologist of Wyoming, wrote to the author on this subject as follows: "It is quite hard to frame a precise definition of the more or less nebulous expression *the Great Divide.* Instead of being limited to some narrow line of critical and immovable location, the foregoing term seems to take in an ever widening territory year by year. At the present time, the entire areas of Wyoming and Colorado are often called the Great Divide. In those two States the Rocky Mountains reached their maximum degree of development, and as a result, their average elevations of 6,700 and 6,800 feet, respectively, are the highest of all the States. Over that vast area of mountainous terrain, quite similar climatic conditions prevail, and as the entire region is traversed in a central position by the Continental Divide, the growing custom of designating it under the name of the most famous geographic feature would appear to be well founded." It should not be presumed that the Continental Divide always follows the highest crests of the mountain ranges. There are places, in Wyoming for instance, where the traveler would never suspect that he was crossing the Continental Divide. Sometimes the divide line traverses a plain or highland plateau many miles from the nearest mountain peak. In such places it is impossible to locate the exact divide line without surveying instruments. Even with such instruments it may be practically impossible to determine the critical level when lakes occur on these great heights. Perhaps the most famous body of water of this kind is Isa Lake (*Isa* from Greek *iso,* meaning equal) in Wyoming on the Yellowstone Park plateau. This appropriately named lake has two outlets of equal elevation, and from one water flows into the Atlantic and from the other into the Pacific. Since North America is bordered by three oceans— Atlantic, Pacific, and Arctic—strictly speaking, says the U. S. Geological Survey, the true Continental Divide should include the little known and probably indistinct water-parting between the streams flowing into the Arctic and streams flowing into the Atlanic. The Atlantic drainage system, of course, includes the Gulf of Mexico.

Do snakes cover their prey with saliva?

Naturalists are agreed that there is no truth in the popular belief that snakes lick their prey with their tongues and cover it with saliva before swallowing it. A considerable quantity of saliva is generated during the process of swallowing, but it does not come from the tongue, which is used merely as a sensory organ. On this subject Raymond L. Ditmars, curator of reptiles at the New York Zoological Park, made the following statement in a letter to the author: "A snake does not cover its prey with saliva before swallowing it, except as the food passes into the throat. Very often a snake will attempt to swallow a large object in the wrong position, and when the reptile releases the portion which has been in its mouth, to grasp the object in a different place, the portion released from the mouth is covered with saliva." Dr. William M. Mann, director of the National Zoological Park at Washington, writes in a similar vein. "The snake," observes Dr. Mann, "has very well developed saliva glands and these function so much during the process of swallowing that the prey is often covered with saliva. The belief that the snake licks the animal before swallowing it has no basis." Waldo L. McAtee, a Government biologist, explained the phenomenon as follows: "Snakes do not customarily cover their prey with saliva before swallowing it. At times, however, they may grasp it in a manner that will not permit it to be swallowed readily. When the snake discovers this, it may regurgitate the material and grasp it again. It is possible that the idea of snakes covering their prey with saliva arose from observing performances such as this."

Why is a British soldier called Tommy Atkins?

Tommy Atkins is the familiar nickname for privates in the British army and is applied to British soldiers collectively. It arose from the fact that *Thomas Atkins* was frequently used as a specimen name in the service record books issued in 1815 and later. In these manuals blank spaces were provided for the soldier's name, address, age, length of service, wounds received in battle, honors won in action—in short a brief résumé of his whole military record. As an aid in filling out these records, model forms already filled out were provided. The fictitious name generally used in the models was *Thomas Atkins,* although *William Jones* and *John Thomas* were also employed. *Thomas Atkins,* however, was used on all model blanks for privates in the cavalry and infantry and consequently it became the most familiar to the soldiers. Many of these old books and blanks are still preserved in the library of the British War Office. One of them dated August 31, 1815, reads as follows: "[Form of a Soldier's Book in the Cavalry when filled up.] Description, Service, &c., of *Thomas Atkins*, No. 6 Troop, 6th Regt. of Dragoons. Where Born . . . Parish of Odiham, Hants . . . Bounty £6. Received, Thomas Atkins, his x mark." The following form was used in the same year for the infantry: "[Form of Soldier's Book in the infantry, when filled up.] Description, Service, etc. of *Thomas Atkins*, Private No. 6 Company, 1st Batt. 23d Regt. Foot. Where born [etc.] . . . Bounty £7.7s. Received, *Thomas Atkins*, his x mark." The War Office has been unable to find any evidence supporting the legend that the original Thomas Atkins was a private whose name became familiar because he dropped dead of wounds while delivering a dispatch to the Duke of Wellington during the battle of Waterloo.

How long was the fast of Terence MacSwiney?

In 1920 Terence MacSwiney, Lord Mayor of Cork, Ireland, was sentenced to two years imprisonment, the chief charge against him being the possession of seditious documents. He was confined in Brixton Prison, London, on August 12, 1920. As a protest against the sentence MacSwiney went on a "hunger strike" and refused to eat food of any kind while in prison. He did not, however, refuse water and medicines. His death occurred on October 25 of the same year—the seventy-fourth day of his fast. Although from time to time he was subject to fits of delirium he retained consciousness until within a few days of his death.

What is the meaning of SS in legal documents?

When used in legal documents the letters *SS*. are the abbreviation of the Latin word *scilicet*, which means *to wit, that is to say, namely*. In English *scilicet* is pronounced *sil-i-set*, with the accent on the first syllable. It is derived from two Latin words, *scire*, to know, and *licet*, it is permitted. Hence *scilicet* literally means "it is permitted to know." *SS*. has various uses in legal documents. Sometimes it means *summons;* when used at the beginning of documents it may indicate the court in which the action or pleading is taking place. Generally, however, it is used in the simple sense of *to wit* and calls attention to what is to follow or introduces explanatory matter pertaining to what has preceded. Like many other Latin abbreviations, it is a relic of the days when all legal documents in England were written in Latin.

Were Robert and Gouverneur Morris related?

So far as known, there was no relationship between Robert Morris, "the financier of the Revolution," and Gouverneur Morris, who distinguished himself as a statesman and diplomat, although historians often erroneously refer to the two as kinsmen. If there was any relationship between them it must have been very distant. Robert Morris was born in Liverpool, England, in 1734, and emigrated to America in 1747. Gouverneur Morris was born in 1752 at Morrisania manor house, in what is now New York City. His great grandfather, Richard Morris, was an officer in Oliver Cromwell's army and came to America upon the restoration of the Stuarts. Robert Morris signed the Declaration of Independence; Gouverneur Morris did not, although the name of his half brother, Lewis Morris, appears on that document. Robert and Gouverneur Morris were members of the Pennsylvania delegation to the Philadelphia convention of 1787, and they both attached their signatures to the Constitution submitted to the States for ratification. When Robert Morris was made minister of finance in 1780, Gouveneur Morris became his assistant.

How did *throwing the hat in the ring* originate?

Throwing the hat in the ring, in the sense of entering a political campaign or announcing one's candidacy for office, came to us from the wrestling and boxing ring. It was popularized in 1912 by Theodore Roosevelt. Early in that year the ex-President was asked to deliver an address before the Ohio Constitutional Convention then in session at Columbus. On February 21, while he was passing through Cleveland on his way to the State capital, newspaper reporters asked him whether he intended to run for President in the coming campaign. "My hat is in the ring. You will have my answer on Monday," replied Roosevelt, who was familiar with Western sporting slang. It was customary in the West a generation ago—and is so even at present in some sections

—for a man to volunteer to enter a boxing or wrestling match by throwing his hat into the ring. This custom is a survival of the old gage of battle. *Webster's New International Dictionary* defines *gage* as "a pledge of a person's appearance to combat, or do battle, in support of his assertions or claims; especially, a glove, *cap,* or the like, cast on the ground to be taken up by the opponent." Among the lumberjacks of the Northwest a fight is often started by the challenger throwing down his hat, coat, or shirt, and *daring* anybody to take it up. A similar custom prevails among the miners in Cornwall, England, where wrestlers from different mines challenge one another by tossing their hats on the ground. In some parts of England and the United States wrestling matches are arranged by having all the contestants throw down their hats, whereupon a blindfolded person shuffles them and hands them out in pairs, the owners thus being paired for a match. In *Tom Brown's School Days,* published in 1856, Thomas Hughes describes the old sport of backswording or singlestick, which is played with sticks handled like medieval heavy swords. The challengers enter the contest by throwing down their hats. Hughes says in Chapter II: "A tall fellow who is a down shepherd, *chucks his hat on the stage* and climbs up the steps."

Is it lawful to dun a person by postal card?

Under the American postal laws it is unlawful to send by mail a card dunning the person to whom it is addressed for a debt or an account past due. This is based on the following provision in Section 471 of the U. S. Postal Laws and Regulations of 1924:

All matter otherwise mailable by law, upon the envelope or outside cover or wrapper of which, or any postal card upon which, any delineations, epithets, terms, or language of an indecent, lewd, lascivious, obscene, libelous, scurrilous, defamatory, or threatening character, or calculated by the terms or manner or style of display and obviously intended to reflect injuriously upon the character or conduct of another, may be written or printed or otherwise impressed or apparent, are hereby declared unmailable matter, and shall not be conveyed in the mails nor delivered from any post office nor by any letter carrier, and shall be withdrawn from the mails under such regulations as the Postmaster General shall prescribe.

The Post Office Department has ruled that this clause prohibiting language calculated to reflect injuriously upon the character or conduct of another forbids the mailing of postal cards on which the addressees are dunned for accounts past due. It does not, however, include cards bearing respectful requests for the settlement of current accounts or giving notice that accounts, assessments, taxes, and bills will be due. Although the provision against matter of a "threatening character" is held by the Department to cover and make unmailable cards which threaten to bring suits or legal proceedings if debts and accounts are not paid, it does not include cards sent out by fraternal and other societies to notify members of assessments and to call respectful attention to the rules of the society prescribing suspension from the society for failure to pay.

Does lightning ever strike twice in the same place?

There is a popular notion that lightning never strikes in the same place more than once. As a matter of fact lightning has been known to strike the same building several times during a single electrical storm. The U. S. Weather Bureau says that trees, steeples, chimneys and other tall objects and structures in elevated and exposed locations are likely to be struck by lightning regardless of the number of times they have been struck in the past. Of course, according to the law of probability it is not likely that lightning will strike again in exactly the same place under ordinary circumstances.

Why do artists depict Moses with horns?

Many medieval painters depicted Moses with horns protruding from his head. Michelangelo's masterpiece of sculpture, the colossal figure of Moses in the Church of St. Pietro in Vincoli at Rome, also represents the leader of the Israelites with horns. This figure was designed for the mausoleum of Pope Julius II and was intended as a compliment to that Pope's warlike prowess. It portrays the painfully restrained wrath and majestic indignation of Moses when he descended from Mt. Sinai and found his people worshipping the golden calf. Although the horns undoubtedly heighten the effect desired, they were really due to a mistake in Biblical translation. In *Exodus 34: 29* and *30* it is stated: "And it came to pass, when Moses came down from mount Sinai with the two tables of testimony in Moses' hand, when he came down from the mount, that Moses wist not that the *skin of his face shone* while he talked with him. And when Aaron and all the children of Israel saw Moses, behold, the *skin of his face shone;* and they were afraid to come nigh him." In Hebrew the word for this shining is *q̂aran* or *karan,* which means "rays of light darting out" or "sending forth beams." The Hebrew word for horn is *q̂eren*. The translators of the Latin version of the Old Testament known as the Vulgate rendered the phrase *quod cornuta esset facies sua,* which means his face was horned. Since *horn* is frequently used in the Bible for strength, the medieval artists represented Moses with horns, thinking the horns were mentioned in the Bible to symbolize his power.

What is the Coudersport ice mine?

About 1894 a shaft was dug several miles from Coudersport, Pennsylvania, with a view of locating silver ore. No silver was discovered and the project was abandoned after a shaft eight by ten feet in diameter had been sunk to a depth of twelve or fifteen feet. Although it was midsummer the crevices in the rocks at this point were filled with ice. The next summer large quantities of ice formed on the walls and bottom of the abandoned pit. As years passed by it was observed that the ice usually begins to form about April and is at its best about June. Then it gradually melts, and by October disappears completely. There is a distinct draft of air out of the mine in summer and into it in winter. This formation of ice in a natural refrigerator proved so interesting to the public that eventually a fence was built around the shaft and a trapdoor was placed over the top. Every year thousands of persons pay a fee to see the famous Coudersport ice mine. The phenomenon, however, is not so rare as commonly supposed and is fairly well understood by scientists. *Glacière* is the name given by geologists to an ice cave like the one in question. In 1921 Edwin Swift Balch, in a paper read before the American Philosophical Society, stated that the mine near Coudersport is the most impressive ice cave in the Eastern part of the United States and exhibits the best ice curtains, ice floor and other glacière phenomena in the spring and early summer. This shaft was sunk at the foot of a hill facing north. The hill is composed of a mass of loose rocks and strata of shale, overlaid with a timber growth which serves to insulate the rocks from the atmosphere. During the winter cold air sinks from its own weight into the hill through apertures and fissures in the rocks. By this means the temperature of the rocks is lowered below freezing. Very little ice is formed then, principally because the air is dry and the surface water is frozen. But during the summer the current of air is reversed, and the cold air passes out. Ice is formed in two ways. Moisture from the humid summer atmosphere collects on the walls and is congealed. Surface water, released by the spring thaws, seeps into the sides of the shaft or trickles over the top and is frozen in the form of ice sheets and icicles sometimes extending the full length of the pit. Frequently the bottom is covered with ice to a depth of several feet. Of course the cold air emerges from the hill through the crevices at many points, but it is most concentrated at the shaft. The temperature in the shaft in midsummer ranges from 25° to 32° Fahrenheit. One investigator states that a bucket of water suspended in the shaft will not readily freeze, a fact which tends to prove the assertion that the chilled rocks cause the moisture and trickling water to congeal. George H. Ashley, State geologist of Pennsylvania, suggested that the cooling effect of evaporation may also play a considerable part in forming the ice.

What great reformer threw an inkstand at the devil?

After Martin Luther appeared at the Diet of Worms in 1521 his friends feared that his safe-conduct would be violated and that he would be seized and punished as a heretic. Therefore his protector, Frederick III, elector of Saxony, had the monk secretly conveyed to the Wartburg, a historic castle at Eisenach. This protective imprisonment lasted for about ten months and Luther took advantage of it to translate the New Testament into German. During this work he fancied that Satan continually appeared before him. The monk, however, refused to desist from his sacred task. According to a legend, one day when Satan appeared Luther became so incensed that he seized his inkstand and hurled it at the intruder. The apparition disappeared and the missile was dashed to pieces against the wall of the castle. In his *History of the Reformation,* which was published between 1835 and 1853, Jean Henri D'Aubigné says: "The keeper of the Wartburg is still careful to call the traveler's attention to the spots made by Luther's inkstand." Such is the case at the present time, and there is reason to believe that fresh ink is occasionally applied to the spot for the benefit of visitors at the Wartburg. Naturally enough, the legend has many refinements and elaborations. According to one version, the devil appeared in the form of a fly, which continually buzzed around the monk's head and so annoyed him that he could not work. The insect vanished after Luther flung his inkstand at it and the ink was splashed over the wall. Another version has it that the wall opened and Satan presented himself as a hideous giant, who pointed his finger at the monk in a threatening manner and gnashed his teeth furiously. When Luther reached for his inkstand Satan was too quick for him. The wall closed behind the giant and received the contents of the ink bottle.

Who invented punctuation?

The present system of punctuation, which divides written language into sections by means of various signs and points, grew out of a system developed by Aldus Manutius, an Italian scholar and printer, who printed Greek classics on his press at Venice in the latter part of the fifteenth century and the beginning of the sixteenth. Manutius was born in 1450, about the time Johann Gutenberg was experimenting with his first movable type; he died in 1515. It should not be supposed, however, that Manutius was the sole inventor of punctuation, no one man being entitled to that honor, although the main features of our modern system are due chiefly to his ingenuity and that of the Greek scholars employed by him at Venice. Among the later ancient Greeks various dots had been used for oratorical and rhetorical purposes. Aristophanes, a Greek grammarian of Alexandria who died about 185 or 180 B. C., is said to have devised a system of punctuation by means of dots. A crude system of prose punctuation was probably employed even before the time of Aristophanes. St. Jerome, who died 420 A. D., knew nothing whatever about punctuation. In the early part of the ninth century the Greek systems had been so completely forgotten that Charlemagne requested scholars to revive them. During the Middle Ages and up to the time of Manutius it was customary to write letters together in lines without breaks or pause marks for either words or sentences. It was only by degrees that words were divided from one another by spacing in the lines. Then came a haphazard division of words into sentences by means of signs and points, borrowed chiefly from the dots of the Greek grammarians. The invention of printing made it very desirable to have a conventional system of punctuation. This Manutius supplied, and his system, with numerous variations, is still in general use.

Does mummy wheat ever grow?

Mummy wheat is the name given to grains of wheat which have lain thousands of years in Egyptian tombs with mummies. Writers and public speakers frequently illustrate the indestructibility of truth by comparing it to such wheat. Now and then somebody announces a new variety of grain which is alleged to have been developed from seed taken from ancient tombs in Egypt. The publication of these stories usually precedes an attempt to sell seed. Botanists and others with sufficient knowledge and experience to form a reliable opinion are unanimous in asserting that there is no evidence that mummy wheat has ever germinated. Dozens of eminent botanists have investigated the subject. The U. S. Department of Agriculture reports: "We do not know of any authentic records of the germination of wheat or other common grain after hundreds or thousands of years." In 1906 a French botanist named Becquerel selected a number of seeds from a museum collection and planted them. These seeds ranged in age from thirty to one hundred and fifty years, the ages being well established. Not a seed of the cereals germinated, although some of the legumes did, which proved that the conditions were favorable for the retention of vitality and for the germination of the seeds. In the same year Alfred J. Ewart, an Australian botanist, made a series of experiments. Some of the seeds used were taken from a collection made in 1856 and had been in a dry, dark, airy cupboard for fifty years. When placed in soil under ideal conditions not a single grain of wheat more than sixteen years old germinated. Ewart did much experimenting in an effort to determine the longevity of various seeds. He estimated that the "probably extreme duration of vitality for any known seed may be set between one hundred and fifty and two hundred and fifty years" for the legume family, and "between fifty and one hundred and fifty years" for the mallow and lotus families. As a general rule the seeds of cultivated plants do not retain their vitality so long as do those of wild plants. Gaston Maspero, a French Egyptologist who spent many years among the ancient tombs, made the following statement: "After repeated and always negative trials, we have arrived at so firm a conviction of the complete death of these grains found in the tombs that now when we find seeds we do not renew our tests of them. It happens sometimes that the seeds, especially of wheat and barley, sold to tourists by the fellahs and the sellers of antiques do germinate, but the fellahs do not have any scruples against mixing fresh or viable seed with that found in the tombs. Not a single seed that we ourselves have picked up in the ancient tombs has ever germinated." The keeper of Egyptian antiquities at the British Museum is emphatic in his statement that the wheat which grows is not ancient Egyptian wheat. He says that the halls of rock tombs are frequently used as dry and secure places in which to store grain and this accounts for some of the modern seeds in the ancient tombs. Sometimes wheat straw is used as temporary packing for mummies and a few seeds are thus scattered about. Dr. C. Stuart Gager, an eminent New York botanist, writes: "In other experiments, carried on with great care, it has been conclusively proved that of several hundred wheat grains stored under the best conditions only eight per cent would germinate at the end of sixteen years, and that at the end of thirty-five years not a single seed would germinate. Microscopic examinations also showed beyond the shadow of a doubt that the embryos of these seeds were dead." Dr. Louis H. Pammel, head of the botany department of Iowa State College, writes as follows to the author: "We have made investigations of seeds of wheat, corn and oats that were on exhibition at the Centennial Exposition in Philadelphia in 1876 and not a single seed germinated after the lapse of twenty years.

A great deal of work has been done on delayed germination in this country and in Europe by such scientists as De Candolle, Arthur, Crocker, Becquerel, Darwin, Nobbe, Duvel, Goss, Ewart, Miss C. M. King, and Haberlandt. This work shows conclusively that the story about mummy wheat germinating is all a myth."

Who said: "You can't eat your cake and have it"?

This oft-quoted saying was suggested by a line in *The Size,* a poem by George Herbert, an English poet and churchman who died in 1633 at the age of thirty-nine. The exact quotation is, "Wouldst thou both eat thy cake, and have it?" In *The Haunted Bookshop* Christopher Morley refers to it as one of "the most familiar quotations in our language." *The Size* is in a collection of Herbert's poems published soon after his death under the title *The Temple: Sacred Poems and Private Ejaculations.* The third stanza of the poem is as follows:

> To be in both worlds full
> Is more than God was, who was hungry here.
> Wouldst thou his laws of fasting disannul?
> Enact good cheer?
> Lay out thy joy, yet hope to save it?
> *Wouldst thou both eat thy cake, and have it?*

Of course the idea expressed by the famous quotation dates back much further than Herbert's time. More than two thousand years ago Titus Plautus, the great comic dramatist of ancient Rome, said in his *Trinummus:* "If you spend a thing you cannot have it."

Is there a tribe of people with tails?

After the close of the Spanish-American War a report came from the Philippine Islands stating that exploring parties sent out by the United States Army had discovered a tribe of tailed people in the jungles of Luzon. These tailed people, according to the report, belonged to the Igorot race. The report further stated that the Government had taken charge of the tailed tribe and was keeping it isolated in the mountains of Luzon until it should completely die out. This report has been repeated so often that it has become a legend. Later what purported to be a photograph of a member of the tailed tribe was published. Postcards containing the picture are still sold in the Philippines and every year thousands of them are carried to different parts of the world by credulous tourists, thus keeping alive the fable about the tailed people of Luzon. Notwithstanding numerous veterans of the Philippine war and many travelers are willing to swear under oath that they have seen members of the tailed tribe, scientists who have investigated the subject are unanimous in asserting that the tailed tribe is a myth. Similar reports have been published concerning tailed races in Borneo, New Guinea and other parts of the Malay Archipelago. Such reports, it is believed, originate either in fraud or in careless observation of the costumes worn by some of the primitive Malay peoples. Many of the Igorot head-hunters of Luzon wear fantastic costumes with tails. That the photograph of the tailed man of Luzon was a fake is proved beyond doubt, according to the U. S. National Museum, which states that it has on file "photographs of the same man both with and without a tail." The same authority asserts that the report of "a tailed tribe in the Philippine Islands is a hoax which we have exposed." Although the tailed race is undoubtedly a myth, it is quite possible that individual persons with tails exist in the Philippines as well as elsewhere. Embryologists inform us that every normal human being has a tail during the embryo stage of his existence. According to Dr. Adolph H. Schultz, a research investigator for the Carnegie Institution of Washington, this tail is usually about one-sixth as long as the embryo itself. There are evidences of this rudimentary tail in the body of every adult human being. As a rule, the tail becomes completely overgrown by neighboring parts as the child develops and it finally disappears from the surface. Occasionally, however, the tail does not completely disappear before birth and a child is born with an external tail. "These so-called soft tails," wrote Dr. Schultz in the *Scientific Monthly* for August, 1925, "contain no vertebræ, but blood vessels, muscles and nerves, and are of the same consistency as the short tail of the Barbary ape." Many authentic cases of children born with such tails are known to science. A baby born in 1928 at Knoxville, Tennessee, had a tail seven inches in length, and several years earlier a boy was discovered in Baltimore with an external tail nearly nine inches long. The longest human tail of which science has authentic record was a nine-inch tail found on a twelve-year-old boy in French Indo-China. Evolutionists argue that this vestigial tail in human beings indicates that man descended from ancestors with well developed tails. Dr. Schultz agrees with other scientists in believing that there is no tribe of people with external tails. In 1928 he said in a letter to the author: "I feel quite certain that there is no group of human beings in which tails are found with particular frequency."

Who said: "I care little who makes a nation's laws if I have the making of its ballads"?

An Account of a Conversation Concerning a Right Regulation of Governments for the Common Good of Mankind was issued anonymously in 1704 by Andrew Fletcher of Saltoun (1655–1716), a Scotch politician and political writer. This treatise, which was addressed to the Marquis of Montrose and the earls of Rothes, Roxburg and Haddington, related an imaginary conversation between Fletcher himself on one hand and the earl of Cromarty, Sir Edward Seymour and Sir Christopher Musgrave on the other. The essay contains the following passage:

Even the poorer sort of both sexes are daily tempted to all manner of lewdness by infamous ballads, sung in every corner of the streets. One would think, said the Earl, this last were of no great consequence. I said, I knew *a very wise man,* so much of Sir Christopher's sentiments, that he believed *if a man were permitted to make all the ballads, he need not care who should make the laws of a nation.* And we find, that most of the ancient legislators thought they could not well reform the manners of any city without the help of a lyric, and sometimes of a dramatic poet.

This is all that is positively known about the origin of the oft-quoted and misquoted saying, "I care little who makes a nation's laws if I have the making of its ballads." Since the publication of Fletcher's treatise there has been much speculation as to the identity of the person alluded to by him as "a very wise man." Perhaps Fletcher had no particular person in mind and merely employed this method of introducing his own idea. Several modern writers have ascribed the famous quotation to Confucius, the Chinese sage, who lived from 550 to 478 B. C. Herbert A. Giles, professor of Chinese at Cambridge University, made the following statement in *A History of Chinese Literature,* published in 1901 : "Confucius may indeed be said to have anticipated the apothegm attributed by Fletcher of Saltoun to a *very wise man,* namely, that he who should be allowed to make a nation's *ballads need care little who makes its laws."* Lord Northcliffe and Samuel S. McClure went even further in *The World's Greatest Books,* published in 1910. In Volume 13 they give the famous quotation as one of the general maxims of Confucius. This is obviously careless editing. There is nothing in the Analects of Confucius or the other Chinese classics which would justify attributing the exact words of the quotation to the great sage. That Confucius emphasized the importance of ballads is a well known fact, and the world is indebted chiefly to him for the preservation of the *Book of Odes.* On one occasion, it is recorded, Confucius told his son that until he learned the Odes he would be unfit for the society of intellectual men. Although Confucius never made any assertion that could be legitimately translated in the words of the quotation in dispute, Chinese scholars inform the author that the quotation does in a general way sum up the great importance which the sage of China attached to the study of ballads and odes.

What causes gossamers?

Gossamers are filmy cobwebs floating in the air or clinging to plants and other objects. Spiders eject them, like other webs, in the form of viscid fluid. Sometimes several threads are produced simultaneously. It is supposed that the gossamers are spun when the spider is on an elevated point and that some of the webs are wafted away by the wind as they are ejected. Not infrequently the spider itself is carried away with a tangle of webs. Often the single strands of the web are so fine that they cannot be seen readily except when the sun is shining on them. *Gossamer* is supposed to be derived from *gos,* goose, and *somer,* summer. It is generally assumed that *goose* in this connection refers to the *downy* appearance of the gossamer; but the theory has been advanced that the word may have alluded originally to the clear warm weather which frequently occurs in the fall when geese were supposed to be in season and to have been extended to the chief characteristic of this period in some sections, namely, the appearance of these webs. Far-fetched as the theory may seem, the fact that *summer-goose* is a localism in England for *gossamer* is pointed out in confirmation. Gossamers are in fact seen chiefly during warm weather in the fall, and this has led some naturalists to the conclusion that these cobwebs are produced only by young spiders. Chaucer refers to the gossamer as an unsolved riddle, and it was once widely believed that this phenomenon was somehow produced by dew.

What is dollar diplomacy?

Dollar diplomacy is a contemptuous phrase which is applied to the foreign policy of a nation when its chief object is to obtain commercial and trade advantages, especially when the negotiations are conducted under the guise of a desire to promote international friendship. In modern diplomacy many political advantages are obtained through commercial treaties.

Did Jesus have brothers and sisters?

Whether Jesus had blood brothers and sisters is a disputed question upon which even the early church fathers differed. Several passages in the New Testament refer to the *brother of the Lord* and the *brethren of the Lord*. For instance, *Matthew 13: 55* and *56* says in part: "Is not this the carpenter's son? is not his mother called Mary? and his brethren, James, and Joses, and Simon, and Judas? And his sisters, are they not with us?" Again in *Mark 3: 31* and *32:* "There came then his brethren and his mother, and, standing without, sent unto him, calling him, and the multitude sat about him, and they said unto him, Behold, thy mother and thy brethren without seek for thee." Thus it will be seen that the Bible mentions by name *four brethren of the Lord,* while it merely refers to *his sisters,* without giving their names or number. The exact relationships intended in these passages, as well as others, are not clear, due chiefly to the fact that the words *brother, brethren,* and *sister* are employed in the Scriptures to indicate various degrees of relationship, such as that between blood brothers and sisters, brothers-in-law and sisters-in-law, cousins, and even more distant relatives. The Catholic

Church, which believes in the perpetual virginity of Mary, the mother of Jesus, holds that the sisters and the brethren of the Lord were his cousins. Many logical arguments have been advanced in support of this position. The Greek Church regards the brethren of the Lord as the children of Joseph by a former marriage, which would make them step-brothers of Jesus. Protestants, however, generally believe that James, Joses, Simon, and Judas, and *his sisters* mentioned in *Matthew 13*, were blood brothers and sisters who were born to Mary and Joseph after the birth of Jesus.

How did *curiosity killed the cat* originate?

Curiosity killed the cat is believed to be a corruption of the older saying *care killed the cat*. It is another of those sayings perpetuated more by sound than sense. A proverb known in England and Scotland from time immemorial says that a cat has nine lives, yet care will wear them all out. "Hang sorrow, care will kill a cat," occurs in *Christmas*, a poem written by George Wither, who died in 1667. The same line is attributed to Ben Jonson, John Taylor the Water Poet, and others. This proverb probably referred originally to the fact that cats are frequently so petted and pampered that they sicken and die. However, nobody familiar with the habits of cats would ever accuse them of being curious. Why *"care* killed the cat" was changed to *"curiosity* killed the cat" is a puzzling question. One writer says a plausible explanation of this change is found in the fact that one of the figurative senses of *cat* is "a human being who scratches like a cat, particularly a spiteful or backbiting woman."

How did Casper in Wyoming receive its name?

Casper, Wyoming, was named after Caspar W. Collins. The original spelling was *Caspar*, with an *a* instead of an *e* in the final syllable. Records in the War Department at Washington show that on July 26, 1865, Lieutenant Caspar W. Collins, commanding parts of Companies D and K of the Eleventh Kansas Cavalry and part of Company G of the Eleventh Ohio Cavalry, engaged in a skirmish with between 1,000 and 1,500 Sioux and Cheyenne Indians on what was known as the Platte River Bridge in Dakota Territory, now the State of Wyoming. The troops under Collins were part of Brigadier General P. Edward Connor's Powder River Indian Expedition of 1865. In a dispatch dated July 27, 1865, General Connor reported that Lieutenant Collins and twenty-five of his men were killed, and that nine men were wounded. Four months later—November 21—Major General Pope issued the following order: "The military post situated at Platte Bridge, between Deer and Rock Creeks, on the Platte River, will be hereafter known as Fort Caspar in honor of Lieutenant Caspar Collins, Eleventh Ohio Cavalry, who lost his life while gallantly attacking a superior force of Indians at that place." According to the U. S. Geographic Board, an examination of old maps running back to 1868, 1870, 1871 and 1876 shows the name uniformly spelled *Caspar* on all military maps, but invariably *Casper* on all others. Coutant, in his *History of Wyoming,* says: "The town which is located about two miles below Old Fort Caspar derives its name from the same source and should be spelled in the same way." The name is correctly spelled on a monument erected July 5, 1920, by the Fort Caspar Chapter of the Daughters of the American Revolution on the supposed site of Caspar Collins's battle with the Indians.

What is a political lobby?

A lobby in the political sense is a group of persons or organizations seeking to influence the members of a legislature in order to obtain the passage or secure the defeat of certain bills. The verb *to lobby* means to solicit the vote of a legislator or to attempt to influence him in the exercise of his official duties. Although in this sense the term is an Americanism, it is occasionally used in England in reference to measures before the House of Commons. It originated before the Civil War and arose from the fact that lobbyists work in the lobbies—halls or vestibules—of Congress, and not actually on the floor of the Senate or House of Representatives. The lobbies are often facetiously referred to as the *third house*. In 1871 M. Scheie de Vere wrote on this subject: "The work done by members of Congress is very largely influenced by agents from without, and by certain established usages of their own. The former is collectively called the *lobby,* a term which, originating in the German *Laube,* a bower or small summer-house, meant for many centuries nothing more than a small hall or entering-room, preceding a larger room. In America, the rooms and passages surrounding the hall, in which legislative bodies hold their meetings, soon monopolized the term, and in a short time the men who assembled there to exercise whatever outside pressure they could bring to bear upon the legislators, were themselves called the *lobby*. All who had petitions to be granted, contracts to be given, or favors of any kind to be bestowed, either went themselves or sent well-qualified agents to Washington, to *lobby* their cause, as it was called. Capitalists used the power which wealth gives, even where no bribery was attempted; high social standing was made serviceable, and even beauty and the charms of a silvery voice were not wanting to secure the votes of susceptible members."

Does the horned toad squirt blood from its eyes?

The horned toad, which is a popular name for a variety of horned lizard, has the power of ejecting fine jets of a reddish fluid from the corner of its eyes. In 1871 the Zoological Society of London published in its proceedings the following statement about the horned toad by John Wallace, of Stockton, California: "Under certain circumstances, apparently as a means of defense, this creature squirts out from one of its eyes a jet of bright red liquid very much like blood. This I have observed three times from three different individuals, although I have caught many that did not do it. They do not generally use this defense when first captured, although I caught one a few days ago which squirted the liquid a distance of six inches over the back of my hand, and another ejected it when I flourished a bright knife before its eyes." Dr. Oliver P. Hay, an eminent authority in the National Museum at Washington, proved with the microscope that the reddish fluid in question is actually blood. This blood, several investigators testify, causes considerable irritation when it lodges in a person's eye. One writer reports that the Mexicans call these creatures "sacred toads" because "they weep tears of blood." In *The Reptile Book* by Raymond L. Ditmars is the following interesting passage about the horned toad: "Occasional specimens, when handled, exhibit a remarkable habit. This consists of the ejection of jets of blood from the corner of the eye. It was after examining several hundred specimens, that the writer's inclination to become skeptical about the alleged habit suddenly received a startling reverse. He received an unusually large and fat specimen of a Mexican species—*Phryno-soma orbiculare,* of a rich, reddish hue—almost a crimson. After photographing the specimen, it was measured. The latter process seemed to greatly excite the creature. It finally threw the head slightly upward, the neck became rigid, the eyes bulged from the sockets, when there was a distinct sound like that produced if one presses the tongue against the roof of the mouth and forces a small quantity of air forward. This rasping sound, consuming but the fraction of a second, was accompanied by a jet of blood at great pressure. It hit the wall, four feet away, at the same level as that of the reptile. The duration of the flow of blood appeared to be about one and a half seconds and toward its termination the force gradually diminished, as noted by a course of drops down the wall and along the floor to a position almost under the spot where the reptile had been held. The stream of blood seemed to be as fine as a horsehair and to issue from the eyelid, which was momentarily much swollen. For some time after the performance the eyes were tightly closed and nothing could induce the lizard to open them. Within two minutes after it was placed on the ground the protruding aspect of the eyeballs and the swelling of the eyelids had disappeared. Most surprising was the amount of blood expended. The wall and floor showed a course of thickly sprinkled spots about one-eighth of an inch in diameter. There were one hundred and three of these spots."

Why is a quarter called two bits?

In England *bit* has been applied to coins for centuries. The term was at one time thieves' slang for money in general. Thomas Dekkar so used it in *A Knight's Conjuring: Jests to Make You Merie,* which was first printed in 1607. Later *bit* was applied to any small silver coin. Even now the British use the term in such phrases as *threepenny bit. Two bits,* meaning a quarter of a dollar, originated in the West Indies where *bit* was applied during the seventeenth and eighteenth centuries to small silver coins forming fractions of the Spanish dollar. It was applied specifically to the real, which was equal to one-eighth of the Spanish dollar. This usage spread to New Orleans and the Southern part of the United States in general. When the Spanish dollar disappeared from circulation in this country *bit* survived only in such phrases as *two bits,* meaning a quarter, and *four bits*, meaning half a dollar. Twelve cents and a half is never called a bit, although in some sections of the United States fifteen cents is called a *long bit*, and ten cents a *short bit*.

What does O.N.T. on thread mean?

The letters *O.N.T.*, which are used as the trade-mark on spools of thread, are the initials of *Our New Thread*. Sewing machines began to come into general use about the time of the Civil War. Their introduction made it desirable for manufacturers to produce a thread that would be suitable for machine as well as for hand sewing. In 1862 the Clark Thread Company developed such a thread and marketed it as *Our New Thread*. Two years later George A. Clark decided to abbreviate the phrase to *O.N.T.* with a view of arousing curiosity as to its meaning. The thread was then advertised as Clark's O.N.T. Spool Cotton, and *O.N.T.* became one of the most popular trade-marks in use. *O.N.T.* was first used in connection with six-cord thread and was not applied to three-cord threads until many years afterwards, and then to threads produced only for manufacturing purposes.

What Revolutionary general requested in his will that he be not buried in any church or churchyard?

Major General Charles Lee, who was second in command under Washington after the resignation of Artemas Ward in 1776, was suspended for one year for his disgraceful conduct at the battle of Monmouth. Later, because of his insolence to Congress, he was dismissed from the Continental service. This Lee, who was born in England, was not related to the famous Lee family of Virginia. He was seized with a violent fever while on a visit to Philadelphia in 1782, and he died in a tavern in that city on October 2 of the same year. His last words, uttered in delirium, were: "Stand by me, my brave grenadiers." Among his papers was his last will, dated 1782, which is still preserved in the office of the clerk of Berkeley County, West Virginia, where Lee owned an estate. This document contained the following remarkable request: "I desire most earnestly that I may not be buried in any church or churchyard, or within a mile of any Presbyterian or Anabaptist meeting house, for since I have resided in this country I have kept so much bad company when living, that I do not chuse to continue it when dead. I recommend my soul to the Creator of all worlds and all creatures, who must from his visible attributes be indifferent to their modes of worship or creeds, whether Christian, Mahometans or Jews, whether instilled by education or taken up by reflection, whether more or less absurd, as a weak mortal can no more be answerable for his persuasions, notions or even scepticism in religion than for the colour of his skin." Lee's wish in this matter, however, was not respected. He was buried in the cemetery of Christ Church in Philadelphia.

Will noise cause bees to settle?

Many bee-keepers believe that a loud noise, such as shouting, beating on pans and ringing cowbells, will induce a swarm of bees to settle. Such noise, in all probability, has no effect on the bees. Naturalists are of the opinion that the sense of hearing in bees, if it exists at all, is very imperfectly developed. "No one knows yet whether bees can hear or not," says the U. S. Department of Agriculture. "At least no one has ever discovered their hearing apparatus. A person is wasting his time when he hammers on a dishpan to bring down a swarm of bees." The belief that serenading will make bees settle is very ancient. It was mentioned by Aristotle, who raised the question whether the insects could hear. He was unable to say whether it was fear or delight that caused the bees to settle upon hearing a loud noise. Virgil alludes to the belief in the Fourth *Georgic,* which treats of bees. "When thou shalt look up and see their hosts, newly freed from the hive, floating through the cloudless summer, . . ." wrote the poet, "wake the jangling bells, and all around clash the cymbals of the Mother of Heaven," and "they will settle of their own accord on the charmed branches." This practice probably sprang from legal difficulties. Originally when a colony of bees left the hive the owner of the land on which the swarm settled would often claim it as his property. Therefore it became a practice, recognized in the law of many nations, for the owner of the bees to follow the swarm and at the same time to raise a clamor to let the neighbors know whose bees they were. The swarm, in other words, was followed with noise in order to retain legal title. Through the passing of the centuries this custom lost its original significance and may have been twisted into the belief that the noise was intended to induce the swarm to light. In England the practice is called tanging the bees, a circumstance which may throw some light on the subject from the standpoint of philology. *Tang* as a verb usually means to strike something such as a bell so as to make it emit a sharp, loud, ringing sound, and most people would assume that such is the application of the word here; but as a noun *tang* is applied to various devices used to hold or clasp. Charles Richardson in his dictionary derived *tongs* from Anglo-Saxon *tang* or *tang-an,* meaning to hold. There is an interesting observation on this subject in *Tom Brown at Oxford,* in which Thomas Hughes describes the efforts of a constable to make a swarm of bees settle by beating a shovel with a huge key. The novelist wrote:

The process in question, known in country phrase as *tanging* is founded on the belief that the bees will not settle unless under the influence of this peculiar music; and the constable, holding faithfully to the popular belief, rushed down his garden *tanging* as though his life depended on it, in the hopes that the soothing sound would induce the swarm to settle at once on his own apple trees.

Is *tanging* a superstition or not? People learned in bees ought to know, but I never happened to meet one who had considered the question. It is curious how such beliefs or superstitions fix themselves in the popular mind of a countryside, and are held by wise and simple alike. David, the constable, was a most sensible and open-minded man of his time and class, but Kemble and Akerman, or other learned Anglo-Saxon scholars, would have vainly explained to him that *tang* is but the old word for to hold, and that the object of *tanging* is, not to lure the bees with sweet music of key and shovel, but to give notice to the neighbors that they have swarmed, and that the owner of the maternal hive means to hold on to his right to the emigrants.

Who divided the Bible into verses?

The early editions of the Bible were not divided into chapters and the smaller sections which are now known as verses. There was even no perceptible space between the words. The author of these divisions in the Old Testament is not known. Euthalius, a deacon and bishop who lived about the middle of the fifth century, divided parts of the New Testament into minute portions similar to the present verses. It is known, however, that the idea did not originate with him. Portions of the Old Testament, and even some parts of the New, had been so divided before his time. Ezra Abbot, an eminent American Biblical scholar, says in his *Critical Essays:* "The first edition of the New Testament divided into our present verses was printed by Robert Stephens at Geneva in 1551, in two volumes, 16mo, the Greek text occupying the center of the page, with the Latin version of Erasmus on one side and the Vulgate on the other." Stephens, whose French name was Robert Estienne, was a member of a famous family of printers in France. His system of dividing the New Testament into verses was adopted by William Whittingham in his translation of the New Testament printed in 1557, and it was followed in the English translation of both the Old and the New Testament known as the Geneva or Breeches Bible, which was printed in 1560. It is supposed that Whittingham was largely responsible for this translation of the complete Bible. In the Geneva Bible it is stated in an introductory note to the reader: "The argumentes bothe for the booke and for the chapters with the nombre of the verse are added."

What is a smock marriage?

A smock marriage is a wedding at which the bride wears nothing but a smock, the old name for the woman's intimate garment now more commonly called shift or chemise. Generations ago it was widely believed in England and New England that if a man married a woman who was in debt he would not be liable to her creditors if he received her from the minister or magistrate without any of her property, including clothing. Modesty compelled those complying with this custom to resort to various expedients. Sometimes the bride stood unclothed in a closet and put one arm out during the marriage ceremony. Frequently the bride would be wrapped only in a sheet or dressed in a smock which had been provided by the bridegroom. Francis Wharton (1820–1889), an eminent American legal authority, wrote: "There is a popular belief that a man who marries a woman in debt, absolves himself from all liability if he take her from the hands of the priest clothed only in her shift. It is a vulgar error." In the records of Lincoln County, Maine, it was stated that John Gatchell and Sarah Cloutman were married in 1767. "Said Cloutman being in debt," attested the justice of peace, "was desirous of being married with no more clothes on her than her shift, which was granted." Sometimes the bridegroom supplied the bride with a complete outfit of clothing in which he retained title. The following is taken from the records of Bradford County, Massachusetts:

Bradford, Dec. ye 24, 1733

This may certifie whomsoever it may concerne that James Bailey of Bradford who was married to the widow Mary Bacon, Nov. 22 last past by me ye subscriber then Declared that he took the said person without anything of Estate and that Lydia, the wife of Eliazer Burbank and Mary, the wife of Thomas Stickney and Margaret, the wife of Caleb Burbank, all of Bradford, were witnesses that the clothes she then had on were of his providing and bestowing upon her.

(Signed) William Balch, Minister of Ye Gospel.

Where is Bedlam?

Bedlam is an old corruption of *Bethlehem*. Eight hundred years ago the birthplace of Jesus was called Bedlam in England. The term, however, is applied particularly to Bethlehem hospital, officially known as the Hospital of St. Mary of Bethlehem, in London. This institution was originally founded as a priory in 1247. We find it referred to as a hospital already in 1330, and as a hospital for lunatics in 1402. When the monasteries and religious establishments were confiscated during the reign of Henry VIII, Bedlam was given to the city of London and was established as a royal institution for the reception of lunatics. Its original site was in Bishopsgate, but later it was rebuilt near London Wall, and in 1815 it was transferred to Lambeth. In Shakespeare's *II King Henry VI*, written about 1593, Lord Clifford says of the Duke of York: "To Bedlam with him! Is the man growne mad?" Centuries ago Bedlam hospital became notorious for the ill-treatment received by its inmates. Patients were discharged partially cured and went about the country begging. In Shakespeare's *King Lear* Edgar, to escape the decree of death proclaimed by his father the Duke of Gloster, assumed the guise of a Bedlam beggar, "the basest and most poorest shape that ever penury, in contempt of man, brought near to beast." Such a beggar was known as a Bedlamite or a Tom o' Bedlam. The reports of brutal treatment of Bedlam patients, although well authenticated, are almost incredible. Sometimes inmates were placed in iron cages like wild animals and exhibited to the public who paid a fee for the privilege of seeing the unfortunate creatures. The word *Bedlam* finally came to be applied to any madhouse or lunatic asylum. It is also applied figuratively to an excited or turbulent crowd.

What is the King drag?

The King drag consists of the two slabs of a split log or two short planks pinned together. Drawing such drags over earth roads after every rain or wet spell is called the King system. The drag received its name from David Ward King, a road specialist of Maitland, Missouri, who strongly advocated the use of this type of road drag. King originally called his invention the *split-log drag*. In *Good Roads at Low Cost,* a paper written in 1910 for the Pennsylvania Railroad Company, King says the King drag was "so named by the road-drag enthusiasts of Iowa." Although King is properly credited with the invention of the modern split-log drag which bears his name, a similar road drag was described in 1851 by William Gillespie in *A Manual of Road-Making.* Gillespie wrote: "A very good substitute for the scraper, in leveling the surface of the road, clearing it of stones, and filling up the ruts, consists of a stick of timber, shod with iron, and attached to its tongue or neap obliquely, so that it is drawn over the road *quartering* and throws all obstructions to one side. The stick may be six feet long, a foot wide and six inches thick, and have secured to its front side a bar of iron descending half an inch below the wood." In a letter to the author dated September 21, 1928, Mary B. King, widow of David Ward King, says: "The drag dates back to 1896—perhaps I can find proof of an earlier date, as I know that Mr. King dragged *his* road long before that with a piece of wooden pump, and something else—I forget what. This he used until it went to pieces. By that time he saw what dragging the roads would do for them, and he made a *split-log drag*—as he called it—which was a log split, the flat sides turned to make the front, and fastened together with wooden pins. Next they began making them of heavy timber, and then came the change to the *King drag* instead of the *split-log drag,* the only difference being the change from the split log to the heavy timber. This change was made because it was so much easier to get the lumber than it was to get the logs. . . . Mr. King died very suddenly in St. Louis on February 9, 1920."

Who are the Gideons who put Bibles in hotels?

The Gideons, the Christian Commercial Travelers Association of America, is a religious association organized, according to its declaration, for the purpose of banding together the Christian travelers and through them winning the commercial travelers for the glory of God; supplying every hotel in America with a Bible in each guest room, and preparing the hearts of travelers for salvation. This society was organized on July 1, 1899, at Janesville, Wisconsin, by three commercial traveling men—John H. Nicholson, W. J. Knights, and S. E. Hill. The name, which was suggested by Knights, is derived from Gideon, one of the judges of Israel, whose history is related in *Judges 6* and *7*. He was a man who did exactly what God wanted him to do irrespective of his own judgment as to methods and results. A pitcher with a lamp inside it was selected as the emblem of the Gideons, in allusion to the pitchers and lamps carried by Gideon and his three hundred followers when the Midianites were delivered into their hands. Only commercial traveling men who are professing Christians and in good standing as members of a church or religious society are eligible to membership. Funds for purchasing Bibles are raised by the members in their local churches or in the towns and cities where they spend their Sundays while covering their itinerary. This work is done gratis and those performing it are not permitted to use any of the money collected for personal expenses. The headquarters of the Gideons at Chicago is maintained by contributions made specifically for that purpose and by money paid as dues by the regular and associate members of the society.

How many Catholics signed the Constitution?

There were two Roman Catholics among those who framed and signed the Constitution. The *Catholic Encyclopedia* says: "He [Daniel Carroll] was also a delegate from Maryland to the convention that sat in Philadelphia, May 14 to September 17, 1789, and framed the Constitution of the United States. Thomas Fitz-Simons

of Pennsylvania was the only other Catholic among its members."
Both Carroll and Fitz-Simons were among the thirty-nine delegates
who signed the document at the close of the convention. Fitz-
Simons was born in Ireland in 1741 and died at Philadelphia in
1811. Carroll was born at Upper Marlboro, Maryland, in 1733, and
died in Washington, D. C., in 1829.

Why is it regarded lucky to find a four-leaved clover?

A four-leaved clover is one that contains four leaflets instead of
the normal three. The superstition that it is a sign of good luck to
find such a leaf is very old. In 1620 Sir John Melton wrote in his
Astrologaster: "That if a man, walking in the fields, find any foure-
leaved grasse, he shall in a small while after find some good thing."
According to an old English rime:

> When sitting in the grass we see
> A little four-leaved clover,
> 'Tis luck for thee and luck for me,
> Or luck for any lover.

Longfellow, in *Evangeline,* speaks of "the marvelous powers of the
four-leaved clover." This belief is not limited to English-speaking
countries. It exists throughout Europe. "He has found a four-
leaved clover" is said proverbially in Germany of a lucky person.
There are many refinements and elaborations of the superstition. In
some countries, for instance, many people believe that the four-
leaved clover, in order to be potent as a good luck charm, must be
plucked on midsummer eve, which is the period near the summer
solstice. This fact has led some writers to suppose that the four-
leaved clover belief originated with the druids, or the ancient sun
worshipers, who gathered clover and other "plants of magic power"
at the summer solstice. Plants undoubtedly played a large part in
the druidic worship and magic, and since clover leaves with four
leaflets were comparatively rare the priests may have attached especial importance to them. The theory has been advanced that the
superstition arose from the fact that four-leaved clovers somewhat
resemble the Christian cross. As a matter of fact, the origin of
the four-leaved clover as a good luck charm has been lost in antiquity and probably is past recovery. Frequently persons ask the

author where the four-leaved clover is mentioned in the Bible. They ask for the book and chapter of the following alleged verse: "Lucky is the one that finds a four-leaved clover, but cursed is the finger that plucks it." Needless to say, there is no such verse and the four-leaved clover is not mentioned in the Scriptures. There is no species of four-leaved clover. On October 4, 1928, an eminent clover specialist associated with the U. S. Bureau of Plant Industry wrote to the author as follows on this subject: "All species of the genus *Trifolium,* including red clover, white clover, alsike clover and several less important species, contain at times individual plants which have a tendency to produce leaves with four leaflets. The tendency is particularly pronounced in white clover, which is the small creeping white-flowered species that occurs commonly in lawns. At Arlington Farm, we have a small patch of white clover grown from a single plant that was found to produce an unusual number of four and five leaves. Possibly ten per cent of the leaves of this plant have more than the normal three leaflets. On the other hand, a great majority of the individual plants of all the species of *Trifolium* never show any tendency to depart from the normal three-parted arrangement of the leaf." Clover leaves with four leaflets, however, are not so scarce as many people suppose. In 1924 a dairy company at Memphis, Tennessee, whose trade-mark was a four-leaved clover, advertised a Four-leaved Clover Week. A pint of ice cream was offered to each person who presented a four-leaved clover at the company's office. On the first day more than 50,000 four-leaved clovers were presented and the distribution was called off because of an ice-cream shortage.

Do human beings ever have a third set of teeth?

Frequently newspapers report alleged cases of what is known as third dentition, that is, a third partial or complete set of natural teeth. The accuracy of these reports is questioned by most dental scientists. It is generally believed by them that these reports refer to teeth really belonging to the second set. The theory is that these teeth failed to emerge at the normal time and appeared late in life when there was sufficient room and when the jaw had atrophied. This theory probably explains most of the cases reported. It is doubtful whether complete third dentition ever occurs in the strict sense of the term. If it does it must be exceedingly rare. The dental department of the U. S. Naval Medical School reports that it knows of no authentic case of persons receiving a third complete set of natural teeth. Dr. Charles C. Hedges, assistant director of the Johns Hopkins Hospital at Baltimore, says in a communication to the author: "The so-called third dentition, after investigation, proves to be one or more supernumerary teeth." However, there are those who believe there have been authentic cases of third dentition. In *Folklore of the Teeth,* published in 1928, Dr. Leo Kanner gives the following interesting summary of the subject: "Speaking of the anomalies of eruption, we must mention further the belief that the cutting of the deciduous teeth is followed occasionally by a third dentition which may appear in very old age. *Third dentition,* described quite often by the older writers on dentistry, was discredited for some time by Scheff and by Busch, who denied its occurrence emphatically and declared that whenever one had one or more teeth come through in older age it was *delayed second dentition.* But since in more modern time Montigel and Kerstig have been able to prove roentgenologically the rightfulness of the older authors' conception and have found at least two undoubted cases of third dentition, we have to believe in its existence."

Is a red evening sky a sign of fair weather?

There is a popular belief that a red sky in the morning is a sign of foul weather and a red sky in the evening is a sign of fair weather. As the old rime has it:

> Evening red and morning gray
> Will set the traveler on his way;
> But evening gray and morning red
> Will bring down rain upon his head.

These signs, says the U. S. Weather Bureau, are far from infallible. Nevertheless there is a slight scientific basis for them and rightly interpreted they may serve as fairly good weather indicators. Their antiquity is indicated by the fact that apparently they were well known and believed by the multitudes who gathered in Palestine to listen to the teachings of Jesus. "When it is evening," Jesus told the people, "ye say, It will be fair weather: for the sky is red. And in the morning, It will be foul weather today; for the sky is red and lowering." At least it is so recorded in *Matthew 16: 2* of the King James version. The passage does not occur in some editions of the New Testament. It is not clear, the Weather Bureau points out, as to exactly what distinction should be made between a sky that is red and one that is "red and lowering." Two kinds of red skies are recognized—a pale or pinkish red, common in the evening; and a much darker red often associated with broken clouds. The former is said to be common during fair weather; the second shortly before a rain. A pale or pinkish red sky in the evening usually means that the atmosphere contains very little moisture and that rain is improbable within the next twenty-four hours. When the evening sky is overcast with uniform gray the dust particles in the air have become loaded with moisture, giving rise to the proverb, "If the sunset is gray, the next will be a rainy day." On the other hand, a gray morning sky generally justifies the expectation of a fair day. Meteorologists explain this phenomenon in connection with the formation of dew. In the morning, however, it is a red sun, rather than a red sky, which is a sign of rain. Any modified appearance of the sun is most conspicuous when it is near the horizon, because the solar orb is then seen through a greater distance of atmosphere. The rays at the red end of the spectrum are refracted to the eye by increased moisture in the atmosphere, and accordingly when the air is heavily charged with dust particles laden with moisture the sun often appears as a fiery red ball, whether it is morning or evening.

How did to *walk Spanish* originate?

To *walk Spanish* refers to an old sport among boys in which one boy seizes another by the collar or the scruff of the neck and the seat of the trousers and forces him along on tiptoe. To *walk turkey* is used in the same sense. Apparently the former expression originated in New England. At any rate, the earliest known uses of *walk Spanish* occur in writings from that section. The application of *Spanish* in the phrase is obscure. It may, as some suppose, allude to the manner in which the old Spanish pirates are reputed to have handled their prisoners when starting them out on the plank. The term has acquired a large variety of meanings in popular parlance. We make another walk Spanish when we discharge him from his job, when we make him step along gingerly, or when we compel him to do something against his will. Likewise a person is said to walk Spanish when he struts, and also when he walks with an unsteady gait. More often the term is equivalent to "toe the line" or "come up to the mark."

How did *show the white feather* originate?

To *show the white feather,* which means to prove cowardly, retreat, or back down, is supposed to be a product of the cockpit. Apparently it was suggested by the old belief that a white feather in the tail of a gamecock was a sign that the fowl was cross-bred and a mongrel, and consequently wanting in courage and pluck. The association of cowardice and cross-breeding is very ancient. We find the idea in *cur,* which is applied to a mongrel dog supposedly inferior because of cross-breeding. It is said by old cockfighters that when a pure-bred bird is pitted in combat against a mongrel bird the mongrel cannot *stand the gaff* and soon shows the white feather, that is, reveals its inferior blood by not being *game.* The Department of Agriculture comments on this subject as follows: "While it seems logical that selective breeding for courage and fighting qualities should result in the production of individual birds or strains best suited to this purpose, it is rather difficult to understand why the phrase to *show the white feather* refers to birds of mongrel breeding. In the old English gamebirds, color and markings were not of great importance, but a hard plumage was desired."

What was Leif Ericcson's religion?

Leif Ericsson, also known as Leif the Lucky, was a son of Eric the Red and was originally a pagan. Most of our information about Leif is derived from the Vineland sagas, a small body of Norse-Icelandic literature consisting of accounts written down between two and three hundred years after the events described. These stories are based on legends and more or less uncertain traditions. According to the *Saga of Eric the Red,* the most trustworthy of these sagas, Leif sailed from Greenland to Norway in the year 999 A. D. He remained some time at the court of King Olaf Tryggvason who converted him to the Christian faith. Leif promised the king that he would proclaim and establish Christianity in Greenland, and for that purpose he took a priest with him on his next voyage. It was while on this expedition that Leif is supposed to have visited the mainland of North America in the year 1000. The saga further relates that Tjodhild, the wife of Eric and supposedly the mother of Leif, received the new faith and she immediately built a church. Old Eric, however, did not like the new doctrine and he found it hard to give up his own. He called the priest a hypocrite and was greatly incensed when his wife refused to live with him after her conversion to the Roman faith. Nevertheless, most of the Norse colonists in Greenland were converted, and churches and monasteries were built and parishes established. In 1110 Greenland was formed into the Diocese of Gardar, Gardar being the chief Norse town on the island-continent. There is a fairly complete record of the Roman bishops of Greenland down to the end of the fourteenth century. The majority of the people of Norway, Sweden and Denmark were converted by the Roman or Western church during the eleventh century.

Of what country is the watermelon native?

The watermelon, it is believed, is a native of tropical Africa where it still grows in a wild state and whence it was carried at an early date to northern Africa, southern Europe, and southwestern Asia. David Livingstone called it the most surprising plant found in the deserts of South Africa. He saw districts literally covered with the vines. The natives are very fond of those varieties which produce sweet fruit. Thus it will be seen that the Negro acquired his decided fondness for the watermelon in the land of his origin. That watermelons were grown by the ancient Egyptians is proved by numerous paintings as well as carvings on monuments. The fruit was probably introduced into England sometime in the sixteenth century. According to Master Graves, it abounded in Massachusetts in 1629, only nine years after the landing of the Pilgrims. The Indians lost little time in adding the watermelon to their list of cultivated plants. In 1664 the Florida Indians were cultivating it in their cornfields, and nine years later Father Marquette found among the Western tribes melons "which are excellent, especially those with a red seed." The tribes on the Colorado River grew watermelons before the death of George Washington. "It is easy to discern," says the U. S. Department of Agriculture, "how both the muskmelon and the watermelon could spread so quickly to all parts of the American continent owing to the ease with which the seeds can be carried and planted. It is notable also that the Indians have from the earliest times shown themselves to be especially fond of watermelons."

How should a baseball bat be held?

Manufacturers of baseball bats place the trade-mark running with the grain of the wood. When a player uses the bat the trade-mark should be held up and the ball struck with the grain of the bat. This protects the bat against splitting. The likelihood of a bat breaking is much greater if it is struck on the trade-mark or on the opposite side.

What is an F.F.V.?

F.F.V. is an abbreviation of First Families of Virginia. An F.F.V. is an aristocratic Virginian who claims descent from Pocahontas or one of the settlers who came over to Jamestown with the first colonists. The designation was originally intended as a good-natured satire upon those natives of the Old Dominion who pride themselves upon their ancestry. It is a common mistake to suppose that F.F.V. was coined by the Virginians themselves. For instance, in 1870 a writer named W. F. Rae published a book in London under the title Westward by Rail, in which he said: "The Virginians had a form which, if clumsy in appearance, answered the purpose nearly as well as any other. The man who, in the Old World, would be dubbed a viscount or a baron was known in the Old Dominion as an F.F.V., that is, he belonged to one of the First Families in Virginia." As a matter of fact, the designation was invented as a joke by Northerners, among whom it came into general use before the Civil War. On April 11, 1857, Harper's Weekly said of John B. Floyd, of Virginia, who had just been appointed Secretary of War by President Buchanan: "Mr. Floyd, as everybody knows, is an F.F.V., and the soul of honor accordingly." On August 2, 1861, while the Federal defeat at the first battle of Bull Run was still fresh in the public mind, the New York Tribune made the following facetious comment: "The famous initials F.F.V.

have had their significance changed by some of our boys in the late campaign, in consequence of their constant alacrity in running, to Fast Footed Virginians."

Did Jefferson ride alone to his first inaugural ceremonies and hitch his horse to a fence?

There is a legend to the effect that when Thomas Jefferson was inaugurated as President the first time he rode to the Capitol on horseback unattended and hitched his horse to a picket fence before entering the building to take the oath of office. This story originated with an English traveler named John Davis, who, though not present at Jefferson's inauguration, pretended that he was in order to make his book of travels more interesting. His book, *Travels of Four Years and a Half in the United States of America During 1798, 1799, 1800, 1801, and 1802,* was published in 1803 and was "dedicated by permission to Thomas Jefferson, President of the United States." In this book Davis wrote:

Let me now come to the object of my journey to Washington. The politeness of a member from Virginia, procured me a convenient seat in the Capitol; and an hour after, Mr. Jefferson entered the House, when the august assembly of the American Senators rose to receive him. He came, however, without ostentation. His dress was of plain cloth, and he rode on horseback to the Capitol without a single guard, or even servant in his train, dismounted without assistance and hitched the bridle of his horse to the palisades.

The fact is that Jefferson, who at the time was lodging in a boarding house on New Jersey Avenue several hundred yards from the Capitol, walked to that building on the occasion in question. It had been planned to have a coach and four for the inaugural ceremony, but John Eppes, Jefferson's son-in-law, did not procure the horses in time. Edward Thornton, then in charge of the British legation in Washington, gave a correct account of the incident in a dispatch which is still preserved in the British archives. Under date of March 4, 1801, Thornton wrote to Lord Grenville, British foreign secretary, as follows: "He [Jefferson] came from his own lodgings to the House where the Congress convenes, and which goes by the name of the Capitol, on foot, in his ordinary dress, escorted by a body of militia artillery from the neighboring State, and accompanied by the Secretaries of the Navy and the Treasury, and a number of his political friends in the House of Representatives." In his *History of the United States* Henry Adams says on this subject: "John Davis, one of many Englishmen who were allowed by Burr to attach themselves to him on the chance of some future benefit to be derived from them, asserted in a book of American travels published in London two years afterward, that he was present at the inauguration, and that Jefferson rode on horseback to the Capitol, and after hitching his horse to the palings, went in to take the oath. This story, being spread by the Federalist newspapers, was accepted by the Republicans and became a legend of the Capitol. In fact Davis was not then at Washington, and his story was untrue."

Does the word *science* occur in the Bible?

The word *science* occurs twice in the Bible, once in the Old Testament and once in the New. *I Timothy 6: 20* reads: "O Timothy, keep that which is committed to thy trust, avoiding profane and vain babblings, and oppositions of *science,* falsely so called." In *Daniel 1: 4* we find: "Children in whom was no blemish, but well favored, and skilful in all wisdom, and cunning in knowledge, and understanding *science,* and such as had ability in them to stand in the king's palace, and whom they might teach the learning and the tongue of the Chaldeans."

Who said: "Public office is a public trust"?

The apothegm "Public office is a public trust" is frequently attributed to Grover Cleveland. It was neither originated nor used by him. Robert M. McElroy, in his life of Cleveland, explains how the saying became associated with the New York statesman. Immediately after Cleveland was nominated for the Presidency in 1884 William C. Hudson, a prominent journalist, was asked to prepare a campaign pamphlet setting forth the outstanding achievements of the candidate's political career. Hudson, who had made a study of Cleveland's state papers and public addresses, headed the appeal with the words, "Public Office is a Public Trust." Although Cleveland had never used the apothegm, he had frequently expressed the same idea in a more roundabout way. For instance, in his first annual message as mayor of Buffalo he said: "We are the trustees and agents of our fellow citizens, holding their funds in sacred trust." And again when he accepted the nomination for governor of New York: "Public officers are the servants and agents of the people, to execute laws which the people have made and within the limits of a constitution which they have established." When Cleveland saw the heading on the manuscript prepared by Hudson he asked: "Where the deuce did I say that?" The newspaperman replied: "You have said it a dozen times, but in different words." Cleveland approved the heading and said he would make it his own, but he continued to express the same idea in his own clumsy way. Daniel S. Lamont, the governor's private secretary, also passed upon the pamphlet before it was published, which accounts for the fact that he is also frequently credited with the authorship of the famous saying. Hudson, of course, did not invent the apothegm. He had undoubtedly heard it many times. Twelve years before—May 31, 1872—Charles Sumner said in the United States Senate: "The phrase *public office is a public trust,* has of late become common property." The Democratic platform of 1876 declared: "Presidents, Vice Presidents, Senators, Representatives, Cabinet officers—these and all others in authority are the people's servants. Their offices are not a private perquisite; they are a public trust." As a matter of fact, the idea was then already old. It had been expressed in different ways by numerous statesmen and writers. In 1835 John C. Calhoun said: "The very essence of a free government consists in considering offices as public trusts, bestowed for the good of the country, and not for the benefit of an individual or party." Even the Constitution associated the terms *office* and *public trust* when, in Article VI, Clause 3, it declared that "no religious test shall ever be required as a qualification to any *office* or *public trust* under the United States."

Did Washington cut down his father's cherry tree?

The story that George Washington hacked his father's cherry tree with a hatchet was originally related in print by Mason Locke Weems, an itinerant preacher, writer and bookseller, who was one of Washington's first biographers. The original edition of Weems's book was published in February, 1800, only about two months after

Washington's death. It was little more than a sketch. The cherry-tree story did not appear until the sixth edition, published in 1808. Unlike the former editions, this one gave an account of Washington's youth, including the following passage:

The following anecdote is a case in point. It is too valuable to be lost, and too true to be doubted; for it was communicated to me by the *same excellent lady to whom I am indebted for the last.* [The italicized words refer to an earlier passage in the book: "Some idea of Mr. Washington's plan of education . . . may be collected from the following anecdote, related to me *twenty years ago by an aged lady,* who was a distant relative, and when a girl spent much of her time in the family."]

"When George," said she, "was about six years old, he was made the wealthy master of a hatchet! of which, like most little boys, he was immoderately fond, and was constantly going about chopping everything that came in his way. One day, in the garden, where he often amused himself hacking his mother's pea-sticks, he unluckily tried the edge of his hatchet on the body of a beautiful young English cherry-tree, which he barked so terribly, that I don't believe the tree ever got the better of it. The next morning the old gentleman finding out what had befallen his tree, which, by the by, was a great favorite, came into the house, and with much warmth asked for the mischievous author, declaring at the same time, that he would not have taken five guineas for his tree. Nobody could tell him any thing about it. Presently George and his hatchet made their appearance. 'George,' said his father, 'do you know who killed that beautiful little cherry-tree yonder in the garden?' This was a *tough question;* and George staggered under it, for a moment; but quickly recovered himself: and looking at his father, with the sweet face of youth brightened with the inexpressible charm of all-conquering truth, he bravely cried out, 'I can't tell a lie, Pa; you know I can't tell a lie. I did cut it with my hatchet.' —'Run to my arms, you dearest boy,' cried his father in transports, 'run to my arms; glad am I, George, that you killed my tree; for you have paid me for it a thousand fold. Such an act of heroism in my son, is worth more than a thousand trees, though blossomed with silver, and their fruit of purest gold.'"

This is the original cherry-tree story. Volumes have been written to prove that Parson Weems was a liar and that the story is a fable. Even such historians as Henry Cabot Lodge and William Roscoe

Thayer joined in the general assault upon the parson's veracity. As a matter of fact, no evidence that disproves the story has been produced. Weems gave it entirely on the authority of the *aged lady* and he thought it was "too true to be doubted" because it was communicated to him by that *same excellent lady*. There is no contemporary statement on the subject. The anecdote, like most anecdotes, may be true or false. There is just as much reason for believing it as there is for disbelieving it. That Weems used his imagination in retelling the story—twenty years after he heard it—is obvious from the detailed manner in which he wrote. But there is no evidence disproving Weems's assertion that he received it from an aged lady who was a distant relative of the Washingtons and who spent much of her time in the family when a girl. It should be noted that, according to the original story, George did not actually cut down the cherry tree; he merely hacked and barked it so the tree probably never "got the better of it."

What is a paper blockade?

When a nation declares a blockade against another nation and does not have sufficient military and naval strength to enforce it, it is called a *paper blockade,* because the blockade exists only in the proclamation. Such a condition is also sometimes called a *cabinet blockade,* referring to the fact that the blockade exists merely as the result of a cabinet decree. The abuse of paper blockades is notorious. Perhaps the most famous paper blockade in history was proclaimed at Berlin by Napoleon in 1806. Great Britain was declared to be in a state of blockade, her subjects and property were made liable to capture and seizure, and all countries under French dominion or allied with France were forbidden to have communication with the British Isles, notwithstanding the fact that Napoleon had hardly a single vessel of war that he could send to support the blockade. It was the beginning of Napoleon's so-called Continental system, which was intended to bar England from trade with continental Europe. Naturally the inconvenience which resulted to neutral nations was great. The blockade, however, continued in effect until 1812, when it was abolished by international agreement. In 1856, to prevent such abuses, the leading powers of Europe, including Great Britain, France, Austria, Prussia, Russia,

Turkey, and Sardinia, signed what is known as the Declaration of Paris. The fourth article of that compact provided: "Blockades, in order to be binding, must be effective—that is to say, maintained by a force sufficient really to prevent access to the coast of the enemy." In other words, a blockade should not be respected unless it is effective enough to make its evasion a dangerous act.

When was Jesus born?

Paradoxical as it may be, Jesus was probably born at least four or five years B.C. *Luke 2:1, 2* says: "And it came to pass in those days, that there went out a decree from Cæsar Augustus, that all the world should be taxed. (And this taxing was first made when Cyrenius was governor of Syria.)" The Cyrenius mentioned here is supposed to have been Publius Sulpicius Quirinius, who was twice governor of Syria, once from 6 to 11 A. D., and once at an earlier period. *Matthew 2: 1* says: "Jesus was born in Bethlehem of Judæa in the days of Herod the king." Historical evidence indicates that this Herod, who was surnamed the Great, died about four years B. C. Therefore Jesus must have been born several years before the beginning of the era which bears his name. Many historians and Bible scholars are of the opinion that Jesus was born several years before the death of Herod, that is, seven or eight years B. C. Others hold that the actual date of Christ's birth should be placed only two or three years B. C. There is not sufficient evidence to justify a definite conclusion. According to *Luke 3: 1,* John the Baptist began his public ministry in the fifteenth year of the reign of Tiberius Cæsar, who succeeded Augustus Cæsar on the throne in 14 A. D. John, who was older by six months, baptized Jesus soon afterwards.

Is Zane Grey the name of a man or a woman?

It is a common mistake to suppose that Zane Grey is the name of a woman. This error is probably due to the similarity of the name and that of Jane Grey, who was queen of England for nine days in 1553. Be that as it may, *Zane* is frequently taken for a woman's name. It is a family name with many historical associations. Zane Grey, the popular novelist, was born at *Zanes*ville, Ohio, in 1875. In 1896 he graduated in dentistry from the University of Pennsylvania and he followed the dental profession in New York

City from 1898 to 1904. His first book, published in 1904, was entitled *Betty Zane*. In a letter to the author, dated August 27, 1927, Zane Grey wrote: "Zanesville was named for ancestors of mine who opened the Ohio Valley and were granted land in various localities. I am a descendant of Colonel Ebenezer Zane who fought in the Revolutionary War. Betty Zane of the famous powder exploit was his sister."

How did *boycott* originate?

Boycott is derived from the surname of Captain Charles Cunningham Boycott (1832–1897), who managed an estate for Lord Erne in Connemara, Ireland. His harsh methods of collecting rents made him exceedingly unpopular with his tenants. Finally, in the fall of 1880, the tenants banded together and demanded a reduction in rents. Boycott refused to comply with the demand, whereupon the tenants began to harass the land agent in every conceivable manner. They refused to work for him and would not permit anybody else to do so. They tore down his fences, intercepted his mail, insulted him personally, and burned him in effigy. The upshot of the affair was that Captain Boycott appealed to the government for protection. A gang of Orangemen, known as *Emergency Men,* came from Ulster and harvested the crops under the protection of 900 soldiers. The methods of the tenants, however, were adopted by the Irish Land League to compel its enemies to comply with its demands, and the word *boycott* immediately became popular in the sense of a commercial or social taboo, especially a combine organized to ostracize an individual or company with a view of making him or it accede to certain demands.

Who were the devil dogs?

Teufelhunde, which is the German equivalent of devil dogs, is the name that the German soldiers are supposed to have given the American Marines after the fighting around Château-Thierry in June and July, 1918. The original *Teufelhunde* were fierce and fiendish dogs mentioned in a Bavarian legend. H. L. Mencken, in *The American Language,* says: "*Teufelhunde* (devil dogs), was invented by an American correspondent; the Germans never used it." The Office of Naval Intelligence, however, states that Marine officers at the front at the time vouch for the fact that German prisoners captured during the battle at Belleau Wood as early as June 8, 1918, said that the American Marines "fought like devil dogs." Unmailed letters found on the bodies of slain German soldiers also referred to the Marines as *devil dogs* and said that they fought like fiends. It is stated by officers who were present in the field that stories of the Marines being called devil dogs or *Teufelhunde* were prevalent in the trenches at the front two or three days after the first attack on June 6, 1918, or very shortly after the first prisoners were taken.

Do elephants shed their tusks?

The projections on an elephant known as tusks are merely elongated incisor teeth in the upper jaw. If these teeth are broken off or extracted they are never replaced. They are preceded, however, by milk teeth, which come out at an early age. Good-sized tusks are produced on both sexes of the African elephant, but they seldom occur on the females of the Asiatic or Indian species. In Ceylon only about one per cent of either sex have any tusks at all. Elephant tusks supply most of the ivory which is so highly esteemed the world over for ornamental purposes.

What is a spoonerism?

A schoolboy once intended to begin an oration with, "The schoolhouse is the bulwark of civilization." He became confused, however, and what he actually said was, "The bulhouse is the schoolwark of civilization." That is a classic example of a spoonerism. *Spoonerism* is the popular name of a kind of metathesis, which is the technical term used to describe an accidental transposition of the syllables or sounds of two or more words. It is derived from the surname of Dr. William Archibald Spooner (1844–1930), who was for many years warden of New College, Oxford, England, and who became notorious among his students for these slips of the tongue. Dr. Spooner was not only a churchman but also a classical scholar of note. In 1879 he announced a hymn as "The Kinquering Congs Their Titles Take." He meant, of course, "Conquering Kings." Dr. Spooner declared in 1928 that this was the only spoonerism of which he was guilty. It was so laughable to the students that it became a fad among them to invent all sorts of similar combinations and attribute them to the doctor. While preaching a sermon Dr. Spooner is reputed to have said, "We all know what it is to have a half-warmed fish within us," meaning "a half-formed wish." On another occasion he said, so it was reported, that "the Lord is a shoving leopard," when he meant "a loving shepherd." At a wedding the warden of New College declared that "It is kistomary to cuss the bride." When a stranger entered the chapel on one occasion Dr. Spooner said to him very courteously, "If you wish, stranger, you may occupew my py this morning." When someone asked the doctor how far it was to London, he replied, "About fifty miles as the fly crows." While telling his students a touching story he said: "Then the mother went down to the gate to guest the parting speed." Examples of these queer slips of the tongue which were invented in fun and attributed to Dr. Spooner could be multiplied indefinitely. It was about 1885 that the students began to call them *spoonerisms,* a word which finally found its way into the Oxford dictionary. True spoonerisms are generally born of stage fright or other forms of nervousness and confusion. In 1925 a distinguished Cabinet official gave an address before the National Press Club of Washington in which he referred to that organization as the "pless crub." During the same year a woman member of Congress delivered an address in which she several times stated what she intended to bring up on "the House of the floor." Once the author, when he was driving along a country road, asked several men walking whether they would like to ride. "No, thank you," came the reply, "cheapings walker." The speaker meant, "walking's cheaper." An Englishman once arrived in New York with no baggage, or luggage as he would call it, except two rugs and a bag. When a porter asked him how many parcels he had, the Englishman replied, "Only two bugs and a rag."

Which is the right bank of a river?

The right bank of a river is the bank to the right of a person looking down stream, that is, in the direction of the current. St. Louis, Missouri, is on the right bank of the Mississippi. In *Old Mortality,* which was published in 1816, Sir Walter Scott wrote: "Monmouth . . . might be discovered on the top of the right bank of the river." The left bank, of course, is the bank to the left of a person looking in the same direction. Memphis, Tennessee, is situated on the left bank of the Mississippi.

Why are rich merchants called merchant princes?

A merchant prince is a merchant who has princely wealth. The name was suggested by *Isaiah 23: 8,* which reads: "Who hath taken this counsel against Tyre, the crowning city, whose *merchants are princes,* whose traffickers are the honorable of the earth."

What is small beer?

Small beer is beer with a small alcoholic content. As applied to liquors *small* means thin, diluted, weak, or mildly alcoholic; as, small ale, small wine, and small beer. The term has been used in this sense for several hundred years. For instance, in 1568 Richard Grafton wrote in his chronicles of England: "For drinke, they had none but small beer."

Why do Chinese in America send their dead to China?

Conservative Chinese in the United States and other foreign countries remove their dead to China because of their belief in ancestor worship. They desire to be reunited in death to their ancestral clan and to receive the reverence paid by descendants to ancestors twice a year. As a rule the dead are not sent to China immediately, but are buried in ordinary cemeteries or in burial grounds owned by groups of their own people. Generally a body is sent back to China only when the deceased has made a request to that effect. Otherwise the burial in this country is permanent. Many Chinese, especially those born here, become so thoroughly Americanized that they neglect this ancient custom of their nation. Transportation of bodies to the homeland has no religious significance other than its relation to the traditional respect for ancestors. The removals are not made by relatives or by religious sects, but by the tong, clan or social organization to which the deceased belonged. All expenses are borne by the organization, which for this purpose has a fund raised by voluntary offerings. After the bodies have lain in cemeteries for a time, usually several years, they are exhumed and shipped in large numbers by special arrangement with steamship companies. Often shipment is made ten, twenty or even thirty years after death, in which case only the bones are gathered and sent in small containers. Cremation before shipment is practiced only by Chinese who are Buddhists. No Chinese is supposed to be buried at sea. China has understandings with other nations whereby the body of a Chinese who dies on the ocean is kept on the ship in a coffin and returned to China by the next vessel. Coffins for this purpose are carried on nearly all Pacific ships.

Who wrote Lincoln's favorite poem?

Mortality, a poem on futility composed by a Scottish poet named William Knox, is remembered chiefly because it was a favorite with Abraham Lincoln. It is often known by its first line, "Oh, why should the spirit of mortal be proud?" Knox was born in Scotland in 1789. From 1812 to 1817 he tried farming in Dumfriesshire but made a failure of it. In 1820 he went with his family to Edinburgh where he became a journalist. Sir Walter Scott admired his genius as a poet and befriended him, frequently giving him substantial pecuniary aid. In his *Journal*, however, Sir Walter says the young poet "became too soon his own master and plunged into dissipation and ruin." His health was broken down by his convivial habits and in 1825 he died of paralysis at Edinburgh at the age of thirty-seven. *Mortality* was first published in 1824 in a volume entitled *Songs of Israel*. Lincoln saw it in a newspaper and committed it to memory. He was very fond of quoting poetry, especially poems expressive of hopelessness, woe and foreboding. Lawrence Weldon, when a young lawyer, traveled with Lincoln on the circuit. Years afterwards he wrote that Lincoln "would frequently lapse into reverie and remain lost in thought long after the rest of us had retired for the night, and more than once I remember waking up early in the morning to find him sitting before the fire, his mind apparently concentrated on some subject, and with the saddest expression I have ever seen in a human being's eyes." When thus gazing into the dying embers, said Weldon, he would often recite *Mortality*. In those days a company of singers known as "the Newhall Family" regularly visited towns in that district and once at Bloomington Lincoln went alone to their show and particularly admired Mrs. Lois E. Hillis, one of the troupe. At her hotel he recited *Mortality* for her and the next day he wrote out the poem and gave her a copy. There is a copy of the poem in Lincoln's handwriting in the manuscript collection of Oliver R. Barrett of Chicago. In 1846 Lincoln sent a poem to Andrew Johnston, a fellow Illinois Whig. This was undoubtedly a copy of *Mortality*. Johnston desired to know who wrote the poem. "I would give all I am worth, and go in debt, to be able to write so fine a piece as I think that is," replied Lincoln. "Neither do I know who is the author. I met it in a straggling form in a newspaper last summer [1845], and I remember to have seen it once before, about fifteen years ago, and this is all I know about it." Several years later he remarked, "I would give a great deal to know who wrote it, but I have never been able to ascertain." Before his death, however, he learned that it was composed by Knox, of whom he probably had never heard. Critics have called *Mortality* a commonplace and pedantic rime, but it will continue to be read by millions because it expressed the thoughts and feelings of Abraham Lincoln. The complete poem is as follows:

Oh, why should the spirit of mortal be proud?
Like a swift-fleeting meteor, a fast-flying cloud,
A flash of the lightning, a break of the wave,
Man passeth from life to his rest in the grave.

The leaves of the oak and the willow shall fade,
Be scattered around and together be laid;
And the young and the old, and the low and the high,
Shall moulder to dust and together shall lie.

The infant a mother attended and loved;
The mother that infant's affection who proved;
The husband that mother and infant who blessed,
Each, all, are away to their dwellings of rest.

The maid on whose cheek, on whose brow, in whose eye,
Shone beauty and pleasure,—her triumphs are by;
And the memory of those who loved her and praised,
Are alike from the minds of the living erased.

The hand of the king that the sceptre hath borne;
The brow of the priest that the mitre hath worn;
The eye of the sage and the heart of the brave,
Are hidden and lost in the depth of the grave.

The peasant whose lot was to sow and to reap;
The herdsman, who climbed with his goats up the steep;
The beggar, who wandered in search of his bread,
Have faded away like the grass that we tread.

The saint who enjoyed the communion of heaven,
The sinner who dared to remain unforgiven,
The wise and the foolish, the guilty and just,
Have quietly mingled their bones in the dust.

So the multitude goes, like the flower or the weed
That withers away to let others succeed;
So the multitude comes, even those we behold,
To repeat every tale that has often been told.

For we are the same our fathers have been;
We see the same sights our fathers have seen,—
We drink the same stream and view the same sun,
And run the same course our fathers have run.

The thoughts we are thinking our fathers would think;
From the death we are shrinking our fathers would shrink;
To the life we are clinging they also would cling;
But it speeds from us all, like a bird on the wing.

They loved, but the story we cannot unfold;
They scorned, but the heart of the haughty is cold;
They grieved, but no wail from their slumbers will come;
They joyed, but the tongue of their gladness is dumb.

They died, ay! they died: and we things that are now,
Who walk on the turf that lies over their brow,
Who make in their dwellings a transient abode,
Meet the things that they met on their pilgrimage road.

Yea! hope and despondency, pleasure and pain,
We mingle together in sunshine and rain;

And the smiles and the tears, the song and the dirge,
Still follow each other, like surge upon surge.

'Tis the wink of an eye, 'tis the draught of a breath,
From the blossom of health to the paleness of death,
From the gilded saloon to the bier and the shroud,—
Oh, why should the spirit of mortal be proud?

Does the Bible mention a person named Dives?

Dives, pronounced *dy-veez,* is the name popularly given to "a certain rich man" who figures in Jesus' parable of the rich man and Lazarus, recorded in *Luke 16: 19–31.* The word *dives,* however, does not occur in any English translation of the Bible, either as a proper name or as a common word. It is merely the Latin word for rich, and accordingly it occurs as an adjective in the Vulgate, a Latin version of the Scriptures translated at the close of the fourth century largely by Jerome and declared by the Council of Trent to be the official text of the Catholic Church. Even in that version *dives* is not employed as a noun or proper name. As a matter of fact in no version of the Bible is the rich man given any name. Apparently it was during the Middle Ages that it became customary to apply the name Dives to the rich man at whose gate Lazarus begged crumbs. This no doubt arose from the fact that the parable was referred to in Latin as *Dives et Lazarus,* which literally means simply the rich man and' Lazarus. It could just as well be written *Lazarus et dives,* in which case *dives* is not capitalized. Since the fourteenth century the word has been used as a proper name even in theological literature.

Why is time indicated on shipboard by bells?

Time is announced on shipboard by striking a bell every half hour. This system dates from the days of the half-hour sandglass, when the ship's bell was struck each time the glass was turned over. It has been retained because seamen are naturally conservative and because it is a convenient method of communicating to the sailors, who are often scattered about the ship. To be able to tell the time of day by bells one must know what watch it is. According to the system used in the American Navy, the twenty-four hours of the day are divided into six watches, which are as follows : First watch, from 8 : 00 o'clock P. M. to midnight; midwatch, midnight to 4 : 00 A. M.; morning watch, 4 : 00 A. M. to 8 : 00 A. M.; forenoon watch, 8 : 00 A. M. to noon; afternoon watch, noon to 4 : 00 P. M., and the dog watch, 4 : 00 P. M. to 8 : 00 P. M. Watches are changed at eight bells, that is, at noon, 4 : 00 P. M., 8 : 00 P. M., midnight, 4 : 00 A. M., and 8 :00 A. M. The dog watch, however, is subdivided into the first dog watch, from 4 : 00 P. M. to 6 : 00 P. M., and the second dog watch, from 6 : 00 P. M. to 8 : 00 P. M. These watches did not receive their name from man's faithful animal friend, but from a mechanical device known as a dog, which is used in reversing motion, such as in a planing-machine. It has been suggested that *dog* in this connection may be a corruption of *dodge,* alluding to the fact that the mechanical dog was introduced to dodge the routine, and the dog watch to prevent the same men from always keeping watch at the same hours. At any rate, the dog watches have the desired effect of changing every night the hours during which the starboard and port watches are on deck. The bells are struck as follows : Twelve o'clock noon, eight bells; 12 : 30 P. M., one bell; 1 : 00 P. M., two bells; 1 : 30 P. M., three bells; 2 : 00 P. M., four bells; 2 : 30 P. M., five bells; 3 : 00 P. M., six bells; 3 : 30 P. M., seven bells; 4 : 00 P. M., eight bells; 4 : 30 P. M., one bell; 5 : 00 P. M., two bells; 5 : 30 P. M., three bells, and so on through all of the six watches of four hours each. This system is uniform on all Navy vessels. A similar arrangement is in use on merchant vessels, although in many cases the details, such as the method of dogging the watches, is left to the discretion of the masters of the various vessels. Bells are struck according to ship's or clock time, which is the time of the zone the ship happens to be in. The earth is divided into time zones, bounded by meridians fifteen degrees apart, and as a ship goes from zone to zone ship's or clock time is set ahead or back, depending on whether the vessel is sailing on an easterly or westerly course, just as railroad time changes in crossing the United States from east to west or vice versa. Navigation, however, is based on Greenwich time, which is kept by the ship's chronometers, the most accurate clocks made. The ship's bell is struck by grasping the clapper tightly in the hand and making the strokes in pairs. For instance, suppose the time is 2 : 30 P. M. The bell is struck twice in quick succession and the hand then placed on the bell to stop vibration. A brief pause follows, when the bell is again struck twice. After another pause the bell is struck only once, making five bells.

Can a whale swallow a human being whole?

This oft-asked question is prompted by the story of Jonah. According to the King James version of the Bible, Jonah was cast into the sea by mariners and swallowed by "a great fish" prepared by the Lord. After the prophet had lived three days and nights in the fish's belly the Lord spoke to the monster, which thereupon vomited Jonah upon the land. In *Matthew 12: 40* the fish is referred to as a whale, which is not a fish but a mammal. The Bible, however, was written when whales were regarded as fishes. *Seamonster* would be a more accurate translation of the Greek word used. We are here concerned with the physical rather than the miraculous character of the narrative. That there are fishes and whales that can swallow a man whole is quite probable. Most whales, it is true, have small gullets, especially those that feed on Crustacea. For instance, the throat of the blue whale, probably the largest species, is only nine or ten inches in diameter. But the sperm whale or cachalot, which feeds chiefly on squids and cuttlefish, has a throat large enough to swallow a human being whole. The manager of a whaling station in northern Britain told Sir Francis Fox in 1914 that the largest thing ever found in a whale was the skeleton of a shark sixteen feet in length. "Whaling captains," according to Sir Francis, "say that it frequently happens that men are swallowed by whales who become infuriated by the point of the harpoon, and attack the boats." One of the largest predaceous fishes, says the American Museum of Natural History, is the white or man-eater shark, which sometimes reaches a length of thirty or forty feet. Basking and whale sharks grow longer and have larger mouths, but they feed on small creatures. A species of shark similar to the basking shark, found in the Indo-Pacific Ocean, is known to attain a length of fifty feet and is said to sometimes attain seventy. Many exaggerated reports have been published concerning a whale shark captured in 1912 near Knight's Key, off Miami, Florida, by Captain Charles H. Thompson. This specimen, when measured in the water, was thirty-eight feet long, eighteen feet in girth and about 10,000 pounds in weight. In preparing the shark for exhibition, however, the skin was stretched to a length of forty-five feet and the mouth and other parts were greatly distorted. This species, says the U. S. Bureau of Fisheries, is doubtless the largest of all fishes. It feeds upon minute animal life and, although its mouth is very large, could not possibly swallow a large fish or a human being. David Starr Jordan, an authority on fishes, states that a fair-sized young sea lion was found whole in the stomach of a white shark. These fish, however, have vicious teeth and it is inconceivable that one could swallow a man without killing him. It is also improbable that a human being could be long retained alive in the stomach of a whale. Although the stomach of these creatures is cave-like in dimensions, the high temperature, the powerful gastric juice, and the spasmodic contraction and expansion of the stomach, would be fatal in a very short time. Certainly a man could not live in a conscious state inside a whale's stomach more than a few minutes. He might be able to live in an unconscious state considerably longer. One authority estimates the normal blood temperature of whales at 104.6° Fahrenheit. Dr. Gerrit S. Miller, curator of mammals at the National Museum, is convinced that no man could survive being swallowed by a whale. That is generally the verdict of scientists, notwithstanding numerous reports that such cases do occasionally occur. On October 4, 1771, the Boston *Post Boy* reported an alleged case in which a whale swallowed a sailor, bit out part of the ship and then vomited the sailor alive on the wreckage. What is often quoted as an *authentic* instance of a man being swallowed by a whale and surviving the experience is recorded in Sir Francis Fox's *Sixty-Three Years of Engineering, Scientific and Social Work,* published in 1924. This account is said to be based on declarations of the captain and another officer of a whaling vessel. The incident, Sir Francis assures us, was carefully investigated by M. de Parville, scientific editor of the *Journal des Débats of Paris,* who died during the World War and who had the original manuscripts in his possession. In February, 1891, according to Sir Francis, the *Star of the East* sent out boats to harpoon a large sperm whale in the vicinity of the Falkland Islands. A lash of the whale's tail upset one of the boats and threw the crew into the sea. One man was drowned and another, James Bartley, could not be found. The crew killed the whale, tied it alongside the ship and began to remove the blubber. The next morning the missing sailor was found unconscious in the whale's stomach after it was hoisted on deck. A sea-water bath revived Bartley, but his mind was not clear and he was placed in the captain's cabin, where he remained two weeks a raving lunatic. He gradually regained possession of his senses and at the end of three weeks was sufficiently recovered to resume his duties. The skin of his face, neck and hands, where it was exposed to the gastric juice, was bleached to a deadly whiteness and did not recover its natural appearance even after being treated in a London hospital, although his health was not unfavorably affected. Bartley affirmed that he lost his senses from fright and not from want of air. He remembered being encompassed in darkness and felt himself slipping along a smooth passage. Then the terrible heat seemed to draw out his vitality and he became unconscious. The other members of the crew thought their comrade survived because he was near the whale's throat and because the whale cooled off rapidly after being killed. Such is the strange story told by Sir Francis Fox, who pronounced it *well accredited*. The incident, however, is not so well authenticated as might at first appear. Neither Sir Francis nor M. de Parville had any first-hand information, and we are given nothing about the character of the unnamed whaling captain and the other officer.

How did *three sheets in the wind* originate?

A drunken person is said to be three sheets in the wind. The term apparently originated among English sailors. It was used in its modern sense already in 1821 by Pierce Egan, who wrote: "Old Wax and Bristles is about three sheets in the wind." In *Dombey and Son,* published in 1846, Charles Dickens wrote: "Captain Cuttle looking, candle in hand, at Bunsby more attentively, perceived that he was three sheets in the wind, or, in plain words, drunk." There is no positive evidence that the term ever had a nautical significance among sailors. In sea parlance a sheet is not a sail, as the landsman would naturally suppose, but a rope or chain attached to a sail to regulate the angle at which it is set in relation to the wind. One writer states that if the sheets are loose the ship will "reel and stagger like a drunken man" and he derives the popular slang phrase from that circumstance. Sometimes *three sheets in the wind* is completed by *and the other one flying,* which suggests that lack of control is the point of the phrase. That the phrase originally alluded to the action of the sails of a ship when the sheets or ropes were loosened is quite probable, but the exact application of *three sheets* is not known for certain. The following theory is advanced by a correspondent: "Sheet means chain. Wind is short for windlass. Therefore three sheets in the wind may simply mean three chains in the windlass. If you ever tried to stand on a boat so rigged in a very mild gale you would certainly see an imitation of a man who had trifled with our noble experiment."

Why do some shoes squeak?

Squeaking in shoes is generally caused by the rubbing together of the different layers of leather composing the soles. Driving pegs into the soles will generally remove the squeak permanently. It can be removed temporarily by soaking the shoes in water to a depth of about three-quarters of the thickness of the soles. Cobblers sometimes take the squeak out of shoes by putting talcum or some other kind of powder between the outer and inner sole.

Where did Noah's ark land?

The average person in replying to this question will say that Noah's ark landed on Mt. Ararat. It is not so stated in the Bible. According to the King James version, *Genesis 8: 4* says that "the ark rested . . . upon the mountains of Ararat." In the Vulgate and Douay versions it says the "mountains of Armenia." The name *Mt. Ararat* nowhere occurs in the Scriptures. It is only a legend that the ark landed on the highest peak of the mountains of Ararat or Armenia. There is no single peak in this range called simply Mt. Ararat, but the highest peak is known as Great Ararat and its nearest rival as Little Ararat. Traditon differs widely as to the exact place where the ark landed. The Kurds, Syrians and Nestorians generally hold that the resting place of the ark was on Mt. Judi in southern Armenia, while the Jews and Armenians have from time immemorial held that it was on Great Ararat. Some ancient writers, including Josephus, located it in Kurdistan. The name *Ararat,* supposedly of Aramæan origin, means supereminence. To the Armenians Great Ararat is *Masis,* meaning sublime. The Turkish name, *Agri-dagh,* signifies steep mountain. Only the Persian name alludes to the Hebraic and Christian tradition. To the Persians the highest peak of the "mountains of Ararat" is *Koh-i-Nuh,* Noah's mount.

How much did the United States pay for Alaska?

By a treaty signed March 30, 1867, the United States agreed to pay Russia $7,200,000 *in coin* for Alaska. There were charges of bribery at the time and vague rumors that the State Department had made a secret deal with Russia. In 1868 the *Worcester Spy* stated: "Of $7,200,000 in gold voted for Alaska, the amount it is now reported Russia actually got was $5,000,000 in gold, about £1,000,000 sterling. This leaves $2,200,000 to be accounted for." The charge led to a Congressional investigation. "The circumstances which led to the transfer are still supposed by many to be enshrouded in mystery," wrote Hubert H. Bancroft in 1890, "but I can assure the reader that there is no mystery about it." The subject might have rested there had it not been for a *Manuscript Note* found in the files of the late Franklin K. Lane. This memorandum, which is dated at Washington, December 29, 1911, was published in 1922 in *The Letters of Franklin K. Lane,* edited by his widow. It reads as follows:

Last night I dined with Charles Henry Butler . . . In the course of the evening Mr. Charles Glover, president of the Riggs National Bank, told me this bit of history. That when he was a boy, in the bank one day Mr. Cockran came to him and handed him two warrants upon the United States Treasury, one for $1,400,000 and the other for $5,800,-000. He said, "Put those in the safe." Mr. Glover did so, and they remained there for a week, when they were sent to New York. Mr. Glover said: "These warrants were the payment of Russia for the Territory of Alaska. Why were there two warrants? I never knew until some years later, when I learned the story from Senator Dawes, who said that prior to the war, there had been some negotiations between the United States and Russia for the purchase of Alaska, and the price of $1,400,000 was agreed upon. In fact this was the amount that Russia asked for this great territory, which was regarded as nothing more than a barren field of ice.

"During the war the matter lay dormant. We had more territory than we could take care of. When England, however, began to manifest her friendly disposition toward the Confederacy, and we learned from Europe that England and France were carrying on negotiations for the recognition of the Southern States, and possibly of some manifestation by their fleets against the blockade which we had instituted, (and which they claimed was not effective and merely a paper blockade), we looked about for a friend, and Russia was the only European country upon whose friendship we could rely. Thereupon Secretary Seward secured from Russia a demonstration, in American ports, of Russian friendship. Her ships of war sailed to both our coasts, the Atlantic and Pacific, with the understanding that the expense of this demonstration should be met by the United States, out of the contingent fund. It was to be a secret matter.

"The war came to a close, and immediately thereafter Lincoln was assassinated and the administration changed. It was no longer possible to pay for this demonstration, secretly, under the excuse of war, but a way was found for paying Russia through the purchase of Alaska. The warrant for $1,400,000 was the warrant for the purchase of Alaska, the warrant for $5,800,000 was for Russia's expenses in her naval demonstration in our behalf, but history only knows the fact that the United States paid $7,200,000 for this territory, which is now demonstrated to be one of the richest portions of the earth in mineral deposits."

The memorandum is not trustworthy evidence. According to the State Department several students have at different times made exhaustive searches in the archives of the Department for evidence indicating that part of the sum paid to Russia in 1868 was reimbursement for a naval demonstration in our behalf during the Civil War. No such evidence has ever been found. Russia was paid in a single draft, not two drafts. It was authorized by a Treasury warrant dated July 29, 1868. The draft itself was dated at the Treasury of the United States, Washington, August 1, 1868, and read as follows: "At sight, pay to Edward de Stoekl, envoy extraordinary, &c., or order, seven millions two hundred thousand dollars. Pay in cash. F. E. Spinner, Treasurer of the United States." It was drawn on the Assistant Treasurer of the United States at New York. Baron de Stoekl, the Russian minister at Washington, acknowledged receipt of the amount on the same date. The investigating committee of 1869 learned that the draft for $7,200,000 was assigned by endorsement to George W. Riggs, a Washington banker, who on the same day took transfer checks on the subtreasury in New York for $7,100,000. Immediately, according to his own testimony and that of Spinner, Riggs transmitted $7,035,000, minus his commission of one-twentieth of one per cent, to the agent of Messrs. Baring Brothers and Company at New York. By direction of Baron de Stoekl he paid $26,000 in gold to Robert J. Walker for a fee, and the remainder was paid by various checks to the Russian minister in person during the months of August and September. The other $100,000 was left in the Treasury subject to Riggs's check, and it was not all drawn out until about the middle of September, 1868. Unfortunately the correspondence on the purchase of Alaska was very meager, because most of the negotiations were oral and informal. The purchase was discussed as early as 1859 and 1861, when the United States made an informal offer of $5,000,000. Although Russia replied that the sum was inadequate, it might have been accepted had not the outbreak of the Civil War interrupted negotiations. After the war Secretary of State Seward offered to pay $7,000,000 for Alaska. He later added $200,000 to the offer on condition that the cession be "free and unencumbered." The offer was accepted. This voluntary addition of $200,000 undoubtedly had much to do with starting the rumors of bribery and a secret deal. Russia attached little value to Alaska, and since we purchased the territory at a time when we were hard up for money, it is not improbable that Russia's friendliness during the Civil War prompted the Government to be more generous than it would otherwise have been.

Will pearls dissolve in vinegar?

Pliny the Elder says in his natural history that Cleopatra once made a wager with Mark Antony that she could spend ten million sesterces on one entertainment. She won by preparing the most expensive carbonated drink in history. Having in her earrings two of the largest pearls in the world, she threw one of them into a vessel of vinegar, which she drank as soon as the pearl had dissolved. Plancus, the umpire, immediately declared the queen winner of the wager and refused to let her dissolve the second pearl. Before Cleopatra's time, Pliny informs us, Clodius, the son of the actor

Æsopus, had done the same at Rome; and, according to Suetonius, the emperor Caligula later exhibited his extravagance by drinking pearls of great price dissolved in vinegar. Some writers regard these stories as historical fictions. Like all carbonates, pearls will dissolve in strong vinegar and other weak acids, evolving carbon dioxide and leaving calcium acetate as dissolved salt. According to the U. S. Bureau of Chemistry and Soils, pearls consist of 91.7 per cent calcium carbonate, 6 per cent organic matter and 2.3 per cent water. Accordingly they should dissolve in vinegar containing six or more per cent of acetic acid. But pearls would dissolve in such vinegar very slowly because of their great hardness. It is not probable that an ordinary pearl would completely dissolve in even strong vinegar in less than three or four hours. Therefore if Pliny's account is correct the Egyptian queen must have waited a long time for the pearl to dissolve or she must have used exceedingly strong vinegar. If the pearl were first pulverized it would not only readily dissolve but effervesce mildly.

Do bees collect wax from flowers?

It is a common mistake to suppose that honeybees collect wax from flowers. Beeswax is a product of digestion and is secreted by the worker bees in the form of tiny scales which appear between the segments on the under side of the abdomen. The notion that bees collect wax from flowers no doubt arose from the fact that many people confuse wax with the pollen that bees collect and carry to the hive in small masses attached to the hairs of the hind legs. This pollen is mixed with honey and converted into bee-bread for the young bees.

What is a four-flusher?

A four-flusher, in common parlance, is a bluffer, braggart, or cheat. The term originated in the popular indoor diversion known as poker. In this game a flush consists of five cards of the same suit, all spades, hearts, diamonds or clubs. If a player gets four cards of one suit and one card of another suit he has a four flush, also called a bobtail flush. Sometimes a player with a four flush pretends to have a full flush and attempts to drive out an opponent by betting heavily. This practice is perfectly legitimate in poker, but such a player is known as a four-flusher. If he succeeds the other players never know what cards he held; if he is *called* he must show his cards and his bluff is exposed. A four-flusher, literally speaking, is merely a poker player who, holding four cards of a suit, bets as if he had five.

Does a baby elephant suck with its trunk?

The young elephant sucks with its mouth, not its trunk. Two teats situated between the forelegs of the female supply the baby elephant with nourishment. When the calf sucks it curls back its trunk. It is a common mistake to suppose that elephants drink through their trunks. The use of the trunk in drinking is confined to taking up water and squirting it into the mouth.

How did *hooch* originate?

Hooch, in the sense of spirituous liquor, is a contraction of *Hoochinoo,* the name of a Tlingit Indian village which formerly stood near the site of the present Killisnoo, on Admiralty Island, near Sitka, Alaska. Both *Hoochinoo* and *Killisnoo,* according to the Bureau of American Ethnology, are corruptions of *Hutsnuwu,* meaning "grizzly bear fort." When Russia transferred Alaska to the United States in 1867 the Indians were acquainted with no hard liquor except Russian rum. The United States Government ordered that all spirituous liquors should be placed under the control of the military commander at Sitka. In 1873 the Attorney General declared that Alaska was Indian country and that no liquor could be introduced into the territory without the permission of the War Department. About this time a man named Sullivan deserted from the American garrison at Sitka and taught the Indians at the Hoochinoo village how to make a mash of brown sugar, spoiled dried fruit and squash flour. This mash was distilled by means of crude stills made from kerosene cans. A chief named Captain Jack, who posed as "the white man's friend," took some of the liquor to Sitka where he sold it to the soldiers and bought more raw materials. The new liquor was called hoochinoo at Sitka, and in the course of a few years the hoochinoo business became the most important industry in Alaska. Molasses was substituted for brown sugar and other ingredients were added. "Before the time of the purchase," wrote Hubert Bancroft in 1890, "the art of making molasses rum was unknown to the natives, but after the military occupation many of the soldiers became proprietors of hoochinoo stills." Ten years later ninety per cent of all the freight going to the territory consisted of molasses, "all for the purpose," says Bancroft, "of making hoochinoo, the other ingredients used being flour, dried apples or rice, yeast powder, and sometimes hops. Sufficient water is added to make a thick batter, and after fermentation has taken place a sour, muddy, highly alcoholic liquor is produced, of abominable taste and odor." Hoochinoo, says Edward R. Emerson in *Beverages, Past and Present,* "if reports can be relied upon, contains more frenzy in one glass than a quart of any ordinary inebriating beverage made."

How did the Amazon River receive its name?

The Amazon River received its name from a tribe of female warriors who were fabled to live on its banks and whom the early explorers called Amazons after the legendary nation of female warriors in Asia Minor. According to Greek tradition the Amazons cut off their right breasts in order to give them greater freedom in using their weapons, and some etymologists derive the name from Greek *a,* without, and *mazos,* breast. In 1541 Francisco de Orellana and fifty followers descended the river from the slopes of the Andes to the sea. Near the mouth of the Trombretas the explorers had a battle with the natives, and in his memorial to the Spanish king Orellana declared that women armed with bows and arrows fought at the head of the men. According to Father Carbajal, who accompanied the expedition, these women appeared to be very tall, robust and fair, and they wore their long hair twisted around their heads. Orellana supposed that these women belonged to the tribe of female warriors whom he had heard about from his guides, and accordingly he called them Amazons and the region they inhabited the land of the Amazons. It was not until many years later that the river itself became generally known as the river of the Amazons, or simply the Amazon. Orellana himself first called it Rio de la Trinidad, and many later explorers mentioned it as the Orellana River. Vicente Yanez Pinson, who in 1500 explored its mouth, had named it Santa Maria de la Mar

Dulce, and for a long period afterwards it was often referred to simply as Mar Dulce, which means fresh-water sea. Rio Grande, El Dorado and Maranon are other names by which the river or stretches of it were known, and in Brazil the principal part of the stream is still known as Solimoes. Whether there was actually a tribe of female warriors along the river remains a disputed question. No doubt the stories about the Amazons had some basis in fact, but the explorers elaborated upon their meager information to aggrandize themselves and to entertain the public. One investigator suggests that Orellana and his companions may have mistaken young men, with long hair, eardrops and necklaces, for female warriors. But among the Caribs and other natives of the New World the women often aided the men in battle, and even at the present time there are native tribes in the Amazon valley whose women are stronger physically and more aggressive than the men.

How much is a *point* in market reports?

Point, as employed in market reports, means a recognized unit of variation in price and is used in quoting the prices of stocks as well as various commodities. In the United States stock market one point ordinarily means $1 a share. The value of a point, however, varies according to the commodity in question. Therefore in order to understand the market reports one must be acquainted with the value of a point in reference to any given commodity. In the coffee and cotton markets, for instance, a point is the hundredth part of a cent; in oil, grain, sugar and pork it is one cent. When cotton goes up 200 points it goes up two cents; when grain goes up five points it goes up five cents.

Why is land at the mouth of a river called a delta?

The triangular tract of land which often forms at the mouth of a river is called a delta because in outline it resembles Delta, the fourth letter of the Greek alphabet, which is shaped like a small triangle and corresponds to D. *Delta* in this sense was originally applied by the Greeks to the three-cornered tract of land formed by the diverging mouths of the Nile and the seacoast. This area was compared to the Greek letter Δ as early as the time of Herodotus, the father of history, who lived in the fifth century B. C. Centuries later Strabo used the term in reference to the alluvial deposit at the mouth of the Indus. The Mississippi, Danube, Rhine, Nile and the Indus are among the great rivers of the world which have clearly defined deltas.

What is the Trench of Bayonets?

On June 10, 1916, two battalions of the 137th French Infantry commanded by Lieutenant Polimann went into position in trenches on the slopes of a ravine near the Thiaumont farm several miles north of Verdun. These troops were subjected to heavy fire by the Germans during the next day and they lost more than half their number in killed and wounded. Throughout the night of June 11 and 12 they were under convergent fire and their losses continued to be heavy. Their rifles being choked with earth the French troops fixed bayonets and determined to resist the enemy to the last man. When the Germans assaulted in the morning many of the French had been buried alive by the explosion of shells. Only their bayonets could be seen protruding from the soft earth. This is the now famous Trench of Bayonets. It is estimated that out of the one thousand men composing the two battalions not more than two hundred and fifty survived. The Trench of Bayonets has been preserved just as it was found after the battle and the bayonets may still be seen projecting from the ground. A monument was erected over the site by the French government to commemorate the heroism of the men who permitted themselves to be buried alive rather than abandon their post.

Does the Pope's crown bear the number 666?

There is a curious though absurd belief held by many non-Catholics that the number 666 appears on the crown or tiara worn by the Pope. The belief is based on the old charge that the Pope is antichrist and identified with one of the allegorical beasts mentioned in the Apocalypse of St. John. *Revelation 13: 18* says in part: "Let him that hath understanding count the number of the beast: for it is the number of a man: and his number is six hundred three score and six." Accordingly 666 is often referred to as the mystical or apocalyptic number. Before the Reformation the Waldensians and Albigensians, as well as John

Wyclif and John Hus, frequently referred to the Pope as antichrist, but usually in a more or less metaphorical sense. After the Reformation the charge was repeated more specifically. According to some early Lutheran writers, antichrist began to reign over the Church between February 19 and November 10 in the year 607 A. D., when Pope Boniface III obtained from the Greek emperor the privilege of calling the Roman church "Head of All the Churches." The charge that the number 666 actually appears on the tiara worn by the Pope followed the assumption that he is antichrist and that the apocalyptic number refers to him. This charge was supported by an odd coincidence. The title of the Pope is Vicar of Christ. On some of the tiaras worn by the Popes this title was written VICARIVS FILII DEI, which is Latin for Vicar of the Son of God. If the letters in this title which are used as Roman numerals are given their respective values and added together, and those not so used are rejected or given the value of zero, they total 666. They may be arranged as follows:

V	5	F	0
I	1	I	1
C	100	L	50
A	0	I	1
R	0	I	1
I	1		
V	5	D	500
S	0	E	0
		I	1

666

This ingenious method of converting VICARIVS FILII DEI into the apocalyptic number is actually accepted by many people as conclusive evidence of the Pope's identity with antichrist. Oddly enough, the Greek letters of *Lateinos* (Pagan Rome) that are also numerals total 666 when added together.

When is the best time to cut trees in order to kill them?

The best time to cut trees in order to kill them is in the spring after the sprouts have started and the tree is in full leaf. Many people believe that there is a certain period in midsummer—a particular day during dog days according to some—when a tree can be killed by merely wounding it, such as cutting off a limb or making a gash in the trunk with an ax. A popular almanac states that "scotching or chipping a tree on the 29th day of August has never been known to fail to kill a tree provided a little of the sap seeped out on the bark." This, of course, is a myth. Some trees have a remarkable capacity for reproducing themselves from shoots and consequently they are hard to exterminate. Among these are the persimmon, sassafras, cottonwood, soft maple, willow, sycamore and yellow poplar or tulip. Owing to their peculiar root systems the stumps of these and certain other species persistently send out shoots and sprouts after the upper trunks have been removed. As a general rule cuts made in trees during the dormant period in winter are not so injurious as cuts made during the spring, summer and early fall. Certain trees, particularly the sugar maple, bleed seriously when wounded in the spring just before the appearance of the foliage, and a large cut at that season might prove fatal, but generally cuts that do not approach girdling of the trunk will not kill trees. "It is a common belief," says the U. S. Department of Agriculture, "that brush cut in the summer or early fall is not apt to sprout again, but investigations have demonstrated that there will always be some second and even third growth, regardless of when the brush is cut." Trees are often cut during the winter because farmers then have more time for such work and the temperature is more favorable for chopping wood. But that is the poorest time of the year to chop down trees with a view of exterminating them. During the growing season trees store up nutritive elements in their roots, and when injured they draw on this reserve to reëstablish themselves. This reserve is at its lowest ebb when the sprouts are starting and the tree is getting into full leaf. Hence that is the best time to cut a tree in order to kill it. The death and decay of some species can be hastened by introducing poison into the circulatory sap system of the living tree.

How do maggots get on meat?

It was once universally believed that maggots are produced on dead flesh by *abiogenesis* or *spontaneous generation,* that is, the production of living from non-living matter. Aristotle taught spontaneous generation and stated as an observed fact that some animals spring from putrid meat. This belief persisted through the Middle Ages and was not disproved until 1668, when an Italian named Francesco Redi advanced the theory that every living thing comes from a preëxisting living thing. Redi exposed meat to the air during hot weather. It soon began to putrify and within a few days was covered with maggots. He then put similar meat in a jar covered with fine gauze and exposed it in the same manner. The meat began to putrify as before, but no maggots appeared on it. Blowflies, however, swarmed over the wire screen covering the jar and within a few days the gauze was covered with maggots. This proved that the maggots were not generated by the corruption of the meat, but were hatched from eggs laid by the flies.

Were cotton bales used at the battle of New Orleans?

One of the most persistent legends in American history is that General Jackson's redoubts during the battle of New Orleans consisted chiefly of bales of cotton. This story is still frequently related as history notwithstanding positive evidence to the contrary. After the night battle of December 23, 1814, Jackson intrenched his army behind the Roderiguez canal several miles below New Orleans. The wet subsoil in this region made it difficult to obtain earth for the breastworks. A creole merchant named Vincent Nolté suggested that cotton bales would materially increase the bulk of the embankments, and Jackson acted upon the suggestion. It happened that a boat loaded with cotton lay in the river near the camp. Accordingly a large number of bales were hurriedly removed and placed in the redoubts. The scheme, however, was not successful. When a heavy cannonade began January 1, 1815, a British cannon ball knocked one of the bales out of the mound and set it on fire. Pieces of burning cotton flying about the camp greatly endangered the ammunition supply. Later several burning bales fell outside the breastworks into the ditch and produced a thick smoke which blinded the American artillerymen. By this time Jackson was as anxious to get rid of the cotton as he had been to get it. Therefore, a few days before the historic fight of the 8th, all the cotton was removed from the redoubts. As early as 1856 Alexander Walker wrote in *Jackson and New Orleans:* "After this no cotton bales were ever used in the breastworks. Yet, a vulgar error has long prevailed that Jackson's defenses were composed chiefly of this great staple." There was probably not a bale of cotton in the redoubts at the time of the final battle.

Who taught *the greatest happiness of the greatest number?*

In 1720 Francis Hutcheson, in his *Inquiry into the Original of our Ideas of Beauty and Virtue,* wrote: "That action is best which procures the greatest happiness for the greatest numbers; and that worst, which, in like manner, occasions misery." This is the earliest known use of the phrase in question. It was employed by Cesare Beccaria in his *Treatise on Crimes and Punishments,* first published in 1764. Later Jeremy Bentham, the English political philosopher, wrote: "Priestley was the first (unless it was Beccaria) who taught my lips to pronounce this sacred truth—that the greatest happiness of the greatest number is the foundation of morals and legislation." The general idea conveyed by the phrase is found in the writings of the ancients, notably Democritus.

Do standing fence posts ever petrify?

Petrifaction of wood through the replacement of wood tissues by silica or other minerals occurs only after long burial under favorable conditions. Water charged with dissolved minerals infiltrates the wood and particle by particle the minerals take the place of the organic matter. This, says the U. S. Geological Survey, does not occur within a short period, nor does it occur while the wood is exposed to the atmosphere. The belief that standing fence posts sometimes petrify evidently arose from the fact that fossil or petrified wood is often used for posts. Many persons who see these posts of petrified wood mistakenly suppose that the posts petrify after being set. Slabs of limestone are used for posts in many parts of the Western States. In Kansas there is a layer of limestone so well adapted to such use that it is locally known as "fence-post limestone." So-called petrified forests are composed of the trunks and branches of trees which were petrified while buried and later exposed. Many of the petrified trees in the western part of the United States rise to heights of twenty or thirty feet. It is believed that the growing trees were covered with volcanic ash and pumice ages ago. Continual rains and nature's chemistry did the rest. The silica-laden water trickled through the volcanic stratum and, particle by particle, the minerals replaced the organic matter of the trees. In Australia Darwin examined petrified trees standing in the position in which they had grown. "According to our view," wrote the naturalist in *The Voyage of the Beagle,* "the beds have been formed by the wind having heaped up fine sand, composed of minute rounded particles of shells and corals, during which process branches and roots of trees, together with many land-shells, became enclosed. The whole then became consolidated by the percolation of calcareous matter; and the cylindrical cavities left by the decaying of the wood, were thus also filled up with a hard pseudo-stalactical stone. The weather is now wearing away the softer parts, and in consequence the hard casts of the roots and branches of the trees project above the surface, and, in a singularly deceptive manner, resemble the stumps of a dead thicket."

Where is the Suwanee River?

The Suwannee or Swanee River, which was made famous by Stephen C. Foster's song by that name, has its source in southern Georgia in the region of Okefenokee Swamp. It flows through part of Florida and discharges its waters into the Gulf of Mexico. In its fifth report, published in 1921, the U. S. Geographic Board says that *Suwannee,* not *Suwanee,* is the correct spelling of this word when it refers to the river and the County and village in Florida, although *Suwanee,* with one *n,* is correct when it refers to a village in Georgia. The Bureau of American Ethnology supposes *Suwannee* to be derived from *Suwa'ni,* a Creek Indian word of uncertain meaning. It is generally translated *Echo.* In 1763 it was the name of an Indian village situated on the right bank of the Suwannee River in Lafayette County, Florida. This village was destroyed during the Seminole War of 1818 and the site is now occupied by Old Town, which was called *Old Suwany Town* in a report sent to the Secretary of War in 1822. Foster used *Swanee* in his song merely because it was euphonious. When he wrote the song in 1851 he had never heard of the river, *Pedee* being the name employed in the first draft. He asked his brother to suggest a euphonious, two-syllable name of a Southern river. *Yazoo* was the first one suggested, but the song writer did not like it. While examining an atlas the brother accidentally came across *Swanee* or *Suwannee,* and that name was adopted. Thus a small and unknown stream was made famous throughout the world. Although the title of the song is *Swanee River,* it is also widely known as *Old Folks at Home.* The first stanza of the song is as follows:

> Way down upon de Swanee Ribber,
> Far, far away,
> Dere's wha my heart is turning ebber,
> Dere's wha de old folks stay.
> All up and down de whole creation,
> Sadly I roam,
> Still longing for de old plantation
> And for de old folks at home.

What does *on the lap of the gods* mean?

This phrase comes to us from the ancient Greeks and means that everything possible has been done and the result depends on a power beyond human control. According to the translation by Andrew Lang and S. H. Butcher, Homer says in the seventeenth book of the *Iliad:* "Yet verily these issues lie on the lap of the gods." A similar expression occurs in the first book of the *Odyssey.* Some translators render the phrase "on the *knees* of the gods."

Why did General Grant expel the Jews from his army?

On December 17, 1862, while General U. S. Grant was in command of the Department of the Tennessee, he issued the following order from his headquarters at Holly Springs, Mississippi: "The Jews, as a class violating every regulation of trade established by the Treasury Department and also department orders, are hereby expelled from the department within twenty-four hours from the receipt of this order." The order was designed to stop illicit trading, especially in cotton. Thousands of traders and peddlers followed the Federal army south with a view of purchasing various commodities from the Confederates and selling them in the North at a large profit. General William T. Sherman referred to this illicit trade in a letter to Secretary of the Treasury Salmon P. Chase. Writing from Memphis under date of August 11, 1862,

Sherman said: "The commercial enterprise of the Jews soon discovered that ten cents would buy a pound of cotton behind our army; that four cents would take it to Boston, where they could receive thirty cents in gold. The bait was too tempting, and it spread like fire, when here they discovered that salt, bacon, powder, firearms, percussion caps, etc., were worth as much as gold . . . and I have no doubt that Bragg's army at Tupelo, and Van Dorn's at Vicksburg, received enough salt to make bacon, without which they could not have moved their armies in mass; and that from ten to twenty thousand fresh arms, and a due supply of cartridges, have also been got, I am equally satisfied." That many of these illicit traders were Jews is not questioned, but that the majority of them were is doubtful. Apparently it was customary around Grant's headquarters to speak of all peddlers and traders as Jews and it was in that sense that Grant used the term in his order. Be that as it may, he was compelled to revoke it. On January 7, 1863, the following order was issued by him: "By direction of General-in-Chief of the Army, at Washington, the general order from these headquarters expelling Jews from the department is hereby revoked." The objection to the order was explained in a letter written under date of January 21, 1863, to General Grant by Henry W. Halleck, General-in-Chief at Washington. "It may be proper," wrote Halleck, "to give you some explanation of the revocation of your order expelling all Jews from your department. The President [Lincoln] has no objection to your expelling traitors [traders?] and Jew peddlers, which, I suppose, was the object of your order; but, as it in terms proscribed an entire religious class, some of whom are fighting in our ranks, the President deemed it necessary to revoke it."

Can bats see?

All bats have eyes and can see. Some species, like the Oriental fruit-eating bats, have large, conspicuous eyes. The common phrase *blind as a bat* leads many people to suppose that bats are unable to see. This alliterative simile probably originated in the old belief that these creatures are totally blind and find their way about by instinct alone. Some authorities, however, believe that the phrase originally referred to the fact that when a bat enters a brilliantly lighted place it seems to be dazed and blunders about. The Oxford dictionary, for instance, defines *bat-blind*, as "blind as a bat in the sunlight." One writer advances the improbable theory that *blind as a bat* was originally *blind as a brickbat*, just as we say *deaf as a stone*. Bats are able to wing their way through darkness with remarkable precision and apparently they can sense objects without seeing or actually touching them. Recent investigations indicate that bats in their night flights are guided chiefly by their ears and their extremely sensitive wings. What part sight plays in guiding them is not known for certain. Many authorities say that a bat's eyes are of little service as organs of sight while flying. In our common insect-eating bats the eyes are small, beadlike and usually hidden in the soft fur. Such eyes, though highly organized, would seem to be comparatively useless during rapid flights in the dark. About 1775 an Italian scientist named Lazaro Spallanzani blinded bats and let them fly in a chamber obstructed with dangling strings and other obstacles. The bats not only avoided the obstructions but turned curves, readily found holes for concealment and in general behaved as if sight were unnecessary. Stopping their ears, on the other hand, caused them considerable embarrassment. But the fact remains that a bat's ability to manage itself is seriously affected by a bright light.

Why is the desert in Africa called the Sahara?

Sahara, the name of the great desert in northern Africa, is believed to be derived from the Arabic *sahira,* which is plural in form and which means deserts, wastes or wilds.

When did tar and feathering originate?

Tarring and feathering is a form of punishment occasionally administered by mobs in the United States. According to the most approved method, after the victim is stripped naked his body is smeared with heated tar and then plastered with feathers from a pillow or feather bed. The phrase *tar and feather* became popular a few years before the Revolution. Richard Thornton lists a notice from the "Committee on Tarring and Feathering," which was printed in the Newport *Mercury* December 20, 1773. In 1774 John Malcomb, customs officer at Boston, was tarred and feathered by a mob. On January 30 of that year the following handbill was posted in the city: "Brethren, and Fellow Citizens: This is to certify, that the modern punishment lately inflicted on the ignoble John Malcomb was not done by our order.—We reserve that Method for bringing villains of greater Consequence to a Sense of Guilt and Infamy." This handbill was signed "Joyce, junr., Chairman of the Committee on Taring and Feathering." Later the British demonstrated that the Bostonians had no monopoly on the popular punishment. Twelve regulars tarred and feathered a minute man. During 1774 Thomas Hutchinson, royal governor of Massachusetts, had an audience with George III. "I see they threatened to *pitch and feather* you," said the king. *"Tar and feather,* may it please your majesty," replied the colonial governor. Although the phrase *tar and feather* apparently originated during this period, it should not be supposed that the practice itself originated at that time. Such punishment was provided in the laws and regulations drawn up in Latin for the English navy by Richard the Lion-Hearted in 1189. James Rymer printed the original statute in *Fœdera.* The following translation of the Latin is from Hakluyt's *Voyages:* "A thiefe or felon that hath stollen, being lawfully conuicted, shal haue his head shorne, and boyling pitch powred vpon his head, and feathers or doune strawed vpon the same, whereby he may be knowen, and so at the first landing place they shall come to, there to be cast vp."

If an earthworm is cut in two will the parts survive?

If an angleworm is cut in two near the middle the front half will usually regenerate another tail which will be normal in length as well as in other respects. The hind half, however, will generally produce a second tail at the mutilated end and the worm will have two tails and no head. Such a worm is incapable of ingesting food and will soon die. Only the fore part of a worm has the organs essential to continued life, the posterior portion containing merely part of the intestines, nerve cords, blood tubes, etc. When only a few of the front segments are cut off the injury is quickly repaired by the remaining part of the worm, although when as many as five or six anterior segments are removed the full number is seldom regenerated. Experiments show that earthworms cut in two behind the nineteenth segment rarely regenerate new heads. When such a posterior portion does regenerate a head the new head is likely to be defective. If a worm is cut in several parts generally only the head end will survive, and then only when this part is not too short. Dr. Thomas H. Morgan, who made extensive researches in the regeneration of parts in earthworms, found no cases of survival of the head ends when the segments were as few as fifteen. When the reproductive organs are removed with the head, the hind part, should it regenerate a head, is incapable of reproduction. These organs lie from the ninth to the fifteenth segment, depending on the species, and once destroyed they cannot be regenerated.

How did *caucus* originate?

Caucus, meaning a preliminary meeting of the leaders of a political party, is supposed to be derived from the name of a club in Boston before the Revolution. John Adams described this club in his diary under date of February, 1763:

This day learned that the Caucus Club meets, at certain times, in the garret of Tom Dawes, the Adjutant of the Boston Regiment. He has a large house, and he has a movable partition in his garret which he takes down, and the whole club meets in one room. There they smoke tobacco till you cannot see from one end of the garret to the other. There they drink *flip,* I suppose, and there they choose a moderator, who puts questions to the vote regularly; and selectmen, assessors, collectors, wardens, pre-wards, and representatives, are regularly chosen before they are chosen in the town. Uncle Fairfield, Story, Ruddock, Adams [Samuel], Cooper, and *rudis indigestaque moles* of others are members. They send committees to wait on the merchant's club, and to propose and join in the choice of men and measures. Captain Cunningham says they have often solicited him to go to these *caucuses;* they have assured him benefit in his business, &c.

William Gordon, the historian, stated that Samuel Adams's father had belonged to such a club fifty years before 1774. Although Gordon published his history in 1788, he could find "no satisfactory origin of the name." Numerous theories have been advanced to explain the name of the original Caucus Club. The use of *caucuses* by Adams suggests that the word may antedate the name of the club; that is, a word already in current use may have been taken as the name of the political society. Because it has long been a common practice to adopt classical names for organizations some derive *caucus* from the Greek *kaukos,* meaning cup. Adams's reference to drinking flip at the Caucus Club is pointed out as evidence of the appropriateness of the Greek word. Since it was also a common practice to give clubs Indian names, others follow a similar line of reasoning and derive the name from the Algonquin Indian *kaw-kaw-was,* meaning talk. J. Hammond Trumbull suggested a derivation from *cawcawaassough,* which in the Virginia dialect of the Algonquin tongue means "one who advises, urges, encourages, pushes on." The earliest theory derived the word from *caulker,* meaning one who drives oakum or old rope into the seams of vessels. According to this theory, which was favored by John Pickering in 1814, *Caucus Club* was merely a corruption of *Caulkers' Club* and the members were contemptuously called caulkers by their enemies because most of them were identified with the shipping interests of Boston. There is no evidence to support any of these theories and the origin of *caucus* remains one of the unsolved puzzles of American etymology. In the latter part of the nineteenth century *caucus* was transported to England, where it is used in the sense of a managing or steering committee of a political party or faction.

What is the purpose of Chinese tongs?

A tong is a secret commercial society among Chinese in America. The tong as we know it does not exist in China; it is an outgrowth of the peculiar conditions under which Chinese have to live in the United States. Primarily the Chinese character standing for *tong* means *hall,* especially a hall where the Chinese family worships its ancestors. Since a clan worships one set of ancestors *tong* came to mean clan, and, by extension, party or association. "The word *tong* in Chinese," says the Chinese Legation at Washington in a letter to the author, "is equivalent to the English word party, i. e., an association of persons having similar objectives." Apparently the first Chinese who came to the New World belonged chiefly to a few families, clans or tongs, and each group had its name, like On Liang Tong and Hip Hsing Tong, which are now two of the most important tongs. Persecutions on the Pacific Coast in the last half of the nineteenth century caused the tongs to develop first into mutual aid societies and later into guilds for the protection of Chinese labor. This is how it happened that *tong*, which in China means only a family group, in the United States means a Chinese trade guild. The word used in China for guild is *hui* or *pang*. In America the Chinese, being isolated and restricted to comparatively few industries, organized their trades in order to distribute the benefits of each occupation in a way satisfactory to the various tongs. A Chinese cannot open a laundry or restaurant indiscriminately in a large city without infringing on the tong controlling that trade. Naturally there is keen rivalry among the various guilds and a breach of agreement in trade matters occasionally results in a so-called *tong war*, in which hired assassins of one tong kill members of rival organizations. A tong war is frequently the outbreak of a feud which has existed for years. One never hears of tong wars in China, where living and business conditions are entirely different. There the guilds have controversies, but they are generally settled by negotiation and public opinion. Most of the tong men in America are Cantonese, who differ widely in language, temperament and customs from the great mass of people in north, central and west China. As a rule they have little confidence in American courts and believe in settling their own difficulties in their own way.

Why was Sir Walter Raleigh executed?

Technically Sir Walter Raleigh was executed for treason. Actually he was executed for shedding Spanish blood and encroaching upon Spanish territory after engaging not to do so. King James I and Raleigh disliked each other intensely. The former favored a policy of peace, the latter wanted war with Spain. Raleigh criticized the king severely after he had been deprived of many of his titles and offices. He asserted on one occasion, it was reported, that a war with Spain would have been preferable to James's ascension to the throne. However that may be, Raleigh was charged with being implicated in a series of conspiracies against the king during the first few months of his reign, and the one-time favorite of Queen Elizabeth was committed to London Tower July 19, 1603. His trial, held at Winchester, was conducted with brutality and manifest unfairness on the part of the attorney general, Sir Edward Coke. Although Raleigh may have known of the conspiracies, no evidence of his guilt was produced. Nevertheless he was convicted and sentenced to death. The execution, however, did not then take place. Instead Raleigh was confined in the Tower, where he remained until 1616. He finally obtained his release by promising the king that he could find a gold mine on the northern coast of South America without encroaching on any of the possessions of Spain. The Spanish ambassador informed the king that Raleigh's promise was impossible of fulfillment, because Spain already had settlements on the coast. James told the ambassador that if Raleigh failed to keep his promise he would have him executed on his old sentence for treason. Accordingly the prisoner was released without a pardon, which left him at the king's mercy. The expedition sailed from England in March, 1617, and reached the mouth of the Orinoco in the following December. Raleigh himself became ill with fever and remained at Trinidad while five small vessels were sent up the river to locate the alleged gold mine. On the way the English found a Spanish settlement and a skirmish took place in which Raleigh's son Walter and several Spaniards were slain. As was expected, the expedition failed and was compelled to return to England with the commander's promise broken. Raleigh was arrested, thrown into the Tower, and October 29, 1618, was executed on the sentence passed more than fifteen years before.

Where is the southernmost point in Europe?

A point near Gibraltar, Spain, is farther south than any other point on the mainland of Europe. It is farther south by many miles than any point in Italy or Greece. It is even farther south than many points on the coast of northern Africa.

What produces cobwebs?

Cobweb means spider web, *cob* being an old English word signifying spider. It is the common name given to the more or less formless webs spun in buildings by certain species of spiders and the larvæ of some insects. Most of the tangled webs which annoy thrifty housewives are produced by the little house spider, *Theridion tepidariorum*. Cobwebs on the ceilings and in the corners of houses are usually not noticed until they become covered with dust, a circumstance which probably gave rise to the popular belief that cobwebs consist merely of dust. The impression was strengthened by the fact that the house spider is seldom observed at work.

What is a gadget?

The slang word *gadget* is synonymous with *thingumbob* or *thingumabob*. It is employed as a convenient name for anything novel or as a substitute word when the speaker is unable to recall the right name. *Gadget* originated in the navy and is applied by sailors to all sorts of small tools and mechanical devices. When a sailor says "Give me that gadget" he may mean anything from a nail to a monkey-wrench. He usually employs the word only when the correct name of the article does not readily occur to him, just as a landsman might say "Give me that thingumbob." Two theories have been advanced to account for the origin of the word, neither being supported by evidence. According to one, *gadget* is derived from French *gâchette*, diminutive of *gâche*, a catch or staple. The other derives it from *gadge*, an obsolete Scotch word meaning gauge.

Do earthworms turn into lightning bugs?

That earthworms turn into lightning bugs or fireflies is a common myth in some sections of the United States. This curious belief no doubt arose from the fact that the lightning bug or firefly is a species of beetle which passes through a larva stage. Adults, larvæ and eggs are all luminous. Observation of the various species of glowworms may also have contributed to the popular belief. None of these luminous creatures are closely related to the common earthworm.

Where is The Little Brown Church in the Vale?

The Little Brown Church in the Vale is the popular name of a small country church at Bradford, two miles northeast of Nashua in Chickasaw County, Iowa. It received its name from Dr. William Savage Pitts's song entitled *The Little Brown Church in the Vale*, which is also known as *The Little Church by the Wildwood*. Dr.

Pitts was born in New England in 1830 and went to Union in Rock County, Wisconsin, when he was nineteen years old. In 1857 he visited Bradford, Iowa, and he afterwards stated that it was while there in the valley of the Cedar River that he received the inspiration for the famous song. "After going back to Wisconsin," he said, "I wrote the words and music of the song, *The Little Brown Church in the Vale*. I made no use of it in public in Wisconsin. In the spring of the year 1862 I came to Iowa, to Fredericksburg. I brought the song in manuscript with me." What particular church, if any, Dr. Pitts had in mind when he composed the song is a subject of controversy. The Bradford church was not yet built when the song was written and it is not in a vale or valley. An old friend of Dr. Pitts, Don Jackson, editor of a Fredericksburg newspaper, always maintained that the song described a country church in Rock County, Wisconsin, where Dr. Pitts's first wife was buried. However that may be, in 1864 Dr. Pitts went to Bradford to teach a class in vocal music. Nine years before a church had been organized in the community and a new frame meeting house was by this time nearly completed. Reverend John K. Nutting, who had been pastor of the congregation since 1862, was a member of the music class, and, naturally enough, he asked the teacher to take part in the dedication exercises at the new church. "It was there," said Dr. Pitts in his account, "I sang the song, *The Little Brown Church in the Vale,* for the first time in public." According to Nutting, the church was painted with warm-brown "Ohio mineral paint" chiefly because the congregation was poor and that kind of paint was cheap. The next spring Dr. Pitts took the manuscript to Chicago and sold it to a publisher named H. M. Higgins. The song immediately caught the popular fancy and soon after its publication became associated in the public mind with the church at Bradford. Dr. Pitts, who wrote many other songs, made his home at Fredericksburg, which is about twenty miles from Bradford, for forty-four years. In 1868 he graduated from Rush Medical College and between that date and 1906 he followed the profession of medicine. He died in Brooklyn, New York, in 1918, and was taken to Fredericksburg for burial. In 1913 the church at Bradford became a branch of the Nashua Congregational Church. It is looked upon as a shrine, and each year thousands of couples go to the Little Brown Church to be married. The complete song which made the church famous is as follows:

There's a church in the valley by the wildwood,
  No lovelier place in the dale,
No spot is so dear to my childhood
  As the little brown church in the vale.

Chorus:
Oh! come, come, come, come,
Come to the church by the wildwood,
  Oh, come to the church in the dale;
No spot is so dear to my childhood
  As the little brown church in the vale.

How sweet on a bright Sabbath morning,
  To list to the clear ringing bell;
Its tones so sweetly are calling,
  Oh, come to the church in the vale.

There, close by the church in the valley,
  Lies one that I loved so well;
She sleeps, sweetly sleeps 'neath the willow,
  Disturb not her rest in the vale.

There, close by the side of that loved one,
  'Neath the tree where the wild flowers bloom,
When the farewell hymn shall be chanted,
  I shall rest by her side in the tomb.

How did *knock into a cocked hat* originate?

To *knock into a cocked hat* means to knock out of shape with a single blow, to alter beyond recognition, or to put an antagonist completely out of a contest, either physically or figuratively. It is generally supposed that the phrase originally referred to striking a thing such a blow that it becomes limp and can be doubled up and carried flat under the arm like the old-fashioned cocked hats worn in the latter part of the eighteenth century and the first part of the nineteenth. Such hats were three-cornered and had the brim permanently turned up. Their name arose from the fact that *to cock* is an old verb meaning to turn, and to cock one's hat still means to turn it up on one side or to set it on the head at a peculiar angle. The British military hat worn by officers with the full dress uniform is still called a cocked hat, although it differs widely from the cocked hats formerly worn by British naval and military officers, as well as those once worn by church dignitaries. Some authorities, however, believe that *knock into a cocked hat* is only indirectly derived from the headgear so called and that the expression originated in the game of tenpins or bowls. Occasionally a player, with a single ball, will roll down all the pins of a frame except the two corner pins and the head pin, leaving a triangular figure. This is called knocking the pins into a cocked hat, which the three-cornered figure is supposed to resemble. On April 29, 1907, Woodrow Wilson, then president of Princeton University, wrote as follows to Adrian H. Joline: "Would that we could do something at once dignified and effective to knock Mr. Bryan once for all into a cocked hat." This letter was published in January, 1912, when Wilson was seeking the Democratic nomination for the Presidency. The purpose of publication was to injure him with William Jennings Bryan and the latter's friends. But Bryan chose to ignore the letter and was largely instrumental in Wilson's nomination at the Baltimore convention later in the same year.

Why is the northern boundary of Delaware curved?

The boundary between Pennsylvania and Delaware forms an arc of a circle of twelve miles radius, with New Castle in Delaware as its center. When Charles II gave Pennsylvania to William Penn in 1681 it was the king's intention to grant to his favorite the territory lying west of the Delaware River and between the 42nd and 39th degrees of latitude. But this would have encroached on the domain of the king's brother, James, Duke of York, who was proprietor of New York and the territory west of Delaware Bay taken from the Swedes by the Dutch. James had no objection to the Pennsylvania grant provided the new province did not come too near his town of New Castle on the Delaware. Therefore the charter specified that the province of Pennsylvania was to be bounded on the south "by a Circle drawne at twelve miles distance from New Castle Northward and Westward unto the beginning of the fortieth degree of Northern Latitude, and thence by a straight Line

Westward." The curved line was to begin on the Delaware River "twelve miles distance Northwards of New Castle." This was the origin of the curved line which now forms the boundary between Pennsylvania and Delaware. Penn, however, was not satisfied with this boundary because it cut his province off from Delaware Bay and gave it inadequate access to the sea. Accordingly, being a royal favorite, he not only succeeded in getting the entire line moved farther south at the expense of Maryland, but persuaded the Duke of York to convey to him his possessions on Delaware Bay, including the town of New Castle and "all that tract of land lying within the compass or circle of twelve miles about the same." Thus Penn became proprietor of the "Three Lower Counties on the Delaware" as well as of Pennsylvania. The curved line between Pennsylvania proper and the lower counties was surveyed and marked in 1701 under a warrant from Penn himself. When these three counties became *Delaware State* in 1776 a dispute over the arc boundary arose and was not definitely settled for nearly one hundred and fifty years. Inaccuracies in the original survey made it impossible to make a single curve pass through the stones set up to mark a radius of twelve miles from the center of New Castle. A joint boundary commission found that a compound curve conformed very closely to the original line and it was finally adopted as the true boundary.

What is a star chamber?

Star chamber is the name often given to any tribunal which assumes arbitrary powers. Sometimes a high-handed and unjust official act is referred to as a star chamber proceeding. It seems that the name was first applied to the room in the royal palace at Westminster, London, where the king's privy council sat in its judicial capacity in the fourteenth and fifteenth centuries. The court of star chamber grew out of these meetings. It was established about 1487 by Henry VII and it gradually assumed jurisdiction over all offenses not provided for by law, and so many of its decisions were high-handed and unjust that the court became proverbial as a typical instrument of tyranny and oppression. This court was abolished by act of Parliament in 1641, during the reign of Charles I. In 1577 Sir Thomas Smith said the apartment where the king's council sat was called the star chamber "because at the first all the roofe thereof was decked with images of starres gilted." Although there were no stars on the ceiling of the room in Sir Thomas's day and there is no confirmatory evidence, the Oxford dictionary regards the theory as "highly probable." Some authorities, however, suppose that the name is derived from Saxon *steoran,* meaning steer or govern. We find it called "the sterred chambre" in 1398, and in the Rolls of Parliament for 1426 we read of "the sterred chambre at Westmynster." William Blackstone, in Book IV of his *Commentaries,* advances a curious theory. Although the Oxford dictionary says the conjecture "has no claim to consideration" it is interesting. After stating the other conjectures, Blackstone says: "It is well known that, before the banishments of the Jews under Edward I, their contracts and obligations were denominated in our ancient records *starra* or *starrs,* from a corruption of the Hebrew word, *shetar,* a covenant. These starrs, by an ordinance of Richard I, preserved by Hoveden, were commanded to be enrolled, and deposited in chests under three keys in certain places; one, and the most considerable of which was in the king's exchequer at Westminster: and no starr was allowed to be valid, until it were found in some of the repositaries. The room at the exchequer, where the chests containing these starrs were kept, was probably called the *star chamber;* and, when the Jews were expelled the kingdom, was applied to the use of the king's council, sitting in their judicial capacity. To confirm this, the first time the star chamber is mentioned in any record, it is said to have been situated near the receipt of the exchequer at Westminster."

What is the unpardonable sin?

This is the name given to the sin against the Holy Ghost because Jesus referred to it as the one sin which admitted of no forgiveness. In *Matthew 12* it is recorded that the Pharisees accused Jesus of casting out devils by the prince of devils instead of by the spirit of God. "All manner of sin and blasphemy," answered Jesus, "shall be forgiven unto men: but the blasphemy against the Holy Ghost shall not be forgiven unto men. And whosoever speaketh against the Son of man, it shall be forgiven him: but whosoever speaketh against the Holy Ghost, it shall not be forgiven him, neither in this world, neither in the world to come." Similar passages occur in *Mark* and *Luke*. Theologians differ as to the exact nature of the unpardonable sin and the subject is an abstruse one among them. The context of the passages referred to indicates that the sin against the Holy Ghost consists of assigning his works to Satan or of denying out of pure malice the divine character of such works. Some theologians interpret the words "blasphemy against the Holy Ghost" in their most literal sense and define the unpardonable sin as the utterance of an insult against the Divine Spirit. By others the sin against the Holy Ghost is held to mean final impenitence or perseverance in "mortal sin" until death. A looser interpretation places in this class all sins committed in downright malice, especially those directly opposed to charity and goodness, supposedly the characteristic qualities of the Holy Ghost. "There is a sin unto death: I do not say that he shall pray for it," says the author of *I John,* and some suppose that *Hebrews 6: 4, 5, 6* refers to the experience that a person must go through to commit that sin, that is, become enlightened and partake of the Holy Ghost and then fall away. A few commentators go so far as to state that "the great transgression" mentioned in *Psalms 19: 13* refers to the same offense, i. e., presuming upon God's mercy and knowingly doing what is wrong, which is held to be sin in the first degree.

What Vice President was elected by the Senate?

Richard Mentor Johnson of Kentucky has been the only Vice President of the United States elected by the Senate. Amendment XII of the Constitution provides that a candidate must receive a majority of the whole number of electoral votes in order to be chosen Vice President. If no candidate for Vice President receives a majority the Senate must then choose a Vice President from the two candidates who have received the largest number of electoral votes, a majority of the whole number of Senators being necessary to a choice. In the election of 1836, when Martin Van Buren was elected President, the candidates for Vice President and the number of electoral votes received by each were as follows: Richard M. Johnson, 147; Francis Granger, 77; John Tyler, 47, and William Smith, 23. The total number of votes received by Granger,

Tyler and Smith was 147, the same number of votes received by Johnson, and no candidate had a majority of the whole number of votes cast. Therefore the election devolved on the Senate, which chose Johnson Vice President.

Is part of a ten-dollar bill redeemable at face value?

Three-fifths or more of a mutilated United States paper currency bill, note or certificate is redeemable at face value by the Treasury Department. When less than three-fifths, but clearly more than two-fifths of the original bill remains it is redeemable at one-half of the face value of the original bill. However, fragments containing less than three-fifths of the original bills are redeemable at full face value by the Treasurer of the United States provided they are accompanied by satisfactory evidence that the missing portions have been totally destroyed. Such evidence must consist of affidavits, subscribed and sworn to before a notary public, setting forth the cause and manner of destruction. Occasionally even the ashes of burned money are identified by the Treasury Department and redeemed at face value. No relief is granted by the Government to the owners of paper currency totally destroyed. Persons wishing to have mutilated money redeemed should communicate with a bank or with the Redemption Division, U. S. Treasury Department, Washington, D. C.

Why is the Belgian king called the *King of the Belgians?*

There are several reasons why the Belgian sovereign is styled *King of the Belgians* instead of *King of Belgium*. The title emphasizes the fact that he is a people's king, and not a king by divine right. Originally the idea of kingship in Europe seems to have been rulership over a nation rather than over territory. The idea of territorial sovereignty, that is, rulership over land instead of people, grew up during the feudal system. Edward the Confessor, Harold, and William the Conqueror were styled *Anglorum Rex,* King of the English. It was not until the reign of Henry II (1154–89) that the English king was known as King of England. Likewise the rulers of western continental Europe, including what is now Belgium, were known as kings of the Franks, not kings of France. The rulers of the Holy Roman Empire bore the title *Ro-*

manorum Imperator, Emperor of the Romans. In the nineteenth century there was a tendency to revert to this earlier practice. Napoleon I styled himself Emperor of the French, and Napoleon III followed his example. When Louis Philippe ascended the French throne he assumed the title King of the French. The kingdom of Belgium came into existence in 1830 when the inhabitants of the Belgian provinces revolted against The Netherlands and declared "the independence of the Belgian people." A constitutional monarchy was established and Leopold of Saxe-Coburg-Gotha was chosen the first king. In the constitution the fact is emphasized that all powers emanate from the people, and upon accession the king must take an oath to "observe the constitution and the laws of the Belgian people." The Belgian people had been known as Belgians for centuries, but when they chose their first sovereign the exact boundaries of the kingdom had not yet been determined. Therefore it was thought that *King of the Belgians* was a more appropriate title for the monarch than *King of Belgium.* In this connection it is interesting to note that in 1928 when Zogu proclaimed himself *King of the Albanians* Jugoslavia protested on the ground that the title might imply that Albanians in Jugoslavia were subjects of the Albanian king.

How did the New Orleans Mardi Gras originate?

Mardi Gras (pronounced *mardee grah*) is French and literally means fat Tuesday. It is the same as Shrove Tuesday, the day before the beginning of Lent. *Shrove* is the past tense of *shrive,* meaning confess, and Shrove Tuesday is the day on which confession or *shrift* was made preparatory to the forty days of Lent. The French name Mardi Gras or fat Tuesday alludes to an old ceremony in which a fat ox, symbolizing the passing of meat, was paraded through the streets of Paris and other French cities on Shrove Tuesday. Lent being a period of fasting Mardi Gras naturally became a day of carnival and revelry. In England the day was formerly observed by eating pancakes and it is still often referred to as Pancake Tuesday, although eating pancakes on this day survives only as a social custom. Pancakes seem to have become particularly associated with Shrove Tuesday because the people desired to use up what grease, lard and similar forbidden foods they had on hand before Lent. Carnivals and pageants still characterize Mardi Gras in many Catholic cities in Europe. Several cities in the United States also observe the day in like fashion, and in two or three States Mardi Gras is a legal holiday. The pageant on Mardi Gras at New Orleans was introduced by the French population. Although pageants were given as early as 1827, it was not until thirty years later that the distinctive ceremonies now associated with the day in that city were introduced. An elaborate street parade and pageant, accompanied by frolicking and merrymaking, is sponsored by civic organizations and the city is on that day ostensibly placed under the control of a king of the carnival.

What kind of wood did the Indians use for bows?

The materials used by the North American Indians for bows varied with different tribes and different sections of the continent. Ash, birch, cedar, cottonwood, elm, hickory, oak, osage orange, walnut, willow, witch-hazel, and yew, all were used for this purpose. Hard woods were generally favored. The northeastern tribes preferred second-growth hickory. Some tribes made compound bows by lashing pieces of bone or horn together; the Eskimos made similar bows by wrapping cord around brittle driftwood. A good bow cannot be made of wood recently cut. It should be seasoned at least three years before the bow is made. The best bows now manufactured are composed of yew imported from Spain and Italy.

What three signers of the Declaration of Independence were imprisoned by the British?

Four delegates from South Carolina signed the Declaration of Independence. They were Edward Rutledge, Thomas Heyward, Jr., Arthur Middleton, and Thomas Lynch, Jr. Three of these signers —Rutledge, Heyward, and Middleton—were later imprisoned by the British. When Charleston was captured on May 12, 1780, the British claimed all the adult male inhabitants as paroled prisoners of war. More than three months later—August 27—thirty-eight prominent citizens of Charleston, including Edward Rutledge and Thomas Heyward, Jr., were seized in their houses early in the morning and taken to the Exchange, from where they were transported a few days later to St. Augustine in Florida, which was then a British possession. Lieutenant Colonel Balfour, the commandant at Charleston, explained that the step was taken "from motives of policy." On November 15 of the same year twenty-three other men, including Arthur Middleton, were dealt with in the same manner, the only charge against them being that "they discovered no disposition to return to their allegiance and would, if they could, overturn the British government." While at St. Augustine the prisoners were given the liberty of the town, but they were not permitted to communicate with their countrymen. The three signers, along with many others, were held by the British until the general exchange of prisoners agreed upon in May, 1781, when they were delivered at the port of Philadelphia and released.

How do broadswords differ from small swords?

The broadsword has a long cutting edge and usually an obtuse or blunt point. It is a distinctively military sword and was originally so called because of its broad blade. In 1842 James Shields challenged Abraham Lincoln to a duel and the latter chose as weapons "cavalry broadswords of the largest size." A thrusting sword, that is, one with which the attack is delivered mainly with the point, is known as a small sword. It is a light sword which gradually tapers from hilt to point and does not have a cutting edge. Such swords are worn on dress occasions and are used chiefly in fencing and dueling. During the eighteenth century small swords were almost universally worn in Europe by civilians of standing.

Is the thumb a finger?

The thumb is a finger, in the most general sense of the term. *Finger* is defined as one of the five terminal members of the human hand, including the thumb. This was probably the original meaning of *finger* as applied to the digits, for the Oxford dictionary suggests that the word may be derived from *penqrós*, related to *penqe*, meaning five. Therefore it is correct to say that a normal person has five fingers on each hand. Likewise it is correct to say the wedding ring is placed on the fourth finger, that finger being the fourth when the thumb is counted. But *finger* has also acquired a specific meaning, namely, one of the four terminal members of the hand *exclusive* of the thumb. It is only natural that the thumb should be singled out and given a special name, because it is more prominent by its somewhat isolated position and because it differs from the other digits in having two instead of three phalanges. Hence it is equally correct to say the normal hand contains five fingers, or four fingers and a thumb, depending on whether one wishes to emphasize the difference between the thumb and the other digits. When *finger* is used in the restricted sense the fingers are numbered from first to fourth, beginning with the one nearest the thumb.

What does *fort* in *fortnight* mean?

Fortnight is a contraction of *fourteen nights*. The latter phrase, in the sense of a period of two weeks, was used in England as early as the year 1000 A. D. In that year it was used in a translation of the laws of Ine, who was a king of the West Saxons in the seventh century. *Fortnight* is probably a survival of an old Teutonic method of reckoning time by nights instead of by days. In 98 A. D. Tacitus wrote as follows of the ancient Germans: "Their account of time differs from that of the Romans: instead of days, they reckon the number of nights. Their public ordinances are so dated; and their proclamations run in the same style. The night, according to them, leads the day."

How did *tip* originate?

A curious story is often told to account for the origin of *tip* in the sense of a small sum of money given for personal service rendered or expected. According to the story, *tip* was derived from the initial letters of the phrase *To Insure Promptness* in the following manner: It was formerly customary to have boxes in English inns and coffeehouses for the receipt of coins for the benefit of the waiters. *To Insure Promptness* or *To Insure Prompt Service* was printed on the boxes to remind guests that a coin deposited inside would bring excellent results in the way of special service. Sometimes the phrases on the boxes were abbreviated to *T.I.P.* and *T.I.P.S.*, and from this circumstance, according to the story, *tip* and *tips* came into use. The quotations given in the Oxford dictionary show the absurdity of this derivation. *Tip* in this sense is probably derived from an old English verb *to tip*, meaning to give.

"Tip me that cheate (booty), giue me that thing," wrote Samuel Rowlands in *Martin Mark-all, the Beadle of Bridewell,* published in 1610. In *The Beaux' Stratagem,* produced in 1706, George Farquhar wrote: "Then, Sir, tips me the Verger with half a crown." By 1755 the word had acquired its modern sense. "I assure you," said a writer in that year, "I have laid out every farthing . . . in tips to his servants."

Who said: "The mills of the gods grind slowly"?

"The mills of the gods grind slowly, but they grind small," is a literal translation of an old Greek aphorism as it appears in the *Oracula Sibyllina.* Friedrich von Logau (1604–1655), the German epigrammatist, appropriated the idea in his *Deutscher Sinngedichte drei Tausend.* As translated in Henry Wadsworth Longfellow's *Poetic Aphorisms* Logau said:

Though the mills of God grind slowly, they grind exceeding small; Though with patience He stands waiting, with exactness grinds He all.

Is a spider an insect?

A spider is not an insect. Spiders belong to the class Arachnida, which also includes scorpions, mites and ticks. They differ from insects in several respects. Spiders have no feelers or antennæ, such as all insects have, and they have four pairs of legs and two pairs of jaws, while insects have three pairs of legs and three pairs of jaws. Professor J. Arthur Thomson, the Scotch naturalist, says: "Spiders are not insects. They are no nearer to insects than reptiles are to birds."

What is meant by *the laws of the Medes and Persians?*

Persia and Media were united under the same ruler after the conquest of the latter country by Cyrus of Persia in the sixth century B. C. The laws of the Medes and Persians are often referred to as a type of the unalterable and irrevocable. This application was suggested by çertain passages in the Bible. *Daniel 6: 8* says: "Now, O king, establish the decree, and sign the writing, that it be not changed, according to the law of the Medes and Persians, which altereth not." Again in the same chapter: "Then these men assembled unto the king, and said unto the king, Know, O king, that the law of the Medes and Persians is, That no decree nor statute which the king establisheth may be changed."

How did *drawing-room* originate?

Drawing-room is merely a contraction of *withdrawing-room*. The original drawing-room was a room to withdraw to. *Withdrawing-room* is still sometimes used and it occurs frequently in the literature of the seventeenth century. For instance, in 1611 Lodowick Barry wrote in *Ram Alley:* "Ile waite in the *with-drawing-room*, Vntil you call."

Which is correct, Smithsonian *Institution* or *Institute?*

Smithsonian *Institution* is the correct name of the establishment of learning at Washington. It is a common error to call it the Smithsonian *Institute*. The name, as well as the institution itself, had its origin in the will of James Smithson (1765–1829), the British chemist and mineralist who bequeathed the greater part of his estate "to the United States of America, to found at Washington, under the name to [of] the *Smithsonian Institution,* an establishment for the increase and diffusion of knowledge among men."

What insects give birth to living young?

Many species of flies deposit larvæ or maggots instead of eggs. The eggs are hatched inside the female's body. Most viviparous flies belong to the family *Sarcophagidæ* and are popularly known as flesh flies because the larvæ feed on flesh. As a rule the female flesh fly lays her young on fresh meat or on the wounds of living animals. Sometimes she deposits maggots in the nostrils of man, where they may cause death.

How does the Curb Market differ from the Stock Exchange?

The New York Curb Market is a market for securities not listed on the New York Stock Exchange. There is no essential difference between the Stock Exchange and the Curb Market either in function or in the general nature of the rules and regulations. The Curb Market, however, developed later historically and it is more a primary market, that is, a market where securities of newer companies are listed. In other words, the requirements for listing securities on the Stock Exchange are more strict. Securities are not listed in the two exchanges simultaneously. Like most of the stock markets of the world, the New York Curb Market had its origin out-of-doors, and it received its name from the fact that from the time of the Civil War until 1921, when a new building was completed, the brokers and their customers met on the street near the curb.

Who said: "When we assumed the soldier we did not lay aside the citizen"?

This quotation is inscribed on the memorial amphitheater in Arlington Cemetery near Washington. It was taken from an address delivered by George Washington on June 26, 1775, to the provincial congress of New York. General Washington was at the time on his way to take command of the Colonial army besieging Boston. He meant that in becoming soldiers the American patriots had not forgotten their duties and obligations as citizens. The idea was not original with Washington. In 1647 the soldiers of Cromwell's army, in a *Humble Representation* addressed to Parliament, declared that "on becoming soldiers we have not ceased to be citizens."

Can a peacock be a female?

In popular speech any peafowl is called a peacock, whether male or female. Strictly speaking, only the male should be called a peacock. The female is properly called a peahen. *Peafowl* is the proper word to apply to the birds when speaking of them generally without reference to sex. The young are known as pea-chicks.

Why is *colonel* pronounced *kurnel?*

The *r* sound in *colonel* is a holdover from the sixteenth century when the word was spelled *coronel* and pronounced *kor-o-nel* to correspond with the spelling. *Coronel* is the form still used in Spanish. This pronunciation was later shortened to *kurn-el,* which became established about 1800. *Colonel* is related to the Italian *colonello,* meaning little column, and the English spelling was gradually changed during the seventeenth century to conform more with the original. The colonel, says Skeat, was so called because he led the little column or company at the head of the regiment.

Why were the Boxers so called?

Europeans applied *Boxer* to members of a secret society in China. The Chinese name for the organization was *I Ho T'uan,* which literally means *Righteousness and Harmony Society.* Although the society originated earlier in the nineteenth century, it did not attract much public attention until 1900, when the members became notorious for their efforts in northern China to rid the country of foreigners. Westerners called them Boxers as the result of a pun. The Chinese name itself has nothing to do with boxing, but the members of the association kept themselves in fighting trim by hand and fist exercises, and it so happens that the Chinese words for *society* and *fist* sound somewhat alike. This accounts for the fact that the name is often incorrectly translated *Righteous and Harmonious Fist Society.*

What is the Sargasso Sea?

Sargasso Sea is the name given to a vast region in the Atlantic Ocean between the Azores and the West Indies where large quantities of seaweed are kept in a slow swirl by the Gulf Stream and the Equatorial Current. Columbus noted the abundance of floating weeds in this region in 1492. The name arises from the fact that the Spaniards called it *Mar de Sargazo,* sea of seaweeds, *sargazo* meaning seaweed in Spanish. It is said that in the days of small sailing vessels navigation was often hindered by the dense collections of seaweed. A French scientist described this part of the Atlantic as "a vast floating meadow," and many writers refer to it as the graveyard of ships. The Sargasso Sea, however, is largely a myth. Early writers evidently exaggerated the size of the seaweed rafts. There is no basis for the common belief that the entire surface of this region is sometimes covered with a mat of seaweed. It is merely a vast area in the North Atlantic, lying roughly between the parallels of 20° and 35° North and the meridians 30° and 70° West, in which patches of seaweed are common. Patches an acre in extent are unusual. William Beebe, who in 1925 explored the Sargasso Sea for the New York Zoological Society, reported that at only certain seasons does the weed collect into the floating meadows reported by trustworthy observers, and these rafts are soon scattered by gales. His observations have been confirmed by numerous competent investigators. Beebe cruised for a month in the Sargasso Sea and saw many patches of weed, but seldom any which were larger than a man's head. He also saw thin streamers of weed, sometimes a mile or two long, undulating over the sea. It is a disputed question whether the seaweed propagates in the open sea or drifts from the coast. Although no seeds or spores are formed in mid-ocean, Beebe concluded that the weed propagates at sea by vegetation for many years, if not perennially. He supposed that the floating seaweed is annually replenished to some extent by fragments torn from rocks of shallow coastal waters and carried into the Sargasso Sea by the Gulf Stream. Rafts of seaweed, though much smaller, are formed also in the Pacific, Indian and Antarctic oceans.

Which sex of the mosquito bites?

The male mosquito does not bite. Only in the female is the proboscis fitted for biting and blood-sucking. The mouth parts of the male are rudimentary and he could not bite no matter how hard he might try. This, at any rate, is true of all the common mosquitoes. Whether blood-sucking is common to both sexes in any rare species is a disputed question. "So far as we know," says the U. S. Bureau of Entomology, "there is no species of mosquito of which the male sucks blood."

What is the difference between flotsam and jetsam?

Miscellaneous articles and odds and ends are often referred to as *flotsam and jetsam*. The phrase is borrowed from the English common law. *Flotsam* and *jetsam* now have about the same meaning and they are usually linked together. Originally, however, the English courts distinguished clearly between the terms. *Flotsam* is derived indirectly from the Latin *flottare,* meaning to float. Flotsam, in the words of Lord Coke, is "when a ship sinks or otherwise perishes, and the goods float on the sea." *Jetsam* is derived from the Latin *jactare,* meaning to throw. Jetsam, to quote Coke again, is "when goods are cast out of a ship to lighten her when in danger of sinking, and afterwards the ship perishes." The distinction was based on how the goods got into the sea, flotsam being swept from the ship by the elements while jetsam was thrown overboard by the crew in an effort to save the vessel.

What was the message to Garcia?

When war between the United States and Spain was imminent early in 1898 the Government desired to communicate as quickly as possible with General Calixto Garcia, commander of the Cuban insurgents, who was somewhere in the eastern mountain districts of the island. He could be reached neither by telegraph nor mail. "Where can I find a man who will carry a message to Garcia?" asked President McKinley. The head of the Bureau of Military Intelligence suggested that Lieutenant Andrew S. Rowan be sent. "Send him," replied the President. Lieutenant Rowan promptly obeyed the order. He left Washington for Jamaica April 8 with instructions to find Garcia and obtain from him full information as to the number, condition and distribution of Spanish troops in eastern Cuba, the character of their officers, the general topography of the region, the condition of the roads and systems of communication, as well as any plans which Garcia might suggest for coöperation with the United States. The message was purely military in character and was not committed to writing, as often stated. Rowan landed by night from an open sail boat on the southern coast of Cuba near Turquino Peak. He was guided through the pathless mountains and jungles by Cuban revolutionists and reached the headquarters of Garcia at Bayamo May 1. Garcia did not reply directly to the message, but sent several of his officers back to the United States with Rowan, who left the island from the northern coast. "You have performed a brave deed," the President told the young lieutenant before a meeting of the Cabinet. Later Rowan was raised to the rank of lieutenant colonel. In recommending the promotion General Nelson A. Miles wrote: "Lieutenant Rowan made a journey across Cuba, was with the insurgent army with Lieutenant General Garcia, and brought most important and valuable information to the Government. This was a most perilous undertaking, and in my judgment Lieutenant Rowan performed an act of heroism and cool daring that has rarely been excelled in the annals of warfare." The prompt and efficient delivery of the message to Garcia by Rowan has become proverbial. *A Message to Garcia,* which was published by Elbert Hubbard in *The Philistine* for March, 1899, immortalized Rowan and the incident. "There is a man," Hubbard wrote, "whose form should be cast in deathless bronze and the statue placed in every college of the land." The essay was widely reprinted and is said to hold the world's record for circulation and translation into foreign tongues. In 1922 Congress awarded Lieutenant Colonel Rowan a Distinguished Service Cross for his heroic exploit twenty-four years earlier.

How many ribs do monkeys have?

In monkeys and apes the number of pairs of ribs varies from eleven in some species to fifteen in others. The orang-utan, like man, has twelve pairs, while gorillas and chimpanzees have thirteen. Only the New World night apes have as many as fifteen pairs of ribs.

How is meerschaum obtained?

Meerschaum is the popular name of sepiolite, a porous, earthy mineral which is known to the public chiefly as a material used in cigarette holders and pipe bowls. In Spain, however, meerschaum is mined for building material, and the Turks often use it for soap in washing. It is not only soaplike to the touch, but lathers well and removes grease readily. Meerschaum is found in certain alluvial deposits in different parts of the world. Deposits on the plains of Eski-Shehr in Asia Minor have been worked for a thousand years or more. The name is from the German *meer,* sea, and *schaum,* foam, and is a literal translation of the Persian *kef-i-daryā,* foam of the sea, referring to the frothy appearance of meerschaum when it is first removed from the earth. Sometimes dried masses of meerschaum will float in water, a fact which probably gave rise to the common story that the ancients first found the substance floating on the sea and supposed it to be "petrified sea foam." Chemically it is a form of hydrous magnesium silicate, being composed of water, magnesia and silica. Most of the meerschaum used in pipes is obtained from Asia Minor, where it is taken from pits twenty-five or thirty feet deep. When first taken from the ground it is grayish white in color, with a faint tint of yellow or red, and the blocks are so soft that they can be cut with a knife like cheese. They are thoroughly dried and then scraped and polished. The chief known deposits of meerschaum in the United States are in New Mexico. Meerschaum taken from these deposits, says the U. S. Geological Survey, is very similar in appearance to that from Asia Minor as it appears on the market ready for carving. The Asia Minor product, however, is somewhat lighter and more spongy.

Is steam visible?

Strictly speaking, steam is invisible. The term is properly applied to the transparent gas or vapor into which water is converted when heated to the boiling point. The visible mist commonly called steam, which consists of minute droplets of water in the air, is not formed until the water vapor has cooled and condensed.

Why do electric light bulbs pop when broken?

If the filament in electric light bulbs were made red hot in air it would oxidize and burn up. Therefore the bulb must consist of a vacuum or it must be filled with a gas in which there is no oxygen. The air is pumped out of ordinary electric light bulbs until a vacuum or nearly a vacuum is produced. When such a bulb is suddenly broken a popping sound is often produced by the outside air rushing into the vacuum. The filament burns up the instant air is admitted into a lighted bulb. Some electric bulbs are filled with nitrogen and they do not pop when broken because the pressure inside tends to equalize that outside.

What was Bryan's *cross of gold* speech?

In 1896 William Jennings Bryan, a former member of Congress from Nebraska, was a delegate to the Democratic national convention at Chicago. He there made a speech which was largely responsible for his nomination for the Presidency. At the time he was thirty-six years old and widely known as "the boy orator of the Platte." In his famous speech he hurled defiance at the Cleveland "sound-money" Democrats and advocated the free and unlimited coinage of silver at the ratio of 16 to 1. It is known as the *cross of gold* speech because it closed with that phrase. "If they dare to come out in the open and defend the gold standard as a good thing," shouted the orator, "we shall fight them to the uttermost, having behind us the producing masses of this nation and the world. Having behind us the commercial interests, and the laboring interests, and all the toiling masses, we shall answer their demands for a gold standard by saying to them: 'You shall not press down upon the brow of labor this crown of thorns; you shall not crucify mankind upon a cross of gold.' "

How did *stealing thunder* originate?

John Dennis (1657–1734), an English dramatist and critic, was responsible for the expression to *steal one's thunder*. In 1709 his play *Appius and Virginia* was produced at Drury Lane, and for its production the playwright introduced a new method of simulating thunder on the stage. Previously stage thunder was produced by large bowls. Dennis produced it "by troughs of wood with stops in them." *Appius and Virginia* was a financial failure and was soon withdrawn by the manager, much to the disgust of its author, who had a high opinion of his work. Soon afterwards he went to Drury Lane to witness a performance of Shakespeare's *Macbeth*, in which the improved method of producing thunder was employed. Dennis was furious when he heard it. He exclaimed: "That's my thunder, by God! the villains will not play my play but they steal my thunder."

Do monkeys have two sets of teeth?

Monkeys like human beings have two sets of teeth. Their first or milk teeth are replaced by a second and more permanent set. This, however, is not peculiar to monkeys and apes in the animal world. "All mammals," says the American Museum of Natural History in a letter to the author, "have two sets of teeth, the first or milk dentition being followed by the permanent set. In the case of most mammals the milk set functions as in human beings and serves the young mammal for an appreciable interval of time. In exceptional cases the milk teeth are almost non-functional and are replaced by the second set so early in life that the milk teeth serve only a very slight useful function. The primates show a condition very similar to that in human beings, the milk dentition persisting for some time and the permanent teeth appearing at a considerable interval after birth, especially the last molars."

What city is known as the Bride of the Sea?

Venice is called the Bride of the Sea from the medieval ceremony known as the "marriage of the Adriatic," in which the doge of Venice threw a ring into the sea, saying: "We wed thee, O sea, in token of perpetual domination." A procession of gondolas, led by the doge in his state bark, was a feature of the ceremony, which was held on Ascension Day. In those days Venice was mistress of the Adriatic and her ships visited nearly every important port in the civilized world. The ceremony, it is supposed, was at first only supplicatory in character and originated during the dogeship of Pietro Orseolo I about the year 1000. Under this doge the prestige of the republic was revived after a lapse. In 1177, when the peace between Pope Alexander III and Emperor Frederick Barbarossa was solemnized at Venice, the Pope gave the ceremony a *nuptial* character by bidding the doge cast a ring into the sea each year. The first ring, according to tradition, was from the Pope's own finger.

How does a capitol differ from a capital?

It is surprising how many people fail to distinguish between *capitol* and *capital* when used in relation to governments. According to American usage, a capitol is a building in which the legislative branch of a government holds its sessions; a capital is the seat of the entire government and hence the city where the capitol or statehouse is located. Thus the United States Capitol, where Congress holds its sessions, is at Washington, D. C., which city is the Capital of the United States. Likewise the New York Capitol, where the State legislature holds its sessions, is at Albany, which city is the Capital of the State of New York. Both words are derived indirectly from the Latin *caput,* meaning head. But *capitol,* like French *capitole,* is borrowed from the form *Capitolium,* which was the name of the national temple in Rome dedicated to Jupiter. It was called Capitolium because it was at the head or top of Saturnian or Tarpeian Hill, which in later times became known as Capitoline Hill. Apparently Governor Francis Nicholson of Virginia, who built a new statehouse at Williamsburg in 1698, was the first to apply *capitol* to a government building in America. In time the statehouse in most of the States came to be called the State Capitol, and it was natural that the Federal Government should have adopted the same name for the home of Congress which was built in the District of Columbia. *Capital* as applied to the chief commercial or political city of a nation or state was originally an adjective used elliptically and means *capital city*, that is, head city.

What does *crossing the Rubicon* mean?

Crossing the Rubicon means committing oneself to a dangerous course from which there is no retreat. In ancient times the Rubicon was a small stream forming the boundary between Italy proper and Cisalpine Gaul, the province allotted to Julius Cæsar. When the senate voted to recall Cæsar in 49 B. C. he decided to march on Rome in violation of a law of the republic which forbade a general to enter Italy with his troops under arms. This act was tantamount to a declaration of war. The Roman historian Suetonius, who wrote early in the second century A. D., says of Cæsar: "Coming up with his troops on the banks of the Rubicon, which was the boundary of his province, he halted a while, and, revolving in his mind the importance of the step he was about to take, he turned to those about him and said: 'We may still retreat; but if we pass this little bridge, nothing is left for us but to fight it out in arms.' While he was thus hesitating . . . a person remarkable for his noble mien and graceful aspect appeared . . . playing upon a pipe. When not only the shepherds but also a number of soldiers flocked from their posts to listen to him, and some trumpeters among them, he snatched a trumpet from one of them, ran to the river with it, and sounding the advance with a piercing blast, crossed to the other side. Whereupon Cæsar exclaimed: 'Let us go whither the omens of the gods and the iniquity of our enemies call us. The die is now cast.' " This may be merely a legend. The historian Froude says: "The vision of the Rubicon, with the celebrated saying that 'the die is cast,' is unauthenticated, and not at all consistent with Cæsar's character." Be that as it may, Cæsar's crossing the Rubicon with his troops precipitated civil war and made him master of Rome. The river in question cannot now be identified positively. It is supposed, however, that the Rubicon's upper course is represented by the modern Pisciatello and its lower course by the modern Fiumicino, which flows into the Adriatic near Rimini. These streams, geological evidence shows, were once united.

Is there such a word as *ornery?*

Ornery and *onery* are corrupted forms of *ordinary*. They are dialectical or colloquial terms meaning insignificant, low, mean, contemptible, and they express a higher degree of contempt and disapprobation than *ordinary* does. *Ornary* as a contraction of *ordinary* was a common provincialism in England in the time of the Stuarts, although it is practically obsolete now. The phrase *uppon ornarie time* occurs in the Easthampton *Records* for 1679. In Ireland and the United States *ornary* persists in the further corrupted forms *ornery* and *onery,* which were brought to the American Colonies and perpetuated largely by the Scotch-Irish immigrants, who settled chiefly in the South and West. This explains the fact that *ornery* and *onery* are generally regarded as Southernisms or Westernisms. In 1830 the New York *Constellation* published the following as a Southern expression: "You *ornery* fellow! do you pretend to call me to account for my language?"

How is *the* pronounced?

There are at least three different ways of pronouncing *the* correctly. Two of these pronunciations depend on whether the definite article is followed by a vowel or a consonant sound. When *the* is used emphatically it is pronounced like the personal pronoun *thee.* It is so pronounced in the following sentence: "There are many portraits of Washington, but Stuart's is *the* portrait of Washington." The word is pronounced in the same way when it is used alone, or when special attention is called to it, as in the question at the head of this paragraph, where the definite article is merely named as a word and is accordingly printed in italics. When it is not emphatic and is used before a word beginning with a consonant sound the *e* is slurred, as in "the man." But when *the* is used before a word beginning with a vowel sound and is not emphatic it is sounded almost like *thi* with the *i* short as in *it.* "The egg," for example. An odd popular error has resulted from a common mispronunciation of the pronoun *thee* in an old prayer in rime. The correct version, which was printed in the *New England Primer* published in 1784, is as follows:

Now I lay me down to take my sleep,
I pray *thee, Lord,* my soul to keep;
If I should die before I wake,
I pray *thee, Lord,* my soul to take.

As generally quoted, however, the definite article *the* is substituted for the pronoun *thee* and the rime is erroneously rendered:

Now I lay me down to take my sleep,
I pray *the Lord* my soul to keep;
If I should die before I wake,
I pray *the Lord* my soul to take.

How did *sirloin* originate?

The derivation of *sirloin,* meaning the upper and choicest part of a loin of beef, is interesting chiefly because of a popular story told in connection with it. *Sirloin,* according to this story, arose from the fact that James I of England, while in a merry mood, knighted a choice cut of loin of beef and dubbed it *Sir Loin.* In 1617 James returned from a visit to Scotland and passed through Lancashire. Some distinguished person was knighted at nearly every place the king stopped. Three days were spent in dining and making merry at Hoghton Tower, near Blackburn, where, says John Roby in *Traditions of Lancashire,* the knight-making monarch "was more witty in his speech than usual." "Whilst he sat at meat," to quote Roby further, "casting his eyes upon a noble surloin at the lower end of the table, he called out, 'Bring hither that surloin, sirrah, for 'tis worthy of a more honorable post, being, as I may say, not *sur*-loin, but *sir*-loin, the noblest joint of all,' which ridiculous and desperate pun raised the wisdom and reputation of England's Solomon to the highest." The story may be true, for other Lancashire writers refer to it as one of the established traditions of the locality, but Thomas Fuller, in his *Church History of Britain,* published in 1655, makes a statement which indicates that a similar story was told of Henry VIII. "Dining with the Abbot of Reading," wrote Fuller, "he [Henry VIII] ate so heartily of a loin of beef that the abbot said he would give one thousand marks for such a stomach. 'Done!' said the king, and kept the abbot a prisoner in the Tower, won his one thousand marks, and knighted the beef." Later writers erroneously attributed the famous pun to Charles II, the merry monarch. Of course the story does not account for the origin of *sirloin,* which is obviously derived from the French *surlonge,* from *sur,* upper or above, and *longe,* loin. "The story about turning the loin into *sir-loin* by knighting it," says Skeat, "is mere trash." Nevertheless the Oxford dictionary believes that the famous pun may have influenced the adoption of the now prevalent spelling. Formerly the word was regularly spelled *surloin,* which Skeat says is still preferable. In 1554, twelve years before James I was born, we find "a surloyn of beef" quoted at 6s, 8d. Samuel Johnson, who was probably the first lexicographer to spell the word *sirloin,* says that *sir* was "a title given to the loin of beef, which one of our kings knighted in a fit of good humor."

Which is cooler, black or white clothing?

Many people believe that light-colored clothing is cooler than dark-colored clothing irrespective of the time it is worn. Such is not the case. Assuming the material to be the same in other respects, there is probably little if any difference in warmth between black and white clothing under ordinary circumstances. Only in bright sunshine are white clothes materially cooler than dark ones. This is because white material reflects more light than dark material does. Thus white clothing affords the body more protection from the rays of the sun than does black clothing. Except in the sunshine, the white fur of the polar bear is just as warm as the dark coat of the black bear. The white coats which nature provides for some animals in the winter are apparently designed for protective coloration without reference to warmth. It is the opinion of some horse experts that black horses are affected more by the heat of the direct sun than white ones are. Garments of closely woven white fabric are worn in tropical countries to protect the body from the hot sun. Such garments have high reflecting powers and prevent the transmission of ultra-violet rays to the skin. According to the U. S. Bureau of Standards, these rays pass through open-weave fabrics more readily than they do through closely woven ones, but it does not make much difference whether the color is black, white, red or green. White, however, has been associated with coolness so long that white garments may have a desirable psychological effect in hot weather.

Why is Yorkshire divided into ridings?

Yorkshire, the largest county in England, is divided into three administrative districts known as ridings—North Riding, East Riding and West Riding. The riding is an old Scandinavian institution and Yorkshire has been so divided since ancient times. In Anglo-Saxon the word was written *thrithing* or *thriding* and it literally meant third—the riding being a third of a larger district. Formerly other English counties also had ridings for purposes of local administration, Lincolnshire being the last to abolish them. Macaulay refers to Charles Duncombe as "one of the greatest land-owners of the North Riding of Lancashire." The divisions of Tipperary in Ireland are known as ridings at the present time. Even districts smaller than counties were subdivided into ridings; Linsey, part of Yorkshire, being formerly divided into the north, south and west ridings.

How did *poor as Job's turkey* originate?

Poor as Job's turkey was apparently suggested by the older phrase *patient as Job*. In *James 5:11* it is said that "Ye have heard of the patience of Job." This, of course, refers to the patriarch whose history is related in the book of *Job* and whose patience is proverbial. Some writers suppose that *poor as Job's turkey* was originated by Thomas Chandler Haliburton in *The Clockmaker: or the Sayings and Doings of Samuel Slick of Slickville*. Haliburton described a turkey gobbler that was so poor that he had only one feather in his tail and so weak that he had to lean against a fence to gobble. This condition was attributed to the gobbler's persistent efforts to hatch chicks from eggs that didn't have chicks in them. *Turkey,* however, was popularly associated with Job in phrases before the Slick stories appeared in 1837. In 1824 the *Sentinel* of Troy, New York, quoted the following extract from a paper called the *Microscope:* "We have seen fit to say the *patience of Job's turkey,* instead of the common phrase, *as patient as Job.* And so it must go for this time at any rate. 'Twould worry out the patience of Job's turkey to be picked and pillaged from in this way." Job could not have had a bird of the species we call turkey, because this branch of the pheasant family was native to America.

How were the pioneers of Utah saved by sea gulls?

The first Mormon settlers under the leadership of Brigham Young arrived in Great Salt Lake valley in July, 1847, and the next spring they sowed hundreds of acres of wheat. In May vast clouds of black crickets or grasshoppers descended upon the fields and began to devour every leaf and blade. The settlers turned out en masse, men, women and children, to combat the pest, but their efforts to beat back the devouring host were in vain. They were eight hundred miles from the nearest settlement, all their seed had been planted, and their food supply for the coming winter was threatened with destruction. Many of them, overcome with despair and exhaustion, fell upon the ground and prayed frantically for help. Suddenly a remarkable thing happened. Myriads of gulls emerged from the islands on the lake and, settling down upon the fields, began to gorge themselves with the insects. Eyewitnesses testified that the birds continued to swallow the crickets after their stomachs were full and great piles of the insects that had been swallowed and regurgitated were later found on the edges of ditches. Thus a portion of the crop was snatched from destruction and the pioneers were saved from threatened starvation. The so-called Mormon cricket is known to science as *Anabrus simplex Hald,* and, according to the U. S. Bureau of Entomology, is really not a cricket at all, but a long-horned grasshopper. The adults are shiny black in color, but the young have longitudinal, gray-colored stripes until after their last molt. A similar species known as the Coulee cricket is common in western Oregon and Washington. Both species still do considerable damage to crops. The Indians used to gather these large black grasshoppers in great numbers and store them for food in the winter. The species of gull responsible for the destruction of the Mormon crickets in 1848, says the U. S. Biological Survey, is the California gull, which breeds on the islands of Great Salt Lake and is common throughout the valley at all seasons of the year. It is a variety of the Franklin gull, *Larus franklini*, which inhabits the interior of North America and breeds in marshes and on islands in lakes and rivers. These birds are jealously protected in Utah by statutes as well as by public opinion. In 1913 a monument commemorating the seagull incident was unveiled in Salt Lake City. It was made by Mahonri Young, a grandson of Brigham Young, and consists of a granite column some sixteen feet in height standing on a granite pedestal in a basin thirty feet in diameter. The column supports a granite ball upon which two gulls, done in bronze covered with gold leaf, are represented as gently alighting. Three sides of the base represent pioneer scenes in Utah, and the fourth contains a tablet with the following inscription: "Sea Gull Monument. Erected In Grateful Remembrance Of The Mercy Of God To The Mormon Pioneers."

Who are the Anzacs?

This is a name often applied to the people of Australia and New Zealand. It originated during the World War. The Australian and New Zealand forces in the British service were officially known as the "Australian-New Zealand Army Corps." In popular usage this name was shortened to *Anzac*, being the initial letters of the words composing the official name. "When I took over the command of the Australian and New Zealand Corps in Egypt [in 1914]," wrote General Sir William Birdwood after the war, "I was asked to select a telegraphic-code address and I adopted the name Anzac." In the following spring the Australian and New Zealand forces made their heroic landing on the Gallipoli peninsula and to commemorate the event General Birdwood named the landing place Anzac Cove. Originally only those Australian and New Zealand soldiers who fought at Gallipoli were called Anzacs, and they jealously guarded the name, but it was gradually extended first to other members of the corps and finally to any Australian or New Zealander. The Anzac Area, a small district on the western side of the Gallipoli peninsula, was dedicated after the war as a permanent memorial to the valor of the members of the Gallipoli expeditionary army who vainly tried to take the western defenses of Constantinople in 1915–1916. By the Treaty of Lausanne, signed in 1923, Turkey granted this area in perpetuity to France, Italy and the British Empire, and these three powers agreed to appoint custodians for the graves and cemeteries. Turkey, however, controls access to the district, which cannot be fortified or built up in any way except to provide shelter for the sole use of the custodians.

How long after mating do elephants produce their young?

Exact knowledge on this subject is not available. Estimates of the period of gestation in elephants range all the way from eighteen to twenty-two months. Dr. William M. Mann, director of the National Zoological Park, says the gestation period in elephants is "about nineteen months, although there are more or less authentic records of twenty-one months." According to Raymond L. Ditmars, curator of mammals at the New York Zoological Park, the period of gestation in the Indian elephant is 641 days, which is considerably more than twenty-one months. There is no evidence to support the belief held by the natives of India and Burma that the gestation period is longer for a male calf than for a female. The scarcity of records is accounted for by two facts. Elephants are very secretive in their breeding habits, and in no country is this species of animal domesticated in the strict sense of the term. The elephants used as beasts of burden in southeastern Asia are maintained under conditions as similar as possible to those of wild animals, and the supply is recruited either by captures from wild herds or by animals born in a semi-wild state. As a rule Indian elephants are tractable, especially if captured young, and they are easily trained for service or show. African elephants are very rarely born in captivity. Indian elephants are not bred in confinement because the process of rearing them from birth to the adult age is slow and expensive and because wild adults captured in the jungle usually soon become gentle and cheerful workers.

Which is correct, game *preserve* or *reserve?*

Areas set aside for the protection and conservation of wild life are variously designated game *preserves, reserves, sanctuaries, reservations* and *refuges.* Game *preserve* originally implied that the area so designated was to be used to preserve game from extermination; game *reserve* implied that the area was to be reserved for breeding game for hunting. However, all five of the terms given above were used interchangeably so frequently that much confusion resulted. Therefore the U. S. Biological Survey adopted *game refuge* as the official name for all areas set aside by the Federal Government for the conservation of wild life. Such names as *game preserve, game reserve* and *bird sanctuary* are retained only in cases where they were employed in the original executive orders or acts of Congress setting the areas aside. The terms are also sometimes used by State and local authorities. Previously to 1905 lands set aside by the Federal Government for forest conservation were referred to as *forest reserves,* but in that year, when such lands were placed under the administration of the Forest Service, the official name was changed to *National forests* to indicate that such lands were not to be locked up and kept from use as the word *reserve* might imply. The States followed suit and now we have not only National forests and National parks, but also State forests and State parks. *Forest preserve* has never been used to any considerable extent.

How long do turtles live?

Giant tortoises are among the few creatures that are known to have an extreme life span greater than that of man. There is unquestionable proof that Giant Galapagos tortoises have lived one hundred and fifty years, and there is reason for believing that they sometimes attain an age of two centuries. Scientists have estimated the age of some specimens at four hundred years, but these estimates are little more than speculations, aided to a limited extent by the scale marks or *rings of growth* on the plates. The London Zoological Gardens contain an Elephantine tortoise from the Seychelles which is supposed to be from one hundred to two hundred years old. Tortoises in the South Seas have been known to have a weight of more than one thousand pounds. Reports of ordinary land turtles bearing dates on their shells cannot be admitted as evidence in determining the extreme life span of these reptiles. There is too much room for mistake and fraud in such cases. Mischievous boys with jackknives are fond of carving *1776, 1812* and other historic dates on the shells of turtles. A case in point is the famous tortoise of Captain James Cook. According to a story which has never been authenticated, Captain Cook captured a tortoise on the Galapagos Islands in 1773 and, after carving that date on its back, released the reptile on one of the islands of the Tonga group. Newspapers periodically publish reports from persons who claim that they have seen this tortoise on different islands in the South Seas. Assuming that the reports are correct in stating that a tortoise bearing the date *1773* is seen occasionally, there is no accurate method by which we could determine how, when or in what region the carving was done.

What birds are trained to fish for their masters?

In the Orient the large sea birds known as cormorants have been trained to fish for man since time immemorial. These birds display remarkable activity under water and they devour fish so greedily that they have become proverbial for their voracity and gluttony. When young they are easily tamed and can then be taught to fish for their masters. A leather collar is placed around their necks to keep them from swallowing their catch. In parts of Japan and China it is a common sight to see a fisherman on a raft with a flock of cormorants in the water controlled by means of cords attached to their collars. During the seventeenth century cormorant fishing was introduced into western Europe, and at one time the master of the cormorants was an official in the royal household of England.

Who discovered soap?

It is generally believed that soap, both as a cleansing and a medicinal agent, was first made by the ancient Gauls, although some writers think that possibly the Gauls learned the art of soap-making from the Phœnicians. In his *Natural History* the elder Pliny says: "Soap, too, is very useful for this purpose [curing scrofulous sores], an invention of the Gauls for giving a reddish tint to the hair. This substance is prepared from tallow and ashes, the best ashes for the purpose being those of the beech and yoke-elm. There are two kinds of it, the hard soap and the liquid, both of them much used by the people of Germany, the men, in particular, more than the women." Before they learned how to make soap from the Gauls or Germans the Romans used fuller's earth as a cleansing agent. Later they greatly improved upon the crude method of soap-making described by Pliny, and a complete soap factory was found in the ruins of Pompeii. Soap, of course, was suggested in a general way by certain plants, shrubs and trees, and the ancient inhabitants of Europe washed with the common plant known as soapwort, which makes a fairly good lather and which will even remove grease stains. The word *soap* occurs in the King James version of the Old Testament, but the Hebrew word *borith,* generally translated *soap,* probably refers merely to the ashes of plants and other simple substances used as cleansing agents. *Savon* is the French word for soap, supposedly from its having been manufactured at an early date at Savona, near Genoa. A factory for making soap from olive oil was established at Marseilles in the thirteenth century, and the manufacture of this product on a large scale was begun in London in the sixteenth century, when it was sold for a penny a pound.

Which is correct, *these* or *this molasses?*

Molasses comes to us through the Spanish from the Latin *mellaceus,* meaning honey-like. Since the singular and plural forms are spelled the same the word is often construed as a plural when it should be construed as a singular. *Molasses are, these molasses* and *those molasses* are common expressions, especially in the South and West. They are incorrect except in those rare cases when the speaker or writer has in mind different kinds of molasses and really desires to use the word in the plural. "These molasses are good" is not correct when the speaker refers to molasses in a container on the dining table. The correct expression is, "This molasses is good." On the other hand, it would be technically correct, though awkward, for a merchant to write, "Please send me ten gallons each of those two molasses I ordered last year," when he refers to different kinds or brands of the product.

How did *Mind your P's and Q's* originate?

The origin of *Mind your P's and Q's,* meaning "Be careful" or "Watch your step," is not known for certain, but there is reason for supposing that it originated in the printing shop. In small roman type *p* and *q* are similar in appearance and easily confused. Apprentices who were just learning type-setting and who had difficulty in distinguishing between the two tailed letters in the type font were told by the printers to mind their *p's* and *q's*. Possibly the expression may have been used for similar reasons in admonishing children just learning the alphabet. Two elaborate theories on this subject should be mentioned here, although neither deserves much consideration from the standpoint of exact etymology. According to one of them, *Mind your P's and Q's* arose from an old custom of keeping track of charge accounts in alehouses and inns. The number of pints and quarts of ale which the various regular customers bought but did not pay for was chalked on the back of the door by the proprietor. Strokes opposite the letters *P* and *Q* indicated the number of Pints and Quarts respectively. After these customers received their weekly wages they were not supplied any more ale until they minded their P's and Q's, that is, paid for the pints and quarts they had drunk during the week. According to the other theory, which is equally absurd, the common expression originated in France during the reign of Louis XIV. When persons were presented at court they wore huge wigs and curtsied very formally. The maneuver consisted of a difficult step and a low bend of the body. In making the steps and bows there was danger that the persons being presented would slip and derange their huge wigs. Therefore the master of ceremonies would admonish them, *Gardez vos pieds et queues,* which translated means to mind your feet and wigs. But *pied,* the French word for foot, is pronounced somewhat like the letter *p,* and *queue,* wig, like *q.* Hence, it is said, the expression was corrupted by the English into *Mind your P's and Q's.*

How long do elephants live?

It is difficult to obtain accurate information as to the extreme age reached by elephants in the wild state. There is no positive evidence that an elephant has ever lived more than seventy or seventy-five years either in captivity or the wild state, although it is supposed that one may occasionally live to an age of ninety-five or one hundred. The age reached by animals in captivity is not always a good criterion of their natural life span because food and temperature are much more regular under such conditions. Dr. W. Reid Blair, director of the New York Zoological Park, says that the extreme life span of animals may be estimated with a fair degree of accuracy by multiplying by four or five the number of years which the young of the species requires to reach maturity. In a general way the age cycle of elephants corresponds to that of human beings. They reach maturity at about twenty-five and begin to get old at sixty or sixty-five.

At what period were the most ex-Presidents living?

Between March 4, 1861, when Abraham Lincoln took the oath as President, and January 18, 1862, when John Tyler died, there were five living ex-Presidents of the United States, a greater number than at any other period in history. They were Martin Van Buren, John Tyler, Millard Fillmore, Franklin Pierce, and James Buchanan. The great number of ex-Presidents living at that time was largely a result of the fact that no President elected between the years 1836 and 1860 served for a longer period than four years.

Why do sea shells roar?

When certain sea shells are held close to the ear a noise resembling the distant roar or rumble of the sea can be heard. Many people believe this rumbling sound is an actual echo of the waves of the ocean. Such, of course, is not the case. The noise is merely a composite of the echoes of a great number of ordinary sounds occurring in the vicinity of the shell. Because of the peculiar shape of the shell and the smoothness of its interior the least vibration produces an echo, and numerous such echoes are blended into the rumble or roar. The effect is heightened by the fact that the shell magnifies the pulses in the head as well as the sounds produced in the vicinity.

Can there be a grammatical error?

Some writers hold that *grammatical error* in the sense of *an error in grammar* violates precision and is incorrect, because *grammatical* means "in accordance with the principles of grammar" and accordingly an error cannot be grammatical. The propriety of the phrase, however, is no longer questioned by the majority of good writers and speakers. The objection to *grammatical error* is based on the mistaken notion that the adjective *grammatical* has only one meaning, namely, "in accordance with the principles of grammar."

As a matter of fact the word now also means "pertaining to grammar," a meaning which is recognized by all unabridged dictionaries. The word is used in this latter sense in the expression under discussion. Because a word has one meaning is no reason why it may not acquire another. Language is in a state of constant change and growth and frequently an expression that is erroneous in its inception becomes correct by long usage. The final arbiter of propriety in language is usage and it has decreed that the convenient and expressive phrase *grammatical error* means "an error in grammar," for which it is a proper substitute.

Are German police dogs descended from wolves?

There is no evidence to support the theory that German shepherd dogs have been developed within recent times by crosses with wolves. They sprang from a union of several kinds of sheepdogs in Germany, five or six root stocks being originally combined to produce the breed. That they may contain wolf or dingo blood inherited from the dim past is not improbable, but if we go back far enough all dogs are civilized wolves. Charles Darwin supposed dogs to be descended from several species of wolves and wild dogs domesticated at different times and in different parts of the world. There is no reason to suppose that the German shepherd has a greater percentage of wild blood in its veins than most other breeds. The impression that it has no doubt arose from the fact that these dogs, due to careful selective breeding, more closely approximate the ancestral type. That they revert more readily to wolfish practices has not been established. They differ materially from wolves in having finer heads, smaller teeth, and shorter, more uniform hair. As a rule they are alert, intelligent, and loyal to their masters, although they are high-spirited and sometimes difficult to control. Their color ranges from black to pure white, but most of them are reddish brown or black and tan in color. At least three distinct varieties are recognized—smooth coated, long coated, and rough coated. In 1896 a number of German shepherd dogs were employed as police dogs at Hildesheim, Germany, and from this date their individuality as a separate breed began to develop. Within the next ten years so many of them were used on police patrols that the breed came to be generally known as German, French or Belgian police dogs, depending on the country where they were bred. During the World War they came into prominence because of their notable work with Red Cross units, and as patrols, messengers and ration carriers on the battlefields, especially on no man's land. About 1916, because of antipathy for Germany, these dogs were identified with Alsace in Allied countries, and they are now known in some parts of the world as Alsatians or Alsatian wolf dogs. In 1918 the American Kennel Club arbitrarily dropped *German* from the name and decided to call the breed simply *shepherd dog.* German *police dog* is not the name of a breed, but merely a popular name for a German shepherd dog trained for police duties.

What are the requirements for Statehood?

Since the thirteen original States ratified the Constitution thirty-five new States have been admitted into the Union. Article IV of the Constitution provides that, "New States may be admitted by the Congress into this Union," and also that, "The United States shall guarantee to every State in this Union a republican form of government." This is all the Constitution has to say upon the subject. There is no general statute prescribing the requirements of Statehood, and whether a given Territory is qualified for admission into the Union as a State must be determined by Congress when the occasion arises. The Northwest Ordinance, enacted in 1787 before the Constitution was framed, provided that the Northwestern Territory should ultimately be divided into States, not exceeding five in number, and that any one of these might be admitted into the Union as soon as its population reached 60,000. In a general way this has since been taken as a criterion in respect to the minimum population of a new State, although Nevada came into the Union in 1864 when it had a population of only about 40,-000. The customary procedure is for the residents of an organized Territory desiring Statehood to send a petition or memorial to Congress asking for admission into the Union. If Congress decides that the Territory has attained sufficient importance and has a population large enough to deserve admission into the sisterhood of States it passes what is known as an *enabling act,* which grants the residents of the Territory permission to formulate a constitution to be submitted to Congress for its approval. Sometimes the first application is turned down. For instance, the residents of Utah Territory, which was organized in 1850, applied for admission several times before their application was finally granted. It was not until 1896, after polygamy had been abolished and its revival made legally impossible, that Utah was formally admitted as a State. Once a Territory becomes a State it has all the rights and duties of its sisters. There is nothing in the Constitution or any statute pertaining particularly to the admission of new States composed of territory not adjacent to continental United States. It is presumed, however, that if the Federal Government saw fit to admit Alaska, Hawaii, Porto Rico, or the Philippines into the Union as States it would have the Constitutional right to do so, although there might be a great difference of public opinion as to the propriety of such a step. Texas was an independent republic at the time of its admission into the Union.

Why are Londoners called cockneys?

Cockney as a popular name for the natives of London has a curious history. It is derived, etymologists believe, from *coken-ey,* Middle English for *Cock's egg,* an old name in parts of England for small, malformed and yolkless eggs often laid by young hens, but formerly supposed by country people to be laid by the cocks. During the fifteenth century the term *cockney,* spelled in various ways, was applied to a child nursed too long by its mother, and consequently one who is over-petted and spoiled. Next the name was applied to any effeminate or sissified person. The transition to a city-dweller was natural, and during the sixteenth century it was applied in derision by country people to any town-bred person to contrast his effeminate, citified ways with the hardier habits of his rural brother. But in the eyes of the English London was "the city," and about 1600 the term *cockney* ceased to be generally applied to the inhabitants of other cities and was narrowed down until it meant Londoners, and particularly those Londoners born within the sound of Bow Bells. Bridges were formerly called *bows,* and Bow Church or St. Mary-le-Bow in Cheapside was so called because it was near a bow or bridge over the Thames. The bells of this church are immortalized in the legend of Dick Whittington, who returned to London and became lord mayor after hearing their chimes in the distance. The process of narrowing the meaning of *cockney* continued until at present it is not only restricted to natives of the old City of London, which comprises an area of only about one square mile, but is seldom used except to denote the uneducated classes of that district, who are noted for their characteristic dialect.

What is a Congressional whip?

A whip in a legislative body is a member who is charged with the task of rounding up the members of his party and getting them to vote on bills in which the party has a special interest. The term *whip* in this sense originated in the British Parliament and was borrowed from the chase. In hunting slang a *whipper-in,* sometimes shortened to *whip,* is a hunter's assistant who manages the dogs and keeps them from straying by driving them back into the pack with a whip. In 1769 the House of Commons engaged in a heated debate on a petition against the admission of H. L. Luttrell in place of John Wilkes, who had been expelled. The ministers of the crown strained every nerve to have their supporters present, and Edmund Burke declared on the floor that they had sent to the north and even to Paris for their friends, "whipping them in." This apt phrase of Burke's caught the public fancy and the patronage secretary of the treasury became known as the *whipper-in,* which was later abbreviated to *whip.* Even at the present time this official is chief of the Parliamentary whips for the ministry. Three years after Burke coined the term the *Annual Register* published a sketch about an imaginary politician who ."first was a whipper-in to the premier, and then became premier himself." Whips play a much more important part in the British Parliament than they do in the American Congress because in the former body defeat on a single measure may turn the ministry out of office.

Who said: "The king is dead; long live the king"?

This expression seems to be of French origin. It was used in announcing the death of a king and at the same time proclaiming his successor, signifying that the people were never without a sovereign. In *Louis XIV and the Court of France in the Seventeenth Century* Julia Pardoe says: "The death of Louis XIV was announced by the captain of the bodyguard from a window of the state department. Raising his truncheon above his head he broke it in the center, and throwing the pieces among the crowd, exclaimed in a loud voice, *Le Roi est mort!* Then seizing another staff, he flourished it in the air as he shouted, *Vive le Roi!*"

Which is correct, *Esthonia* or *Estonia?*

The name of the country on the Baltic Sea is variously spelled *Esthonia* and *Estonia* in English. According to the consul general of Estonia at New York, *Estonia,* without the *h,* is the official and correct spelling of the name, and it has been officially adopted by the Department of State at Washington.

How old was Jesus when he was crucified?

It is difficult to determine the age of Jesus at the time of his crucifixion. *Luke 3: 23* says that "Jesus himself began to be about thirty years of age." This was when he began his ministry and after he had been baptized in the Jordan by John the Baptist. John was six months older than Jesus and began to preach in the wilderness of Judæa in the fifteenth year of the reign of Tiberius, who succeeded Augustus during the year 14 A. D. The duration of the ministry of Jesus is likewise unsettled. Historians have placed it at various periods ranging from one year to fifteen. The probabilities are that it lasted between two and three years, which would make Jesus thirty-two or thirty-three years of age at the time of his death.

Did the pre-Columbian Indians ever smoke merely for personal enjoyment?

Students of ethnology differ on this question. There is very little if any evidence to justify the common belief that the Indians of pre-Columbian days smoked habitually and privately merely for personal enjoyment. To the Indians the tobacco plant had a sacred character and was smoked on solemn occasions, accompanied with suitable invocations to their deities. In this respect the smoking of tobacco and other materials had a significance somewhat similar to the burning of incense among other peoples. Tobacco was also smoked by the Indians ceremonially to cure disease, aid in distress, ward off danger, bring good luck, and to allay fear. "It is our opinion that the American Indians did not smoke in private for pleasure, as we do today," says George G. Heye, director of the Museum of the American Indian, in a letter to the author. "Smoking by the Indians seems to have been reserved for treaties, councils, public functions, social and religious intercourse, divination and the cure of disease. When we consider the endless variety of material used by the Indians in smoking, such as twigs, bark, leaves, roots, etc., other than the true tobacco, *Nicotiana,* it seems very doubtful if they smoked for the mere enjoyment of it as we do." But Matthew W. Stirling, chief of the Bureau of American Ethnology, believes that the pre-Columbian Indians smoked privately as well as ceremonially, although he offers no evidence dating further back than the eighteenth century, when the aborigines of this continent had been in contact with the whites for many generations. "There are many notices of the use of tobacco in social ceremonies, as distinguished from ceremonies purely religious," he informs the writer, "but not so many of its use privately because in most cases it was so common as to attract little comment." He then proceeds to quote John Lawson, who, in his *History of Carolina* published in 1714, speaks of the Congaree women as smoking much tobacco under conditions that could hardly have been ceremonial or religious, and who states that among the Siouan and Iroquoian tribes visited by him both men and women were much addicted to the use of tobacco. He further quotes Robert Beverly who says in his *History of Virginia,* published in 1705, that the ceremonial pipes used by the Indians are bigger than "those for common use." But this was after the Indians in question had learned many of the ways of the white man. If habitual private smoking was known at all among the pre-Columbian Indians it must have been confined to a few individuals or to certain isolated tribes. Smoking as a personal habit apparently originated among Europeans who adopted and modified an Indian custom which they did not thoroughly understand.

What is a charley-horse?

In sports slang *charley-horse* is the name given to a painful stiffness in the body, especially in an arm or a leg. The typical charley-horse is a sudden bunching of muscle fibers into a hard knot, caused by the fibers being first torn apart by overstrain. A muscular hemorrhage is produced and the injury manifests itself by a swelling, and any attempt to exercise the injured part is generally attended with severe pain. Anybody may be afflicted with a charley-horse, but this type of injury is most prevalent among athletes engaged in strenuous sports. The term was suggested by the fact that *Charley-horse* is a common name for a horse, particularly an old plug that is afflicted with sweeny or other stiffness.

What was the mark set upon Cain?

When Cain was sentenced for killing Abel he complained that he would become a fugitive and vagabond in the earth and "every one that findeth me shall slay me." Therefore, according to *Genesis 4: 15,* "the Lord set a mark upon Cain, lest any finding him should kill him." The Lord said: "Whosoever slayeth Cain, vengeance shall be taken on him sevenfold." The Bible narrative does not give us the least hint as to the nature of the protective sign. Numerous speculations on the subject supply us with little that is worthy of consideration. Bernhard Stade, the German critic, supposed that the sign or mark set on Cain was an incision in the forehead. Another scholar suggests that it may have consisted of circumcision. Perhaps it was a tribal mark or clan totem analogous to the cattle marks used by the Bedouins and other nomadic peoples. In the East such marks often had a religious significance and denoted that the bearer was a follower of a certain deity. Cain apparently feared that if he left his people without a mark of identification he would be slain by members of other tribes or clans. Still it is difficult to see what purpose a scar or brand on the body would serve except to aid the revengeful in detecting the culprit. Therefore some have supposed that the Lord did not set a mark on Cain's body, but merely gave out a protective sign to guide others. This sign, it has been suggested, consisted of the words: "Whosoever slayeth Cain, vengeance shall be taken on him sevenfold." The theory is supported by the fact that the Hebrew word for sign is *oth,* and it means a sign set up, such as a road sign to guide travelers. Only in the passage about Cain is the word *oth* translated mark instead of sign. *Tav* is the Hebrew word meaning an actual brand on the body. In Ezekiel's vision the Lord sent a man with a writer's inkhorn through Jerusalem to "set a mark (tav) upon the foreheads of the men" that grieved because of the wickedness of the city. According to a curious popular belief, Cain was the progenitor of the colored race and the mark set upon him consisted of Ethiopian or African characteristics. This, however, contradicts another common belief, namely, that Cain's hair and beard were yellow or reddish yellow, which gives us the word *cain-colored*.

How was the State of West Virginia formed?

The Constitution, Article IV, Section 3, says: "No new State shall be formed or erected within the jurisdiction of any other State; nor any State be formed by the junction of two or more States, or parts of States, without the consent of the legislatures of the States concerned as well as of the Congress." The question often arises: Since West Virginia was created in 1863 from the territory of Virginia when the latter State was a member of the Confederacy and at war with the Union, how did Congress admit the new State without violating the Constitutional provision just quoted? As a matter of fact, the transaction was given the color of Constitutionality by an extraordinary proceeding. That part of Virginia which became West Virginia had been settled largely by Northern people. Slavery was economically impractical in that region. In 1860 the slave population of Virginia was nearly half a million. Less than 13,000 of these slaves were owned in the Counties now comprising West Virginia. Nature provided a boundary between the two sections and the question of dividing the State along the lines finally accomplished had been discussed in the Virginia legislature from time to time for fifty years before the outbreak of the Civil War. But the people in the western Counties knew that Virginia would never consent to such dismemberment. After Virginia seceded in 1861, the western Counties remained loyal to the Union. They sent delegates to Wheeling, and the convention not only declared secession revolutionary and illegal but proceeded to set up what it claimed to be the true government of Virginia. A governor and other officials were elected, United States Senators were sent to Washington, and this "restored" government of Virginia acted in every respect as if it were the legal government of the State, and the Federal Government recognized it as the only legitimate government of Virginia. It was this government at Wheeling which gave the necessary technical consent to the formation of the State of West Virginia from its territories. On December 31, 1862, President Lincoln approved a bill admitting the new State into the Union, and the following year a proclamation announcing the admission of the new State was issued. The "restored" government of Virginia was transferred to Alexandria, where, under the protection of the Federal Government, it continued to function as the *recognized* government of the State until it was transferred to Richmond after the fall of that city in 1865.

How did *cabal* originate?

Five of the ministers of Charles II—Clifford, Arlington, Buckingham, Ashley, and Lauderdale—are known in English history as the *Cabal* from the accidental coincidence that the initials of their names spell that word when arranged properly. Many writers assert that this was the origin of *cabal* in the sense of a small clique or faction engaged in intrigue. Such is not the case. *Cabal* was used in practically the same sense long before the reign of Charles II and it was first applied in 1673 to five of his ministers merely as a witticism. As a matter of fact the five men referred to were not the only members of the famous Cabal in the Privy Council of King Charles. It is probable, however, that the popular witticism added to the sinister character of the meaning conveyed by the word. *Cabal* is a shortened form of *Cabbala,* which is derived from the Hebrew *qabbālāh,* meaning reception or tradition. In ancient times it was applied to the oral tradition handed down from Moses to the Jewish rabbis, and later, during the Middle Ages, it was specifically applied to the pretended tradition of the mystical interpretation of the Old Testament. Gradually it acquired the meaning of any secret, mystic or esoteric doctrine, and was finally extended to a group or faction engaged in intrigue and private machination. The *Committee for Foreign Affairs* in the time of Charles II was popularly called, first, the Cabala, and later, the Cabinet. "In the large and balanced Council which was formed after the Restoration," says the historian Green, "all real power rested with the Cabala of Clarendon, Southampton, Ormond, Monk, and the two Secretaries; and on Clarendon's fall these were succeeded by Clifford, Arlington, Buckingham, Ashley, and Lauderdale. It was by a mere coincidence that the initials of the latter names formed the word *Cabal,* which has ever since retained the sinister meaning their unpopularity gave to it."

Why is the Black Sea called black?

Black Sea is a literal translation of the Turkish *Kara Deniz.* This body of water was so named by the Turks supposedly because of its dense fogs and violent storms, *black* being used in the sense of bleak, gloomy and forbidding. In winter the waters are often covered with heavy fogs which obscure the sun and lend a dark aspect to the entire sea. The early Greeks called it *Pontus Axenus,* meaning inhospitable sea or sea unfriendly to strangers, because of its barren shores and its want of islands where navigators could find shelter from the frequent storms. Later, however, after Greek colonists had settled on the shores, the name was changed to *Pontus Euxinus,* meaning hospitable sea or sea friendly to strangers. It does not seem probable, as sometimes stated, that the Black Sea was originally so called from the black or dark rocks on its shores.

What is meant by fiddling for worms?

This is the name given to an odd method used by fishermen to induce angleworms to come to the surface. A stake or piece of board is driven into the ground and a rasping or shuddering vibration is produced by drawing an iron bar or a board over the stake or upright piece. In a short time earthworms begin to emerge from the earth within a radius of twenty or twenty-five feet of the stake. Similar results are sometimes obtained by merely tapping or hammering on the ground in a place where there are evidences of the presence of worms. An electrical process used consists of vibrating the soil by sending a current through two rods connected by wires. Scientists are not agreed as to what causes the worms to emerge from the agitated soil. Earthworms are very sensitive to vibrations in the earth and if they happen to be on the surface the least jar will send them to their burrows. The worms may come to the surface to escape the vibration; or they may, as one authority supposes, mistake the vibration for that produced by rain. It has been also suggested that the worms may mistake the disturbance for that caused by the burrowing of their worst enemy, the mole. Whether the so-called fiddling process is successful depends on the species of worm and the character of the soil. In most parts of the United States it is not successful, although it is often employed by fishermen in parts of Florida and the other Gulf States.

How did Ash Wednesday get its name?

Ash Wednesday, the first day of Lent, is so called from the Roman Catholic ceremony in which the priest on that day dips his thumb into ashes previously blessed and makes the sign of the cross upon the forehead of the faithful. The ashes used are made by burning the remains of the palms blessed on the Palm Sunday of the preceding year. Ashes are the symbol of penitence, and the ceremony is undoubtedly an outgrowth of the penance in "sackcloth and ashes" referred to by the Old Testament prophets. The ceremony from which Ash Wednesday gets its name is intended to remind mortal man that "thou art dust and unto dust thou shalt return." Both the custom and the Latin name of the day, *dies cinerum* (day of ashes), probably date back to the eighth century, if not to the time of Pope Gregory the Great.

What was John C. Frémont's religion?

John C. Frémont, known in American history as *The Pathfinder*, was an Episcopalian. He was born near Savannah, Georgia, January 21, 1813, while his parents were camping on a journey among the Southern Indians. His mother, whose maiden name was Ann Beverly Whiting, was a member of an old Virginian family. She was a member of the Episcopal Church and she brought her children up in her faith. Frémont's father, Charles Frémon(t), was a political refugee from France. He was not a Roman Catholic, as popularly supposed. In 1929 Allan Nevins, author of *Frémont, the West's Greatest Adventurer,* wrote to the author as follows: "Frémont's father was unquestionably a French Huguenot. All the family records and traditions agree upon this point, and Frémont himself so stated." The erroneous belief that John C. Frémont was a Catholic dates from 1856, when he was the Republican nominee for President. His enemies circulated a report that he was a Catholic in order to injure him with the Know Nothing Party, which was strongly anti-Catholic. Frémont's French name and several other circumstances made the report plausible. He would make no public statement on the subject, taking the position that, regardless of what his own religion was, no religious faith disqualified anybody from office under the Constitution. On October 19, 1841, he had been married in Washington to Jessie Benton by Father Van Horseigh, a Catholic priest. As a matter of fact, it was a runaway marriage and the couple applied to the priest only after several Protestant clergymen had refused to perform the ceremony on the ground that it was a secret marriage to which Senator Benton was bitterly opposed. Further evidence that Frémont was a Catholic was found in the fact that he had carved a cross on Rock Independence during his first expedition in the West! Frémont describes the incident in his journal under date of August 23, 1842. "Yesterday evening," wrote the explorer, "we reached our encampment at Rock Independence, where I took some astronomical observations. Here, I engraved on that rock of the Far West a symbol of the Christian faith. Among the thickly inscribed names, I made on the hard granite the impression of a large cross, which I covered with a black preparation of India rubber, well calculated to resist the influence of wind and rain."

What is a swan song?

A swan song is the last work of an author, artist or composer, especially a work produced just before death. The phrase alludes to the old belief that the swan sings beautifully while dying. According to a Greek legend, Apollo, the god of music, passed into a swan. Plato, in *Phaedo,* has Socrates say that swans sing at their death "not out of sorrow or distress, but because they are inspired of Apollo, and they sing as foreknowing the good things their god hath in store for them." Aristotle and other early Greek philosophers accepted the belief that swans sing before death as having a proper place in natural history. Much has been written to prove or to disprove the belief. There may have been a slight basis for it. Although most species of swan make no sounds at any time that could be described as musical, there are a few exceptions. In his *Account of Iceland* Nicol says of the whistling swans of that island that "during the long, dark nights their wild song is often heard resembling the tones of a violin, though somewhat higher and remarkably pleasant." A statement even more to the point is found in Georg Adolf Erman's *Travels in Siberia*. He says that the *Cygnus olor* or whooping swan "when wounded, pours forth its last breath in notes most beautifully clear and loud." The U. S. Biological Survey makes the following interesting statement on this subject: "It seems now that notwithstanding swans do not have notes that are particularly musical, on rare occasions wounded or dying swans do produce notes which are very different from the ordinary notes of the species and which might readily give rise to the story that the bird sings when dying. This may have been the original basis for the story, and it is vouched for by the field observations of a very competent observer, in comparatively recent years."

Where do eels go to spawn?

All fresh-water eels found in America and Europe, no matter how remote from the coast, are hatched from eggs deposited in the Atlantic Ocean in the neighborhood of Bermuda, not far south of 30° North and 60° West. It is supposed that species found in other parts of the world have similar spawning habits. Conger eels, as well as other salt-water species, never enter fresh water. The fresh-water eel is the only known creature that spends most of its life in fresh water and goes to the sea to spawn. Aristotle stated that eels had no sex, eggs nor semen and that they arose from the entrails of the sea by spontaneous generation. The mystery of the eel's spawning was finally unraveled by Johannes Schmidt, an eminent Danish scientist who spent eighteen years studying the habits of these interesting fishes. Adult eels leave their fresh-water abodes and go to the ocean to spawn, after which they die. The newly hatched young are flat, ribbon-shaped, transparent creatures, so totally unlike their parents that they were long supposed to be the adults of another species of fish. In this stage at least two species begin to swim slowly northward, completing their metamorphosis before they reach fresh water. They reach the latitude of Bermuda within the first year and then separate into two streams. One stream swings westward. The eels composing it develop rather rapidly and soon after the first year they have reached the stage when they are known as elvers. A mysterious instinct guides them into the various streams from Florida to Canada, from which their parents emerged a year or two before. There are no eels in the streams on the Pacific Coast. The other stream swings eastward. The eels in this stream belong to a different species and they develop much more slowly. Not until about three years later do the elvers wriggle up the streams of northern and western Europe. A dozen years or so elapse before they leave their fresh-water homes and return to the Sargasso Sea to spawn and die. It should be mentioned in this connection that the lamphrey or lamphrey eel is not a true eel.

Did the Pope's picture once appear on a one-dollar bill?

One of the most curious stories relating to American currency is to the effect that a Catholic engraver secretly incorporated a picture of the Pope and other Catholic symbols in the design of the one-dollar greenbacks or legal tender Treasury notes of the "Series of 1917." This bill is often referred to as the Catholic dollar bill by anti-Catholics and it is whispered around that the engraver responsible for it was sentenced to a term in the penitentiary. It is hardly necessary to state that the story is pure fiction. The first plate for greenbacks bearing this face was designed and engraved in 1868 by the Columbia Bank Note Company of New York and the first bills bearing the design were issued in 1869 when Grant was President. With different signatures, seals and other trifling changes the same plate was used to print bills in 1874, 1875, 1878, 1880, and again in 1917. On the left-hand side of this bill is a picture of Columbus discovering the New World, and in the upper left-hand corner is a figure which many take to be a human face—perhaps that of the Virgin Mary or of the Pope! This figure, according to the Bureau of Engraving and Printing, was not intended to be a face at all. When viewed at a different angle, or under a magnifying glass, the figure ceases to resemble a face and becomes merely a floral decoration, apparently a flower with the petals fallen back. Figures such as this frequently occur in engravings, especially in the older designs, without any intent on the part of the artist to produce such an effect. The designer of currency resorts to all sorts of figures and fancies for the purpose of making counterfeiting difficult. The cross that appears on at least two *E's* on the reverse side of the same bill is explained in a similar manner and is merely a fancy design in lettering. Likewise the so-called rosary around the border of the design in the center of the reverse is nothing more than a conventional engraving pattern and does not resemble a rosary. There is no reason for supposing that the serpent in the lower right-hand corner of the face was intended to be a Catholic symbol. The story about the Catholic dollar bill received wide circulation after a number of employees were dismissed from the Bureau of Engraving and Printing during President Harding's administration. The trouble was not in connection with paper money, but Liberty Bonds, and all the dismissed employees were later exonerated. In 1924 William Gibbs McAdoo, who was Secretary of the Treasury in 1917 when the bill was issued, declared that "the Catholics had no more to do with the design of this one-dollar bill than the man in the moon." More one-dollar bills were needed and, according to McAdoo, "it became necessary to resume the one-dollar greenbacks." An old design was used and the words "Series of 1917" were substituted for "Series of 1880" merely "to indicate that the reissuance was not counterfeit."

What does *of that ilk* mean?

Probably the majority of people who use this phrase do not know the real meaning of *ilk*. It does not properly mean kind, sect, family, or race, as often supposed. *Ilk* is from the Anglo-Saxon *ilc* and signifies identical or same. In Scotch *of that ilk* denotes that a person's surname is the same as the name of his estate. *Knockwinnock of that ilk* means simply *Knockwinnock of Knockwinnock,* the name of the proprietor and his property being identical. The improper usage in which *ilk* is employed to mean kind or sort probably originated in carelessness or facetiousness and has been perpetuated through ignorance of the true meaning.

Is there such a word as *alright?*

No such word as *alright* is recognized in modern English usage. It is branded by reputable dictionaries as an erroneous form of the phrase *all right*. For a period during the twelfth and thirteenth centuries—before the invention of printing—*alright* was employed to some extent by English writers, but *all right* had been previously preferred and it has been regarded as the correct form ever since.

Large numbers of writers, however, insist on employing *alright* in place of *all right,* and eventually we may have both *alright* and *all right,* on the analogy of *already* and *all ready,* with a corresponding distinction in meaning.

What king of England could speak no English?

George I, king of England from 1714 to 1727, could neither speak nor write the English language. He was the son of Ernest Augustus, elector of Hanover, and Sophia, granddaughter of James I of England. The German prince became the nearest heir to the English crown on the theory that the blood of James II in the direct line was *corrupted.* When he succeeded Queen Anne as sovereign of England he was fifty-four years old and he made no attempt to learn the language of his kingdom. William of Orange, who reigned jointly with his wife Mary from 1689 to 1694 and as sole sovereign from 1694 until 1702, was Dutch in nationality and knew very little English. "William," says Macaulay, "was not sufficiently master of our language to address the Houses from the throne in his own words; and on very important occasions, his practice was to write his speech in French, and to employ a translator." French, of course, was the native language of the English kings for many generations after the Norman conquest.

What Vice President first attended Cabinet meetings?

It is often stated that Calvin Coolidge was the first Vice President of the United States to attend meetings of the President's Cabinet. That is not strictly correct. When the Federal Government was inaugurated under the Constitution President Washington invited Vice President John Adams to attend the meetings of the Cabinet. Apparently Washington's original plan was to regard the Vice President as a member of his official family. Adams was present once at least, probably twice, but after that he was not again invited. There is no record of Washington's reasons for not renewing the invitation. Whatever his reasons were, the result was that no Vice President again attended Cabinet meetings until President Wilson went to Europe in December, 1918, when Vice President Thomas R. Marshall was requested to preside over the Cabinet meetings during the President's absence. Marshall complied with the request. The second time President Wilson went to Europe the Vice President was invited neither to preside over nor to attend the meetings of the Cabinet. On February 9, 1925, Mr. Marshall wrote to the author as follows: "The first time the President was at Paris I presided over the Cabinet meetings. I did not do so when he returned the second time." Calvin Coolidge, elected on the Harding ticket in 1920, was the first Vice President to attend Cabinet meetings regularly. This precedent was not followed in the case of Charles G. Dawes, who was elected Vice President in 1924, nor in the case of his successor, Charles Curtis, elected in 1928.

How long is the longest elephant tusk on record?

The longest elephant tusk of which there is authentic record is eleven feet five and one-half inches in length, and eighteen inches in circumference at its maximum girth. This tusk and its mate, which is somewhat shorter, weigh together two hundred and ninety-two pounds. They were taken from an elephant of the Sudan species —*Loxodonta oxyotist*—which was shot by an American a short distance from the border of Abyssinia at the beginning of the nineteenth century. King Menelik of Abyssinia obtained possession of the pair, which finally, by way of the London ivory market, found their way to the National Collection of Heads and Horns in New York City, where they are now on exhibition. The longest Indian elephant tusk on record is eight feet nine inches in length. Its maximum circumference is seventeen and one-fourth inches and it weighs eighty-one pounds.

Is there a man-eating tree?

The man-eating tree is a myth. There is no species of tree that captures and devours human beings and large animals. Many of the stories of man-eating trees are probably based on a letter written in 1878 by a traveler named Carle Liche to a Polish doctor named Omelius Fredlowski. In this letter Liche asserted that a native tribe in Madagascar worshiped a devil tree whose trunk resembled a thick pineapple standing on end. At the apex was a receptacle filled with a highly intoxicating fluid, and huge leaves hung from the trunk like doors swung back on their hinges. Long hairy tendrils stretched out in every direction from beneath the receptacle, and above it were numerous palpi which projected upward and twirled and twisted incessantly. Liche says he saw the natives compel a woman to mount the trunk, which was eight feet tall, and drink some of the liquid, after which the tendrils and palpi seized her with savage fury and crushed her to death. Then the broad leaves slowly arose like the arms of a derrick and closed about the victim with the force of a hydraulic press. Fluid from the receptacle, mingled with the blood and viscera of the woman, trickled down the trunk and was collected and drunk by the warriors as they danced around the tree and became frantically intoxicated. When Liche returned ten days later all trace of the victim had disappeared from the receptacle and nothing but a skull at the foot of the tree remained as evidence of the awful rite that had taken place. Liche's letter was printed in numerous scientific publications and because of its circumstantial style was widely accepted as authentic, notwithstanding the fact that it bore many of the earmarks of pure fiction. Similar carnivorous trees that obtain nourishment by reaching out with tentacles and capturing animals and human beings have been reported from South and Central America, the Philippines, Australia and other parts of the world. These tales may have been suggested by various poisonous trees in the tropics, as well as by certain plants that entrap and consume insects, such as the well known pitcher plant. The largest known plant of this kind was found in tropical India and exhibited at Horticultural Hall in London. It attracts large insects and even mice by an odor from its blossom and then entraps and consumes them by dissolving them in a liquid. In 1924 Chase Salmon Osborn, former governor of Michigan, published a book entitled *Madagascar, Land of the Man-Eating Tree*. He states that in his extensive travels on the island he never saw a man-eating tree, but he heard stories about such trees from all the native tribes that he met. His conclusion was that "while a man-eating tree is an unlikely thing, it is not an impossibility." The legend of the man-eating tree was investigated and proved baseless by Dr. Ralph Linton, an anthropologist, who was in Madagascar from 1925 to 1927 as leader of the Captain Marshall Field Anthropological Expedition. Later Charles F. Swingle of the U. S. Bureau of Plant Industry investigated the story. "After traveling through much of Madagascar and asking on many occasions about the man-eating tree, I concluded that this fable has no more basis of fact than any ordinary fairy tale," wrote Swingle to the author in 1929. "I did hear of the fable on several occasions in Madagascar, but, like the end of the rainbow, the plant always grew in some other part of the island. It is, of course, always difficult to disprove stories such as this, but it seems to me that there is no basis of truth for the story of the man-eating tree."

What does *Ibid* mean?

Ibid is a contraction of the Latin adverb *ibidem* and literally means "in the same place." It is employed chiefly to avoid repeating a reference, particularly after a quotation to indicate that it is taken from the same book, chapter, passage or other source as the preceding one. In this sense the term came into general use during the seventeenth century when it was still fashionable to borrow freely from the classical languages upon the slightest provocation. It is not uncommon to meet with persons who suppose *Ibid* to be a noted author whose writings are frequently quoted.

What causes the tides?

The tides are caused by the gravitational action of the sun and moon upon the rotating earth. Theoretically all the stars, planets and satellites in the universe produce separate and distinct tides, but their influence, of course, cannot be detected. The moon is nearly two and a quarter times more potent as a tide-producing agent than the sun, because the tide-generating force of a body depends not only on its mass but also on its distance from the earth. Although their effect may not always be appreciable, the tide-producing forces exert themselves on all bodies of water in proportion to their size and depth, even on ponds and pools. It is not true, as sometimes stated, that there are no tides in such bodies as the Mediterranean Sea and the Great Lakes. The same forces produce tides in these bodies, but their area is relatively small and the tides are so slight that they are generally masked by differences in mean level resulting from winds, changes in atmospheric pressure, and the discharge of rivers. At Chicago the tide in Lake Michigan rises only about two inches. The subject of tides is exceedingly complex because of the motions of the earth and moon and because the actual operation of the tide-producing forces is modified by numerous local factors, particularly the location and configuration of the oceans. The pull of the moon tends to separate the solid part of the earth from the more mobile waters, which therefore pile up. When the moon is over a body of water it pulls the fluid upward and sets a tidal wave in motion. But the earth and the moon are swinging around a common center of gravity and pulling against each other, the moon actually causing the earth to deviate slightly from what would otherwise be its normal path. Therefore, while the moon is piling up the water on its own side of the earth it appears to push it out on the opposite side. In reality the more mobile water merely takes a slightly greater orbit than the solid part of the earth does when the entire earth is held back by the moon. The more or less free water on the opposite side of the earth bulges away from the moon much as the passengers in the rear seat of an automobile are thrown outward when the machine suddenly turns a sharp corner. Thus two vast tidal waves originate at the same time on opposite sides of the earth and sweep through the oceans. The crests of these waves are 180° apart, but their troughs vary in width, depending on the position of the moon. These tidal waves continually sweep through the seas as the earth rotates and produce two high and two low tides in every period of 24 hours and about 51 minutes. During a great part of the time the sun and the moon pull in different directions, or at angles to each other, but twice each lunar month—at new and full moons—they pull in the same line and then the highest tides occur. When it is low tide on the coast of California it is also low tide on the Pacific coast of northern Japan; but, owing to the location, size, and configuration of the Atlantic, there is several hours difference between low tide on the eastern coasts of the United States and low tide on the western coasts of Spain and France.

Why doesn't the Christian era begin on Jesus' birthday?

Our calendar is supposed to be based on the birth of Christ, but the year begins on January 1 instead of December 25, the supposed day on which Jesus was born. Paradoxical as it may be, Jesus was born between two and eight years B. C. This anomalous situation is due to the fact that the Christian era was calculated about 532 by Dionysius Exiguus, a learned monk of Rome, who came to the conclusion that Jesus was born on December 25, 753 *Anno Urbis Conditæ,* i. e., from the founding of Rome. Dionysius began the Christian era with the following year 754 A. U. C. because he wanted to leave the Roman year and months intact and did not desire to confuse established chronology. His system of computing the Christian era did not come into general use in Christendom until about 1000 A. D. Later researches proved that the monk had wrongly calculated the birth year of Jesus and that his figures were in error from two to eight years. But meanwhile the Christian calendar had assumed definite form with the birth of Christ set at December 25 and it was found impractical to upset the entire system of historical chronology by changing the date of the beginning of the Christian era, which was already well established.

Do bees make or gather honey?

This is a disputed question. Some authorities are of the opinion that the liquid collected by bees from the nectaries of flowers does not differ materially from honey, and that accordingly it is correct to say that bees gather honey rather than make it. Others insist that the nectar undergoes considerable elaboration in the honey stomach or sac of the bee before it is deposited in the wax cells in the form of the sweet viscid liquid which we call honey, and that therefore it is more accurate to say that bees gather nectar and make honey. To what extent the nectar is altered in the crop of the bee is difficult to determine because there are so many different kinds of nectar and honey. The chemical composition of both varies widely. Nevertheless nectar is the raw material used by bees in manufacturing honey. The U. S. Department of Agriculture officially defines honey as "the nectar and saccharine exudations of plants, gathered, *modified,* and stored in the combs by honeybees." Under this definition nectar in its original state is not honey, although in popular parlance it is so regarded. It is erroneous to suppose, as some people do, that honey is nectar which has been partly digested by bees. Honey is not a product of digestion in the accepted sense of the term. Bees have two stomachs, or more accurately speaking, they have a stomach and a honey sac. The first performs the ordinary processes of digestion, while the second merely receives and retains for a time the nectar, which may or may not be essentially modified and which is regurgitated and deposited in the honey-cells.

How often does the year contain fifty-three Sundays?

According to the Gregorian calendar every year has fifty-three days of the one it begins on. Generally speaking, the year contains fifty-three Sundays every five or six years. This occurred in 1928 and will occur again in 1933, 1939, 1944, 1950, 1956, 1961, 1967, etc. "In any continuous series of twenty-eight years," says the U. S. Naval Observatory, "five have fifty-three Sundays, unless the series includes a year whose number ends in two ciphers without its being a leap year, as 1700, 1800, 1900." When leap year begins on Saturday two of the six-year periods fall consecutively.

What animals have no gall bladder?

The gall bladder is absent from all common members of the deer family. Deer have livers but no organ takes the place of the gall bladder. This anatomical peculiarity, however, is not found in the Asiatic musk deers, which for that reason are sometimes classed in a separate family closer to the cattle. Likewise antelopes, which are not true deers, have gall bladders.

How did Halloween originate?

Halloween as we know it may be said to date from 837 when Pope Gregory IV instituted All Saints' or All Hallows' Day on November 1 in place of the earlier festival of the Peace of the Martyrs. The day was set aside to honor all saints, known and unknown, and to supply any deficiencies in the annual calendar of saints' feasts. *Halloween*, which is now the preferred way of writing the word, is merely a shortened form of *All Hallows' E'en*, that is, October 31, the evening before All Hallows' Day. It is often stated that Halloween antedates Christianity. This is true only in the sense that certain pagan customs were grafted on the vigil of All Hallows' Day. In southern Europe Halloween apparently absorbed some of the customs formerly associated with the festival of Pomona, the Roman harvest feast, which fell about the first of November. This probably accounts for the popular association of fruits, nuts, grain and other products of the autumn with Halloween. During the Middle Ages there seems to have been a widespread belief that the souls of the departed on this night revisited their former abodes on earth to warm themselves by fires and to partake of good cheer provided for them by their kinsfolk and friends. Even today in countries where Catholicism is the prevailing faith Halloween is associated with the dead and graves are decorated with flowers on All Saints' Day. There it is not, as it is in America and some other countries, a time for revelry, youthful pranks and practical jokes played on unsuspecting neighbors. In northern countries, however, the early characteristics of Halloween were the lighting of great bonfires on the hills and the superstition that on this of all nights spirits and witches go abroad. It is very probable that these features of Halloween were derived from the practices of the druids, the pagan priests of the Celts of Gaul and Britain, who set aside one night each year after the gathering of the harvest for the purpose of feasting and making merry. Huge fires were built and the druids drank, ate and danced throughout the night. Our pumpkin lanterns may represent the various witches and hobgoblins associated with these pagan celebrations. The ringing of bells and the burning of fires on Halloween probably were originally intended to attract wandering spirits. In the mountains of Scotland and Wales the custom of lighting huge fires on the hills on Halloween survived until a generation or two ago. The Irish sometimes call Halloween *Oidhche Shamhna,* which is Gaelic for Shamhna's vigil. Shamhna was the druidic god of death who once every year called together certain wicked souls.

What are dew ponds?

Dew pond is the name applied to certain shallow saucer-shaped basins which usually contain a supply of water even during prolonged drouths when ordinary ponds at lower levels dry up. The mode of replenishment is somewhat mysterious because the most successful dew ponds are situated on the highest points of the chalk downs of southern England, where the soil is extremely porous, where there are no springs, where evaporation proceeds more rapidly than in the valleys, and where many cattle and sheep consume large quantities of the water daily. They received their common name from the belief that they are replenished chiefly by the deposit of dew on the surface of the water, a belief which probably arose from the fact that during the hottest weather the vegetation in the vicinity of such ponds is often thickly covered with dew after nightfall. Scientists who have investigated the subject report that dew has little if anything to do with the mysterious replenishment of the ponds during drouths. It is believed that they receive water from downland fogs and mists from the sea, in addition, of course, to the regular supply from rain. That fog or mist is the source of some water is confirmed by the fact that the ponds contain considerable quantities of sodium chloride and other salts. This theory would also explain why those ponds on the highest points of the chalk downs are usually the last to dry up during a drouth. Apparently the ponds have the power of attracting water from the mists, fogs, and low clouds, and accordingly in some sections of England they are known as mist ponds, fog ponds and cloud ponds. It is commonly believed by the people on the downs that dew ponds were made in prehistoric times. Certainly some of the ponds still in existence date back many generations. Even at the present time they are constructed along certain traditional lines. The essence of the typical dew pond is its waterproof bottom, which is made by puddling clay tempered with chalk or lime. Sometimes layers of straw are elaborately laid beneath the puddled clay bottom, but the purpose and value of this feature is a question of dispute among the pond builders themselves. Usually a layer of loose chalk rubble is placed over the clay to prevent cattle from perforating the bottom with their hoofs. As a rule the pond is filled the first time by artificial means.

How are the sizes of stockings determined?

The size of hose is based on the distance in inches between a point on the toe and a point on the heel measured in a straight line. Size 8 is eight inches more or less from the tip of the toe to the end of the heel. Both men's and women's stockings are measured in this manner. According to the U. S. Bureau of Standards, the standard method of measuring hosiery is as follows: After the hose has been pressed and is flat and unwrinkled, a ruler is placed along a line in which the tip of the toe and the bottom of the heel gore are connected. The hosiery size is the distance in inches along this line from tip of toe to the intersection of the ruler with the back of the heel. Only inches ,and half inches are represented in size numbers. Preference is given to the lower number. For instance, if the exact measurement is 10¼ inches the stocking is called size 10 rather than 10½.

Why is cement called Portland?

Portland was first applied to a cement made in 1824 by John Aspdin, a bricklayer of Leeds, England, who mixed clay and lime in definite proportions, burned them in a kiln, and pulverized the resulting mass. He called his product Portland cement because concrete made from it somewhat resembled Portland stone, a famous building limestone obtained from the isle or peninsula of Portland on the coast of Dorsetshire. Aspdin, however, was not the first to make the comparison. More than fifty years earlier John Smeaton had stated that cement made of such materials would "equal the best merchantable Portland stone in solidity and durability." The cement made by Aspdin was not clinkered but merely calcined, while modern Portland cement is made by burning a natural or artificial mixture of clay and lime to a clinking temperature and then grinding up the clinker.

Which is correct, *Havana* or *Habana?*

The name of the capital of Cuba is correctly spelled either *Havana* or *Habana*. *Habana* is the preferred spelling in Spanish, and *Havana* in English, but both spellings occur frequently in both languages. This variation arises from the fact that in Spanish *b* and *v* are pronounced almost alike, being uttered with the lips close together but not completely touching each other. Many words besides *Habana* and *Havana* are spelled indifferently with *v* or *b*. "Oddly enough," says I. A. Wright in *Cuba,* "the spelling (with *v*) which is usual in English seems to have been the original, the present Spanish version (with *b*) being, I judge, a corruption occasioned by local mispronunciation of *v* and its consequent confusion with *b*." On July 25, 1514 (?), a group of Spaniards settled on the site of the present port of Batabanó on the south shore of Cuba, almost directly across the island from the present site of Havana. This settlement was named *San Cristóbal de la Havana,* because the date was the feast day of St. Christopher and *Havana* or *Avana* was the Indian name for that part of the island now comprising the province of Habana. Thus it will be seen that Havana was not so named because the name literally means *haven,* as often erroneously stated. In 1519 Diego Velázquez, conqueror and first Spanish governor of Cuba, repaired his ships in the present Havana harbor. He found the place especially desirable as a haven and therefore caused the San Cristóbal de la Havana settlement to be removed across the island, first to what is now La Chorrera, and finally to its present site.

What is no man's land?

No man's land as used during the World War was merely a new application of an old term. In the fourteenth century *no man's land* was a piece of waste ground just outside the walls of London which was often used for executions. Later we find the term frequently employed to describe any debatable territory, especially on the boundary of two countries. In *Robinson Crusoe,* published in 1719, Daniel Defoe wrote: "This was a kind of Border, that might be called *no man's Land."* The term has been used as the specific name of districts in Great Britain, South Africa, Australia, the United States and other countries. In the United States alone *No Man's Land* has been the name of several districts, including an island near Martha's Vineyard in Massachusetts. Our most famous *No Man's Land,* however, was a large strip of territory north of Texas thirty-five miles wide and one hundred and sixty-seven miles long. It was ceded by Texas to the Federal Government in 1850, and between that date and 1890, when it was incorporated with Oklahoma, it had no particular form of government and became notorious as the refuge of outlaws and recalcitrant Indians. It was natural that a descriptive term so widely known should be revived during the World War to designate the narrow strip of unoccupied land lying between the front line trenches of opposing armies. Modern trench warfare on a large scale made the term peculiarly apt. No man's land, which on the Western front varied in width from a few yards to a quarter of a mile or more, was usually strewn with dead bodies, fragments of shells, broken fences, riddled trees and other wreckage of war. In 1922 a man named J. Howard

Randerson, of Albany, New York, published a book in which he stated that he was the first to use the term *no man's land* in connection with the World War. He coined the phrase, he said, in the fall of 1914 while attending a conference of the members of a foreign order of chivalry at Lake George. His claim is disproved by the fact that *no man's land* in this connection appeared in print in London on September 15, 1914, in a narrative signed *Eyewitness*. This date, according to Randerson's own story, must have been before the Lake George conference took place.

Why are some girls called flappers?

Flapper as the slang designation of a girl of a certain type came into general use in the United States between 1912 and 1920. It occurs many times in Harry Leon Wilson's *Bunker Bean,* first published in 1912. The author makes Bulger say: "See the three skirts in the back? That's the Missis and the two squabs. Young one's only a *flapper,* but the old one's a peacherine for looks." Later, according to the novelist, Bunker Bean "saw that she was truly enough a *flapper;* not a day over eighteen, he was sure." The term was further popularized in 1920 when *This Side of Paradise* and *Flappers and Philosophers,* two books by Francis Scott Fitzgerald, were published. *Flapper* originated in England and was introduced into America with a somewhat different meaning. Literally a flapper is something that moves with a loose, flapping motion. Therefore, some authorities suppose, girls were so called in allusion to the flapping of their bobbed hair and the motion of their jaws while chewing gum. It is almost certain, however, that *flapper* in this relation was suggested by *flapper* in the sense of a fledgling bird. In British sporting slang a flapper is a young partridge, wild duck or other bird which has wings but is yet unable to fly, being able merely to flap. According to the Oxford dictionary, the term has been used in that sense since 1773 at least. Before the World War the term was applied in Great Britain to a sub-débutante, that is, a young, unsophisticated girl. During the War it was employed to denote young girls who defied convention by bobbing their hair, dressing in boyish costumes, smoking cigarettes, and substituting for men in driving trucks and doing other work. *Flapper's delight* was Tommy Atkins's name for inferior officers or subalterns who prided themselves on their popularity with flappers. In the United States the word was applied to sophisticated, venturesome girls who go to extremes to attract attention, especially in matters of dress. During the nineteenth century *flapper* was applied to young girls of questionable morals. For instance, in *Passing English of the Victorian Era,* James Redding Ware defines *flapper* as "a very immoral girl in her early teens."

What is the Iron Gate in the Danube?

The famous Iron Gate in the Danube is not a gate at all. That is merely the picturesque name given by the Turks to a gorge or pass where the river has cut its way through a spur of the Transylvanian Alps a few miles below the city of Orsova in Rumania. A real gate of iron could not have more effectively prevented the passage of Turkish fleets up the Danube than the dangerous rapids and massive rocks which obstructed the narrow channel for nearly two miles. In 1890 a Hungarian company began the removal of many of the boulders and other obstructions by a series of great blasting operations. The river through the Iron Gate or the Iron Gates was declared open for navigation in 1896.

Why do men lift their hats to women?

It is believed that the custom of uncovering the head as a mode of salutation originated in the military practices of the ancients. In the days when men wore heavy armor a man would take off his helmet or headgear to show that he was not afraid to stand with head uncovered in the presence of another; it was an act expressive of confidence. Later it became customary to remove the headgear to show deference to a superior or as a mark of respect to a person of distinction. It was only a step further to lift the headdress as an act of politeness or gallantry to ladies, and thus raising the hat gradually became a general method of greeting women. The practice retains some of its earlier significance and many people still take off their hats to salute distinguished persons of either sex, and respect for the national flag is shown in the same manner. Quakers do not believe in raising the hat. George Fox, the founder of the Society of Friends, taught that a Christian should submit to persecution and even face death itself rather than touch his hat to the greatest of mankind, whether male or female. When asked to produce Scriptural authority for his dogma on this subject, Fox cited the Biblical passage in which it is stated that Shadrach, Meshach and Abednego were thrown into the fiery furnace with their hats on. The Quaker leader also pointed out that the Turks never show their bare heads to their superiors and said that they should not be permitted to surpass Christians in virtue.

How does adjective law differ from substantive law?

Substantive law consists of the general and fundamental laws enacted for the regulation of human conduct. Adjective law consists of certain rules and regulations governing court procedure and the administration of the substantive law. In other words, adjective law is a set of rules by which the substantive law is executed. Sometimes, as in the case of the rights and privileges of Congress, it is not easy to distinguish clearly between the two classes of law. The acts embodying the privileges, usages, practices and regulations of the Senate and the House of Representatives combine some of the features of a substantive law of rights, and some of the features of an adjective law of procedure.

What is meant by the free coinage of silver at 16 to 1?

During the Presidential campaign of 1896 William Jennings Bryan, the Democratic nominee, ran on a platform demanding the free and unlimited coinage of silver at the ratio of 16 ounces of silver to 1 of gold. This would have meant, if adopted, that a person having silver could take it to a mint and have it converted into coins free of charge, 16 ounces of silver being presumed to have the same value as 1 ounce of gold. The United States is on a gold basis and the Government is under obligation to purchase unlimited quantities of this metal at the rate of $20.67 a fine ounce. Accordingly we have free and unlimited coinage of gold, but not of silver. Any person who has gold of the value of one hundred dollars or more may take it to a mint or assay office and demand in return the exact equivalent in the form of coins or bars. Gold is purchased in various degrees of fineness, but no metal containing more than 800 parts of base metal is accepted. Coinage gold is 900/1000 fine. The Government makes an alloy charge when it is necessary to treat a deposit in order to reduce it to the standard fineness of coins. All gold received at a mint or assay office is first melted and assayed to determine its fineness, and a "melting charge" is made for this process. All charges for treating gold at the mint, however, are merely nominal and are deducted from the value of the deposit when the depositor is paid.

How is a minority President elected?

Minority President is the name applied to a President of the United States who has been elected by a minority, or less than half of the total number of popular votes cast. This is possible because the President and the Vice President are not elected directly by popular vote, but by electors who are chosen by popular vote. Each State is entitled to as many electors as it has Senators and Representatives in Congress, and the electors vote by States. A candidate for President receives all or none of the electoral votes cast by a State, except in the rare cases when the electoral vote of a State is split. Hence it is possible for a minority of the voters of the country as a whole to elect a majority of the Presidential electors. This is likely to occur especially when more than two candidates are in the field. In the early days of the Federal Government under the Constitution the State legislatures elected or *appointed* the Presidential electors, the preference of the people being expressed indirectly by their votes for members of the State legislatures. There is for that reason no trustworthy record of the popular vote for President previous to 1824. In the election of that year none of the four candidates for President received a majority of either the electoral or the popular votes, and John Quincy Adams was chosen by the House of Representatives in accordance with the method prescribed by the Constitution for such cases. Since then James K. Polk, Zachary Taylor, James Buchanan, Abraham Lincoln (1860), Rutherford B. Hayes, James A. Garfield, Grover Cleveland (in 1884 and 1892), Benjamin Harrison, and Woodrow Wilson (in 1912 and 1916), were elected President without receiving a majority of the total popular vote. In most of these cases minority Presidents were elected because several candidates were running. But in 1876 Tilden actually received more popular votes than Hayes did and still Hayes became President. Likewise in 1888 the Cleveland electors received 5,-

540,050 popular votes and the Harrison electors received only 5,-444,337, but Harrison received 401 electoral votes as compared with 168 received by Cleveland and Harrison became President. Since the election of 1876 was somewhat irregular the election of 1888 is the best illustration of how a candidate may receive more popular votes and fewer electoral votes than an opponent. Suppose, for illustration, that there were only two States in the Union at the time—Georgia and New York. The Harrison electors—speaking in round numbers—received 40,000 votes in Georgia; the Cleveland electors received 100,000. In New York the Harrison electors received 650,000; the Cleveland electors 635,000. Thus from these two States Cleveland received a total of 735,000 popular votes as compared with only 690,000 received by Harrison. But a majority, even of only one, usually carries with it the entire electoral vote of a State. Accordingly Cleveland received only the 14 electoral votes of Georgia while Harrison received the 45 electoral votes of New York. When this principle is applied to a large number of States it is easy to understand how a candidate may receive a majority or a plurality of the popular votes without receiving a majority or even a plurality of the electoral votes.

Are honeybees native to America?

Honey or hive bees, which belong to the genus *Apis,* are not native to the New World. Wild honeybees in America all sprang from domesticated bees imported from abroad. It is supposed that colonies of these insects were first introduced into North America about the middle of the seventeenth century, and into South America much later. From the beginning the Indians associated the honeybee with the colonists and called it "the white man's fly." The prevalent idea that honeybees are indigenous to the American continents is undoubtedly due to the fact that swarms escaped at an early date and established themselves in hollow trees in the wilderness. Honeybees, however, should not be confused with the native wild bees of America. Many species of social bees belonging to the families *Melipona* and *Trigona* are indigenous to the New World, especially its tropical and semi-tropical regions. These insects, which make their nests in trees or in the ground, are called stingless bees because their stings are only vestigial, and they are often known as "mosquito bees" because of their small size. They are not hive bees and produce honey and wax in small quantities only. Honey and wax referred to in the records of the conquest of Mexico by Cortez may have been produced by these insects. Fossilized bees dating back to prehistoric periods in America probably belonged to the same families.

Do bees know their master?

Entomologists hold that there is nothing in the common notion that honeybees recognize the beekeeper and distinguish him from other individuals. Although some of the bees hatched late in the fall survive the winter, the average life of a worker during the active honey season is only about six weeks, two of which are spent in the hive. It is not likely that a beekeeper would examine a hive frequently enough to be recognized by creatures so short-lived even if they had the ability to distinguish between different human beings. A good beekeeper does not provoke bees so much as inexperienced persons do because he is familiar with their habits and knows how to handle them.

Where is the tree that is said to own itself?

A large white oak tree in Athens, Georgia, is known as "the tree that owns itself." The ground on which the tree stands was once owned by William H. Jackson, a professor at the University of Georgia. He was born about the close of the Revolutionary War and was the father of James Jackson, who was chief justice of the State supreme court at the time of his death in 1887. Professor Jackson was so fond of his oak tree that about 1820 he wrote a deed conveying to the tree full possession of itself and the land on which it stands. The original of this so-called deed is not a matter of record and it is not probable that it was ever actually registered. According to a well established tradition it was to the following effect: "I, William H. Jackson, of the County of Clarke, State of Georgia, of the one part, and the oak tree (defining the location) of the County of Clarke of the other part: Witness, that, for and in consideration of the great love I bear this tree and the great desire I have for its protection for all time, I convey entire possession of itself and of the land within eight feet of it on all sides." Of course a tree, like other chattels and things, cannot legally own property, but Jackson's admiration for the tree led him to adopt this unique, and perhaps whimsical, means of preserving it after his death. His sentiment has been respected. However defective the tree's title may be in law, it is recognized by the people of Athens who cherish and protect the tree as if it were a *freeholder* of the city. Soon after the beginning of the twentieth century a private citizen at his own expense had granite posts connected by chains placed around the Jackson oak for its protection, and a white marble block, inscribed with part of the words of the traditional deed, was erected near by.

How did *halcyon days* originate?

Halcyon days, meaning days of peace and tranquillity, is an ancient phrase which came to us from Greek mythology. Ceyx, according to the most usual version of the myth, was drowned at sea and his body was cast upon the shore, where it was discovered by his wife Alcyone or Halcyone. The gods, out of compassion, transformed them both into birds known as halcyons, popularly identified with a species of kingfisher. This bird, it was believed, spent seven days during the coldest time of the winter in building a floating nest upon the sea and laying its eggs. Seven days more were then required for brooding. During the fourteen days when the halcyon was building its nest and brooding, the winds ceased to blow, the sea subsided, and the weather became calm. The period was therefore called the halcyon days. Later it was supposed that the halcyon or kingfisher itself had the power to calm the weather and the sea by charming the wind and waves. According to another curious belief, if a kingfisher was dried and hung up by the head its bill would always point in the direction from which the wind was blowing.

How is the number of thread determined?

Sewing thread is numbered according to the size of the single strands or cords which compose the thread. A single strand 840 yards in length is taken as the unit. The number is computed from the number of such hanks in one pound of the thread. For instance, suppose a pound of thread contains one hank of 840 yards. It is No. 1 thread. If it contains 60 hanks, it is No. 60, and so on. Thus the number increases as the size decreases. Early cotton sewing thread was composed of three strands of No. 30 single yarn; No. 40 was composed of three strands of No. 40 single yarn, and so on. Domestic sewing machines, introduced during the Civil War, made it necessary to develop a smoother and stronger thread than was possible with three strands. Therefore, in 1862 a six-cord thread was produced. This was the original O.N.T. sewing thread. Since the size and number of thread were well established it was found advisable to make the new six-cord thread the same size in diameter as the prevailing size of the three-cord thread. For that reason No. 30 six-strand was composed of six strands of No. 60 single thread, which makes the diameter of No. 30 the same as the original No. 30 thread of three strands.

How did the turkey fowl get its name?

There is probably no truth in the oft-repeated assertion that turkeys were originally so called because the English supposed these fowls came from Turkey. The fact is that before the discovery of America the terms *Turkey cock* and *Turkey hen* were applied to the guinea fowl, which is native to Africa. Apparently these two species of bird were confused and the name was transferred from the African to the American species. When the American fowl was first introduced into the Old World is not known definitely. In a letter to his daughter under date of January 26, 1784, Benjamin Franklin said that the first turkeys seen in Europe were "brought to France by the Jesuits from Canada, and served up at the wedding table of Charles IX." This French king was married to Elizabeth of Austria in 1570. There is evidence, however, that the American turkey fowl was known in Europe at an earlier date. It is frequently stated that a lieutenant of Sebastian Cabot took some of the birds to Europe during the first years of the sixteenth century. Be that as it may, there is authentic record of their introduction into Spain in 1524. When Juan Grijalva discovered Mexico in 1518 he observed that the natives had domesticated the turkey, and when the Spaniards conquered that country a few years later they found turkeys in the zoological gardens of the Aztecs. The modern domesticated turkey is believed to be descended from the Mexican variety—*Meleagris mexicana*. Among the Pueblo Indians of the

Southwest turkeys were raised before the coming of the Spaniards, and these fowls had reached about the same degree of domestication that pigeons have reached among us. By 1541 the turkey had found its way to England, and a generation later it was already a favorite Christmas dish among the English. The earliest known use of the word *turkey* as applied to the American bird occurred in 1555. Many curious theories have been advanced to account for the term. One writer suggested that the name *turkey* may have been adopted because of the supposed resemblance between the adornments of the fowl's head and the fez formerly worn by Turkish men. Another derived the name from the bird's call notes—*turk, turk, turk.* According to still another theory, the name arose from the fact that turkeys were first handled largely by Jewish merchants who called the new birds by the Jewish name for the peacock, *tukki,* which was corrupted into *turkey* by gentiles. These theories are of little value because, as previously pointed out, the word *turkey* was applied to the guinea fowl before it was to the turkey. An English writer supposes that guinea fowls were called Turkey cocks and Turkey hens from the fact that they were introduced to London and Bristol by traders who dealt chiefly with the Near East and who were popularly known as *Turkey merchants.*

Why was Thursday chosen for Thanksgiving Day?

Our national Thanksgiving Day falls on Thursday as the result of a long chain of circumstances. Thanksgiving as an annual festival is a legacy from the New England colonists. Of course they brought the general idea with them from England, where it was customary to observe special thanksgiving days after events of national importance. For instance, after the defeat of the Spanish Armada two separate days were set apart by the English church as special days for offering thanks. The Puritans, who professed to be more spiritual than their more ceremonious brethren, were especially fond of offering thanks after a good harvest, the arrival of a ship, or their deliverance from an enemy. Even the earliest Puritans who came to New England generally selected either Wednesday or Thursday for these combined religious and festive occasions, probably because they desired to have them as far as possible from the Christian Sabbath, which they observed with severe simplicity. After the first harvest in the fall of 1621 the Pilgrim Fathers at Plymouth set aside a period for feasting and offering thanks. Four hunters sent out by Governor Bradford returned with a large supply of game. Hospitality was extended to the Indians, and Massasoit with ninety of his people came to the festivities, which lasted three days. Conspicuous among the game on the tables were numerous wild turkeys, then common in the woods of Massachusetts, and from this circumstance arose the popular association of these birds with thanksgiving days. Notwithstanding the meager records of such occasions in New Plymouth, it is probable that the Pilgrim Fathers held such a festival after each harvest. Speaking of the abundant harvest of 1622, Governor Bradford wrote: "For which mercie (in time conveniente) they also sett aparte a day of thanksgiving." A day of public thanksgiving in 1623 is alluded to, and Bradford preserved a letter referring to "a day of thanksgiving to our merciful God" in 1631. Among the Puritans of Massachusetts Bay, however, thanksgiving days were from the first observed with more solemnity. February 22, 1630, was publicly appointed a day of thanksgiving for "friend-bringing and food-bearing ships," and November 4, 1631, after the harvest, Winthrop wrote: "We keep thanksgiving day today in Boston." June 19, 1633, was also set apart as a day of thanksgiving, although there is no record of the special reason. In 1639 Connecticut observed a similar day of thanksgiving, and in 1644 the Dutch of New Netherland proclaimed a public day for giving thanks. Although for many years they were held at irregular intervals, there was a tendency almost from the beginning for thanksgiving days to become annual events in both Massachusetts and Connecticut. Naturally the Puritans proclaimed special days of thanksgiving after every important event affecting the welfare of the colonies. The news of the capture of Louisburg by the British and colonial troops reached Boston July 3, 1745, and the following Thursday was appointed a day for public thanksgiving. During the Revolution the Continental Congress appointed at least one day of thanksgiving nearly every year, and these were our first national thanksgiving days. These days, of course, were governed largely by the events of the war. In 1789 Congress by joint resolution requested the President "to recommend to the people of the United States a day of public thanksgiving and prayer, to be observed by acknowledging with grateful hearts the many and signal favors of Almighty God, especially by affording them an opportunity peaceably to establish a form of government for their safety and happiness." Washington, in the first thanksgiving proclamation issued by a President of the United States, designated Thursday, November 26. His selection of the last Thursday in November was later adopted as a precedent. In the same year the Protestant Episcopal Church of America adopted a new prayer book in which the *first* Thursday in November was recommended as a day of thanksgiving, and that day was generally observed by that church in States where no official day was appointed. In 1795 President Washington designated Thursday, February 19, as a day of thanksgiving on account of the suppression of the Whiskey Insurrection. The elder President Adams appointed Wednesday, May 9, 1798. With this single exception all of our national thanksgiving days since the adoption of the Constitution have fallen on Thursday. Adams also designated Thursday, April 25, 1799. Another proclamation of this kind was not issued by a President for thirteen years, when President Madison appointed the third Thursday in August, 1812, as a day for public thanksgiving. He appointed two other such days, the last being the second Thursday in April, 1815, after the restoration of peace with Great Britain. No more national days of thanksgiving were designated by the President for forty-nine years, when President Lincoln issued a proclamation dated April 10, 1862, in which he "recommended to the people of the United States that at their next weekly assemblages in their accustomed places of public worship which shall occur after notice of this proclamation shall have been received they especially acknowledge blessings, etc. . . . ." This proclamation, it will be noted, did not specify a particular day. There was a good reason why no President between Madison and Lincoln designated national days of thanksgiving. The Southern States objected to such days, especially by Presidential proclamation, on the ground that they were relics of Puritan bigotry. The result was that this festival during these years was confined chiefly to the Northern States. In 1863 Lincoln set aside Thursday, August 6, as a definite day of thanksgiving, and later in the same year he returned to the precedent set by Washington and designated the "last Thursday of November next as a day of thanksgiving." This may be regarded as the beginning of our annual national Thanksgiving Day as we now know it. Lincoln appointed the last Thursday in November again in 1864. There seems to have been no particular reason for choosing Thursday except that it was the day chosen by Washington and had been a favorite day for that purpose among the Puritans. President Johnson, in his first Thanksgiving proclamation, departed from the precedent of Washington and Lincoln and designated the "first Thursday of December, 1865," but the following year he returned to the precedent of his predecessor and appointed the last Thursday in November, and that day has been chosen by all his successors. Thanksgiving Day is now observed in all the States of the Union and it is a legal holiday in most of them. The Dominion of Canada adopted an annual day of thanksgiving. At least one such day has been proclaimed nearly every year since 1872. By parliamentary statute adopted in 1921 thanksgiving day in Canada is the Monday of the week containing Armistice Day or November 11. Lower Canada began to observe public thanksgiving days as early as 1799.

Does the Bible mention the witch of Endor?

Contrary to popular belief, the phrase *the witch of Endor* does not occur in the text of the Bible, although in some English editions it is used in the heading for Chapter 28 of *I Samuel*. The person commonly called the witch of Endor is referred to merely as "a woman that hath a familiar spirit at Endor." She brought up the prophet Samuel from the dead upon the request of Saul, who wished to inquire as to the fateful battle in which he was to lose his life. Her function was not exactly that of a witch, who is supposed to hold communion with the devil and other evil spirits, but rather that of a spiritualistic medium, who claims to have power to convey messages from the dead to the living.

Who said: "He who would bring home the wealth of the Indies must carry the wealth of the Indies with him"?

The following inscription appears on the facade of the Union Station in Washington, D. C.: "He that would bring home the wealth of the Indies must carry the wealth of the Indies with him. So it is in traveling; a man must carry knowledge with him if he would bring home knowledge." This inscription, along with others on the building, was suggested and edited by President Charles W. Eliot of Harvard University. It was taken from James Boswell's *Life of Johnson,* which contains the following passage under date of 1778:

I said to him that it was certainly true, as my friend Dempster had observed in his letter to me upon the subject, that a great part of what was in his *Journey to the Western Islands of Scotland* had been in his mind before he left London.

Johnson: "Why yes, Sir, the topics were; and books of travels will be good in proportion to what a man has previously in his mind; his knowing what to observe; his power of contrasting one mode of life with another. As the Spanish proverb says, 'He, who would bring home the wealth of the Indies, must carry the wealth of the Indies with him.' So it is in traveling; a man must carry knowledge with him, if he would bring home knowledge."

Boswell: "The proverb, I suppose, Sir, means, he must carry a large stock with him to trade with."

Johnson: "Yes, Sir."

How did *by the skin of the teeth* originate?

This is the literal translation of an ancient Hebrew phrase which occurs in the Bible only once. To escape by or with the skin of the teeth means to escape by the narrowest possible margin. "My bone cleaveth to my skin and to my flesh," says the patriarch in *Job 19: 20,* "and I am escaped with the skin of my teeth."

What is a Cheshire cat?

The Cheshire cat has no existence except in the expression to *grin like a Cheshire cat,* which refers to a forced or sneering grin in which the teeth and gums are shown. Some reference works give the impression that the phrase was coined, or at least popularized, by Lewis Carroll (Charles L. Dodgson) in *Alice's Adventures in Wonderland.* A grinning cat appears on the scene to give Alice advice and then suddenly disappears. But the animal is persuaded to return, after which it disappears very gradually, the grin being the last thing to vanish. When Alice asked the Duchess why her cat grinned like that she was told that it did so because it was a Cheshire cat. The author of *Alice's Adventures in Wonderland* was merely making use of a proverbial phrase. The origin of *grinning like a Cheshire cat* had been discussed many years before his book was published. Thomas C. Haliburton, in *The Sayings of Samuel Slick,* had previously written: "Lavender was there . . . *grinnin like a chessy cat.*" The true origin of the phrase has never been determined. In 1852 a writer supposed that it originated from the unhappy attempts of a Cheshire sign painter to represent a rampant lion on the signboards of several inns in the county. The result was a grotesque grinning cat, which became the source of many jokes. Another theory associates the phrase with Cheshire's most famous industry since time immemorial—cheese making. Early in the nineteenth century some Cheshire cheeses were made in the shape of cats, with bristles inserted for whiskers; others bore the imprint of a grinning cat. That the grinning Cheshire cat may have originated from such a trade device is not unlikely, but it is more probable that an enterprising cheese manufacturer was only taking advantage of a device already proverbial.

Who said: "What's the Constitution between friends"?

This cynical bit of political philosophy originated with Timothy J. Campbell, a Tammany politician who represented a New York City district in the Federal House of Representatives for several terms between 1885 and 1895. There are two different stories as to what the circumstances were that provoked the celebrated query. Traditionally, says William Tyler Page, who has spent half a century in the service of the House of Representatives, it was uttered when the Tammany boss called on President Cleveland and asked him to sign a certain bill. The President explained that compliance with the request would necessitate a violation of the Constitution. "But what's the Constitution between friends?" replied Campbell. Charles Willis Thompson, however, says the incident occurred on the floor of the House during Cleveland's second administration, when the Democrats were split into several factions. On one occasion, about 1895, two Democratic members became involved in an unusually bitter verbal encounter. They faced each other in an aisle, waving their fists wildly and yelling loudly. It looked as if they surely would come to blows. One of them shouted that the other's proposal was in flat defiance of the Constitution. At that happy moment the affable and genial "Tim" Campbell edged in between the quarrelsome pair and asked in his bland way, "Ah, but what's the Constitution between friends?" A roar of laughter throughout the House restored everybody to good humor.

What is the check-off system?

Check-off was originally applied in the coal-mining industry to a system whereby the operators make deductions from the wages of employees for sharpening tools, house rent, professional fees, and merchandise bought in company stores. This system originated in the British coal fields and is peculiarly adapted to that industry. Coal, particularly bituminous coal, is generally produced in isolated communities where the miners and their families are largely dependent on facilities provided by the mine owners. In time the term was extended to include the system by means of which an employer, by agreement with a trade union, deducts union dues, fines and assessments from the wages of workers on pay day and turns them over directly to the officers of the union. Suppose, for instance, a union requires each of its members to pay one dollar a week in dues. Under the check-off system the union collects that sum from the company by which the member is employed and the company in turn deducts it from the employee's weekly pay check. The check-off system has never been widely adopted except in the soft coal industry, although the feature relating to the collection of dues is used by the Alaska Fishermen's Union, and in 1929 Seattle adopted it for its street-car system. Union leaders favor the check-off system because it solidifies and strengthens their organizations by insuring the prompt payment of dues, and the soft coal operators who employ union labor exclusively accept it because it aids the unions to live up to their contracts and to discipline recalcitrant members.

When was rice introduced into America?

Rice, according to a legend, was introduced into South Carolina accidentally in 1693, when a vessel bound for Liverpool from Madagascar was driven from her course by a storm and compelled to put in Charleston harbor for repairs. The captain, says the legend, presented Landgrave Thomas Smith and the settlers a small bag of rough rice for seed, and from this seed sprang the entire American rice industry. Even John Fiske accepted the legend as authentic history. In *Old Virginia and Her Neighbors* he wrote: "The value of the former crop [rice] was discovered in 1693, when a ship from Madagascar, accidentally stopping at Charleston, had on board a little bag of rice, which was planted with very notable success." There is ample evidence to prove that the story is a myth, and it is surprising that it should have been so generally accepted by historians. Two years before the incident is supposed to have occurred—1691—the rice industry had become so important in South Carolina that the provincial assembly granted a patent to Peter Jacob Guerard, who had "lately invented and brought to perfection, a Pendulum Engine, which doth much better, and in lesse time and labour huske rice, than any other heretofore hath been used within this Province." As a matter of fact, a considerable quantity of rice was being raised in South Carolina within a few years after the first settlements were made. The promoters of the colony in England had not overlooked the possibilities of rice culture in the new territory. "The Meadows are very proper for Rice," said *A Brief Description of the Province of Carolina,* written in 1666, supposedly by Robert Horne. By 1699 the cultivation of rice in the Carolinas had reached such dimensions that transportation of the crop across the Atlantic was a serious problem. Sir William Berkeley had made an unsuccessful attempt to raise rice in Virginia as early as 1647.

What is whalebone?

Whalebone is not bone and it has none of the properties of bone. The term is merely a popular but inaccurate name for an elastic, fibrous substance that grows on the roof of the mouth of the right and certain other species of whales. Whalebone, more properly called baleen, consists of a series of thin parallel plates on the palate and is a horny exaggeration of the ridges found on the roof of the mouth of most mammals. Baleen plates have been known to reach a length of fifteen feet, although they seldom exceed twelve feet even in the largest whalebone whales. They take the place of teeth and their function is to strain the water that the creature takes up in large mouthfuls. Because of its combined lightness, flexibility and toughness, whalebone is used in corsets, stays and other articles for stiffening women's dresses. It has been supplanted by steel in the manufacture of umbrellas. Whalers prepare the product for the market by boiling it until it is quite soft and then cutting it into strips of the required size. Formerly the whale was often confused with the walrus and other sea animals and the expression "white as whale's bone" originally meant white as walrus ivory.

Why do we have a best man at weddings?

The custom of having a best man at weddings is believed to be a survival of primitive marriage by capture, when a man seized a woman and carried her away by force. He would naturally, under such circumstances, select a faithful friend or follower to go with him and ward off the attacks of the girl's kinsmen while he stole away with her. Thus the appearance of the groom with his grooms-man or best man at the bride's home really represents a prehistoric marauding expedition. The term *best man* is of Scotch origin and probably does not date back further than the eighteenth century.

When was Black Friday?

Black Friday does not refer to a particular date, as often supposed, but is the name given to several Fridays on which financial panics have occurred. Apparently the term was first applied to the Friday in December, 1745, when the news was received in London that Charles Edward Stuart, the Young Pretender, had reached Derby, only ten days' march from the capital. A panic immediately ensued. *Black Friday* was probably suggested by Black Monday, an old name for the Monday following Easter. In a London chronicle written about 1435 we read: "In the same yere [1360] the xiiii day off April and the morning after Ester, Kyng Edward with his Oost lay before the Citee off Parys: the which was a ffoule Derke day . . . so bytter colde, that syttyng on horse bak men dyed. Wherefore, vnto this day yt ys called *blak monday*." According to another account, Black Monday received its name from the fact that the Black Prince's army sustained heavy losses from a storm on Easter Monday in 1357. Be that as it may, analogy with *Black Monday* was undoubtedly responsible for *Black Friday* as used in 1745. This term was revived in England for Friday, May

11, 1866, when a commercial panic in London followed the failure of Overend, Gurney and Company. In the United States the term *Black Friday* generally refers to September 24, 1869, when a panic resulted from the efforts of Jay Gould and James Fisk to corner the gold market by buying all the gold in the banks of New York. On the day referred to the financial district of the city was a veritable bedlam and men went insane from the excitement. Business firms feared that they would have to close their shops because of the fluctuations in prices. The panic ceased when it was announced that the Government was placing part of its gold reserve on the market. *Black Friday* was later also applied to September 19, 1873, the worst day of the panic following the failure of Jay Cook & Company.

What did *F* and *Y* stand for on Columbus's flag?

The letters *F* and *Y* inscribed on the banners of Columbus and his captains were the initials of Ferdinand and Ysabella, the sovereigns of Castile and Aragon, under whose auspices the great navigator sailed. In old Spanish *I* and *Y* were interchangeable and the queen's name was correctly written either Isabella or Ysabella.

Are timothy and clover seed used in making dyes?

There is a widespread but erroneous belief that large quantities of timothy and clover seed are used in the manufacture of dyes. At the present time no dyes are made of timothy and clover seed. "Many references to such use of these and various grass seeds," says the U. S. Bureau of Plant Industry, "have reached this Bureau, but in spite of every effort to trace this information to some reliable source it has been found impossible to do so." The U. S. Bureau of Chemistry and Soils also investigated the subject and was unable to find a single manufacturer who utilizes timothy and clover seed for such a purpose. Vegetable colors, the latter Bureau says, are generally very fugitive in respect to light and washing. There is some evidence, however, that clover seed was at one time used to a limited extent in dying cloth, especially calico. A grain dealer suggests that the popular notion that timothy seed is used for coloring purposes may have arisen from the common practice of preparing seed for the market by mixing new seed with old in order to brighten up its appearance, a process known as coloring seed. Dealers who purchased seed "to color up their stock" may have created the impression that it was to be used in the manufacture of dyes.

Why are certain ships called schooners?

Schooner is believed to be derived from *scoon,* an old Scotch and dialectical word meaning to skip or skim over the surface of the water. According to a popular story, the first vessel of this type was built at Gloucester, Massachusetts, in 1713 by Captain Andrew Robinson, a Scotchman. When the ship was being launched a bystander exclaimed, "Oh, how she scoons!" Captain Robinson replied, "A scooner let her be!" The word soon came into general use as the name of vessels of this type. Although the story was first recorded in 1790 on the authority of tradition, the derivation that it suggests is not improbable. There is good reason for believing that *schooner* originated in Massachusetts, and probably in Gloucester, about 1713, and early examples show that it was originally sometimes spelled *scooner* and *skooner.* In 1721 a man named Moses Prince wrote: "Went to see Capt. Robinson's lady. This gentleman was the first contriver of schooners, and built the first of the sort about eight years ago." In point of fact similar vessels had been previously built in England during the seventeenth century.

Who was Mrs. Partington?

According to a popular story, Mrs. Partington was an old lady who lived in a cottage on the beach at Sidmouth in Devonshire. During a great storm in 1824 she tried to keep the high tide out of her house with a mop. She failed to stem the torrent and was compelled to take refuge in her attic. Hence those who attempt what is obviously futile are reminded of Mrs. Partington and her mop. Whether there was actually such a person as Mrs. Partington is doubtful. She was probably created especially for the anecdote. Sidney Smith popularized the story when in an address delivered at Taunton in 1831 he drew a comparison between the rejection of the Reform Bill by the House of Lords and Dame Partington's effort to keep back the Atlantic. "I do not mean to be disrespectful," said the speaker, "but the attempt of the Lords to stop the progress of reform, reminds me very forcefully of the great storm of Sidmouth, and of the conduct of the excellent Mrs. Partington on that occasion. In the winter of 1824, there set in a great flood upon the town—and everything was threatened with destruction. In the midst of this sublime and terrible storm, Dame Partington, who lived upon the beach, was seen at the door of her house with mop and pattens, trundling her mop, squeezing out the sea water, and vigorously pushing away the Atlantic Ocean. The Atlantic was roused. Mrs. Partington's spirit was up; but I need not tell you that the contest was unequal. The Atlantic Ocean beat Mrs. Partington. She was excellent at a slop or a puddle, but she should not have meddled with a tempest." Like Mrs. Grundy, Mrs. Partington has no first name. In 1847 Benjamin P. Shillaber, the American humorist, began the publication of *Mrs. Partington's Sayings* in the Boston *Post*. She is portrayed in these sketches as an old lady of amusing affectations, a sort of Mrs. Malaprop, who makes all kinds of laughable mistakes and ridiculous blunders in the use of words.

How do tree frogs change their color?

The change of color in certain frogs, chameleons and fishes to simulate their background is one of the most interesting phenomena in nature. Many tree frogs can, within a few minutes, alter their color from nearly black to white to harmonize with an object on which they are resting. Dr. Samuel O. Mast says that the fishes known as flounders can assume shades, patterns and colors remarkably similar to their background within a certain range of colors and hues. In the *Voyage of the Beagle* Charles Darwin mentions the extraordinary, chameleon-like power of the octopus or cuttlefish to change its color in order to escape detection. This creature, writes the naturalist, appears to vary its tints according to the nature of the ground over which it is passing. Many complicated factors enter into these color changes, but in a general way it may be said that they are produced by the expansion and contraction of the pigment cells in the superficial layers of the skin. All the cells are linked up with the sympathetic and central nervous system by means of nerve fibers and they can all act in harmony as the result of a common stimulus. The stimulus may be due to moisture, light or temperature acting directly on the skin; cerebral excitement; food or the creature's physiological condition; or the surroundings acting through the eyes. One investigator reports that blind tree frogs do not change color as rapidly as those with normal sight, and Dr. Mast attributes the color adaptations in flounders to stimuli received through the eyes. The simplest color changes in frogs and chameleons are probably caused by the direct action of moisture, light and temperature on the skin. Heat or a bright light will make a frog lighter in color because the black pigment cells just below the epidermis contract and retreat. On the other hand, the frog will become dark if it is subjected to darkness and cold, because darkness and cold expand the cells and force the black pigments toward the surface. It is supposed that the black pigments in a frog are largely excretory in nature, consisting of waste products deposited in the skin through the action of light and heat instead of being carried off in the usual way.

What is pigeon's milk?

This is the name given to a milky secretion which is ejected from the crops of both male and female doves and pigeons and fed to their young during the early stages. Pigeon's milk is not composed of food that has been partly digested and then regurgitated, as often supposed, although it may serve to moisten such food. Certain cells in the double walls of the crop undergo a cheese-like degeneration and this substance when mixed with mucus and perhaps another juice makes up the white fluid fed to the young. If the young die or are removed during this period both parents suffer severely and are liable to die from the turgid congestion of the excessively developed walls of the crop. *Pigeon's milk* also has a figurative meaning, being applied to something that does not exist, such as an imaginary article for which a novice is sent on a fool's errand.

What causes white specks on fingernails?

White spots and lines appearing on the fingernails are popularly known as "good luck spots" and they are said to be a sign of coming good fortune. They are merely imperfections in the nail. Nails are formed by the gradual fossilization of living cells into the non-living horny tissue called keratin. The specks result when some of the cells near the root of the nail fail to be converted completely into nail substance. As the nail grows these blemishes are pushed outward. They may be natural imperfections or they may be produced by any slight cut, bruise or injury near the line where the fresh nail is being formed. Not infrequently they are due to careless manicuring.

What archbishop is primate of England?

The archbishop of York is "the Primate of England." "Primate of *All* England" is the title borne by the archbishop of Canterbury. The salary of the former is £9,000 a year; that of the latter, £15,000.

Are many acts of Congress declared unconstitutional?

Comparatively few of the many acts passed by Congress are later declared unconstitutional by the Supreme Court of the United States. It is estimated that between 1789 and 1929 Congress passed about 55,000 separate acts, considerably more than half of which were of a public nature. During this period of 140 years the Supreme Court, according to its librarian, declared 56 acts and parts of acts of Congress unconstitutional.

What is the Giant's Causeway?

The Giant's Causeway is a remarkable group of basaltic rocks on the north coast of Ireland. These rocks project into the North Channel near Bengore Head, about eight miles from Portrush. They received their name from a legend that they were once part of a bridge or causeway over which giants passed between Ireland and Scotland. The interesting formation, according to geologists, seems to have some natural connection with the basaltic formations on Staffa Island near the coast of Scotland, and it is apparently the result of an upheaval of basalt during the Tertiary period. Ages of erosion have left a line of perpendicular cliffs five hundred feet in height. The individual columns of the Giant's Causeway are cut as if by mathematical calculation and it is hard for the average spectator to realize that they were not carved by human hands. Within an area of several hundred square yards there are some 40,-000 vertical columns of basalt ranging in diameter from fifteen to thirty inches. Most of the pillars, which form an uneven pavement extending three hundred feet out into the water, are six sided, although some of them have five, seven, eight and even nine regularly formed sides. Some of them are twenty feet in height. Strictly speaking, the Giant's Causeway consists of three groups of columns, known respectively as the Little Causeway, the Honeycomb Causeway, and the Grand Causeway.

Do Negroes have holidays peculiar to their race?

The anniversary of their emancipation from slavery is the only date widely observed by the colored people of the United States as a peculiarly racial holiday. This event, however, is not universally commemorated on the same date, due to the fact that emancipation did not result from a single act but from a series of legislative and executive acts stretching over a period of years. January 1 is the date most widely observed by Negroes as Emancipation Day. That was the date in 1863 on which President Lincoln proclaimed the slaves free in all the States or parts of States then in rebellion. September 22, the date of the preliminary proclamation, is also widely observed by Negroes. In some States the colored people observe either December 18, the date on which Amendment XIII of the Constitution was adopted, or the date on which that Amendment was ratified in a particular State. Likewise many Negroes celebrate on the date on which slavery was actually abolished in their State. In Texas, for instance, June 19 is Emancipation Day, that being the date on which the Federal commander, General Robert S. Granger, issued a proclamation telling the colored people that they were free. By coincidence June 19 is the date on which Congress, in 1862, passed an act forever prohibiting slavery in the Federal Territories.

How did Sunset Cox get his nickname?

Samuel S. Cox (1824–1889), politician and writer, was called "Sunset" because of a florid description of a sunset which he wrote for the *Ohio Statesman,* published at Columbus. He became editor of that paper in 1853 when only 29 years old and on May 19 of the same year he published an article entitled *A Great Old Sunset.* This article fastened upon its author a nickname which clung to him throughout his long and distinguished career as a member of Congress, first from Ohio and later from New York. The complete article follows:

What a stormful sunset was that of last night! How glorious the storm and how splendid the setting of the sun! We do not remember ever to have seen the like on our round globe. The scene opened in the west, with a whole horizon full of golden impenetrating luster, which colored the foliage and brightened every object in its own rich dyes. The colors grew deeper and richer, until the golden luster was transformed into a storm-cloud, full of finest lightning, which leaped in dazzling zigzags all around and over the city. The wind arose with fury, the slender shrubs and quaint trees made obeisance to its majesty. Some even snapped before its force. The strawberry beds and grass plots "turned up their whites" to see Zephyrus march by. As the rain came, and the pools formed, and the gutters hurried away, thunder roared grandly, and the fire-bells caught the excitement and rung with hearty chorus. The south and east received the copious showers, and the west all at once brightened up in a long, polished belt of azure, worthy of a Sicilian sky. Presently a cloud appeared in the azure belt, in the form of a castellated city. It became more vivid, revealing strange forms of peerless fanes and alabaster temples, and glories rare and grand in this mundane sphere. It reminds us of Wordsworth's splendid verse in his *Excursion:*

> The appearance, instantaneously disclosed,
> Was of a mighty city—boldly say
> A wilderness of buildings, sinking far
> And self-withdrawn into a wondrous depth,
> Far sinking into splendor without end.

But the city vanished only to give place to another isle, where the most beautiful forms of foliage appeared, imaging a paradise in the distant and purified air. The sun, wearied of the elemental commotion, sank behind the green plains of the west. The "great eye in heaven," however, went not down without a dark brow hanging over its departing light. The rich flush of the unearthly light had passed and the rain had ceased; when the solemn church bells pealed; the laughter of children, out in the air and joyous after the storm, is heard with the carol of birds; while the forked and purple weapon of the skies still darted illuminations around the Starling College, trying to rival its angles and leap into its dark windows. Candles are lighted. The piano strikes up. We feel that it is good to have a home—good to be on the earth where such revelations of beauty and power may be made. And as we cannot refrain from reminding our readers of everything wonderful in our city, we have begun and ended our feeble etching of a sunset which comes so rarely, that its glory should be committed to immortal type.

What does *Baraca* mean?

Baraca, pronounced *ba-rak-a* with the accent on the second syllable, is the name of an international organization of young men's Sunday-school classes, the first of which was organized in 1890 at Syracuse, New York. Baraca Bible classes, consisting of thousands of local groups, now exist in many different religious denominations. The name is derived from a Hebrew word meaning *blessing.* In a different form it appears as a proper name in *I Chronicles 12: 3,* and also in *II Chronicles 20: 26,* which reads: "And on the fourth day they assembled themselves in the valley of Berachah; for there they *blessed* the Lord; therefore, the name of the same place was called, The Valley of Berachah, unto this day."

What does it mean to *turn state's evidence?*

State's evidence is the evidence produced by the government in criminal prosecutions. The term is also applied to a *person* who gives such evidence. When a person implicated in a crime voluntarily confesses his share in the illegal act and gives testimony tending to incriminate his accomplices he is said to *turn state's evidence,* that is, he becomes a witness for the state. In such cases there is often an express or implied promise on the part of the authorities that they will not prosecute the witness who thus testifies, or that they will at least deal leniently with him. It is not customary for prosecutors to promise such immunity unless there is insufficient evidence to convict a defendant without the testimony in question.

Why is a necktie called a cravat?

Cravat is derived from *Cravate,* the French name of the inhabitants of Croatia, who in English are called Croats (pronounced *kro-ats,* in two syllables). *Khrvat* is the Croato-Serbian form of the name. The original cravat or cravate was a linen or muslin scarf worn around the neck by members of a regiment of Croat mercenaries in the service of Austria. About 1636 France organized a regiment of light cavalry dressed in uniforms with neckware patterned after that of the Croats. This mode of neckware was immediately adopted by fashionable men in Paris, and the style later spread throughout the civilized world. When first introduced among civilians the cravat consisted of a simple scarf, but cravats edged with lace and tied in a bow with long flowing ends later became the fashion.

How did *by-law* originate?

By in *by-law* is believed to be derived from the old Danish word *by* or *bye,* meaning town or dwelling place, which still survives in numerous English place names, such as Whit*by,* Grims*by,* Der*by,* Rug*by,* Apple*by* and Nether*by,* all of which were named by the Danes. In Lincolnshire, one of the chief seats of the Danish settlement in England, the names of about a hundred towns and villages end in *by,* and the coast in that region is studded with these relics of the Danish occupation. The original by-laws were the laws of the town or *by,* that is, the local ordinances as distinguished from the general laws of the realm. Gradually *by-law* came to mean any minor or subordinate law or regulation. This transition was undoubtedly hastened by the analogy between the term and such words as *by-path* and *by-way.* Later the real origin of *by-law* was lost sight of and it was mistakenly supposed that *by* in this connection was merely an adverb meaning aside or secondary.

What was the Boxer indemnity?

In 1900 the Boxers, members of a Chinese secret society, began open hostilities against foreigners in northern China. All foreign ministers were warned to leave Peking. They did not do so, because they were afraid to go to the coast unprotected. The German minister was assassinated in the street and many other crimes against Europeans followed. Most of the foreigners in the capital, as well as many native Christians, barricaded themselves in the British legation. Great Britain, the United States, Germany, Russia, France and Japan sent about 16,000 troops to relieve the besieged and put down the uprising. China was compelled to pay the powers a large indemnity, secured by the customs revenue and the salt tax, which were taken over and administered by the powers. The United States received a bond, dated December 15, 1906, for the sum of $24,440,-778.81 as her proportionate share of the indemnity. China agreed to pay this sum in annual installments, with interest at four per cent, within a period ending in 1940. When the indemnity was imposed it was intended to be punitive as well as compensatory. The share allotted to this country greatly exceeded the actual pecuniary losses and expenses due to the Boxer disturbances, and the Government had no desire to punish the entire Chinese nation for what about 40,000 Boxers had done. Therefore, in 1908 the United States limited the total bond to $13,655,492.69, plus interest, and remitted to China the remaining $10,785,286.12 as an act of friendship. At the same time $1,175,835.64 of the money already paid was returned to China. It is a mistake to suppose, as many do, that America relinquished her entire share of the indemnity. The Chinese government, not to be outdone in graciousness, expressed its appreciation by setting this money aside as a fund for the education of Chinese students in the United States. Hundreds of Chinese supported by the Boxer fund have been educated in this country, and a college has been established in China to prepare students for work in American institutions of learning. Under international law China was compelled to pay the whole amount of the indemnity according to the agreement with the powers, but the United States solved this difficulty by accepting the full installment each month and immediately returning a portion of it. China made regular annual payments until December, 1918, when a five-year moratorium was granted. The payments were resumed in January, 1923, and continued until July, 1925. In 1924 Congress passed a joint resolution remitting to China all further payments of the indemnity. Under this and a subsequent act the sum of $1,469,284.43, which had already been paid, was returned to China.

Do bats carry bedbugs?

That bats carry bedbugs is a rather common belief. It arises from the fact that many bats are infested with a species of insect very similar to but distinct from the ordinary house bedbug. Bugs resembling bedbugs found on bats, swallows and pigeons, according to entomologists, belong to species peculiar to those creatures and do not ordinarily attack human beings. There is no evidence that bats ever carry common house bedbugs. "The bat bedbug," says the U. S. Bureau of Entomology, "is very frequently found in bat roosts, and when these roosts are in the attics or walls of houses the insects have been known to stray into bedrooms and cause some annoyance to the occupants. So far as we know, the bat bedbug never becomes a serious pest in houses unless the bats are exceedingly abundant."

What determined the width of the climatic zones?

The earth is divided into five grand divisions in respect to latitude and temperature. They take their name from the prevailing climate and are known as the torrid, north and south temperate, and north and south frigid zones. Their boundaries are parallels of latitude and their width is determined by the amount of inclination of the earth's axis to the plane of the ecliptic—about 23° 27'. The torrid zone is 46° 54' wide, and is all the earth's surface between the parallels known as the Tropic of Cancer and the Tropic of Capricorn, which are 23° 27' north and south of the Equator. Because the sun is always vertically overhead at some point in this zone a warm climate prevails. The north and south frigid zones lie between the poles and the polar circles, which are 23° 27' from the poles. Here the climate is cold because the sun strikes the earth obliquely and at every point in each zone there is at least one day in the year when the sun does not rise and one when it does not set. The north and south temperate zones lie between the polar circles and the torrid zone and each is about 43° 6' wide. Their climate is variable because the sun is always south of the zenith at noon in the north temperate zone and north of it in the south temperate zone, but it rises and sets daily in each throughout the year. Due to the flattened figure of the earth the length of a degree of latitude varies from 69.407 miles near the poles to 68.704 near the Equator. Thus the width of the torrid zone is about 3,225 miles, and the frigid zones are each slightly more than half that width. This classification of the earth into zones is very ancient. J. K. Wright, in a work published by the American Geographical Society in 1925, says: "Parmenides [about 500 B. C.] may have been the first to conceive of zones upon the earth's surface corresponding to the zones into which the astronomers had divided the heavens. Eratosthenes is said to have been the first to place the theory of terrestrial zones upon a firmly scientific footing, 'by determining exactly upon the sphere the position of the fixed circles which mark the limits of each zone.' Ancient geographers set the number of terrestrial zones at five, though they differed as to the character of the climates within them. The general opinion—one which was shared by Aristotle—was that the polar caps and the equatorial regions were incapable of sustaining life, the first on account of cold, and the second on account of heat."

Why is thirteen called a baker's dozen?

During the thirteenth, fourteenth and fifteenth centuries many stringent laws were passed to regulate the baking and selling of bread in London. Several of these regulations are preserved in *Liber Albus, the White Book of the City of London,* compiled in 1419 and translated into English from the Latin in 1859 by Henry T. Riley. Dealers, when purchasing bread, says Riley, "were privileged by law to receive thirteen batches for twelve, and this would seem to have been the extent of their profits. Hence the expression still in use *a baker's dozen.*" Some authorities, however, hold that the phrase arose from the fact that the bakers gave an extra loaf for each dozen in order to avoid all risk of incurring the heavy fine for short measure. *Baker's dozen* may be simply a corruption of *devil's dozen,* an older name for thirteen. That was the number of witches formerly supposed to gather at the evil conclaves to receive their master's commands. The London bakers had a bad reputation in olden times and it is not improbable that the consumers substituted *baker's* for *devil's* in the common phrase.

What is Dead Sea fruit?

Anything pleasing to the eye but worthless when acquired is called Dead Sea fruit or apples of Sodom. These phrases allude to a deceptive fruit described by Josephus and supposed to grow in the land of Sodom on the shores of the Dead Sea. "Still, too," wrote the Jewish historian, "may one see ashes reproduced in the fruits, which from their outward appearance would be thought edible, but on being plucked with the hand dissolve into smoke and ashes." Tacitus wrote as if this condition were true of all vegetation in that region. "Whatever the earth produces, whether by the prolific vigor of nature, or the cultivation of man," said the Roman, "nothing ripens to perfection. The herbage may shoot up, and the trees may put forth their blossoms; they may even attain the usual appearance of maturity; but with this florid outside, all within turns black, and moulders into dust." The Dead Sea fruit of Josephus cannot be definitely identified. No known plant answers to his description completely. Perhaps the ancient writer merely recorded a "traveler's tale" which had but slight basis in fact. Some authorities think Josephus referred to *Solanum sodomeum*, a prickly shrub with fruit resembling a small yellow tomato. Others suppose the original Dead Sea fruit to have been the Bussorah gall, which is produced on certain oaks. Edward Robinson, an American Biblical scholar, was of the opinion that the singular fruit known to the Arabs as *'osher* is the true apple of Sodom or Dead Sea fruit. This plant is the *Asclepias procera* of botanists. "Its fruit," says Dr. John C. Geikie in *The Holy Land and the Bible*, "is like a large smooth apple or orange. . . . When ripe it is yellow and looks fair and attractive, and is soft to the touch, but if pressed, it bursts with a crack, and only the broken shell and a row of small seeds in a half-open pod, with a few dry filaments, remain in the hand."

Where was the first theater built in the United States?

The first building in the United States designed primarily as a theater was erected in 1716 at Williamsburg, the colonial capital of Virginia. In the records of Yorktown for 1716 is a contract by which William Levingston, merchant, agreed with Charles Stagg and his wife Mary, actors, to build in Williamsburg a theater "for the enacting of comedies and tragedies in said city." Stagg and his wife were dancers and they had previously conducted a peripatetic dancing school in New Kent County. This playhouse, undoubtedly the first in the country, was sold to the city for a town hall in 1748 and a new building was erected to replace the theater. It was this second Williamsburg theater that George Washington frequently attended, as shown by his diary, and it was here that the *emperor, empress* and *crown prince* of the Cherokees were present at a performance of Shakespeare's *Othello* in 1752. The

Indian empress became so alarmed when she saw the actors fighting on the stage with swords that she sent an attendant to prevent them from killing one another. John Fiske was mistaken when he wrote in *The Dutch and Quaker Colonies in America* that "the first theater in America was established in Beekman Street, about the middle of the eighteenth century." The Beekman Street theater, built in 1761, was not the first playhouse even in New York, although it may have been the first building erected there primarily for that purpose. A theater existed in that city as early as 1732. It is mentioned in the New England and Boston *Gazette* for January 1, 1733, in a New York news item dated December 11, 1732. "On the 6th instant," said the item, "the *New Theater* in the building of the Hon. Rip Van Dam, Esq., was opened by the ingenious Mr. Thos. Heady, Barber and Peruque maker to his Honor."

Why are small places called jerk-water towns?

The origin of *jerk-water* as applied to small towns is obscure. It is supposed that the original jerk-water town was a place where trains stopped to take on water. In the early days of railroads the engine was often stopped at wayside streams to replenish the water supply. This was called *jerking water* because the water was carried to the locomotives in leather buckets. In time *jerk-water* came to be applied to small towns noted for nothing in particular except that trains stopped there to take on water.

What is a berserker rage?

In Norse mythology Berserk was the nickname of the grandson of the eight-handed Starkadder. He always went into battle without armor and was famed for the reckless fury with which he fought. *Ber-serk* in old Scandinavian probably meant *bare-shirt,* that is, one clothed only in his shirt and not protected by armor or heavier clothing. Among those slain by Berserk was King Swafurlam, by whose daughter he had twelve sons equal to himself in bravery. These sons of Berserk were called berserkers, a term which thus became synonymous with fury and reckless courage. Later *berserker* was applied to a class of heathen warriors who were supposed to be able to assume the form of bears and wolves, from which fact some etymologists derive the term from *bera-sark,* meaning bear-shirt or armor of bearskin. Dressed in furs these berserkers would fall into a frenzied rage, foam at the mouth and growl like wild beasts. They were said to have prodigious strength and to be invulnerable to fire and iron. From this latter myth we get the phrase *berserker rage.*

Why is the Pope's palace called the Vatican?

The Vatican received its name from an old name of the site on which it stands. In ancient times a low, level region on the right bank of the Tiber was known as *Ager Vaticanus,* Vatican Field. This name, it is believed, was derived from Vaticum, an Etruscan settlement which had vanished centuries earlier. Be that as it may, *Vatican* came gradually to be attached specifically to the neighboring eminence. The Popes acquired possession of large portions of the old Vatican Field, as well as of Vatican Hill, by purchases during the Middle Ages. A papal residence was built on the site already in the time of Symmachus, who was Pope from 498 to 514 A. D.

How did the owl become the symbol of wisdom?

The owl figures extensively in the legends and folklore of nearly all peoples and it has been regarded as the symbol of wisdom since the dawn of history. Its nocturnal habits, its noiseless flight, its mournful call, and its large, stationary eyes have all contributed toward making this bird an object of superstition. Some of the ancients considered the appearance of an owl near a sick chamber as an omen of death. Among the Greeks the owl became the symbol of meditation and counsel because it was one of the attributes of Athena, the deity who presided over the whole intellectual side of human life. It is probable that the owl represents the original form under which that goddess was first worshiped and that the idea of its being her favorite bird developed subsequently. *Glaukopis,* meaning keen-eyed, was applied to Athena by Homer, and there is reason for supposing that the epithet originally signified owl-faced. Although many people think that the owl looks wise, as a matter of fact this bird is rather stupid compared with some others. There are several curious things about the owl. Its eyes are fixed immovably in their sockets by strong cartilaginous cases; to compensate for this inability to move the eyes the bird's neck is so jointed that it can readily turn its head almost in a complete circle. Owls, like other birds of prey, eject through the mouth in the form of elongated pellets all hard, indigestible portions of the food which they swallow, and these pellets of regurgitated food can generally be found around the haunts of the birds.

Who was the Laughing Philosopher?

Democritus, a Greek thinker who lived in the time of Socrates, was known as the Laughing Philosopher. Just why he was so called is not known for certain. His moral philosophy was very stern and taught the absolute subjection of all passions. According to a legend, probably unfounded, Democritus put out his own eyes so that he might think more clearly and not be diverted in his meditations. Some ancient writers say that he became so perfect in his teachings that he went about continually smiling, from which circumstance he became known as the laughing philosopher; but others say that the inhabitants of Abdera, the colony in Thrace where Democritus was born, were notorious for their stupidity, and that he was called the derider or laughing philosopher because of the scorn and ridicule which he heaped upon his townsmen for their ignorance. Perhaps he acquired his popular title from his habit of laughing at the follies of mankind in general.

What was the value of the widow's mite?

The value of ancient coins cannot be given exactly in terms of modern money, but it is supposed that the Greek *lepton,* which is rendered *mite* in English translations of the New Testament, was worth about one-sixth of a United States one-cent piece. Therefore the contribution made by the widow was worth about one-third of a cent, because, according to *Luke 21,* she cast *two mites* into the treasury. Strictly speaking, we should speak of the widow's *mites* instead of *mite.* In *Mark 12: 42* we also read: "And there came a certain poor widow, and she threw in *two mites,* which make it a farthing." One commentator states that the Jewish coin referred to as *lepton* in Greek and *mite* in English was worth only about one-eighth of a cent. *Mite,* it seems, was never the name of a specific coin in England. The original mite (Dutch *mitj*) was a Flemish copper coin of very small value, being worth, according to some early Flemish writers, only one-third of a penning. It is improbable, says the Oxford dictionary, that *mite* was ever in English mercantile use, although in books of commercial arithmetic during the sixteenth and seventeenth centuries it appears as the lowest denomination of English money of account, usually ½₄ of a penny. *Mite* was used rather as a general name for any extremely small unit of money value. The popular belief that a mite is half a farthing is based entirely on the use of these words in translations of *Mark 12: 42,* quoted above.

How did *meander* originate?

Meander, meaning winding or crooked, is derived from the ancient name of a river in Phrygia. This stream, which is proverbial for its winding and tortuous channel, is now known as the Menderez. It flows into the Ægean Sea opposite the island of Samos off the coast of Asia Minor. "We speak of meandering streams," says Mark Twain in *Innocents Abroad,* "and find new interest in a common word when we discover that the crooked river Meander, in yonder valley, gave it to our dictionary."

Which is correct, *Tangier* or *Tangiers?*

Tangier, pronounced *tan-jeer,* is the correct spelling of the name of the city in northwestern Africa. A generation ago it was commonly spelled and pronounced *Tangiers,* with a final *s,* and that usage is still quite common. *Tangier* is the French form of the name and it has prevailed. Among the inhabitants the city is called Tanjah. An ancient city near this site was known to the Romans as Tingis.

What great orator put pebbles in his mouth?

When the ancient Greek orator Demosthenes was a young man he not only had very weak lungs and a shrill voice, but he was unable to pronounce the sound expressed by the letter *r.* The methods adopted to overcome these handicaps are related by Plutarch. "As for his personal defects," says that writer, "Demetrius the Phalerean gives us an account of the remedies he applied to them; and he says he had it from Demosthenes in his old age. The hesitation and stammering of his tongue he corrected by practicing to speak with pebbles in his mouth; and he strengthened his voice by running or walking uphill, and pronouncing some passage in an oration or a poem, during the difficulty of breath which that caused."

How did *something rotten in Denmark* originate?

"There is something rotten in Denmark" is said of a concealed evil. Thousands of persons use this expression continually without having the least suspicion of its true source. It is based on a passage in Shakespeare's *Hamlet*. In Scene 4, Act I of that play Marcellus, an officer of the watch, says to Hamlet's friend Horatio: "Something is rotten in the state of Denmark." The statement was made after Hamlet had followed the ghost of his father from the platform before the royal castle.

What was the sign that Constantine saw?

In his *Life of Constantine,* written twenty-six years after the Roman emperor's death, Eusebius relates an incident that is alleged to have occurred in 312 when Constantine was in the neighborhood of Rome shortly before the battle of Milvian bridge. While the emperor was praying, writes Eusebius, "a most marvelous sign appeared to him from heaven, the account of which might have been hard to credit had it been related by any other person. But since the victorious emperor himself long afterwards declared it to the writer of this history, when he was honored with his acquaintance and society, and confirmed his statement by an oath, who could hesitate to accredit the relation, especially since the testimony of after-time has established its truth? He said that about mid-day, when the sun was beginning to decline, he saw with his own eyes the outline of a cross of light in the heavens, above the sun, and bearing the inscription, *Conquer By This.* At this sight he himself was struck with amazement, and his whole army also, which happened to be following him on some expedition, and witnessed the miracle." Eusebius is not always trustworthy and this passage is not confirmed by contemporary writers, but an actual meteorological phenomenon may have been the basis of the legend. Shining crosses do occasionally appear in the sky in the daytime. On Good Friday, 1929, thousands of persons saw a fiery, blood-red cross against the sunset sky in England. The upright bar was formed by a vertical *sun pillar* and the horizontal bar by an incomplete solar halo. Sun pillars and solar halos are produced by the reflection of the sun's rays from tiny particles of ice or droplets of water suspended in the atmosphere. Science, of course, has nothing to say about the alleged inscription. It would seem, however, from a subsequent paragraph that Eusebius confused this part of the story with the dream in which Constantine was said to have been commanded to place the monogram of Christ on the shields of his soldiers. Lactantius, who spent several years in Constantine's household and who tutored his son Crispus, says: "Constantine was directed in a dream to cause the heavenly sign to be delineated on the shields of his soldiers, and so to proceed to battle. He did as he had been commanded, and he marked on their shields the letter X, with a perpendicular line drawn through it and turned at the top thus, ⚴ being the cipher of Christ. Having this sign, his troops stood to arms." Many later writers attribute Constantine's conversion to Christianity to the vision of the cross.

Who was the Millboy of the Slashes?

Henry Clay was known as *the Millboy of the Slashes*. He was born and brought up in Hanover County, Virginia, in a neighborhood known locally as *the Slashes,* because of the numerous slashes—swampy thickets or sloughs—in the vicinity. As a boy Clay used to carry sacks of grain on horseback to a near-by mill. From this circumstance he received his famous sobriquet, which did much to increase his popularity among the common people during his campaigns for the Presidency.

How did *pinchbeck* originate?

The original pinchbeck was a copper and zinc alloy having the appearance and luster of gold. It received its name from its inventor, Christopher Pinchbeck (1670?–1732), a famous London clock and toy maker, who first made cheap jewelry from such alloy. An ordinary person could distinguish the imitation from gold only by its lightness and lack of resonance. Cheap jewelry is still made of pinchbeck, which generally contains from ten to twenty per cent zinc, the remainder being copper, although tin and other elements are sometimes added. No contemporary record has been found showing just when Pinchbeck invented the metal which bears his name. Dictionaries and reference books, without sufficient reason, give 1732, the year of his death, as the date. On November 27 of that year the London *Daily Post* contained an advertisement announcing "that the toys made of the late ingenious Mr. Pinchbeck's curious metal . . . are now sold only by his son and sole executor, Mr. Edward Pinchbeck." Although *pinchbeck* is still employed in the sense of cheap jewelry, it is now more often applied figuratively to anything counterfeit or spurious. "Where in these *pinchbeck* days," asked Anthony Trollope in *Framley Parsonage*, "can we hope to find the old agricultural virtue in all its purity?"

What is a free lance?

A free lance is a person not permanently affiliated with an organization. Free-lance writers are persons who write on their own account and not as members of the staff of any publication. Sir Walter Scott and later writers applied the term to professional soldiers of the Middle Ages whose services were purchasable by any feudal lord willing to pay the required price. Sometimes the free lance was a roving knight who had a handful of armed horsemen under his command.

What is the meaning of *V.D.B.* on Lincoln pennies?

The letters *V.D.B.* on some Lincoln one-cent pieces minted in 1909 are the initials of Victor David Brenner, the medalist and sculptor who designed the coin. This part of the design was soon withdrawn by the Treasury Department and consequently the artist's initials appear on only part of the Lincoln pennies bearing the date 1909. Brenner was born at Shavly, Russia, in 1871, and he died in New York in 1924.

How did Buttermilk Channel get its name?

Governors Island in New York Bay is separated from Long Island by a deep arm of water known as Buttermilk Channel. How this unusual name originated is not known for certain. There is, however, a tradition on the subject. It is believed that Governors Island was once connected with Long Island. At any rate, when

Wouter van Twiller was governor of New Netherland the channel
was so narrow and shallow that cattle could easily wade across it.
Van Twiller became governor of the colony in 1633. According to
one historian, four years later he purchased Governors Island
(then known as Nooten or Nutten Island) from the Indians for
"an axe-head or two, a string of beads, and a few nails." The only
boats that could navigate the channel in those days were flat-
bottomed craft drawing little water. Such boats made regular trips
across the channel to carry buttermilk, a favorite drink among the
Dutch, from the dairies of Long Island to Governors Island and
New Amsterdam. They were popularly called buttermilk boats, and
from this circumstance the channel received the name Buttermilk
Channel.

What is meant by the black ox?

The black ox symbolizes old age, ill luck, adversity, or trouble
and misfortune in general. "The black ox has trod on his foot," is
a proverbial expression recorded already in 1546 by John Heywood.
It means that one knows the meaning of sorrow, such as having been
visited by death. The phrase *black ox* alludes to the black cattle
sacrificed by the ancient pagans to the infernal deities, especially to
Pluto, supreme judge and lord of the nether world. White cattle
were sacrificed to Jupiter. At Rome the altar on which the black
oxen were sacrificed was twenty feet below the level of the ground
and was never exposed to public view except when the sacrifices were
being made. Among the Arabs the black camel is the symbol of
murder and death by violence.

How do shears and scissors differ?

In the United States the terms *shears* and *scissors* are often
used interchangeably. As a rule, however, *shears* is employed when
the implement is large, and *scissors* when it is small. All such instruments having a total length of six inches or less are called scissors
in the hardware trade; those exceeding six inches in length are
called shears. In Scotland all sizes are called shears, the word
scissors being seldom used. The Oxford dictionary says: "The
larger instruments of this kind, especially those which are too large

to be manipulated with one hand, are called shears." *Scissors,* since the name is applied to a single implement, is sometimes construed as singular although it is plural in form; thus we may say "the scissors are sharp" or "the scissors is sharp."

Why do snakes dart out their tongues?

Many people believe that snakes sting with their tongues. This, of course, is not true, the tongue of a snake being perfectly harmless. Snakes do not sting; they bite with their fangs. The continual motion of this organ is known to have some sensory significance, the exact nature of which is not yet fully understood, according to Waldo L. McAtee, a biologist associated with the U. S. Bureau of Biological Survey. Apparently the long, delicate, forked tongue enables the reptile to feel its way over the ground. The projecting of the snake's tongue, says Dr. William M. Mann, director of the National Zoological Park at Washington, is supposed to be sensory in function. "It has been suggested," he asserts, "that the sense of smell is present, to some extent, in the snake's tongue, though I do not believe this has been very well substantiated." Raymond L. Ditmars, curator of reptiles at the New York Zoological Park, says on this subject: "The tongue of the snake is an extremely sensitive organ, and serves to trace scents over the ground by taste. It also is sensitive to sound vibration." In Shakespeare's time the belief that snakes sting with their tongues was almost universal. The dramatist makes King Richard II say:

> And when they from thy bosom pluck a flower,
> Guard it, I pray thee, with a lurking adder
> Whose double tongue may with a mortal touch
> Throw death upon thy sovereign's enemies.

INDEX